REALIZING ISLAM

ISLAMIC CIVILIZATION AND MUSLIM NETWORKS

Carl W. Ernst and Bruce B. Lawrence, editors

Highlighting themes with historical as well as contemporary significance, Islamic Civilization and Muslim Networks features works that explore Islamic societies and Muslim peoples from a fresh perspective, drawing on new interpretive frameworks or theoretical strategies in a variety of disciplines. Special emphasis is given to systems of exchange that have promoted the creation and development of Islamic identities—cultural, religious, or geopolitical. The series spans all periods and regions of Islamic civilization.

A complete list of titles published in this series appears at the end of the book.

Realizing Islam

The Tijaniyya in North Africa and the Eighteenth-Century Muslim World

Zachary Valentine Wright

THE UNIVERSITY OF NORTH CAROLINA PRESS
CHAPEL HILL

Set in Times New Roman by PageMajik
Manufactured in the United States of America

The University of North Carolina Press has been a member of the Green Press Initiative since 2003.

Library of Congress Cataloging-in-Publication Data
Names: Wright, Zachary Valentine, author.
Title: Realizing Islam: the Tijāniyya in North Africa and the eighteenth-century Muslim world / Zachary Valentine Wright.
Other titles: Islamic civilization & Muslim networks.
Description: Chapel Hill: The University of North Carolina Press, 2020. | Series: Islamic civilization and Muslim networks | Includes bibliographical references and index.
Identifiers: LCCN 2020010716 | ISBN 9781469660813 (cloth: alk. paper) | ISBN 9781469660820 (pbk.: alk. paper) | ISBN 9781469660837 (ebook)
Subjects: LCSH: Tijānī, Abū al-ʻAbbās Aḥmad ibn Muḥammad, 1737 or 1738–1815. | Tijānīyah—Africa, North. | Sufism—Africa, North. | Islam—History—18th century.
Classification: LCC BP189.7.T5 W75 2020 | DDC 297.4/8—dc23
LC record available at https://lccn.loc.gov/2020010716

Cover illustration: Zawiya ceiling. Photograph by author.

Portions of this book were previously published in a different form as "On the Path of the Prophet: Shaykh Ahmad Tijani and the Tariqa Muhammadiyya" (master's thesis, American University in Cairo, 2005) and "Secrets on the Muhammadan Way: Transmission of the Esoteric Sciences in 18th Century Scholarly Networks," *Islamic Africa* 9, no. 1 (May 2018): 77–105. Both are used here with permission.

S|H M|P **The Sustainable History Monograph Pilot**
Opening up the Past, Publishing for the Future

This book is published as part of the Sustainable History Monograph Pilot. With the generous support of the Andrew W. Mellon Foundation, the Pilot uses cutting-edge publishing technology to produce open access digital editions of high-quality, peer-reviewed monographs from leading university presses. Free digital editions can be downloaded from: Books at JSTOR, EBSCO, Hathi Trust, Internet Archive, OAPEN, Project MUSE, and many other open repositories.

When you cite the book, please include the following URL for its Digital Object Identifier (DOI):
https://doi.org/10.5149/9781469660844_Wright

We are eager to learn more about how you discovered this title and how you are using it. We hope you will spend a few minutes answering a couple of questions at this url:
https://www.longleafservices.org/shmp-survey/

More information about the Sustainable History Monograph Pilot can be found at https://www.longleafservices.org.

CONTENTS

Acknowledgments, ix

Note on Orthography, xi

Introduction
The Tijāniyya and the Verification of Islamic Knowledge, 1

CHAPTER ONE
Sufism and Islamic Intellectual Developments in the Eighteenth Century, 18

CHAPTER TWO
Portrait of a Scholar:
An Intellectual Biography of Shaykh al-Tijānī, 53

CHAPTER THREE
The Actualization of Humanity on the Muḥammadan Path, 100

CHAPTER FOUR
The Seal of Muḥammadan Sainthood and Hidden Pole, 142

CHAPTER FIVE
Abundant Blessing in an Age of Corruption, 175

Conclusion, 208

Notes, 219

Bibliography, 265

Index, 291

ACKNOWLEDGMENTS

Alḥamdulillāh wa ṣalāt wa salām ʿala rasūlillāh. I have been honored in completing this work by the assistance of many guides, mentors, and scholars better than myself. First and foremost, my gratitude to the late Shaykh Ḥasan Cissé and the current Imam of Medina-Baye Senegal, Shaykh al-Tijānī Cissé, who graciously provided me access to their knowledge and archives. Scholars of the Tijāniyya who also helped me with this work include Shaykh Muḥammad al-Māḥī Cissé of Senegal, the late Dr. Abdelaziz Benabdallah of Morocco, the late Shaykh Aḥmad b. Muḥammad al-Ḥāfiẓ of Egypt, and Shaykh Muḥsin Shalaby of Egypt.

I am graced by a supportive academic community, many of whom gave substantive feedback on this manuscript. I thank Ousmane Kane, Rüdiger Seesemann, Rudolph Ware, and Mark Sedgwick for reading this work or earlier versions of it, and for their invaluable comments, resources and mentorship over the years. I also thank Souleymane Bachir Diagne, Andrea Brigaglia, Oludamini Ogunnaike, Khaled El-Rouayheb, John Voll, Joseph Hill, Ahmad Dallal, Louis Brenner, Zekeria Ould Salem, Said Bousbina, Nelly Hanna, Carl Petry, Mohamed Serag, Justin Stearns, Omar Edward Moad, Erin Pettigrew, Mamadou Diouf, Ismail Warcheid, Farah El-Sharif, Amir Syed, Sean Hanretta, Will Caldwell, and Brannon Ingram for pointed interventions in the development of my research on the Tijāniyya and the eighteenth-century Islamic world. I am grateful to UNC Press editors Elaine Maisner, Carl Erst, and Bruce Lawrence for their invaluable feedback through the revision process, and for supporting the publication of this book.

I am honored by a rich research network, with Sohaira Siddiqui, Jonathan Brown, Abdel Rahman Azzam, Joseph Lumbard, Gavin Picken, Mauro Nobili, Ibrahim Abusharif, Alexandre Caeiro, Henry Lauziere, Rebecca Shereikis, Ousman Kobo, Rasul Miller, Samiha Rahman, Patrick Laude, Jonathan Glassman, David Schoenbrun, Nate Matthews, Rogaia Abusharaf, Anto Mohsin, and Sami Hermez deserving special mention for sharing their insights on Islamic intellectual history, and African and

Middle East Studies more broadly. I also thank the Muslim intellectuals and readers who gave feedback and provided resources on various parts of this research: Fakhruddin Owaisi (South Africa), Muḥammad al-ʿIrāqī and his uncle Anas b. Idrīs al-ʿIrāqī (Morocco), Ibrāhīm Khalīl al-Tijānī (Morocco), Muṣṭafa Sané (Senegal), Ashaki Taha-Cissé (USA), the late Sayyid Abdussalam (USA), Selma Bennani (Morocco), Abu Bakr Kindi (Ghana/Morocco), Talut Dawud (USA/Mexico), Ibrahim Dimson (USA), Hicham Hall (USA), ʿAbd al-Ṣamad Uruzzi (Italy), Yahya Weldon (USA/Qatar), and Khalīfa al-Khulayfī (Qatar).

This research has been supported by a number of grants and institutions over the years: Fulbright Hayes and IIE grants in Senegal and Morocco, Northwestern in Qatar research grants, and visiting fellowships at Northwestern's Institute for the Study of Islamic Thought in Africa and Harvard's Divinity School. For hosting my presentation of various sections of this book, I especially thank Northwestern's ISITA and Middle East and North Africa programs, the Harvard Divinity School, Columbia University's Institute for African Studies, Georgetown's Alwaleed Center for Muslim-Christian Understanding, the University of Michigan's IKHLAS initiative, NYU-Abu Dhabi's Arab Crossroads program, and Hamad Bin Khalifa's College of Islamic Studies. During my time at Northwestern in Qatar, I am especially indebted to the support of Marwan Kraidy, Hariclea Zengos, Craig LaMay, Kathleen Hewett-Smith, Elizabeth Lance, Iman Khamis, Mark Paul, Everette Dennis, and Sandra Richards. I must also recognize the generosity of the Qatar Foundation, and especially the vision of Shaykha Moza bint Nasser and Shaykha Hind Al Thani, in the ongoing support for research and scholarship in Qatar's Education City.

Lastly, I am grateful for the support of my family, without whom this book would not have been possible. To my children: this work is for you.

NOTE ON ORTHOGRAPHY

Transliteration of Arabic words complies with the system utilized by Cambridge's *International Journal of Middle East Studies*. This system is reproduced for reference purposes below.

Place names rely on the French spelling (thus Oujdah, not Wijda), unless the name has been previously Anglicized (thus Fez, not Fès). Family names from sub-Saharan Africa are preserved as earlier represented in literature for the sake of continuity. Thus Niasse, Sy, and Cissé appear as they would on government passports and in earlier academic literature, rather than the Wolof spelling Ñaas, Sii, and Seesay or the Arabic transliteration Anyās, Sih, and Sīsi. I have otherwise opted for the Arabic transliteration of first names in most cases (thus Tijānī rather than Tidiane, Ḥasan rather than Assane, Aḥmad rather than Amadou).

All dates mentioned in the text have been converted to "Common Era" (CE). Translations from Arabic and French into English are my own, unless otherwise indicated.

Arabic Transliteration Chart

Arabic letter	*Transliteration*	*Phonetic equivalent*
ا	ā	talk
ب	b	boy
ت	t	table
ث	th	bath
ج	j	joy
ح	ḥ	-
خ	kh	-
د	d	day
ذ	dh	then
ر	r	run

Arabic letter	*Transliteration*	*Phonetic equivalent*
ز	z	zebra
س	s	sun
ش	sh	shine
ص	ṣ	-
ض	ḍ	-
ط	ṭ	-
ظ	ẓ	-
ع	ʿ	-
غ	gh	-
ف	f	feast
ق	q	-
ك	k	key
ل	l	love
م	m	mother
ن	n	none
ه	h	health
و	w/ū	weather/food
ي	y/ī	yes/street
ء	ʾ	(glottal stop)
ة	-/t	(silent)/hat
َ	a	bag
ِ	i	big
ُ	u	bug

REALIZING ISLAM

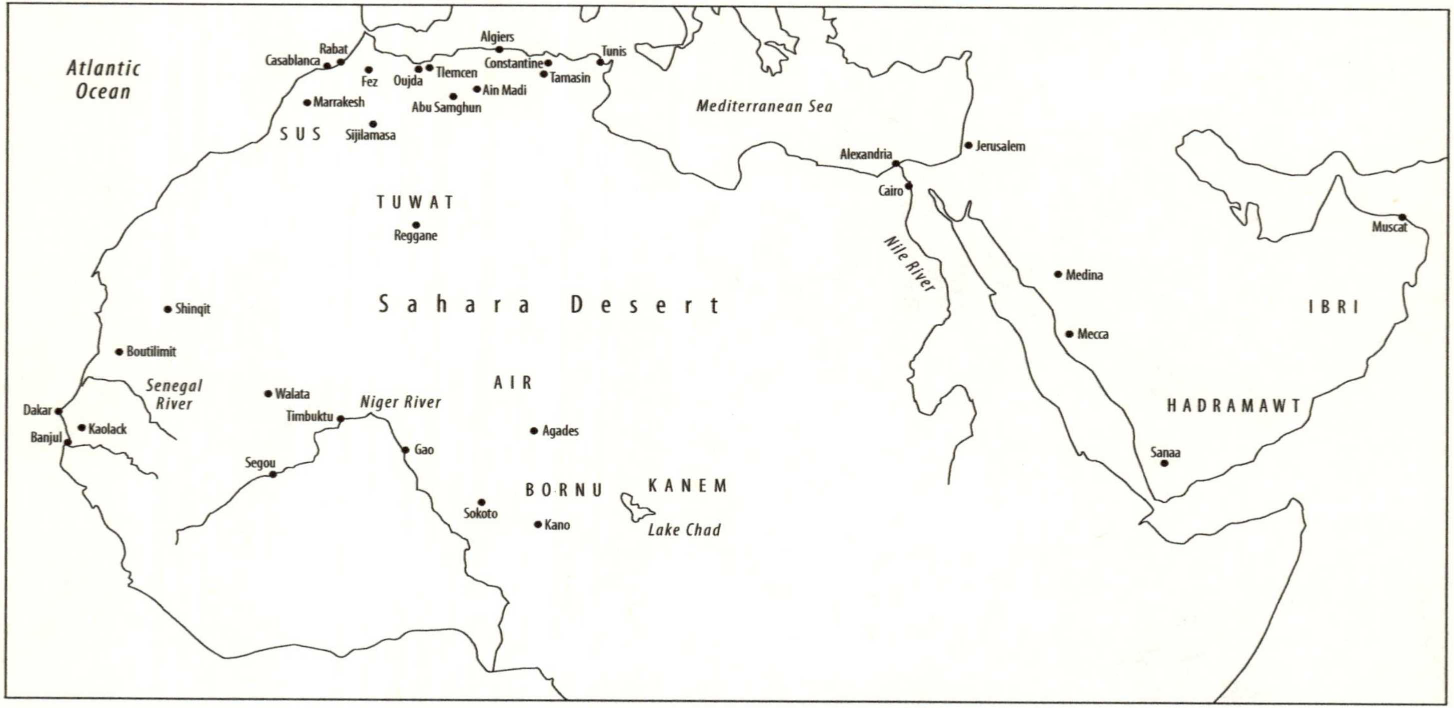

Muslim Africa and the Middle East in the eighteenth century.

Introduction

The Tijāniyya and the Verification of Islamic Knowledge

What is the reality of Sufism?" asked a disciple of Shaykh Aḥmad al-Tijānī. "Know that Sufism is to exemplify the command (of God) and to flee from what is prohibited, both externally and internally, in what pleases God, not in what pleases you."[1] It seems extraordinary that a learned student of a reputed scholar-saint in late eighteenth-century Morocco would be asking to verify the basic reality (*ḥaqīqa*) of the Sufi path. But for followers of the nascent Tijāniyya in late eighteenth-century North Africa, verification, realization, or actualization (*taḥqīq*) of Islamic religious identity appears at the center of their search for knowledge. To a student of Islamic learning, al-Tijānī thus wrote, "May God . . . cause us to seek the way of realization (*taḥqīq*) and sincerity (*sadād*), and may He allow us to die on the religion pleasing to Him."[2]

For al-Tijānī, the establishment of his own "Muhammadan spiritual path" (*Ṭarīqa Muḥammadiyya*) was the means to share the realization of human potentiality, exemplified by the Prophet Muḥammad, at a time when humanity was perceived to be distant from God. The Tijānī Muḥammadan path (or Tijāniyya) emphasized the individual self's acquisition of divine satisfaction by following the external and internal example of the Prophet Muḥammad. Verification of the external Muḥammadan law (Sharīʿa) thus paralleled verification of an enduringly important prophetic spiritual presence. The resultant activation of the Muḥammadan essence at the core of human identity made an individual the recipient of divine grace, even in a perceived age of social and political corruption.

Such realization of the human condition (*taḥqīq al-insāniyya*) was not unique to al-Tijānī and his followers. But even if the Tijānī version of the *Ṭarīqa Muḥammadiyya* drew upon similar articulations within an eighteenth-century global scholarly network, the Tijāniyya developed a distinctive rendition of this concept. Al-Tijānī's notion of the consummation, perfection, or "sealing" of the Muḥammadan path in the Tijāniyya both responded to regional Maghrebi intellectual and social currents and facilitated the global spread of the order in a manner perhaps unrivaled by contemporary articulations. With a vibrant and growing presence in West and North Africa, the Middle East, India, Indonesia, Malaysia, and Muslim minority communities in Europe and the Americas, the Tijāniyya has certainly become one of the world's most widespread Sufi orders.

The Tijāniyya came with nothing new in relation to earlier Islamic and Sufi ideas: adherents conceived their affiliation to the "way of Muḥammad" as the fullest actualization of a very old and basic concept. In most Arabic dictionaries, the meaning for *ḥaqqaqa* or *taḥqīq* is to "act according to the truth," or to "verify; confirm."[3] To make *taḥqīq* is thus to put knowledge into practice, or confirm a religious truth through its performance. The notion of actualization as a form of knowledge beyond rational verification was associated with Sufism in opposition to Hellenistic philosophy at least since the thirteenth-century formulations of the Andalusian Ibn al-ʿArabī and his Anatolian disciple Ṣadr al-Dīn al-Qūnawī.[4] According to William Chittick:

> Sufi teachers frequently spoke of the goal of the Islamic tradition as "realization" (*taḥqīq*), a word derived from the same root as the Divine Name *al-Ḥaqq*, the Real, the Right, the True, the Appropriate. Grammatically, realization means to actualize truth (*ḥaqq*) and reality (*ḥaqīqa*), and in Sufism it came to designate the end result of following the path to God. To achieve realization means to reach the Real, to see and understand all things in light of the Real, and to act rightly and appropriately in all situations. This demands the transformation of the very being of the seeker.[5]

A *muḥaqqiq* is thus one in whom truth has become manifest: he is the living proof of the truth's verification.

The spiritual claims of the Tijāniyya—that al-Tijānī was the Seal of Saints, that the "stamp" of the Tijāniyya is over all other Sufi paths till the end of time, for example—is best understood through the concept of *taḥqīq*. Sufi actualization was part of a more general accent on scholarly verification for al-Tijānī. According to al-Tijānī's close disciple ʿAlī Ḥarāzim:

> Among his concerns was verification (*taḥqīq*) and scrutiny (*tadqīq*) in everything, large or small, in order to establish the real truth. By this,

> he departed from the yoke of imitation (*taqlīd*) and (blind) acceptance (*taṣdīq*) . . . until he came to encompass all of the official sciences (*al-ʿulūm al-rasmiyya*), with verification, investigation, understanding, and contemplation; solving problems and enigmas. He became the imam of all types of knowledge. People sought him out for his explanations, for he was knowledgeable of the cause, judgement, sources, branches, derivative issues, understandings, pronouncements, abrogating and abrogated matters [in all fields of learning]. He plunged into the depths of all transmitted and official learning . . . just as [he did in] the knowledge of divine reality.[6]

In other words, the appeal of eighteenth-century scholar-saints such as Aḥmad al-Tijānī was their perceived ability to offer a comprehensive realization of an Islamic religious identity. These exemplars were guides to the truth in a time of confusion. "The true scholar," al-Tijānī said, "gives form to what is clear, and clarifies what is ambiguous, from the strength of his knowledge, the breadth of his understanding, the soundness of his spiritual vision (*naẓr*) and his verification (*taḥqīq*)."[7] Al-Tijānī's Sufi claims are illegible without an appreciation of this vibrant discourse on the verification and realization of Islamic knowledge, by which scholars justified their prominence in the eighteenth-century Muslim world.

Al-Tijānī's *Ṭarīqa Muḥammadiyya*, allegedly gifted directly by the Prophet in a waking encounter to al-Tijānī, was thus meant to verify the essence of all Sufi paths. The shaykh's own realization of paradigmatic sainthood was articulated as simply the reflection of his spiritual proximity to the Prophet Muḥammad as the source of all divine realization. While such claims to saintly authority were no doubt controversial to an external audience, they were certainly not illegible. Sufi saints, and premodern Islamic religious authority more generally, were "presences" thought to be inscribed not only with the knowledge they taught, but with the aspirations of their students and followers. "Without saints, there is no Sufism," a prominent historian of Sufism observed.[8] But too often observers have decontextualized the spiritual claims of saints from disciple investiture in sainthood as a participatory medium.[9] "If the greatest of the perfected saints (*aqṭāb*) came to know what has been given to our companions," al-Tijānī assured his disciples, "they would cry to God and say, 'Our Lord, you have given us nothing.'"[10] In partial explanation, the shaykh reported the Prophet Muḥammad's words to him: "Anyone who loves you is the beloved of the Prophet, God's blessing and peace on him, and he will not die until he becomes a saint."[11] For followers of the Tijāniyya, the rank of their shaykh was thus a medium to actualize the Prophet's own invitation to get closer to God.

The Eighteenth-Century Islamic World

The Tijāniyya emerged at the end of the intellectually vibrant eighteenth century. New research on this period in the Muslim world concurs in overturning an earlier orientalist and Islamic modernist assumption of scholarly stagnation in the seventeenth and eighteenth centuries. "It was a period," John Voll observes, "of major developments in key aspects of the Islamic tradition, providing both a culmination for the first millennium of Islamic history and the foundation for many dynamic aspects of Islam in the modern world."[12] Ahmad Dallal makes a similar observation in his overview of Islamic intellectual history in the period: "The Islamic eighteenth century was a period of great intellectual vitality comparable in its scope, intensity, and quality to the cultural activities of the classical period. Intellectuals from virtually all the regions of the Muslim world systematically attempted to scrutinize the epistemological foundations of inherited knowledge and to reformulate the traditional Islamic disciplines of learning."[13] Such scrutiny shares much, then, with an emphasis on "verification" (*taḥqīq*) that Khaled El-Rouayheb locates in the seventeenth century,[14] but which arguably blossomed as the eighteenth century progressed.

Researchers have focused on different aspects of scholarly renewal: Voll on chains of prophetic narrations (*ḥadīth*) and juristic interpretations (*ijtihād*), Dallal on juristic methodology (*uṣūl al-fiqh*) and evaluation of ḥadīth transmissions (*uṣūl al-ḥadīth*), and Rouayheb on theology (*kalām*) and Sufism, for example. Understandably, the exercise of *taḥqīq* employed different epistemological strategies for different intellectual disciplines: transmission (*ʿilm al-naql*) for ḥadīth and jurisprudence (*fiqh*), rational proof (*ʿilm al-ʿaql*) for theology and legal methodology, and experiential witnessing (*kashf, maʿrifa*) for the spiritual realities referenced in Sufism.[15] Verifying transmitted knowledge prioritized the search for alternative sources of narrations, authenticating existing ḥadīth literatures through the "science of transmitters" (*ʿilm al-rijāl*), and the acquisition of the shortest possible chain of knowledge transmission (*sanad*) from licensed scholars.[16] Verifying theological premises or legal theory required "rational demonstration" and the ability to "critically assess received views,"[17] most particularly, for Dallal, through a "consistent historicization" of legal thought: the eighteenth-century scholar's observation of the inherited intellectual tradition's ability to respond to historically diverse circumstances, but also the necessity for contextualizing received opinions in their own time and place.[18] Verifying spiritual realities required the direct experience of the unseen: "In a Sufi context, 'verification' typically denoted the mystical-experiential authentication of the truths to which ordinary believers—including exoteric theologians—abstractly assent."[19]

This overview does not mean to collapse significant distinctions between studies of the eighteenth century. Researchers have disagreed most notably on how widely ideas were shared, and whether or not global scholarly exchanges have any relevance in understanding the local formulation and reception of diverse scholars. Even so, such differences can risk exaggeration. According to John Voll, "these connections [between scholars] can be overstated as well as underestimated, and it is important to set a balance. The eighteenth century Muslim world was . . . [not] composed of totally separate and isolated parts."[20] Elsewhere, Voll adds, "there is enough interaction among revivalists in the eighteenth century" to conclude that "revivalist movements . . . did not emerge in isolation."[21] Ahmad Dallal's emphasis on understanding local and regional contexts over global exchanges, while critical of Voll's work on networks, nonetheless concedes, "none of these movements was totally detached from outside intellectual currents of the Muslim world."[22]

The foundation of the Tijāniyya is a key case study, only superficially referenced in earlier research on eighteenth-century intellectual history, that emphasizes the importance of verification or realization of knowledge. It also suggests both the significance of global scholarly exchanges and the importance of regional historical context in understanding the reception of eighteenth-century Islamic scholarship. Aḥmad al-Tijānī traveled throughout North Africa and the Middle East and had meaningful connections with Arab, Kurdish, and Indian scholars in Egypt and the Hijaz. But clearly, his teachings responded to regional historical developments in Algeria and Morocco in the late eighteenth and early nineteenth centuries. The spread of the Tijāniyya during his life and around the world today may have much to do with al-Tijānī's ability to make the inherited intellectual tradition speak to a perceived new historical era of unprecedented corruption. The emphasis on realization or authentication provides a useful lens through which to understand scholarly exchange, local context, and perception of historical specificity at the foundation of the Tijāniyya. Al-Tijānī in fact emphasized the same aforementioned *taḥqīq* in all three epistemological strategies—transmission, rational proof, and spiritual experience—in promoting Islamic religious revival. Even if Sufism remained, for al-Tijānī as for al-Ghazālī, the privileged method of verifying the truth of religion, the foundational sources of the Tijāniyya give important insight into the ways in which the disciplines of ḥadīth, legal theory, theology, and Sufism interfaced and mutually supported one another in eighteenth-century scholarship.

The *Ṭarīqa Muḥammadiyya*

As suggested above, al-Tijānī's notion of the "Muḥammadan Way" was useful in focusing Islamic learning on individual religious realization. For the shaykh, the *Ṭarīqa Muḥammadiyya* was the Prophet's own chosen path for the actualization of divine knowledge. Such external and internal emulation of the Prophet necessitated both the learning of the Prophet's transmitted behavior (Sunna) and the emulation of his spiritual state in the presence of God. The Tijānī Sufi path thus presupposed a degree of legal and theological knowledge, though it certainly accentuated the methodology of the self's purification in order to experience unseen realities. In this, the Tijāniyya was no different than most Sufi orders. Indeed, the Tijāniyya's most visible distinguishing characteristic—the waking encounter with the Prophet and the claim to Seal of Sainthood—do not result from any ideological or practical innovation. Al-Tijānī perceived his own "Muḥammadan Way" as nothing new, only the ultimate fulfillment of Sufism's promise to connect the worshipper to God. But Rüdiger Seesemann's analysis of nineteenth-century Tijānī literature is instructive here: "even if the 'old-hat-argument' holds true, we still need to consider the possibility that the same idea (or text) can assume a different meaning or relevance in a different context."[23]

Al-Tijānī was not the first to employ the terminology of the *Ṭarīqa Muḥammadiyya*, nor was he the first to claim the waking vision of the Prophet or the Seal of Muḥammadan sainthood. While the proliferation of self-proclaimed *Ṭarīqa Muḥammadiyya* movements in the eighteenth and nineteenth centuries certainly suggests shared influences, there is little shared coherence to the term to indicate a globally transmitted "Muḥammadan Way" in the period. Discussion of shared influences and global intellectual currents invoking the concept is useful to understand the context and later reception of the Tijāniyya, particularly in Africa. But there is nothing in Tijānī primary sources to substantiate the notion that the Tijāniyya was part of a global "movement" or network of *Ṭarīqa Muḥammadiyya* scholars visibly distinct from the larger Sufi tradition. Nonetheless, the Tijāniyya drew on the intellectual resources of eighteenth-century thought—themselves the crystallization of earlier ideas—and offered its own version of the *Ṭarīqa Muḥammadiyya* as having particular relevance to Muslims of the period.

Aḥmad al-Tijānī (1737–1815) and the Tijāniyya

Aḥmad b. Maḥammad b. Mukhtār al-Tijānī al-Ḥasanī[24] was born in the southwestern Algerian oasis of ʿAyn Māḍī and traveled throughout North Africa and the Hijaz before taking up permanent residence in Fez, Morocco, in 1798. Before leaving ʿAyn Māḍī at age twenty-one, he completed the standard curriculum of Qurʾān memorization and study of jurisprudence, theology, prophetic traditions, Qurʾān exegesis, and Arabic literature. His travels in search of further knowledge (mostly prophetic narrations and Sufi training), led him to stays in several North African centers of knowledge, such as Fez, Tlemcen, Tuwāt, and Tunis. During these years, he received initiation into various branches of the Shādhiliyya, the Qādiriyya, and the Khalwatiyya. He accomplished the pilgrimage to Mecca in 1774. During this trip, he received initiations from prominent Khalwatī shaykhs Maḥmūd al-Kurdī (d. 1780) in Cairo and Muḥammad al-Sammān (d. 1775) in Medina, as well as an Indian Sufi, likely of the Naqshbandiyya, Aḥmad al-Hindī (d. 1774) in Mecca. His combination of Islamic learning and Sufi knowledge eventually distinguished him as "one of the greatest imams of his time," according to Tijānī sources.[25]

While making spiritual retreat (*khalwa*) in the Algerian town of Abū Samghūn in 1781–82, he experienced his first waking encounter with the Prophet Muḥammad. Al-Tijānī reported that the Prophet told him to leave aside his previous Sufi initiations and gave him the distinctive litany (*wird*) of the Tijāniyya Sufi path.[26] The claimed direct involvement of the Prophet Muḥammad in the establishment of the Tijāniyya, as well as the disciple's constant visualization of the Prophet's enduring spiritual presence, meant that followers of the Tijāniyya considered the Prophet Muḥammad to be the ultimate Sufi shaykh of their "Muḥammadan way."

Upon his final establishment in Fez, al-Tijānī joined Sultan Mawlay Sulaymān's council of scholars and initiated several prominent Moroccan figures into the Tijāniyya, such as the jurist and theologian Ḥamdūn b. al-Ḥājj, several government ministers, and perhaps even the sultan himself. The most comprehensive biographical dictionary of Moroccan scholars relating to the period, Muḥammad al-Kattānī's *Salwat al-anfās*, describes al-Tijānī as "the grounded gnostic," "the rope of the Sunna and the religion," and the "comprehensive saintly pole" before continuing: "He was among the scholars who put his knowledge into action, the imams of independent scholarly opinion (*al-aʾimma al-mujtahidīn*), among those who combined the nobility of origin with the nobility of the religion, the nobility of knowledge, action, certainty, divine spiritual states (*aḥwāl*) and lofty saintly stations (*maqāmāt*)."[27] Such descriptions, although not uncontested, suggest al-Tijānī's reception among elements of both general and elite audiences. A number of Moroccan sultans have since maintained close relations with the Tijāniyya, most recently funding the restoration of al-Tijānī's final burial place and main lodge (*zāwiya*) of the Tijāniyya in Fez, as well as al-Tijānī's original house in the city, the "House of Mirrors," that Mawlay Sulaymān gifted to al-Tijānī upon his arrival in Fez.

The Tijāniyya first spread primarily in North and West Africa. By the early twentieth century, it had become the most popular Sufi order in Morocco.[28] By the nineteenth century, it had made significant inroads among established clerical lineages of Mauritania, Senegal, Mali, and Nigeria; and by the mid-twentieth century, under the leadership of the Tijānī revivalist Ibrāhīm Niasse (d. 1975, Senegal), had displaced the Qādiriyya as the dominant Sufi order in West Africa.[29] It is today found all over the Muslim world and beyond, with notable Tijānī communities (besides North and West Africa) in Indonesia, Singapore, India, Turkey, Palestine, Arab Gulf states, Egypt, Europe, and North and South America.[30]

If the Tijāniyya has become one of the Islamic world's most popular Sufi orders, it is certainly a testimony to the success of eighteenth-century Islamic scholarly revival. The lack of serious academic consideration of the Tijāniyya in historical overviews of Sufism, or its place in eighteenth-century revivalism, is an astounding oversight in both fields. In elaborating the notion of the "Hidden Pole" (*al-quṭb al-maktūm*), the Tijānī tradition seemed unconcerned by such opacity: "The secret with me," al-Tijānī said, "is locked in a house whose doors are shut and whose key has been lost."[31] But full understanding of the shaykh's secret knowledge is not necessary to appreciate the rapid spread of the order and the dynamic intellectual production it inspired.

Literature and Sources on the Tijāniyya

Generalist studies of Sufism or of eighteenth-century intellectual history have undoubtedly been limited by incomplete or problematic prior research on the Tijāniyya. The primary English monograph on the Tijāniyya, Jamil Abun-Nasr's *The Tijaniyya: A Sufi Order in the Modern World* (1965), framed an otherwise notable exposition of primary source material with an uncritical belief in the inevitable "demystification" of the modern world. For Abun-Nasr, the Tijāniyya was an example of Sufism's incompatibility with modern, postcolonial Muslim rationalized sensibilities. "Their story is," Abun-Nasr noted in accusing the Sufi orders and the Tijāniyya in particular with colonial collaboration, "that of adjustment and reconciliation, which would have enabled them to survive politically had it not been that the doctrines which they preached and the functions which they performed were no longer suited to modern times."[32] Themes of colonial collaboration, political posturing, and intellectual irrelevance remained consistent refrains for subsequent mentions of the Tijāniyya, as they did for African Sufi communities more broadly. A later introduction to a series of conference papers on the Tijāniyya remarks on the order's "theological arrogance" and its "long 'concubinage' with French colonial power" permitting it to become "one of the greatest beneficiaries of the colonial period." And unlike other orders, the Tijāniyya "remains exclusively African—this is another one of its characteristics."[33] Generations of later scholarship thus appear to have remained beholden to Abun-Nasr's reading of the Tijāniyya.

My 2003 master's thesis, "On the Path of the Prophet: Shaykh Ahmad Tijani and the Ṭariqa Muhammadiyya," was later published (2005) without peer review. It hoped to recontextualize Tijānī primary source material within the intellectual history of the eighteenth century. The work stands, I believe, as a useful introduction to the Tijāniyya, but is limited by a surface-level reading of primary source material and an exaggeration of the *Ṭarīqa Muḥammadiyya* as an intellectually coherent scholarly network. In any case, the book has received some academic attention, with two reprints and a French translation reflecting its apparent usefulness to non-academic audiences and the undergraduate classroom.[34]

The only other published academic monograph to narrate the history of the Tijāniyya (in a European language[35]) is Jilali El Adnani's *La Tijāniyya, 1781–1881*.[36] While Adnani recognizes the significance of the Tijāniyya in the modern history of Morocco, his utilitarian focus on shaykh-disciple relationships at the foundation of the order reduces Sufi affiliation to a form of false consciousness. Like Abun-Nasr, Adnani's citation of primary source material focuses on provocative statements to substantiate an apparent narrative of Tijānī heterodoxy, failing to balance such citations with others that might allow him to read these statements differently. Adnani thus concludes, "the rehabilitation of Ahmad al-Tijānī resided in the reinforcement of his superior rank over his disciples, something impossible without recourse to miracles and magic . . . testimony to a strategy destined for the masses, which was much more receptive to invisible actors than to Sufi erudition."[37] Alexander Knysh has usefully bracketed such understandings of Sufi communities based on crude power dynamics: "'Power' is too general a concept to account for construction, justification, and performance by Sufi masters of their claims to knowledge and guidance across centuries. Commanding respect and awe, being listened to in silence by a captive and respectful audience without necessarily 'dominating' or 'exploiting' it, is a motivation that does not fit neatly into the narrowly conceived grid of power relations envisioned by neo-Marxian sociologists of various stripes."[38] Knysh concludes that such an understanding "fails to do justice to the complexity of human aspirations." Abun-Nasr's and Adnani's apparent reduction of the religious identities of millions of Tijānī adherents may fit various instrumentalist understandings of the Tijāniyya's social and political role in Africa from the nineteenth century, but their dismissal of the intellectual contributions of al-Tijānī and his early disciples has left a void in more general overviews of Sufi thought and history. This tendency to selectively ignore formative teachings from primary sources, in preference for decontextualized controversial statements, necessitates a more balanced narration of one of the Islamic world's most important Sufi orders.

It must be admitted, however, that the works of Abun-Nasr and Adnani provide a window into intriguing polemical debates surrounding Sufi doctrine and practice in modern contexts. Some of these debates—such as the implications of seeing the Prophet—appear specific to the Tijāniyya, but most are more general to Sufism (the hierarchy of saints or the power of Sufi prayers, for example) and perhaps to "traditional Islam" broadly defined (the authority of scholars, the enduring spirit of the Prophet beyond the grave, or the present-essence of God, for example). Full exploration of such polemics, and the voluminous literature they have produced, deserve a separate and more focused inquiry that is beyond the scope of this work. However, I hope that the disciplined situation of the Tijāniyya's emergence in eighteenth-century Islamic intellectual history can provide a more stable foundation for such further explorations.

In addition to the problematic decontextualization of primary sources in earlier academic accounts, a new history of the Tijāniyya is also warranted from the perspective of newly available or edited Arabic source material. While Aḥmad al-Tijānī, like many Sufi shaykhs, left few writings himself, there are a number of central primary sources written or collected by his disciples. Foremost among them is the "Pearls of Meanings and Obtainment of Hopes in the Spiritual Floods of Sayyidī Abū l-ʿAbbās Aḥmad al-Tijānī" (hereafter referenced as *Jawāhir al-maʿānī*) written by al-Tijānī's closest disciple, ʿAlī Ḥarāzim al-Barrāda (or al-Barāda, d. 1804), and completed in 1798.[39] The work contains al-Tijānī's biography, his interpretations of various Qurʾān verses and sayings of the Prophet, and responses to a variety of questions from disciples. In writing the book, Ḥarāzim recycled short, formulaic sections from an earlier Moroccan Sufi text, ʿAbd al-Salām b. al-Ṭayyib al-Qādirī's (d. 1699), *Kitāb al-maqṣad al-Aḥmad*, concerning the seventeenth-century Shādhilī saint Aḥmad b. ʿAbdallāh Maʿn al-Andalūsī (d. 1708).[40] While Abun-Nasr concludes that the fact that Ḥarāzim "drew heavily" on this earlier text constitutes an "act of plagiarism,"[41] close comparison between published versions of the *Jawāhir al-maʿānī* and the 1932 publication of *Kitāb al-maqṣad* reveal that Ḥarāzim borrowed roughly 2.5 pages of *al-Maqṣad*'s formulaic introduction: a few of the introductory paragraphs, and a few of the poems probably themselves recycled from past writings.[42] Considering the roughly 680 pages of the 2011 publication of the *Jawāhir*, this borrowing (0.3 percent) hardly qualified as plagiarism by the standards of the classical Arabic textual tradition,[43] but it nonetheless became part of a Salafi-inspired attack against the Tijāniyya in early twentieth-century Morocco.[44] In any case, the *Jawāhir al-maʿānī* has enjoyed unrivaled authority in the Tijāniyya, due to Ḥarāzim's designation as al-Tijānī's "greatest deputy" (*al-khalīfa al-aʿẓam*) and on account of the Prophet's appearance to al-Tijānī to order the book's compilation: "Preserve it," Ḥarāzim records the Prophet's words to al-Tijānī, "in order to benefit the saints after you."[45] Elsewhere, al-Tijānī was reported as saying,

"The Prophet ordered me to collect the *Jawāhir al-maʿānī*, and he told me, 'This is my book, and it is I who authored it.' "[46]

There are significant divergences among published copies of the *Jawāhir al-maʿānī*, and some Tijānī scholars claimed that earlier publications dating to the beginning of the twentieth century departed from the original manuscript.[47] But the claim of interpolation is difficult to substantiate: divergent publications appear to be primarily the result of various manuscript versions penned by ʿAlī Ḥarāzim himself, or prominent early Tijānī scholars from Ḥarāzim's work. The Moroccan Tijānī scholar Rāḍī Kanūn's 2012 republication of the *Jawāhir al-maʿānī* identified no fewer than four original manuscripts of the text in Ḥarāzim's handwriting: one held in ʿAyn Māḍī, two located in Tlemcen (Algeria), and one found in Kaolack, Senegal.[48] This latter version had already been published in 2011 by the Senegalese shaykh Tijānī b. ʿAlī Cissé, based on the manuscript his grandfather Ibrāhīm Niasse had obtained from his father ʿAbdallāh Niasse, who was gifted the copy in Fez in 1911 by al-Tijānī's descendant Bashīr b. Muḥammad b. Aḥmad al-Tijānī.[49] While Kanūn privileges the ʿAyn Māḍī manuscript as the "mother" text, the "Kaolack" manuscript arguably deserves precedent recognition: this was the copy kept in al-Tijānī's possession, from which he read, for the last sixteen years of his life.[50] The initial page contains al-Tijānī's handwritten testimony: "Everything written in this manuscript (*al-kunnāsh*), each letter appearing from the beginning to the end, I have authorized."[51] While Kanūn's recent publication presents a useful comparison between various versions of the *Jawāhir*, the amalgamated text he published does not reproduce any one version of a manuscript original.[52] For these reasons, I primarily rely on Cissé's 2011 edition from the original *Jawāhir al-maʿānī* kept in al-Tijānī's possession during his life for all citations.

Another disciple, Muḥammad b. al-Mashrī (or Mishrī) al-Sāʾiḥī (d. 1809), left two separate collections of al-Tijānī's teachings that remained unpublished until 2012. The first is "The Garden of the Annihilated Lover in what has been transmitted from our Shaykh Abū l-ʿAbbās al-Tijānī" (hereafter *Rawḍ al-muḥibb*), written around 1792.[53] The second is "The Collection of the Pearls of Knowledge overflowing from the Seas of the Hidden Pole" (hereafter *al-Jamiʿ*), completed in 1804.[54] It is clear Ḥarāzim and Ibn al-Mashrī shared notes between them, for much of the three books contain similar passages and sometimes share organizational features. However, Ibn al-Mashrī's texts add much to our understanding of al-Tijānī's intellectual contributions beyond the Ḥarāzim's *Jawāhir al-ma'ānī*, particularly in regard to theology and jurisprudence. To prove the point that Ibn al-Mashrī's writing contained value in its own right, a later Tijānī scholar published a separate book collecting everything from the *Jāmi'* not contained in the *Jawāhir*.[55]

Primary sources written by direct disciples of al-Tijānī also include a collection of the shaykh's sayings, collected by the scholarly disciple al-Ṭayyib al-Sufyānī (d. 1843, Fez), "The Aḥmadan Blessing for the Aspirant of Eternal Happiness" (hereafter *al-Ifāda al-Aḥmadiyya*), and gathered shortly after the shaykh's passing in 1815.[56] There is also the "Book of Divine Guidance" (*Kitāb al-irshādāt al-rabbāniyya*), al-Tijānī's commentary on al-Buṣayrī's (d. 1294, Alexandria) poem in praise of the Prophet (*al-Hamziyya*) dictated to 'Alī Ḥarāzim.[57] The significant collections of the Moroccan Tijānī scholar Aḥmad Sukayrij (d. 1944) detailing the biographies of al-Tijānī's students should also be considered as foundational primary sources. Sukayrij's "Removal of the Shroud" (*Kashf al-ḥijāb*)[58] and his expanded "Raising the Veil" (*Raf' al-niqāb*)[59] include rare source material, such as letters between al-Tijānī and various disciples, treatises, poetry, and prayers composed by the shaykh's students, and meticulously researched oral narrations concerning al-Tijānī's relationship with his community of students. A later descendant of al-Tijānī collected all of his ancestor's letters found in various other collections and published a separate volume, the "Selected Letters" (*Mukhtārāt min rasā'il al-shaykh*), that also serves as a useful primary source.[60]

Other later Tijānī scholars published Arabic source materials that played important roles in the explanation and spread of the Tijāniyya. Some of these sources that inform this book include the "Lances of the Party of the Merciful" (*Rimāḥ*) of the nineteenth-century West African 'Umar Fūtī (Tal),[61] the "Fulfillment of Beneficience" (*Bughyat al-Mustafīd*) of the nineteenth-century Moroccan scholar al-'Arabī b. al-Sā'iḥ,[62] and the "Removal of Confusion" (*Kāshif al-ilbās*) of Ibrāhīm Niasse.[63] While these varied published sources were certainly written with different audiences and historical contexts in mind, they nonetheless form an impressive trove of information from which to reconstruct the intellectual history of the early Tijāniyya.

Many years of field research have afforded access to other manuscript sources still unpublished and unknown to previous academic research. The most notable is a forty-nine-page untitled "travel notebook" (hereafter referred to as *Kunnāsh al-riḥla*) written in al-Tijānī's own handwriting.[64] The work collects various prayers al-Tijānī received from scholars he visited while traveling in North Africa and Arabia. The date of this compilation is unknown, but it appears from most of the scholars mentioned that it was written during his pilgrimage east in the years 1773 and 1774, or shortly thereafter upon his return to the Maghreb. A second important manuscript is the *Mashāhid* ("spiritual encounters") of ʿAlī Ḥarāzim, a 212-page account detailing Ḥarāzim's own spiritual training and experiences at the direction of al-Tijānī, written in 1799 or 1800, soon after the completion of the *Jawāhir al-maʿānī*.[65] Other various "notebooks of secrets" (sing. *Kunnāsh*) attributed to al-Tijānī, to which the contemporary Senegalese shaykh Tijānī Cissé granted me access in his personal archive,[66] also inform my understanding of al-Tijānī's scholarly influences and breadth of knowledge, especially in the field of esotericism.

There are a few Arabic sources, external to the Tijāniyya, that tangentially reference al-Tijānī and the early Tijāniyya, most notably Abū l-Qāsim al-Zayānī's (d. 1833) *al-Tarjumāna al-kubrā*, Aḥmad al-Nāṣirī's (d. 1897) *al-Istiqṣā li-akhbār duwal al-Maghrib al-aqṣā* (completed 1894), and Muḥammad Jaʿfar al-Kattānī's (d. 1927) *Salwat al-anfās* (completed 1887).[67] I make reference to these external perspectives, but the fact is that external sources on the Tijāniyya are simply too sparse to rely on to the same degree as internal sources.[68] The false equivalence between the secondhand, often contradictory reports in external sources, and firsthand internal narratives—the historical value of which can be too easily dismissed as imagined hagiography—is an oversight, I believe, that has limited prior research on the Tijāniyya. This question of historiography is sometimes addressed by Sufi communities themselves, notably by Ibrāhīm Niasse in his first encounter with a French historian. Niasse said, "I heard you mentioned me in your book. I have also written many books, but I never mentioned you. Do you know why? Because I do not know you."[69] Of course, external narratives are indispensable; the point is simply that internal accounts cannot be immediately dismissed as providing unreliable historical data. Just as Ibn Khaldūn's observations of Muslim societies cannot be discounted simply because he was a practicing Muslim, so too must historians take seriously the internal narratives of Sufi communities despite the fact their authors were practicing Sufis. Alternately, clearly defined genres of Sufi writing—such as hagiography, advice on etiquette or spiritual training, and prayer manuals—certainly have audiences other than critical historians in mind.

Nonetheless, several internal sources clearly cross disciplinary boundaries: the multivolume biographical dictionaries of Aḥmad Sukayrij, for example, contain critically researched oral traditions cross-referenced with alternative narrations and textual references. This book situates internal sources within the context of externally established historical narratives but focuses more on exploring the process of religious realization captured in internal sources, than it does on reconciling or disproving every external fragment. This is a story of religious identity in historical context; I make no claim to writing the definitive history of the Tijāniyya.

The spread of the Tijāniyya, particularly in vibrant scholarly contexts of nineteenth-and twentieth-century Mauritania, Mali, Senegal, and Nigeria, produced a veritable explosion of Arabic literature.[70] Full analysis of this literature,[71] which includes treatises, letters, and poetry both for and against the Tijāniyya, is not attempted in this book. Nonetheless, this literary production, including the controversies it preserves, should be more systemically considered in accounting for the later spread of the Tijāniyya. Charismatic Sufi authority, as Rüdiger Seesemann observes in the later Tijānī community of Ibrāhīm Niasse, sometimes consciously risked public censure to provide spiritual realization to greater numbers of people. "His most important task consisted of finding a balance between attracting followers and controlling their experiences. The internal sources leave no doubt that he [Niasse] was up to the task, but apparently not all of the deputies were. Yet if some of the latter were less successful in walking the tightrope between captivating the followers and curbing their enthusiasm and talkativeness, the resulting attacks of the deniers helped to reinforce the cohesion of the community. This very mechanism eventually drove the large-scale expansion."[72] Such controversies arguably played a role in the expansion of the Tijāniyya from its foundation. But as I argued in relation to the community of Ibrāhīm Niasse,[73] I believe that polemics surrounding the teachings of al-Tijānī are the later reflection of an underlying appeal, not the generative mechanism for spread of the Tijāniyya by themselves. Liabilities of the polemical frame include an ahistorical reading of later polemics into the foundational sources, or an overemphasis of polemical sources, most often marginal to lived experiences of most disciples, to the exclusion of more central preoccupations. This book thus concerns the ideal of religious actualization that attracted disciples to al-Tijānī in a late eighteenth-century North African context and leaves the (mostly) later controversies that this ideal produced, or failed to produce, to other researchers.

Structure of the Book

This work begins with situating the emergence of the Tijāniyya in a broader eighteenth-century intellectual context. While I hope to avoid generalizing across divergent local contexts and scholarly articulations, much of Aḥmad al-Tijānī's teachings clearly responded to currents of global exchange in the Muslim world. Topics such as independent scholarly reasoning (*ijtihād*), the verification of divine oneness (*tawḥīd*), or the Sufi's privileged connection to the Prophet were all ideas in wide circulation, even if scholars had different understandings of these ideas. This chapter summarizes new research on the eighteenth-century Muslim world, but I also make direct recourse to the primary sources of this period, including the writings of seminal figures like Ibrāhīm al-Kūrānī, Muṣṭafā al-Bakrī, ʿAbd al-Ghanī al-Nābulusī, Muḥammad al-Sammān, and Maḥmūd al-Kurdī. Discussions of eighteenth-century intellectual history frequently privilege the Middle East and India, with only marginal reference to North or West Africa. Here I consider intellectual developments in North Africa, sub-Saharan Africa, the Middle East, and India as all playing a role in the shared scholarly discourses that informed the emergence of the Tijāniyya.

The second chapter considers Aḥmad al-Tijānī's formation as a Muslim scholar in eighteenth-century Algeria and Morocco. While al-Tijānī was of course primarily remembered as a Sufi, his scholarship was imprinted by a long engagement with the broader scholarly tradition, including Qur'ān and ḥadīth study, Islamic law, theology, and esotericism or "talismanic sciences." Sources for this discussion include the core primary sources of the Tijāniyya, but read from the perspective of specific Islamic disciplinary specialization. I also consider al-Tijānī's opinions on esotericism from the vantage point of previously unavailable manuscript sources.

Chapter 3 returns more explicitly to the notion of actualization or *taḥqīq*, but this time with a pronounced emphasis on the realization of humanity (*taḥqīq al-insāniyya*). I argue that the reflection on the human condition evident in primary sources of the Tijāniyya is what informed conceptions of witnessing the unseen world, particularly the experience of seeing the Prophet Muḥammad. Perhaps most significant, this actualization of human potentiality was not restricted to the shaykh alone but included his disciples in sometimes surprising ways.

In chapter 4, I take up the challenge of understanding Aḥmad al-Tijānī's claims to spiritual authority and the asserted preeminence of the Tijāniyya over other Sufi orders. As reflected in primary sources themselves, these claims raised difficult questions in al-Tijānī's early community: did the shaykh mean to confirm or to abrogate the earlier Sufi tradition? How could disciples be warned against spiritual complacency while being assured of the new order's ascendant value? Such dynamic tensions deserve balanced analysis to comprehend the reception and continued meaning the Tijāniyya has had for millions of Muslims.

The final chapter considers the question of historical context in both practical and philosophical terms. Aḥmad al-Tijānī, like many others in the late eighteenth century, perceived his time as being one of unprecedented sinfulness and corruption. The Tijāniyya was thus conceived as a cure for the ailing Muslim community, giving hope to those who had despaired of obtaining divine grace in such a time. Not surprising, such an understanding has had heightened meaning for subsequent generations of Tijānī adherents, who perhaps cannot help but observe increased corruption and an enduring need for God's bountiful grace in their own diverse historical contexts. The conclusion reflects on the remarkable spread of the Tijāniyya as a testimony to the intellectual vibrancy of the eighteenth century.

CHAPTER ONE

Sufism and Islamic Intellectual Developments in the Eighteenth Century

THE IDEAS THAT BECAME CENTRAL to the Tijāniyya had wide currency in the Muslim world by the late eighteenth century. Such ideas were sometimes sourced in texts, but more often they were transmitted through personal investiture, accompanied by texts or without. It is no accident, then, to find al-Tijānī personally connected to those whose ideas were later integrated in the Tijāniyya. This is not to suggest a static continuity between teachers and students across generations and vast geographical space. But it does suggest that personal connections cannot be ignored in the sharing of ideas between scholars.

The eighteenth century represented the culmination of centuries of Islamic scholarly prestige in the Muslim world. Later generations witnessed the rise of the modern state and its confiscation of the endowments (*awqāf*) that gave financial independence to the scholarly class and the promotion of Western-influenced schooling that created new intellectuals who displaced traditional scholars as teachers, writers, and bureaucrats. But before this state-centric (and often colonially inspired) modernization, scholars confidently asserted their ascendant rank over sultans in best ensuring the Islamic authenticity of their societies. "In Muslim society *vox* ʿulamāʾ is legally *vox dei*," wrote an historian of eighteenth-century Egypt, "and practically *vox populi* for they had it in their power to rouse or placate public opinion."[1]

Global scholarly exchange gave intellectuals the opportunity to hear new ideas, access new textual sources, and invest themselves with "heightened" (shorter) chains of knowledge transmission. These events usually occurred when individuals accomplished their pilgrimage rites in the Hijaz, often stopping in other scholarly centers, such as Cairo, along the way. It may be true that the culmination of such activities in the eighteenth century eventually caused regional scholarship to assert its sufficiency from continued travels in search of knowledge.[2] But it is also true that global scholarly exchange after the eighteenth century was limited by European colonial occupation: non-Muslim authorities generally began to restrict and surveil the travels of Muslim scholars even during the pilgrimage season.[3] Global networks of Muslim scholars were well established on the eve of colonial conquest, and intellectual exchanges figured prominently in the biographies of scholars written during the period even if such exchanges were less pronounced in later generations.

It was primarily the desire for verification (*taḥqīq*) that motivated the intellectual vibrancy of the eighteenth century. Verification or religious actualization took on different meanings depending on the field of knowledge involved, whether jurisprudence (*fiqh*), theology (*ʿaqīda*, *ʿilm al-kalām*), or Sufism (*taṣawwuf*).[4] In Islamic law, *taḥqīq* meant ascertaining the relationship between a definitive sacred text (*naṣṣ*)—usually a saying of the Prophet (*ḥadīth*)—and a scholarly opinion (*ijtihād*) from the schools of law (*madhhab*, pl. *madhāhib*). Much has been made about transmission of ḥadīth and calls for *ijtihād* in the period, but these can arguably be categorized as renewed discussions of legal theory (*uṣūl*).[5]

In theological terms, *taḥqīq* meant the verification of God's oneness (*tawḥīd*) and the eradication of hidden idolatry (*shirk al-khafī*). Of course, the "Muḥammadan" Sufis of the eighteenth century had different understandings of this process than did the nascent "Wahhabi" movement of central Arabia: namely the purification of the heart from other than God in order to experience *tawḥīd*, versus a form of Protestant-style confessionalism.[6] But the shared intention to cleanse the belief of Muslims is undeniable in eighteenth-century scholarly networks, and theology was a primary preoccupation of most of the era's scholars.

The *taḥqīq* of Sufism meant the endeavor to connect Sufi practices and understandings with the spiritual path of the Prophet (*Ṭarīqa Muḥammadiyya*). Even the followers of Muḥammad b. ʿAbd al-Wahhāb were quick to assert that they never suggested this purified Sufism was blameworthy or that they denied the miracles of the saints,[7] and Ibn ʿAbd al-Wahhāb insisted in his letters, "I know of nothing that makes a person closer to God than the spiritual path (*ṭarīqa*) of God's Messenger."[8] Once again, the students of the eighteenth-century scholarly networks shared similar aspirations, even if the understanding of the "Muḥammadan Sufism" or *Ṭarīqa*

Muḥammadiyya diverged sharply between mainstream scholarly Sufism of the time and radical outliers.

Aḥmad al-Tijānī's own interjections in the verification of legal opinions, theology, and Sufism comprise later chapters of this book. But here it is useful to outline the knowledge circulation within eighteenth-century scholarly networks, particularly as they related to al-Tijānī. Such superficial descriptions are suggestive at best, and no one book, whatever its pretension, can delve into the intellectual content of all eighteenth-century scholars with any meaningful depth. This chapter thus limits itself to discussing the teachings of al-Tijānī's most significant scholarly contacts within these networks, and the broader spectrum of ideas out of which al-Tijānī's *Ṭarīqa Muḥammadiyya* emerged.

Scholarly Networks

Most, if not all, prominent eighteenth-century scholars were connected with each other through person-to-person chains of knowledge transmission. This highly ritualized form of knowledge investiture and authorization, represented in the personalized *ijāza/sanad/silsila* model, emphasized the internalization of learning and the formation (or recognition) of exemplary disposition.[9] However, students, especially those with a variety of learned influences, rarely reproduced the exact practice or doctrine of their teachers. Rather such networks shared a common discourse loosely based on verification through heightened connection to the Prophet. "Some think sharing a discourse means that people are part of a homogenous organization. But a community of discourse is not an organization, and people within that community of discourse can disagree strongly even though they utilize the same discourse."[10]

With such caution in mind, the following summarizes the remarkable constellation of scholars who shared teacher-student relationships during the period. Our particular focus here is the situation of al-Tijānī within these networks, so these summaries are far from definitive. The particular traditions with which al-Tijānī connected include: the "Muḥammadan" Sufism of the North African Shādhilī master Muḥammad b. Nāṣir (d. 1674, Tamagrut, Morocco) and his student Ḥasan al-Yūsī (d. 1691, Marrakesh); the West African Sharīʿa-based, visionary Sufism emerging in scholarly centers such as Timbuktu by the sixteenth century; the *Ḥaramayn* (Mecca and Medina) *hadith* and *ijtihād* transmitters emerging from the "school" of

Ibrāhīm al-Kurānī (d. 1693, Medina); the renewal of the Khalwatiyya Sufi order in Egypt under the leadership of the Damascene Muṣṭafa al-Bakrī (d. 1748, Cairo); and the Indian Shaṭṭariyya and Naqshbandiyya networks transmitting the teachings of Muḥammad al-Ghawth (d. 1563, Ahmedabad). The Tijāniyya was an heir to all of these often-overlapping traditions. Its later global spread, especially in West Africa, reflects the resonance of the Tijāniyya with prior traditions as much as it does the unprecedented divine grace it claimed to transmit.

Shādhilī Sufism in North Africa

Of the several branches of the Shādhiliyya in North Africa, the Nāṣiriyya and Wazzāniyya both stand out for their similarity to the later emergence of the Tijāniyya. These branches, as opposed to the initially antinomian Darqawiyya,[11] were distinguished by their good reputation in scholarly circles for societal involvement and orthodoxy. Muḥammad b. Nāṣir, who established his following as the Nāṣiriyya in seventeenth-century southern Morocco, cautioned against extreme acts of renunciation as well as music and dance in Sufi practices, balancing an emphasis on "the Islamic sciences, respect for the Sunnah and scrupulous imitation of the Prophet's example on the one hand, with initiation and mystical knowledge on the other."[12] He stressed the importance of having a spiritual guide to actualize one's Muslim identity: "If you do not have a shaykh, Iblīs [Satan] must be near to you, and if Iblīs is near to you, you are not a true Muslim."[13] The shaykh offered his own path as a remedy: "My path is easy, and the benefits large."[14] Later Nāṣirī followers would claim that initiation gave the aspirant salvation in the afterlife.[15] For these reasons—and due to the order's success in facilitating trade—the Nāṣiriyya seems to have been the most popular Sufi order in North Africa by the late seventeenth century.

Ibn Nāṣir's close disciple, al-Ḥasan al-Yūsī, was arguably Morocco's most famous scholar of the seventeenth century. He advocated the scholar's active verification of Islam's central theological doctrine of divine oneness (*tawḥīd*) to obtain certainty (*yaqīn*), although methodologically he favored rational proofs according to the Ashʿarī theological school as opposed to the mystical experience of the "unity of being" (*waḥdat al-wujūd*).[16] Al-Yūsī's treatment of the visionary experiences claimed by Sufis reflects a sober balance between the verification provided by such experiences and the fact that such experiences were themselves subject to verification.

Al-Yūsī argued that, because saints were not immune to error, they could misinterpret spiritual unveilings. While waking visions were more reliable than dreams or states of spiritual intoxication, they could also be subject to delusion. A person should test his own visions, as well as what he hears from others, on the basis of their scholarship and character: "He should not be deluded by every prattler, nor think poorly of every Muslim. Such recondite matters can only be grasped by the intelligent and those blessed with guidance, and it all must be explained with the assistance and guidance of Exalted God." True visions should be concealed to avoid causing discord, unless the vision could bring benefit to others or unless the visionary was ordered by his teacher to reveal the vision.[17]

The Nāṣiriyya thus came to be associated with a sober, sharīʿa-compliant Sufism that rearticulated the importance of saintly authority and scholarship in the verification of knowledge and spiritual states. By the late eighteenth century, the Nāṣiriyya remained a predominate religious force in North Africa and beyond. The Moroccan sultan Mawlay Sulaymān (r. 1792–1822) was initiated into the order, and it became established within the circles of scholarly renewal in the Middle East, probably after the pilgrimage east of Ḥasan al-Yūsī in the late seventeenth century. The Indian scholar resident in Cairo, Murtaḍā al-Zabīdī (d. 1791), had been initiated into the order while studying ḥadīth in Medina, Arabia, and would later pass knowledge authorizations to the head of the Nāṣiriyya who visited him in Cairo.[18]

The Wazzāniyya was less known outside of Morocco,[19] but similar to the Nāṣiriyya, enjoyed good relations with the Moroccan political and scholarly establishment. This branch of Shādhiliyya, founded by ʿAbdallāh b. Ibrāhīm al-Idrīsī (d. 1678) in the northwestern Moroccan town of Wazzān, differed little from Shādhiliyya-Jazūliyya into which the *Sharīf* ʿAbdallāh had been initiated.[20] As such, it emphasized the saint's role in social and soteriological intercession, the notion of the Sufi path as a "universalistic spiritual path in which the authority of the Sufi shaykh was based on an explicit analogy between the saint and the Prophet Muhammad," and the paradigmatic sainthood of one who had become "the veritable personification of the Messenger of God."[21] The early Jazūliyya also made specific reference to the notion of the *Ṭarīqa Muḥammadiyya*, although the association meant to emphasize the Sufi saint's social obligations rather than the direct inspiration of his path from the Prophet.[22] ʿAbdallāh al-Idrīsī himself did not publicly teach his version of the Shādhiliyya until being given permission by the Prophet directly. Indeed, al-Idrīsī's own Jazūlī shaykh

ʿAlī Ṣarsī (d. 1628) had once declared, "If we are unable to visit him (the Prophet), he will come to us in our place."[23] The Jazuliyya's imprint on the Wazzāniyya was perhaps best reflected in the person of the third Wazzānī shaykh Mawlay al-Ṭayyib (d. 1767), under whose leadership the town of Wazzān became an established center of religious learning and economic development, seeing the Wazzāniyya further spread throughout Morocco and Algeria.[24]

Aḥmad al-Tijānī received initiation in both the Nāṣiriyya and Wazzāniyya during his travels to Morocco prior to the foundation of his own *Ṭarīqa Muḥammadiyya*. His earliest Sufi affiliation, "the first whom he met among the distinguished masters," was Mawlāy al-Ṭayyib of the Wazzāniyya, "the famous axial saint" (*al-quṭb al-shahīr*), whom he visited in Wazzān on his way to Fez sometime around 1760.[25] Still in his early twenties, al-Tijānī was apparently surprised to receive, along with initiation, an immediate authorization to initiate others (*ijāza fī l-taqdīm*). His reaction was to "abstain" from practicing the order's litanies "in order to work on (purifying) himself."[26] A disciple of al-Tijānī later asked, "Why did you leave his litany (*wird*) when he was one of God's saints (*awliyāʾ*)?" Al-Tijānī responded, "I did not (then) know the spiritual states (*aḥwāl*) of the saints, and when I saw him in a (certain) state, I thought that a saint could not be in such (a state)."[27] This is likely a reference to the reputed worldly wealth of the Wazzānī shaykhs by the eighteenth century.[28] Nonetheless, he would later attest to the high spiritual attainment of the Wazzānī tradition, declaring that five Wazzānī shaykhs had obtained axial or paradigmatic sainthood (*quṭbāniyya*), including Mawlāy al-Ṭayyib.[29]

Al-Tijānī took the litany (*wird*) of Ibn Nāṣir through Muḥammad b. ʿAbdallāh al-Tuzānī (d. 1778). Al-Tuzānī, whose grave remains a site of pious visitation (*ziyāra*) in northeastern Morocco, had initiation through his father, from his uncle, from Ibn Nāṣir's son Aḥmad, with the uncle having a separate initiation in the Nāṣiriyya from Ḥasan al-Yūsī.[30] Al-Tijānī did not practice the Nāṣirī *wird* long, but he continued to commend, consistent with Nāṣirī litanies, the recitation of al-Jazūlī's *Dalāʾil al-khayrat* long after the establishment of the Tijāniyya.[31] The legacy of the North African Shādhiliyya thus was clearly a significant background to the emergence of the Tijāniyya. Although he claimed the ascendency of his Sufi path over the Shādhiliyya, al-Tijānī encouraged the respect for past Shādhilī masters and continued to practice much of the devotional supplications of the Shādhiliyya.[32]

Muḥammadan Sufism and Scholarly Verification in Sub-Saharan Africa

Aside from the Nāṣiriyya and the Wazzāniyya, another central influence on Moroccan Sufism in the eighteenth century was the teachings of ʿAbd al-ʿAzīz al-Dabbāgh (d. 1719, Fez), collected by his disciple in the widely circulated book "Pure Gold" *(Dhahab al-ibrīz)*.[33] Al-Dabbāgh, whom al-Tijānī referred to as the "axial saint" (*quṭb*) of his time,[34] claimed to be in frequent visionary communication with the Prophet and emphasized the superiority of taking knowledge from the Prophet directly.[35] Although he never used the term *Ṭarīqa Muḥammadiyya* himself, he transmitted his own Sufi path inspired in part by prayers given to him by the guide of Prophet Moses (Khiḍr), with the express purpose of joining with the presence of the Prophet Muḥammad.[36] A formative influence on al-Dabbāgh was a sub-Saharan African scholar named ʿAbdallāh b. ʿAbd al-Jalīl al-Burnāwī, who appeared in Fez in order to train him to experience the waking vision of the Prophet Muḥammad. Al-Burnāwī then departed from him, saying: "O Sayyid ʿAbd al-ʿAzīz, before today I was afraid for your sake. But today since God the Sublime, through his mercy, has united you with the lord of creation—God's blessing and peace upon him—my heart feels safe and my mind is assured. I therefore leave you in the hands of God the mighty and glorious."[37] Despite his departure from Fez, al-Dabbāgh remained in spiritual contact with al-Burnāwī after he returned to Bornu. Al-Dabbāgh was spiritually informed of the day Burnāwī died, saying, "When Sayyid ʿAbdallāh al-Burnāwī died, I inherited the secrets he possessed."[38]

This example points to the important role sub-Saharan African scholars played in the scholarly exchanges culminating in the eighteenth century. But there is much more to the story, in both the particulars of al-Burnāwī here, and the general portrait of African Muslim scholarship in the period. While the *Ibrīz* appears to subtly exoticize al-Burnāwī's sudden appearance ("behold there was a black man at the gate. He began to stare at me."[39]), other sources, such as al-Kattānī's *Salwat al-anfās*, give depth to al-Burnāwī's scholarly background. Here, I follow Bobboyi's suggestion that the al-Burnāwī who appeared to al-Dabbāgh was a post-mortem apparition of ʿAbdallāh b. ʿAbd al-ʿAzīz al-Burnāwī (d. 1677), who had established an influential Sufi community at the northern frontier of the Bornu empire.[40] Soon after al-Dabbāgh's al-Burnāwī left Fez, another of al-Burnāwī's more ordinary students appeared in the city: the traveling

Sudanese-Yemeni scholar Aḥmad al-Yamanī (d. 1712, Fez).[41] Al-Yamanī, who had studied with al-Burnāwī in the central-western African kingdom of Bornu before arriving in Fez, referred to his shaykh as "the master of his time" (*ṣāḥib waqtihi*) and the "wonder of his age."[42] Al-Burnāwī, according to another contemporary account, *Rīḥān al-qulūb*, was sometimes in a state of spiritual ecstasy (*majdhūb*), but nonetheless the "pole of the Sufi way" (*quṭb al-ṭarīqa*) who was in constant contact with the Angel Isrāfīl.[43] He was also an accomplished scholar of the exoteric sciences: he had knowledge of theology, Qur'ān exegesis, and linguistics. He had a photographic memory, taught an Arabic grammatical work, the *Alfiyya* of Ibn Mālik, and "gave commentary on the Qur'ān like the exegesis of the great scholars."[44] Al-Burnāwī claimed nonetheless that all his knowledge was a result of his friendship with God (*walāya*): "God does not make a saint (publicly) manifest, except that He supports him with knowledge."[45] Al-Burnāwī's portrait thus emerges here in more detail than in the *Ibrīz*. Taken as a whole, this African intellectual appeared in Fez as an eminent scholar-saint who emphasized the scholar's direct connection to the Prophet Muḥammad, the importance of Sufi training under a shaykh, and the balance between Sufism and the sacred law.

But al-Yamanī had more to say about African scholarship than his testimony of al-Burnāwī. Al-Yamanī came to Fez from East Africa across the Sahel. According to *Salwat al-anfās*, "He spent a long time in the land of the blacks (*bilād al-sūdān*)." Aside from al-Burnāwī, he studied with other African scholars, such as Aḥmad al-Tārikay ("the Tuareg"), from the town of Agades (Adkaz), allegedly of the Suhrawardiyya Sufi order.[46] This is no doubt a reference to al-Yamanī's contact with the legacy of the sixteenth-century West African scholar Sidi Maḥmūd al-Baghdādī, another alleged "axial saint" of his age,[47] who may have been the first to introduce a recognizable Sufi order in black Africa. According to H. T. Norris, the "Maḥmūdiyya" Sufi order was probably a combination of the Suhrawardiyya and Khalwatiyya (and perhaps Qādiriyya) Sufi orders but came to be identified with "an original Muḥammadiyya ṭarīqa, a theory in vogue at a much later date."[48] Sidi Maḥmūd's teachings were collected by a Tuareg scholar Aḥmad b. Uways in the book *al-Qudwā*, written between 1670 and 1680. This author was undoubtedly the same Aḥmad that served as al-Yamanī's teacher in Agades. Here is the *Qudwā*'s description of the preeminent *Ṭarīqa Maḥmūdiyya*:

> The meaning of *Ahl al-Tarīqa al-Maḥmūdiyya* is "those who call upon the people of Allah to a clarity of vision." A clarity of vision and of awareness is the gift which was brought by him [the Prophet]—the blessing and peace of Allah be upon him—to teach mankind about Allah. It was his sunna and the word of his Lord. As for the *Ṭarīqa* of Sīdī Maḥmūd, it is the original path and the other paths have borrowed from it. It is the way of the sons of the world to come, in canonic law, in mystical discipline, and in ultimate truth. All else is but the following of a wayward fancy.[49]

Interesting here is the notion that the preeminent, "original" Sufi order would teach the knowledge of God as a gift from the Prophet in order to "clarify" or verify the religion of Islam. There is no specific mention that the Prophet Muḥammad appeared to Sīdī Maḥmūd to teach him the Ṭarīqa Maḥmūdiyya. But the *Qudwā* elsewhere asserts that Sīdī Maḥmūd claimed the Sufi circles of remembrance in the "western lands" (thus those of Sidi Maḥmūd) were "organized and made ready by the Prophet."[50] According to Norris, al-Yamanī likely brought a copy of the *Qudwā* with him to Fez after studying it in Agades.[51] If so, the idea of a transcendent *Ṭarīqa Muḥammadiyya* that defined the purest form of Sufism, as a gift from the Prophet, had an earlier resonance in sub-Saharan Africa and may have influenced the idea's popularization in Fez with ʿAbd al-ʿAzīz al-Dabbāgh and Aḥmad al-Tijānī.[52]

Moreover, the *Ṭarīqa Maḥmūdiyya* was not the only sub-Saharan African-based Sufi order to make an appearance in Fez. There was later a *muqaddam* of the Kuntiyya-Qādiriyya from Mukhtār al-Kuntī (d. 1811), a resident of Fez, a certain Sharīf Muḥammad b. al-Hadi al-Dabbāgh (d. 1867).[53] Several of al-Kuntī's students were active participants in the eighteenth-century scholarly circles, and al-Kuntī himself corresponded with Murtaḍā al-Zabīdī in Cairo.[54] Al-Kuntī's discussion of saintly miracles privileged the waking encounter with the Prophet Muḥammad, and he claimed that the Algerian Qādirī ʿAbd al-Karīm al-Maghīlī (d. 1505, Tuwāt), who allegedly brought the Qādiriyya to the Kunta people south of the Sahara, was in constant communication with the Prophet Muḥammad.[55] West African scholars thus clearly saw themselves as equal participants in the global scholarly exchanges of the eighteenth century, particularly when it came to the idea of the *Ṭarīqa Muḥammadiyya*.

The popularity of "Muḥammadan Sufism" in West Africa is further substantiated by analysis of the Timbuktu chronicles, which detail scholarly life in this key center of scholarship from the fifteenth century.[56] Although these sources do not mention the presence of any Sufi order in West Africa prior to the eighteenth century, the strict Mālikī scholars described therein are frequently associated with Sufi gnosis (*maʿrifa*), sainthood (*walāya*), and visionary encounters with the Prophet Muḥammad. The renowned fifteenth-century scholar Yaḥyā al-Tadillisī, whose mosque still stands in the center of Timbuktu,[57] was known as "the jurist and scholar, the *quṭb*, the Friend of God Most High"[58] who experienced nightly visions of the Prophet.[59] Of particular note is the Aqīt lineage that provided Timbuktu's most eminent scholars, such as Aḥmad Bābā (d. 1627). In the late sixteenth century, several Aqīts had close relations with the Egyptian saint Muḥammad al-Bakrī (d. 1585), the transmitter of seminal Tijānī "Prayer of Opening" (*ṣalāt al-fātiḥ*). Al-Bakrī attested to the sainthood of the Aqīt scholars of his time,[60] and both hosted these scholars in Egypt on their way to Mecca and visited them in Timbuktu.[61]

Al-Bakrī's apparent role as a "spiritual mentor for the scholars of Timbuktu"[62] and his influence on the Tijāniyya suggest a degree of intellectual continuity between the Islamic scholarship of Western Africa and later reception of the Tijāniyya. Muḥammad b. ʿAlī al-Bakrī was a shaykh at Azhar University and one of the most renowned scholars of sixteenth-century Egypt. Al-Bakrī was so named because his family claimed descent from the Prophet's companion Abū Bakr Siddīq. Al-Shaʿrānī referred to his contemporary al-Bakrī as the "reviver" (*mujaddid*) of the sacred law and esteemed his famous collection of Sufi prayers, the *ḥizb al-bakrī.*[63] Al-Saʿadī's *Taʾrīkh al-sūdān* describes al-Bakrī in several places as "the friend of God" (*walī-Allāh*) and the "axial saint" (*quṭb*) of his time "who had great affection for the scholars of Timbuktu."[64] Intellectually, al-Bakrī emphasized the Sufi's involvement in society, the study of the law from a variety of *madhhab* perspectives, and the possibility of direct spiritual unveiling, particularly in relationship to the spirituality of the Prophet.[65] He was also interested in the writings of Ibn al-ʿArabī, although he distanced himself from the external meaning of "the unity of being" (*waḥdat al-wujūd*), suggesting, "The unity is experiential, not ontological."[66] Al-Bakrī's role in the unveiling of *ṣalāt al-fātiḥ* is discussed later in this book, but the Tijāniyya's popularization of al-Bakrī's most valuable secret would have certainly made an impression on a West African scholarly legacy that had, at least in Timbuktu, earlier associated itself with al-Bakrī's reputation.

African scholars had other subsequent contacts with Arab counterparts that played key roles in eighteenth-century intellectual exchange. A certain Aḥmad Bābā (named after the more famous Aḥmad Bābā al-Massūfī who died in 1627) from Timbuktu met the Syrian Naqshbandī Shaykh ʿAbd al-Ghanī al-Nābulusī in Medina in 1694. At the Timbuktu scholar's request, al-Nābulusī composed a commentary on the versified rendition of al-Sanūsī's (d. 1490, Algeria) *ʿAqīda al-ṣughra* by the Timbuktu student of the original Aḥmad Bābā, Muhammad Baghrūʿu.[67] The contact between Aḥmad "al-Timbuktī" and Nabulusī is significant, as the latter's ideas on the *Ṭarīqa Muḥammadiyya*, transmitted through a book on the subject and his student Muṣṭafa al-Bakrī (d. 1749), helped define many eighteenth-century articulations of the concept,[68] including those of Maḥmūd al-Kurdī, the later initiator of al-Tijānī in Cairo.

Another African scholar, Muḥammad al-Kashnāwī, became well known in Egypt as the teacher of Ḥasan al-Jabartī, the father of the famous Egyptian historian ʿAbd al-Raḥmān al-Jabartī. Al-Jabartī's formative Sufi shaykh was Maḥmūd al-Kurdī. Al-Kashnāwī is mostly known for his authorship of an important treatise on the esoteric sciences: *al-Durr al-manẓūm wa khulāsat al-sirr al-maktūm fī l-siḥr wa l-ṭalāsim wa l-nujūm*.[69] While certainly known as an esotericist in Egypt, he received comprehensive scholarly training in central west Africa before leaving Katsina around 1730. Among his teachers were Muḥammad al-Walī al-Burnāwī and possibly Muḥammad Fūdī, the father of ʿUthmān b. Fudī.[70] Al-Walī (flourished during the late seventeenth century) was among the most famous scholars of Kanem-Bornu. Aside from his writings on Ashʿarī theology, his legal opinions prohibiting smoking made him one of the few Mālikī scholars of his age to take such a stance,[71] anticipating the prohibition of tobacco by several eighteenth-century scholars, including al-Tijānī himself.[72]

Al-Kashnāwī's disposition toward the esoteric sciences appears to resonate with later Tijānī articulations: he accepted their role in the actualization of religious knowledge, but he cautioned against their misuse. Al-Kashnāwī was hesitant to teach students his esoteric knowledge, having been warned previously: "If I reached the countries of the East and especially the Ḥaramayn, I should not reveal to any of their inhabitants that I know something of those letter-based sciences, and what resembles them of the sand-based sciences, on account of their prevalent [mis]uses in these countries for causing corruption, tribulations and dissension [among people], in plain sight of those of discerning minds."[73] Al-Kashnāwī's book is thus not merely a collection of esoteric sciences, but a moral pronouncement on the "virtues and misuses of the secret sciences."[74] He laid out twelve preconditions for practicing such secrets, ranging from initiation, concealment, seriousness of need to the fear of God.[75] This was no doubt important advice: by the eighteenth century, the esoteric sciences were studied throughout Egypt by "leading members of the establishment."[76] The appearance of a sub-Saharan African scholar in Cairo as a foremost teacher and moral guide to the use of esoteric sciences in Cairo demonstrates once again that Africans in the Middle East were central figures to the intellectual debates of their age.

Ṣāliḥ al-Fullānī, a Fulani scholar from Futa Jallon (modern-day Guinea), came to reside in Medina and garnered a wide reputation for Islamic scholarship. The later Indian scholar, Muḥammad ʿAẓīmābādī (d. 1905), referred to al-Fullānī as the scholarly "renewer" (*mujaddid*) of his age,[77] and his legacy has been variously appropriated by India's *Ahl al-Ḥadīth* movement as well as Arab Salafism. But al-Fullānī was also the ḥadīth teacher of Muḥammad al-Ḥāfiẓ al-Shinqītī (d. 1830), the student of al-Tijānī, and famous propagator of the Tijāniyya into the Sahara, as well as of the Moroccan Tijānī scholar Ḥamdūn b. al-Ḥājj (d. 1817).[78] Al-Fullānī was also an associate of al-Tijānī's Khalwatī Shaykh in Medina, Muḥammad al-Sammān.[79] While several of al-Fullānī's students no doubt rejected the Sufi orders and the schools of law (*madhāhib*), perhaps influenced by their teacher's stance against "following the schools of law with zeal and narrow-mindedness,"[80] others remained defenders of such institutions. Al-Fullānī's prominent Mauritanian student, Imam ʿAbd al-Raḥmān b. Aḥmad al-Shinqītī (d. 1809), established himself in Morocco as a prominent Mālikī jurist and later accepted the Tijāniyya, confirming al-Tijānī's scholarly credentials to countrymen like Mūḥammad al-Ḥāfiẓ. "By God," Imam ʿAbd al-Raḥmān swore of al-Tijānī, "there is no one more knowledgeable on the face of the earth than him."[81] Indeed, al-Fullānī's argument for *ijtihād* by reading established textual sources (*naṣṣ*) in dialogue with scholarly opinion was similar to al-Tijānī's own legal methodology, although al-Tijānī himself otherwise remained a practicing Mālikī.[82] Al-Fullānī exemplifies the ability of African scholars to situate themselves at the center of *ijtihād* and *hadith* renewal networks that were often closely related to an accent on "Muḥammadan Sufism." Rather than reading Fullānī's stance on *ijtihād* as evidence of his influence by Salafi-Wahhabism, he in fact evidenced a critical West African engagement with the *madhāhib* that dates at least back to Aḥmad Bābā al-Massūfī and the scholars of Timbuktu, who had earlier criticized the Moroccan scholars' fanatical attachment to the Mālikī school.[83] Such a stance was formative for eighteenth-century currents of scholarly verification.

While al-Tijānī had no direct links to the African scholars mentioned here, their ideas clearly influenced the eighteenth-century scholarly networks to which al-Tijānī was connected. As al-Dabbāgh's relationship with Shaykh al-Burnāwī indicates, the scholarly atmosphere of eighteenth-century Fez was infused with references to Islamic scholarship south of Morocco. A collection of nine biographical dictionaries of Moroccan scholars, mostly concerning the eighteenth and nineteenth centuries, presents no fewer than nineteen separate Saharan scholars, with the designation "al-Shinqītī," residing in Morocco.[84] Al-Tijānī himself left Fez in the later years of his life to visit the Saharan oasis town of Tuwāt, where he exchanged knowledge with scholars there, perhaps of the Kuntī-Qādiriyya scholarly lineage, originating farther south, which had an established presence in the town by the late eighteenth century.[85] If such references were lost on later generations of Moroccans, sub-Saharan Islamic scholarship certainly remembered its long-standing dialogue with Moroccan intellectual history, and with eighteenth-century revivalism more broadly. The reception of the Tijāniyya south of the Sahara must be seen as the continuation of this earlier trend.

Egypt and the Hijaz in the Eighteenth Century

Shaykh Aḥmad al-Tijānī arrived in Medina, the city of the Prophet, in 1774. After "God fulfilled his longing" in accomplishing the pious visitation (*ziyāra*) of the Prophet's grave,[86] al-Tijānī sought out Muḥammad al-Sammān (d. 1775), the holder of the keys to the Prophet's tomb, whom al-Tijānī had been informed was the axial saint of the age (*quṭb al-zamān*). Al-Tijānī's companionship with al-Sammān demonstrates his connection to two overlapping scholarly networks in the Middle East in the eighteenth century. The first was the "school" of Ibrāhīm al-Kūrānī: al-Sammān had studied with Muḥammad Ḥayāt al-Sindī (d. 1750), who studied with his countryman also resident in Medina, Muḥammad Sindī (d. 1727), who studied with Ibrāhīm al-Kūrānī. This was the same knowledge network—emphasizing in varying degrees ḥadīth study, scholarly reasoning outside of the *madhhab* (*ijtihād*), and the Sufism of Ibn al-ʿArabī—that included the likes of Shāh

Walī-Allāh, ʿUthmān b. Fūdī, Aḥmad b. Idrīs, Muḥammad al-Shawkānī, and (perhaps more tangentially) Muḥammad b. ʿAbd al-Wahhāb.[87]

The second was with the Khalwatiyya as taught by the Syrian shaykh Muṣṭafa al-Bakrī (d. 1749): Muḥammad al-Sammān was initiated by al-Bakrī, and his primary Sufi affiliation remained the Khalwatiyya. Al-Bakrī's students in Egypt had helped to spread the order throughout Egypt and North Africa. Although al-Bakrī stressed exclusive allegiance to the Khalwatiyya, he himself was one of only two fully authorized students of ʿAbd al-Ghanī al-Nābulusī. Al-Sammān, like al-Nābulusī, authored a major treatise on the notion of a *Ṭarīqa Muḥammadiyya*. Al-Tijānī's own teachings often reference the scholars and ideas of these Middle East networks associated with al-Kūrānī and Muṣṭafā al-Bakrī. I attempt here, therefore, to briefly explore the primary sources relevant to the scholars of the "Kūrānī school" and the Khalwatiyya with particular reference to ideas shared by al-Tijānī. My point here is not that al-Tijānī simply reflected the teachings of his initiators in the Middle East, but that these teachings provide an important context to al-Tijānī's own articulations later on.

The Legacy of Ibrāhīm al-Kūrānī

By most accounts, Ibrāhīm b. al-Ḥasan al-Kūrānī al-Kurdī—"one of the towering figures of seventeenth-century Sufism"[88] and known as the "seal of verifiers" (*khātimat al-muḥaqqiqīn*)[89]—was a central influence on the intellectual dynamism of the eighteenth century. Al-Kūrānī and his students "dominated ḥadīth scholarship and its chains of authority"[90] during the period. His teaching of ḥadīth—as evidenced from al-Kūrānī's recently published (2013) commentary on the Prophet's words, "Actions are by intentions"—invoked dense theological discussions (free will versus predestination), debates among legal schools (what constitutes the formation of intention), and Sufism (sincerity and the heart's purity as the prerequisite of all action).[91] While ḥadīth certainly constituted a foundation for his teaching, al-Kūrānī's most influential writing was in the disciplines of theology and Sufism. The latter was mostly associated with the defense of Ibn al-ʿArabī, particularly in articulating the controversial notion of "the oneness of being" (*waḥdat al-wujūd*). Many eighteenth-century scholars celebrated their connections to al-Kūrānī in their own teaching of Ibn al-ʿArabī, such as the Indian revivalist Shāh Walī-Allāh (d. 1762)[92] and the Yemeni legal theorist Muḥammad al-Shawkānī (d. 1839).[93] Al-Tijānī himself would defend the concept of *waḥdat al-wujūd* despite the conspicuous absence of prior reference in Moroccan texts such as the *Ibrīz*, and the more skeptical stances of Moroccan Shādhilī scholars like Ḥasan al-Yūsī or of the Timbuktu students of Muḥammad al-Bakrī. It is thus useful to consider al-Kūrānī's bold articulation of the concept, as it likely informed al-Tijānī's teachers in the Middle East. Similar to the writings of al-Nābulusī, al-Kūrānī's work went beyond a selective restatement of the idea,[94] but presented a masterful exploration, ending with the concept of divine manifestation (*tajalla*) that may have influenced al-Tijānī's own understanding.

Al-Kūrānī argued that *waḥdat al-wujūd* was reconcilable to orthodox Ashʿarī theology since "God, whose quiddity and existence are identical, is both distinct from all contingent quiddities and manifests Himself in them."[95] Newly published treatises of al-Kūrānī on the subject, "The Bountiful Ascension in the Verification of Divine Transcendence in the Oneness of Being" (*Maṭlaʿ al-jūd fī taḥqīq al-tanzīh fī waḥdat al-wujūd*) and "The Splendorous Insight into the Persistence of Divine Transcendence with God's Manifestation in Created Forms" (*Jalāʾ al-naẓr fī baqāʾ al-tanzīh maʿa l-tajallī fī l-ṣūr*),[96] permit further exploration. Al-Kūrānī tasks himself with explaining several mysterious statements of Ibn al-ʿArabī, such as "Glory to Him who made things manifest, while He is their essence (*ʿayn*)," or "The Real, Most High, is present (*mawjūd*) in His Essence (*bi-dhātih*), for His Essence (*li-dhātih*)."[97] He presents the logical precept, "The world exists through God (bi-Llāh) and not through itself, nor for itself: (all) existence is bound (*muqayyad*) to the existence of the Real,"[98] and cites a poem: "Surely the creation is an illusion (*khayāl*); only real in the (divine) reality." The nonreality of creation, or its lack of reality except in God, is due to its inescapable state of transition (*istiḥāla*).[99] The creation, however, does not encompass God, for He is beyond comprehension (*taʿaqqul*) or specification (*taʿayyun*).[100] What manifests from specified entities, when they appear in a state of fixation and unscented with the "fragrance of divine being," is not divine appearance but rather God's rules (*aḥkām*) and effects (*athār*) specific to that entity.[101]

It is the concept of divine manifestation (*tajalla*), al-Kūrānī suggests in the conclusion of both texts (*Maṭlaʿ al-jūd* and *Jalāʾ al-naẓr*), which permits a person to grasp the simultaneous omnipresence and transcendence of God: the divine manifests in any manner He chooses without compromising His transcendence.[102] The manifestation of the sun's light on the moon, al-Kūrānī cites Ibn al-ʿArabī to say, does not mean that the moon has the light of the sun "in" itself, nor has the sun moved to join its identity (*dhāt*) with that of the moon. Divine manifestation thus represented neither the fusion between God and creation (*ittiḥād*), nor the incarnation (*ḥulūl*) of God in creation.[103] The obvious conclusion here is that divine manifestation is not the act of God "coming down" (*tanzīl*) upon a created entity, or moving from one place to another: it is when the veils of a creation's dependent (or nonessential) reality disappear before the presence of God's ultimate being (*al-wujūd al-muṭlaq*). This witnessing is subjective (*shuhūdī*), because few perceive divine manifestation; but it is also ontological (*wujūdī*), because nothing has intrinsic reality except God's ultimate being. As demonstrated later in this book, al-Kūrānī's explanation closely anticipated that of al-Tijānī in late eighteenth-century Maghreb.

While later inheritors of the "Kūrānī school," such as the Medina-based Indian ḥadīth scholar Muḥammad Ḥayāt al-Sindī, may not have transmitted the depth of al-Kūrānī's commitment to the teachings of Ibn al-ʿArabī, neither were they entirely untouched by it. Al-Sindī, a Naqshbandī Sufi who taught ḥadīth behind the Prophet's tomb in Medina,[104] wrote a number of Sufi works, including a lengthy commentary on a seminal text of the Sufi tradition, the *Ḥikam* of Ibn ʿAṭā-Allāh (d. 1309, Alexandria).[105] In explaining Ibn ʿAṭā-Allāh's aphorism, "You are only veiled from the suns of gnosis by the clouds of effects," al-Sindī wrote: "As for the gnostics (*al-ʿārifūn*), they see secrets in [God's] effects (*āthār*), the witnessing of which increases them in illumination, until witnessing created beings does not prevent them from witnessing the Creator. Rather they see effects as reflections of the Sovereign Lord of effects, as if they were Him, except that in reality they have no attribution to Him. Exalted is God beyond that. So understand the secret of this matter if you are its custodian (*ahl*)."[106] Elsewhere, al-Sindī is emphatic in his denial that such knowledge entails God's fusion (*ittiḥād*) with or indwelling (*ḥulūl*) in the creation.[107] But al-Kūrānī, as mentioned above, was no less insistent that the idea of *waḥdat al-wujūd* did not mean blasphemous denial of God's transcendence. Although he did not so openly endorse the concept, al-Sindī was clearly not opposed to *waḥdat al-wujūd*. His open discussion of Sufi gnosis necessitates reframing the alleged reformist impulse he supposedly shared with Muḥammad b. ʿAbd al-Wahhāb.[108] He was certainly not the proto-Wahhabi who transmitted the extreme theology of the earlier Kadizade movement to Ibn ʿAbd al-Wahhāb.[109] Indeed, al-Sindī's shaykh in the Naqshbandiyya, the Yemeni scholar of Medina ʿAbd al-Raḥmān al-Saqqāf Bā-ʿAlawī (d. 1713), claimed to only initiate Sufi aspirants with the permission of the Prophet, saying, "There is no veil remaining between me and the Prophet."[110] There is no doubt, then, that al-Sindī's gnostic understandings were the result of his Sufi training at the hands of a consummate Sufi shaykh. Muḥammad al-Sammān and Aḥmad al-Tijānī, and not Muḥammad b. ʿAbd al-Wahhāb, were most certainly the clearer mirrors of al-Sindī and eighteenth-century Medinan scholarship.

Muṣṭafā al-Bakrī and the Egyptian Khalwatiyya

Al-Tijānī's most significant Sufi initiation in the Middle East was the Khalwatiyya, obtained from Muḥammad al-Sammān and Maḥmūd al-Kurdī, who were the students of Muṣṭafā Kamāl al-Dīn al-Bakrī (d. 1749, Cairo). While the extent of al-Bakrī's identification with an eighteenth-century Khalwatī revival has been debated,[111] he initiated significant numbers of Muslims into the Khalwatiyya, including the head of Egypt's Azhar University Muḥammad al-Ḥifnī (d. 1767), and was indisputably "one of the most prominent Khalwatī Sufis of the eighteenth century."[112] Al-Bakrī's spiritual genealogy in the Khalwatiyya passed through ʿAlī Qarabāsh (d. 1686, Edirne), who emphasized the practice of a regular litany, the *wird al-sattār*, and vigilant combat against the lower self through fasting and periodic retreat (*khalwa*).[113] But al-Bakrī had previously been initiated into the Naqshbandiyya, connecting him to the Indian rival of Aḥmad Sirhindī, Tāj al-Dīn ʿUthmānī (d. 1640), through "the seal of ḥadīth scholars" ʿAbdallāh b. Sālim al-Baṣrī (d. 1722, Mecca).[114] Al-Baṣrī was also the student of al-Kūrānī.[115] As previously mentioned, al-Bakrī was also only one of two students to receive full authorization (*ijāza*) from the noted Naqshbandī Sufi and scholar ʿAbd al-Ghanī al-Nābulusī (d. 1731), with whom he studied the works of Ibn al-ʿArabī.[116] Confirmed in his attachment to the Khalwatiyya by al-Nabulusī,[117] al-Bakrī would later require his disciples' exclusive attachment to the order.[118] He experienced nineteen separate visions of the Prophet, and three of Khiḍr—the latter who designated him as the "axial saint of the east." His saintly authority allegedly extended to the spirit-world, and he initiated seven kings of the jinn into the Khalwatiyya.[119] Al-Jabartī thus describes al-Bakrī: "He was granted the keys of all sciences, so that the saints of his age and the seekers of the truth, east and west, submitted to him. He bound the chiefs of the jinns by compact and his help prevailed." Once the Prophet appeared to al-Bakrī and asked him about his composition of prayers (presumably the *wird al-saḥar*), "Where did you obtain this help?" He answered, "From you, O Messenger of God." The Prophet nodded.[120] Although he may have focused more on training disciples than did al-Nābulusī, he was also a prolific writer, authoring some 220 works.[121]

Al-Bakrī's teaching was characterized by the transmission of Sufi gnosis within an enduring emphasis on shaykh-disciple relations. One of his more significant works appears to have been "The Epistle on Sufi Companionship" (*al-Risāla fī suḥba*), beginning with the words, "Praise be to God who made the companionship with the elect (*akhiyār*) the reason for success and happiness."[122] When giving spiritual training to his designated deputy (*khalīfa*) al-Ḥifnī, al-Bakrī stressed the importance of grateful companionship over individual exertions: "Give heed to what I say. If you wish to fast and pray, practice spiritual discipline and exercises, do so in your home country. While you are with me, do not busy yourself with anything but us. Do not devote all your time to the spiritual disciplines you wish to perform, but let it be done in proportion to your capacity. Eat, drink, and be happy."[123] But this emphasis on Sufi etiquette (*adab al-sulūk*) did not preclude al-Bakrī's public defense of gnosis, including the notion of *waḥdat al-wujūd*.[124] In his poetry, he explained the concept's reconcilability with divine transcendence (*tanzīh*) as follows:

Everything upon which the Real manifests
In His Essence, (that thing) passes away from its (attribute of) creation
For the (creation's) taste of this manifestation is prevented
Just as Divine oneness (*aḥadiyya*) is free from all earthly nourishment.[125]

The experience of annihilation in God, this passage confirms, was central to al-Bakrī's teachings. His "daytime litany" (*wird al-saḥar*) emphasized such Sufi gnosis in imploring God: "Free [our] interior senses from the tendency to behold things other than you. Exterminate us so that we will not perceive ourselves."[126] Gnosis thus presupposed the self's purification. Al-Ḥifnī would explain al-Bakrī's teachings to one of his own inheritors: "Always pay careful attention to the workings of the ego-self (*nafs*) in every outward action and breath, and this especially when you are approached for teaching and guidance. Since (the *nafs*) lies in wait even for old men, one must never put away the sword of spiritual combat against it."[127] Al-Bakrī's visionary experiences, association with the teachings of Ibn al-ʿArabī, and apparent claim to paradigmatic sainthood, thus were grounded in a "traditional" Sufi foundation of spiritual purification and gnosis.

Muḥammad al-Ḥifnī, al-Bakrī's favored disciple, had remarkable success in spreading the Khalwatiyya in Egypt. The Egyptian historian ʿAbd al-Raḥmān al-Jabartī considered him "the pole of Egypt," whose death released affliction on the land.[128] The prominent Moroccan ḥadīth scholar ʿAbd al-Qādir al-Kūhan (d. 1837, Fez) traced his own reception of al-Ghazālī's *Iḥyāʾ ʿulūm al-dīn* in the Maghreb through students of al-Ḥifnī.[129] Aside from Maḥmūd al-Kurdī, al-Ḥifnī had several prominent lieutenants, including the Egyptian Mālikī scholar Aḥmad al-Dardīr (d. 1786), the Algerian Muḥammad b. ʿAbd al-Raḥmān al-Azharī (d. 1793, Kabylia), and the Moroccan saint Aḥmad al-Ṣaqillī (d. 1764, Fez). Aḥmad al-Tijānī met both al-Ṣaqillī and Ibn ʿAbd al-Raḥmān in Fez and Algeria respectively prior to his meeting with al-Kurdī and was even initiated into the Khalwatiyya by Ḥifnī's Algerian representative.[130] Al-Tijānī did not spend long in al-Ṣaqillī's company, but allegedly attested to his high spiritual rank: "There is no axial saint (*quṭb*) buried within the walls of Fez except our master Aḥmad al-Ṣaqillī."[131] It is clear then that the al-Bakrī and al-Ḥifnī's Khalwatiyya already had a significant reception in North Africa, and that al-Tijānī had developed a favorable opinion of the order before traveling to Egypt and the Ḥijāz.

Muḥammad al-Sammān, Quṭb of Medina

Another of al-Bakrī's disciples was to have a lasting influence on al-Tijānī. Muḥammad b. ʿAbd al-Karīm al-Sammān (d. 1775, Medina), whom al-Tijānī referred to as the axial saint (*quṭb*) of his age,[132] was certainly one of more significant figures of late eighteenth-century Sufism. Al-Sammān was a scholar of the Shāfiʿī legal school who lived in Medina, Arabia, and held the keys to the Prophet's tomb.[133] His teachings were later popularized in the Sudan and Indonesia as the Sammāniyya Sufi order, although there is no evidence from Tijānī sources that al-Sammān transmitted anything other than the Khalwatiyya during his own lifetime. Nonetheless, other sources indicate a variety of Sufi affiliations, and his transmission of a spectrum of Sufi practices, including his own invocations of blessing on the Prophet (*ṣalawāt*),[134] were doubtless the grounds on which several close disciples formed distinctive "Sammānī" Sufi communities. He appears to have tolerated a variety of Sufi initiations, so long as the disciple only really "belonged" to one.[135] His own writings demonstrate that he was primarily devoted to Muṣṭafa al-Bakrī, whom he referred to as "the seal of sainthood" (*khātim al-walāya*) among other "verifiers" (*muḥaqqiqīn*) of Sufism.[136] Al-Sammān's connections to al-Bakrī and al-Sindī have already been mentioned above, but among his students there were many notable Sufi scholars besides al-Tijānī: the aforementioned West African resident of Medina Ṣāliḥ al-Fullānī, the Indian resident of Cairo Murtaḍā al-Zabīdī, and the well-connected Moroccan scholar al-Tāwudī b. Sūda.[137]

Significant elements of al-Sammān's teachings that give context to al-Tijānī's later articulations center primarily on the practical methodology of connecting to the spiritual presence of the Prophet. Following earlier Ḥijaz-based Sufis such as Ḥasan al-ʿUjaymī, this methodology of continuously invoking prayers on the Prophet, for al-Sammān, was the definition of *Ṭarīqa Muḥammadiyya*. "You should continuously recite *ṣalawāt* with perfect concentration," al-Sammān emphasized. "This means that you spend your time in loving the Prophet. Because of this, God opens the most beautiful thing to you; that is, the reality of Muhammad, peace be upon him."[138] The aspirant should "make present" (*istaḥdar*) both the physical form of the Prophet and the "Muhammadan reality": "When you recite *ṣalawāt*, remember that it is not you who recites it, but rather the Prophet himself. Every atom, including your organs, is created from him (his light)."[139] The desired result was for the aspirant to behold the form (*dhāt*) of the Prophet: "He will then stand directly before your eyes. You will perceive him, speak to him, put questions to him, and converse with him. He will give you answers, speak to you, and converse with you; in this way, you will attain the rank of the *Ṣaḥāba* [Prophet's companions]."[140] Al-Sammān himself reported a waking encounter with the Prophet Muḥammad as a result of this practice, a narration that emphasized the pervasive light of Muḥammad gradually taking physical form.[141] The result was that al-Sammān, in his own words, became possessed of "a strong love for the Prophet even in my bones, my spirit, my hair and my eyes, like cold water refreshes in terribly hot temperatures."[142]

This form of "annihilation" (*fanāʾ*) in the Prophet presupposed the precedent annihilation in God. For al-Sammān, the Prophet Muḥammad's reality represented the most perfect manifestation (*tajalla*) of God among the "grades of existence" extending from the undifferentiated divine essence (*aḥadiyya*) to the realm of bodies (*ʿālam al-ajsād*).[143] This notion thus meant to further explain the notion of the unity of being (*waḥdat al-wujūd*), God as the "one true existence"; although al-Sammān, like al-Tijānī, otherwise tried to avoid the polemical exchanges concerning *waḥdat al-wujūd*.[144] Concentration on the Prophet, and devotion to him, allowed for the aspirant to experience divine manifestation, for the Prophet was "the appearance of the real essence of God in mankind."[145]

For al-Sammān, the *Ṭarīqa Muḥammadiyya* was not a distinct, transcendental Sufi order but rather a practice that reinforced the traditional shaykh–disciple relationship in Sufi training, normally within an established order. For the Sufi disciple, the shaykh stood in the place of the Prophet: Sufi disciples with their shaykh were simply replicating the relationship between the Prophet and his companions. In his primary text on Sufi practice, al-Sammān cites an older Sufi adage also used in Tijānī circles in the present day: "All of Sufism is etiquette (*adab*): there is a proper etiquette for every time, state and spiritual station. Whoever persists in good etiquette reaches where the distinguished folk (*rijāl*) have attained. Whoever forsakes etiquette is far (from God) even while he thinks himself close, and is rejected even while he hopes for acceptance."[146] The etiquette of the disciple with the shaykh was to "not move in any of your affairs except with his permission" and perceive oneself "between his hands like the corpse in hands of its funeral washer, or the baby with its mother."[147] Clearly, al-Sammān's notion of the *Ṭarīqa Muḥammadiyya* reinforced traditional notions of Sufi affiliation rather than superseded them. God's saints (*awliyā'*) were the inheritors of the Prophet: "All who show enmity to God and His Messenger and His saints are expelled from the straight path and from sound faith (*al-īmān al-qawīm*). All who love God and His Messenger and His saints have grasped the firm handhold and are guided to the straight path."[148] Al-Sammān's notion of the saint's proximity to the Prophet's physical form and spiritual reality, and the *Ṭarīqa Muḥammadiyya* as an emphasis on invoking prayers on the Prophet, provide context to al-Tijānī's later articulations.

Maḥmūd al-Kurdī, Guide on the Path

Whatever al-Sammān's fame in the Hijāz, the leading Khalwatī shaykh in Egypt at the time of al-Tijānī's pilgrimage in the 1770s was most certainly Maḥmūd al-Kurdī (d. 1780, Cairo). Besides al-Tijānī, notable students included 'Abd al-Raḥmān al-Jabartī, the Moroccan student of al-Dabbāgh

ʿAbd al-Wahhāb al-Tāzī (d. 1792),[149] and the later shaykh al-Azhar ʿAbdallāh al-Sharqāwī (d. 1812). Al-Jabartī memorialized al-Kurdī as follows: "He was praiseworthy in his deeds and known for his perfection. He was invested with the crown and became (al-Ḥifnī's) lieutenant authorized to teach and accept aspirants. He gave spiritual guidance and removed temptations from men's hearts. He was famous for his sanctity, believed in by small and great alike, and had many visions of the Prophet. It was a sign of divine favor toward him that he could see the Prophet in a vision whenever he wanted to. Remarkable revelations were made to him."[150] Al-Ḥifnī seems to have directed aspirants to al-Kurdī for spiritual training during his own lifetime and brought his favorite Iraqi student to receive direct instruction from al-Bakrī himself.[151] He was not as prolific a writer as al-Bakrī or al-Sammān, but his teaching—some of which has been preserved in his "Letter of Aphorisms" (*Risāla fī l-ḥikam*), commented on by al-Sharqāwī—evidently left an impression on his students. Al-Kurdī's instruction was characterized by an emphasis on shaykh-disciple relations, visionary experience, and humility on the Sufi path.

Maḥmūd al-Kurdī's book of aphorisms is a summary of etiquette on the Sufi path, written in masterfully concise Arabic rhyme. "Strive (against yourself) and you will witness (the Divine)," is a good example; in Arabic *ijhad tashhad.*[152] Al-Kurdī's central focus was this jihad against the self: "Self-contentment is a sign of ignorance,"[153] he warned. "Cling to work," he added, "Avoid wagging the tongue over the words of the path without endowing yourself with the character traits of its folk,"[154] for proper etiquette (*adab*) "returns to the Real."[155] He warned disciples against the self's "hidden idolatry" (*al-shirk al-khafī*), which al-Sharqāwī explained means doing good deeds for other than God's sake.[156] "Avoid making claims, even if you are truthful: *adab* is to be free from claiming a rank (*maqām*) before attaining it, and even after attaining it."[157] This entails, al-Sharqāwī cites Ibn al-ʿArabī to explain, the prohibition of claims emerging from the *nafs*, even if truthful.[158] Al-Kurdī thus emphasized: "To be steadfast in worship is better than a thousand spiritual unveilings or saintly miracles."[159] The shaykh summarizes this instruction in his last aphorism: "The (Sufi) aspirant is the one who cuts the throat of his ego-self."[160]

For al-Kurdī, knowledge of God and the Sufi path could only be partially learned from books: "Knowledge is of two types: a knowledge from sheets of paper (*awrāq*), and a knowledge by spiritual experience (*adhwāq*). The first is loved if accompanied by action. The second is a (divine) gift from pre-eternity."[161] But self-purification could only be realized by the companionship with a perfected guide: "The Shaykh is the one who causes you to ascend by his secret, and who guides you, prepares you, and takes possession of your heart to purify it from other than God."[162] Al-Kurdī emphasized, "The path is prolonged without a guide."[163] For al-Kurdī, submission to one's shaykh meant the abandonment of other paths, whatever their blessing. He himself initially resisted relinquishing the prior litany (*wird*) of al-Qushayrī (d. 1074, Nishapur) he had continued practicing after taking the Khalwatiyya, until meeting with Muṣṭafā al-Bakrī. After meeting with al-Bakrī, al-Kurdī dreamed that Qushayrī was complaining to the Prophet about al-Bakrī's request for exclusive commitment to his version of the Khalwatī *wird*. To solve the dilemma, the Prophet's companion Abū Bakr came to al-Kurdī with al-Bakrī's *wird* written on light and filling up the heavens. It appears al-Bakrī experienced the same dream, and al-Kurdī thereafter devoted himself exclusively to the Khalwatiyya.[164]

Al-Kurdī's emphasis on the practical purification of the self may indicate he was less inclined toward the theosophical exposition of al-Kūrānī and other eighteenth-century scholars. But he was no less committed to the legacy of Ibn al-ʿArabī, as demonstrated by the legend surrounding his writing of his aphorisms in the first place: "The reason for its composition was that he saw Shaykh Muḥyī al-Dīn (b.) al-ʿArabī in his dream giving him a key, and he said to him, 'Open the treasury.' When he awoke, [the book] came to his tongue and mind, and he wrote it."[165] Al-Kurdī clearly connected the necessity of self-purification at the hands of a spiritual master with the heights of gnosis referenced by Ibn al-ʿArabī. "Purity from metaphorical filth," the *Risāla fī l-ḥikam* insists, "is by the soul's submission to the shaykhs, and the delight of souls is in the purification from the phantoms of creation (*ashbāḥ*)."[166] Although only referenced briefly, al-Kurdī's text clearly suggests that the desired goal is a type of divine knowledge where God is revealed as the only true reality. Al-Tijānī's affiliation to al-Kurdī may require no other explanation than al-Kurdi's appearance to al-Tijānī in a dream in Tunis before the two met in Cairo.[167] But al-Kurdī's sober combination of visionary experience, Sufi purification and etiquette, exclusive affiliation to a shaykh, and the highest aspirations of divine knowledge clearly resonated with al-Tijānī's own inclinations.

The Islamic Esoteric Sciences and *The Book of Five Jewels*

The Islamic "esoteric sciences" (*ʿulūm al-asrār*) were never far beneath the surface in eighteenth-century scholarly exchanges. Islamic esotericism can be defined as the use of talismans (*tilsām, taʿwīdh*), letter-science (*ʿilm al-ḥurūf*), "magic squares" (*awfāq, jadwāl*), and geomancy (*khaṭṭ al-raml*).[168] Practitioners often sourced these sciences to Prophet Enoch (Idrīs), and sometimes to the Prophet Muḥammad.[169] There is no doubt about their general scholarly acceptance and wide circulation in eighteenth-century networks. The "Shaykh al-Azhar" at the time of al-Tijānī's arrival in Egypt, Aḥmad al-Damanhūrī (d. 1778), had evidently inherited from his Moroccan teachers in the line of Ḥasan al-Yūsī a profound knowledge of this field, authoring at least three elaborate works on the subject.[170] The Yemeni ḥadīth scholar Muḥammad al-Shawkānī admitted his study of these subjects with a Tunisian shaykh.[171] The Indian scholar Murtaḍā al-Zabīdī studied the esoteric sciences with an Anatolian shaykh as well as the West African Cairo resident Muḥammad al-Kashnāwī and later freely corresponded with diverse scholars on such topics.[172] The Moroccan Shādhilī-Darqāwī scholar Aḥmad Ibn ʿAjība (d. 1809) included a lengthy discussion of talismans and esotericism in his autobiography (*Fahrasa*), where he cited al-Yūsī's approval of studying such sciences (see below).[173] Although modern critics of Sufism often explicitly associate these practices with Sufis, they were traditionally linked to the study of mathematics, philosophy, and spiritualism (*ʿilm al-rūḥāniyyāt*). In reproducing a "magic square" for ease in childbirth, the Persian Sufi Abū Ḥāmid al-Ghazālī (d. 1111) thus chastises philosophers for their belief in its efficacy while denying knowledge gained by direct experience of the unseen (*kashf*).[174] Just as ḥadīth transmission and Sufi affiliation were often mixed in eighteenth-century scholarly networks, so too were the esoteric sciences often part of broader intellectual inquiry and exchange during the period.

The proliferation of the esoteric sciences has not been without controversy, most noteworthy being in Sufi circles themselves. Later Tijānī texts cite none other than Ibn al-ʿArabī, in the explanation of the Shādhilī scholar Aḥmad Zarrūq, in cautioning against their use: "Shaykh al-Ḥātimī said, 'The science of letters is a noble science, but it has become blameworthy in this world and the next, so beware of this, and with God is all success.' As for its blameworthiness in this world, it is because the one who practices this science becomes preoccupied with illusionary secondary causes (*asbāb*) without verification. This diminishes his reliance on God, due to the effort expended for the secondary cause."[175] Ibn al-ʿArabī's sixteenth-century popularizer, the Egyptian Sufi ʿAbd al-Wahhāb al-Shaʿrānī (d. 1565) similarly protested against the misuse of these "sciences of the philosophers," though he did not question their overall efficacy.[176] Muḥammad b. ʿAbd al-Wahhāb would of course take this censure further, declaring that "whoever wears an amulet has committed idolatry (*shirk*)," even though he admitted some scholars permitted the practice "if the amulet contains verses of the Qurʾān or God's names or attributes."[177]

Despite instances of controversy, the dominant opinion by the eighteenth-century was probably best articulated by Ḥasan al-Yūsī: "We do not heed those who prohibit some of these sciences, for science in itself is food for the mind and the joy of the spirit and the attribute of virtue. . . . Even magic, which all jurists agree may not be used, if one were to learn it . . . just to know it, and be able to distinguish between it and miracles . . . studying it would be permissible, or even a duty."[178] A similar opinion of the Azharī Mālikī scholar Aḥmad b. al-Ghunaym al-Nafrāwī (d. 1713) became famous in West Africa: "there is no doubt that whatever is proven to be beneficial cannot be disbelief (*kufr*)."[179] The influential work of the Ottoman scholar Mehmed Birgivi (or Birkawī, d. 1573),[180] thought to have inspired the anti-Sufi crusades of the seventeenth-century Kadizadilite movement, in fact includes "charms and spells" under a chapter on medical knowledge: "It is possible that charms and spells are forbidden only to those who think that they are the only means of cure. Those who believe that both sickness and its cure are from God, and that medical intervention is in the hand of God, may also use charms and spells."[181] Al-Birkawī's text was popularized in eighteenth-century scholarly circles through the commentary of ʿAbd al-Ghanī al-Nābulusī: *al-Ḥadīqa al-nadiyya sharḥ al-Ṭarīqa al-Muḥammadiyya*. Al-Nabulusī explained al-Birkawī's words by differentiating between incantations (*ruqya*) performed by Muslims and that performed by non-Muslims: "As for *ruqya* with Qurʾān verses and established utterances, there is no prohibition in this, indeed it is the *sunna*. . . . All *ruqya* is permitted if it is with the words of God or with his remembrance."[182] He cites Yaḥya al-Nawawī (d. 1277) in saying that the Angel Gabriel once made *ruqya* for the Prophet when he got sick. Al-Nābulusī then suggests a difference of opinion concerning the incantations of non-Muslims: Imam Shāfiʿī permitted the *ruqya* of Jews and Christians, while Imam Mālik disliked it. Al-Nābulusī, again citing al-Nawawī, concludes that seeking good health justifies an open mind: "Seeking medicine is loved and it is the path of the Prophet and his companions, and of the righteous forefathers (*salaf*) . . . unlike the exaggerators (*ghilāt*) among the Sufis who do nothing claiming everything is fated."[183] In explaining the permissibility of going to Jewish or Christian healers, al-Nābulusī cites al-Shaʿrānī to say: "Know that the subsidiary causes (*asbāb*) are all in the hand of God, and He is the healer, none other . . . everything other than Him is a but a means (*sabab*)."[184] This sort of discussion has interesting theological implications, and it is important to note the dialogue between theological verification, especially within the Ashʿarī school, and esoteric exploration to which eighteenth-century scholars found themselves the heirs.[185]

Aḥmad al-Tijānī's handwritten *Kunnāsh al-riḥla*, documenting the prayers he received from the mysterious Indian *quṭb* resident in Mecca, the Naqshbandī shaykh Aḥmad ʿAbdallāh al-Hindī, makes frequent reference to a significant work of the esoteric sciences, *The Book of Five Jewels* (*Kitāb al-jawāhir al-khams*).[186] The Shaṭṭariyya Sufi order to which its author Muhammad al-Ghawth and his more famous successor Ibrahim al-Kurānī belonged has largely disappeared. But as the order's most famous text, *The Book of Five Jewels* has ensured the Shaṭṭariyya's lasting influence within the Sufi networks of the eighteenth century, becoming "a staple reading among his (al-Ghawth's) spiritual descendants."[187] Indeed, the book seems to have circulated throughout the Islamic world, from India to Morocco.[188] Al-Zabīdī's celebrated dictionary of the Arabic language, *Tāj al-ʿarūs*, contains a citation from *al-Jawāhir al-khams*.[189] Today, the work is widely known within Tijānī circles, and the most popular published version of the work in West Africa was prepared under the auspices of the twentieth-century Moroccan Tijānī scholar Idrīs al-ʿIrāqī, for many years the head of the central Tijānī *zāwiya* in Fez, Morocco.[190] Tijānī scholars may have been the primary source for the book's popularity in West Africa. The sultan of Sokoto, Muhammad Bello b. ʿUthmān Fūdī (of the Qādiriyya), apparently requested permission in the book from his friend ʿUmar Tāl,[191] the renowned propagator of the Tijāniyya in nineteenth-century West Africa.

Al-Jawāhir al-khams appears to have been primarily circulated through the networks connected to Ibrāhīm al-Kūrānī. Al-Kūrānī had studied the book with his teacher Aḥmad al-Qushāshī (d. 1660), who had received it from Aḥmad al-Shinnāwī (d. 1619), and he from Sibghat-Allāh al-Barwajī (d. 1606), the successor of the book's author Muḥammad al-Ghawth (d. 1562, India).[192] Sibghat-Allah brought the book with him from India to Arabia, where he first translated the book from its original Persian to Arabic, although al-Ghawth himself may have written a first draft of the text in Arabic.[193] Reference to *al-Jawāhir al-khams* in Morocco prior to al-Tijānī, in the seventeenth-century travelogue of Abū Sālim ʿAbdallāh al-ʿAyyāshī (d. 1679) for example, links the book's transmission to this same spiritual lineage: al-ʿAyyāshī was the student of al-Qushāshī during the Moroccan pilgrim's stay in Medina.[194]

The Egyptian al-Shinnāwī's commentary on the *Jawāhir*, sometimes referenced as *Taḥliyat al-baṣāʾir bi-tamshiya ʿalā l-jawāhir* or *Ḍamāʾir al-sarāʾir ḥāshiyat al-Jawāhir*,[195] often appears in Tijānī accounts as the means of *al-Jawāhir al-khams*'s transmission.[196] Nonetheless al-Shinnāwī's unpublished commentary is now almost impossible to locate, except for a barely legible copy in the Bibliotheca Alexandrina in Maghrebi handwriting.[197] The commentary appears to add substantial information to the currently published version of *al-Jawāhir al-khams*, and a report circulates within the Tijāniyya that al-Shinnāwī had once declared no one would find his commentary except that God had given him permission to use the prayers it contained.[198] Al-Tijānī's transcription of sections of *al-Jawāhir al-khams* was evidently based on direct access to al-Shinnāwī's explanation. The latter portions of al-Shinnāwī's commentary may in fact have been the work of his Yemeni student, Sālim b. Shaykhān Bā-ʿAlawī (d. 1636, Mecca). Al-Tijānī's manuscript, presumably copying from an earlier text provided him by al-Hindī, in fact cites this Yemeni scholar's writing on the source for his access to *al-Jawāhir al-khams*: "The direct source (*min aṣlihi mubāshira*) for this book has been the beloved brother (*shaqq al-ḥabīb*) in knowledge of the people of spiritual witnessing of the unseen, the gnostic (*al-ʿārif bi-Llāh*) al-Sayyid (Aḥmad) Sālim b. Aḥmad Shaykhān Bā-ʿAlawī."[199] According to accounts from within the Bā-ʿAlawī tradition, Sālim read the entire *Jawāhir* with Shinnāwī seven times, and himself wrote the commentary (under his teacher's name) on the fourth and fifth of the "jewels" as Shinnāwī had only been able to write commentary on the first three.[200] Al-Tijānī's *Kunnāsh al-riḥla* contains a separate short treatise from Sālim explaining the intricacies of the saintly hierarchy and reconciling the understanding of Muḥammad al-Ghawth with that of Ibn al-ʿArabī.[201] Al-Tijānī's *Kunnāsh* thus appears to recognize an intellectual debt to the Bā-ʿAlawī scholar, as well as to al-Shinnāwī, in the transmission of *al-Jawāhir al-khams*.

While the exact connection between Bā-ʿAlawī and the later al-Hindī remains unclear, al-Tijānī's reception of the *al-Jawāhir al-khams* appears inherited directly from al-Shinnāwī even if its transmission through

Bā-ʿAlawī likely bypassed intervening figures like Ibrāhīm al-Kūrānī. According to the contemporary Moroccan Tijānī researcher al-Rāḍī al-Kanūn, al-Hindī was one of the great scholars (*aʿlām*) of the Naqshbandiyya, whose spiritual arrival (*wuṣūl*) had been at the hands of an unidentified saint from Tanta, Egypt.[202] Tanta was also the origin of the Aḥmad al-Shinnāwī, who transmitted both Shaṭṭariyya and Naqshbandiyya Sufi affiliations. The *Kunnāsh al-riḥla* specifically references al-Hindī for lines of transmission for certain prayers through al-Shinnāwī's teacher, Sibghat-Allāh al-Barwajī (d. 1606, Bijapur), and al-Shinnāwī's student Aḥmad al-Qushāshī (d. 1660, Medina).[203] Aḥmad al-Hindī thus appears to have been a part of the network associated with Ibrāhīm al-Kūrānī in Medina, many of whose members were Indian residents in the Ḥijāz and who alternated Sufi affiliations between the Shaṭṭariyya and the Naqshbandiyya. Al-Hindī's separate inheritance of *al-Jawāhir al-khams* suggests that this network was not beholden to al-Kūrānī alone, but that al-Kūrānī was just one notable scholar in a larger constellation circulating through the Hijaz.

The book *al-Jawāhir al-khams* situates discussions of the esoteric sciences within a broader understanding of the aspirant's ordinary worship of God. Beginning sections of the book are "clearly aimed at the ordinary [Muslim] believer," while "succeeding parts increasingly aim at more elite audiences."[204] Of the five "jewels" or chapters of the book, the first two deal primarily with prayers or supplications to be performed at specific times of the year or for certain needs. For example, there are prayers for forgiveness (*ṣalāt al-tasbīḥ*), for guidance (*ṣalāt al-istikhāra*), for making up missed prayers (*ṣalāt kafārat al-ṣalāt*), for "illuminating the heart" (*ṣalāt tanwīr al-qalb*), and for "encountering the prophetic presence" (*malāqāt al-ḥaḍra al-nabawwiyya*). There are also different prayers for the beginning of each lunar month, and for other special days of the year, such as the nights of Ramaḍān, the fifteenth of Shaʿbān, or the tenth of Muḥarram.

The book's more "esoteric" accent develops in last three chapters. The third "jewel" introduces the reader to the system of numerological equivalences to the Arabic letters (*ḥisāb abjada*) that comes to characterize the rest of the book. Muḥammad al-Ghawth suggests that the divine response (*ijāba*) to the worshipper's supplication is connected to the spiritual "weight" of letters and words, which connect the divine kingdom (*malakūt*) to the seen world (*mulk*). Each letter is in fact linked to a divine name, an angelic presence, and—by way of indicating influence over the worldly kingdom—to a phase of the moon:

> The twenty-eight letters (of the Arabic alphabet) are, at their source, twenty-eight comprehensive divine names. Every letter has a spiritual presence (*rūḥānī*) entrusted with that letter and occupied with the remembrance of the (respective) divine name . . . so when they (saints) became engrossed with invoking the names, they found the trustees and spiritual presences of these names by way of unveiling and ocular witnessing. They found twenty-eight divine names, from which manifested the twenty-eight phases of the moon (*manāzil al-qamar*). Just as there are twenty-eight letters, there are (a like number of) determinative, comprehensive names (*asmāʾ kawniyya kulliyya*), and so there are twenty-eight lunar abodes. What is found among the influences in the world: they are due to the determinative names, for what is seen is the (worldly) kingdom (*mulk*), and what is unseen is the spiritual kingdom (*malakūt*).[205]

Al-Tijānī considered this discussion significant enough to copy portions of it, along with the elucidation of al-Shinnāwī: "The excellence of every supplication is in its letters and words . . . and the efficacy (*ḥukm*) of the letters is by the efficacy of the angelic names (*al-asmāʾ al-jabarūtiyya*) attached to them." The logic behind the "science of letters" emerges then from a deep reflection on the relationship between the letters comprising the revealed text and the unseen spiritual world.

In the context of eighteenth-century scholarship's search for "realization" or "verification" (*taḥqīq*), the work provides significant evidence to the way in which ḥadīth study and the search for divine grace (*faḍl*) were combined in knowledge acquisition. *Al-Jawāhir al-khams*, like other books of its genre, thus mines the ḥadīth corpus for special prayers to attain divine satisfaction. Al-Tijānī's first reference to *al-Jawāhir al-khams* in his *Kunnāsh al-riḥla* is to the aforementioned *ṣalāt al-kafāra*, a prayer that could make up for any ritual prayers missed in a Muslim's lifetime. The following citation is taken from al-Tijānī's *Kunnāsh*, with divergences from the published *Book of Five Jewels* based on Shinnāwī's commentary rendered in italics:

> Whoever has missed a ritual prayer and does not know[206] how many, let him pray on Friday four extra prayer cycles (*rakaʿāt*) with one final salutation (*taslīm*), uttering as his intention: "I pray for the sake of God four cycles to cover the obligation (*takfīran li-qiḍāʾ*) of what I have missed in all of my life from obligatory and supererogatory prayers

> together." Then he reads in each cycle "the throne verse" (*ayat al-kursī*) seven times and "surely we have granted you the abundance" (*kawthar*) fifteen times,[207] *with full presence of heart.*
>
> The prince of the faithful, ʿAlī b. Abī Ṭālib, may God ennoble his countenance, said: "I heard God's messenger, peace and blessing upon him, say: 'Even if a person has missed seventy years of prayer, this will cover him.' They said, 'O messenger of God, mankind's lifespan does not exceed seventy or eighty years, *so what is the meaning of this description*?'[208] [He replied] 'Then *it covers* his prayer and the prayer of his parents and children, *and the prayers of all are accepted.*' "
>
> Then he offers the invocation of blessing on the chief of the world (*sayyid al-ʿālam*), peace and blessing upon him, one hundred times, and reads the following supplication [. . .].
>
> *In another narration: "Whoever prays on Friday before the afternoon prayer four cycles, in each the opening chapter of the Qurʾān (fātiḥat al-kitāb) once, the throne verse once, and 'surely we have granted you the abundance' fifteen times, and when done asks God's forgiveness ten times, and invokes blessing on the Prophet fifteen times, it covers (all) prayers missed." ʿUthmān, may God be pleased with him, said: "I heard the Prophet, peace and blessing upon him, say, 'This prayer covers the missed prayers, even those for one hundred years.' " And ʿAlī, may God be pleased with him, said: "I heard the Prophet, God's blessing and peace upon him, say: 'This prayer covers the missed prayers of five hundred years.' " And ʿĀʾisha said, "I heard the Prophet, peace and blessing upon him, say: 'This prayer covers the missed prayers of one thousand years. Who makes this prayer without further need of compensation, it covers the missed prayers of his father and mother.' "*[209]

Noteworthy here is that a book of "esoteric sciences" elaborates on different narrations from the Prophet concerning a prayer to fulfill a basic obligation of Islamic law. An obvious question would be why such a prayer would be transmitted through secret manuscripts (and thus by initiation) rather than more public ḥadīth transmission. The likely answer is that scholars could thereby ensure a lay audience did not misinterpret this special prayer to avoid praying the five daily prayers altogether. The passage also demonstrates the role of al-Shinnāwī, referred to in al-Tijānī's text as "the eye of (Muḥammad) al-Ghawth's spiritual presence," in heightening the later scholarly reception of *al-Jawāhir al-khams* by providing a variety of mutually supportive narrations.

There are other places where al-Shinnāwī departs entirely from the original text, for example, in discussing the invocation of blessing on the Prophet Muḥammad (*ṣalāt ʿalā l-nabī*). By all accounts, this practice became an integral component of various *Ṭarīqa Muḥammadiyya* articulations in the eighteenth century. Here is an example of al-Shinnāwī's writing on the topic as it appears in al-Tijānī's handwritten transcription:

> Whoever desires to have the light of (Muḥammad) Muṣṭafa's beauty, peace and blessing upon him, illuminate him like the rising sun, let him bath every night from Friday to Friday, wear clean clothes and perfume himself. And every night (for a week), let him read the following prayer one thousand times: "O God, send blessings and peace upon the body (*jasad*) of Muḥammad among all bodies, and upon the tomb of our master Muḥammad among all tombs, and upon the earth (around the grave) of our master Muḥammad among all earth." He who embarks on the preceding will become acquainted with (regularly) meeting him (the Prophet), God's blessing and peace upon him, and he will obtain from him what he desires, finding true honor and elevation from him directly.[210]

This "commentary," appearing at the end of the second chapter of the *Five Jewels*, bears no real connection to Ghawth's previous discussion on prayers to avoid unfortunate astrological alignments (*dafʿ nuḥusat al-kawākib*). Al-Shinnāwī here provides a practical method for encountering the enduring presence of the Prophet Muḥammad so important for the Tijāniyya and many Sufi communities of the eighteenth century. *Al-Jawāhir al-khams*, especially through al-Shinnāwī's commentary, became popular during the period because of this accent on religious "verification" (*taḥqīq*) that deftly weaved between ḥadīth, Sufi unveiling, and the esoteric sciences.

Conclusion: *Madhhab* and the *Ṭarīqa Muḥammadiyya*

This chapter has explored the eighteenth-century intellectual traditions to which al-Tijānī was connected. What emerges is a portrait of scholarly vibrancy and inquiry in the period of both noteworthy local depth and nuance, but also with intriguing correspondences across vast distances. The accent here has been on scholarly articulations unencumbered by presupposed notions of shared reformist impulses across space and time. But al-Tijānī's own intellectual background reflects several important themes of eighteenth-century scholarship that appear to have received increased attention during the period. These themes include the centrality of ḥadīth study, the realization of divine oneness (*tawḥīd*), and perhaps most important: the notion of "Muḥammadan Sufism" or the *Ṭarīqa Muḥammadiyya*. Scholars in different places may have reached different conclusions concerning these ideas, but they nonetheless were asking similar questions that invariably stressed the verification or actualization (*taḥqīq*) of religious knowledge.

It is remarkable that the many Sufi exchanges of the eighteenth century often consciously relativized affiliation to the established schools of jurisprudence (*madhāhib*). Despite his Mālikī training, most of al-Tijānī's contacts in the Middle East appear to have been Shāfiʿī, even if al-Sammān and al-Kurdī traced their Khalwatī affiliation to the Ḥanafī-trained al-Bakrī.[211] Al-Bakrī also appeared to have students of the Ḥanbalī school.[212] Other scholars within these eighteenth centuries freely changed *madhhab* affiliations, one claiming permission from a dream of Imam al-Shāfiʿī to leave the Shāfiʿī school and join the Ḥanafī school.[213] A prominent student of al-Ḥifnī changed from the Shāfiʿī school to the Mālikī, and then back to the Shāfiʿī.[214] The aforementioned Shaykh al-Azhar al-Damanhūrī, originally trained as a Shāfiʿī, gave legal opinions in all four schools and wrote separate books on both Ḥanbalī and Ḥanafī legal interpretations.[215] The permissibility of continued scholarly reasoning (*ijtihād*) was generally accepted, and al-Zabīdī's call for restricting *ijtihād* appeared to have been a minority opinion.[216] While Morocco was most certainly less welcoming of non-Mālikī affiliation, the Moroccan sultan Mawlay Muḥammad (d. 1790) encouraged the increased study of ḥadīth and suggested the equal validity of all four legal schools. His son Mawlay Sulaymān retained this emphasis on ḥadīth, while returning to official support for the Mālikī school.[217] This rhetorical return to the text (Qur'ān and Ḥadīth) appeared to be the substance of the hesitant approval for the Wahhābīs by Fez's most eminent Mālikī jurist and disciple of al-Tijānī, Ḥamdūn b. al-Ḥājj (d. 1817).[218]

As central as legal questions remained to most scholars of the eighteenth century, law was not a hermeneutically sealed category. *Ijtihād* was not always the only solution to "blind imitation" (*taqlīd*): "verification" (*taḥqīq*) could also be a relevant exercise.[219] In the eighteenth century, scholars specifically identified as jurists frequently related visions of the Prophet,[220] or arguments derived from reflections on Sufi etiquette. Muḥammad Ḥayat al-Sindī's argument for placing the hands on the chest in prayer (*qabḍ*), instead of below the navel in the Ḥanafī school, demonstrates the blurred categories of ḥadīth, legal practice, and Sufism. Al-Sindī first cited numerous ḥadīth in support of *qabḍ*, suggested that even Imam Mālik was well aware of the practice's grounding in the Sunnah (thus his inclusion in the *Muwaṭṭā*) despite later North African Mālikī interpretations, and then concluded: "Indeed, the breast is the place of the light of Islam, so its protection by the hands (over it) in prayer is more appropriate than pointing toward the private parts by putting the hands below the navel. And it is closest to humility, and humility is the beautification of prayer."[221] Like the almost identical argument for *qabḍ* of the twentieth-century Tijānī scholar Ibrāhīm Niasse,[222] al-Sindī's ends by returning the discussion to inward disposition so often emphasized by Sufism. Part of the ingenuity of eighteenth-century legal thought is thus the inclusion of multiple epistemological perspectives, not only a reworking of juristic methodology (*uṣūl*).

The *Ṭarīqa Muḥammadiyya* was another idea of wide circulation, but which meant different things in different contexts. Al-Nābulusī's commentary on al-Birkawī's book on the subject may have reclaimed the "Muḥammadan Way" from the anti-Sufi Kadezadilites, but al-Nābulusī otherwise remained committed to al-Birkawī's overall project of associating the essence of Islamic spirituality with ethics, for Sufis the *adab al-sulūk*.[223] This idea of the Sufi's exemplification of the character of the Prophet was also the meaning of reference to the *Ṭarīqa Muḥammadiyya* in North and West Africa in the seventeenth century, along with a shared accent on paradigmatic sainthood. Later students in the tradition of the Moroccan ʿAbd al-ʿAzīz al-Dabbāgh, such as Aḥmad b. Idrīs and Muhammad al-Sanūsī, clearly associated the *Ṭarīqa Muḥammadiyya* primarily with "meeting" the Prophet. Ibn Idrīs's teacher ʿAbd al-Wahhāb al-Tāzī thus first became attached to al-Dabbāgh when al-Dabbāgh met him and asked, "Do you want to see God's Messenger? . . . Raise your head and look!"[224] Murtaḍa al-Zabīdī cites the *Ṭarīqa Muḥammadiyya* as a separate Sufi order into which he was initiated, but he used this reference to emphasize the individual's practice of "prayer upon the Prophet" (*ṣalāt ʿalā l-nabī*) that "illuminates the darkness of the open spaces and clears away the shadows of the late night."[225] The Naqshbandī Ḥasan al-ʿUjaymī, who with Ibrāhīm al-Kūrānī shared Aḥmad al-Qushāshī as a shaykh, emphasized the spiritual state to be engendered through the *Ṭarīqa Muḥammadiyya*:

> The basis of this path [the tarīqa Muḥammadiyya] is that the inner being of the one who follows it is absorbed in the vision of Muḥammad's *dhat* (being), while he is zealously imitating the Prophet outwardly in word and deed, busying his tongue invoking blessings upon him, and devoting himself to him at all times whether in seclusion or in public, until honouring the Prophet comes to dominate his heart and to permeate his inner being to such an extent that he need only hear the Prophet's name and he starts trembling, his heart is overwhelmed beholding him and the visible appearances of the Prophet emerge before his inner sight.[226]

Such an idea was later echoed by Muḥammad al-Sammān, who stressed above all the "Muḥammadan Way" as a method of increasing the aspirant's love for the Prophet. Al-Sammān's fellow Khalwatīs whom al-Tijānī met in Egypt did not specifically reference a *Ṭarīqa Muḥammadiyya*, but they emphasized similar teachings and certainly reported regular encounters with the Prophet.

Another version of the *Ṭarīqa Muḥammadiyya*, to which al-Tijānī had no verifiable connection, was that of the Indian Naqshbandī shaykh Nāṣir al-ʿAndalīb (d. 1758), who was connected to the spiritual lineage of Aḥmad Sirhindī. Close to al-Tijānī's birth (1737), al-ʿAndalīb had a vision of the Prophet's grandson Ḥasan, who gave him a distinct spiritual path, better than all others: "My dear grandfather has sent me specially to you so that I may fill you completely with interior knowledge and sanctity."[227] When his son Mir Dard asked him how to name the path, he responded: "Our love is the love of Muḥammad and our claim is the claim of Muḥammad. One must call this order the ṭarīqa Muḥammadiyya, the Muḥammadan path. It is exactly the path of Muḥammad, and we have not added anything to it. Our conduct is the conduct of the Prophet, and our way the Muḥammadan way."[228] Al-ʿAndalīb's example is perhaps an exception to Radtke's nonetheless valid observation: "The tarīqa Muḥammadiyya is not a Sufi order but a path, a form of spiritual concentration."[229] By the late eighteenth-century, the *Ṭarīqa Muḥammadiyya* had come to mean various things: conformity with the Sunnah of the Prophet, prayer upon the Prophet, loving the Prophet, seeing the Prophet, and a distinct inheritance or investiture from the Prophet. Al-Tijānī's own version of the *Ṭarīqa Muḥammadiyya* included all of these elements. But it was al-ʿAndalīb's version that best foreshadowed al-Tijānī's own claims for having been given a distinct Sufi path directly by the Prophet.

The point here is not that the Tijāniyya replicated a coherent eighteenth-century philosophy or intellectual movement. It is that al-Tijānī's ideas were distinctly legible within multiple, overlapping eighteenth-century Islamic intellectual discourses. Following recent academic research, the exploration here of Muslim intellectuals also permits some significant correctives to earlier understanding of the eighteenth century. Al-Tijānī did not inherit an intellectual tradition, for example, that was at odds with the theosophy of Ibn al-ʿArabī;[230] nor one that de-emphasized shaykh-disciple relations;[231] nor one that had begun to relativize or subject Sufi affiliation to skeptical distance;[232] nor even one that held esotericism in increasing suspicion.[233] This chapter's discussion of intellectual developments in the Moroccan Shādhiliyya, West African saintly scholasticism, and a particular Middle Eastern conflation of Sufi knowledge, ḥadīth, and esotericism, demonstrates multiple rich discursive fields. Muslim intellectuals such as al-Tijānī were clearly animated with a desire to verify, explore, and actualize the depths of the Islamic intellectual tradition. The emergence of the Tijāniyya, like other scholarly communities during the period, must be understood within these rich intellectual currents, while also appreciating the distinct contributions of individual scholars. The rest of this book takes up the challenge of doing justice to al-Tijānī's thought in the context of late eighteenth- and early nineteenth-century historical contexts.

CHAPTER TWO

Portrait of a Scholar

An Intellectual Biography of Shaykh al-Tijānī

IN THE LATE EIGHTEENTH CENTURY, a Mauritanian jurist and ḥadīth scholar named Muḥammad al-Ḥāfiẓ al-ʿAlawī (d. 1830) was in Mecca performing Hajj. His most fervent prayer was "to meet a perfected shaykh among the folk of God the Exalted." As he circumambulated the sacred house, an unknown man approached him and said, "Your shaykh is Aḥmad al-Tijānī." Surprised, and never having heard this name before, al-Ḥāfiẓ began to inquire of other pilgrim groups about this shaykh. Finally, he encountered some "riffraff" from Fez (*sūqat ahl al-Fās*), who told him, "as if they wanted to belittle" the shaykh: "There is a jurist (*faqīh*) with us in Fez (by that name), who is associated with philosophy (*al-ḥikma*) and alchemy (*al-kīmiyāʾ*)." They continued in this manner until one of them finally admitted they knew little about him and referred al-Ḥāfiẓ to a group of Moroccan scholars, "for they have more direct knowledge of him than us." This second scholarly group held the shaykh in great esteem and informed al-Ḥāfiẓ of al-Tijānī's learning and saintliness. Upon accomplishing his pilgrimage, al-Ḥāfiẓ came to Fez and apprenticed himself to the shaykh he had so ardently sought.[1] In Fez he found his attachment to al-Tijānī confirmed by his countryman ʿAbd al-Raḥmān al-Shinqītī, the former student of Ṣāliḥ al-Fullānī, who declared of al-Tijānī (as earlier mentioned), "By God, there is no one more knowledgeable on the face of the earth than him."[2] This story tells how an influential Mauritanian scholar became a student of Aḥmad al-Tijānī, in turn serving as perhaps the most important conduit for the spread of the Tijāniyya in nineteenth-century sub-Saharan Africa.[3]

Reference to the "knowledge" of eminent Sufi leaders, so important for their initial recognition within circles of Islamic scholarship, is often reduced to distinctive "mystical" or Sufi understandings in later narrations. Even if al-Ḥāfiẓ was directed to al-Tijānī by a mystical encounter, it was al-Tijānī's scholarly reputation that confirmed al-Ḥāfiẓ's affiliation to the Tijāniyya. This chapter explores a comprehensive intellectual biography of al-Tijānī, confirming the theme of eighteenth-century scholarly vibrancy at the foundation of the Tijāniyya. For al-Tijānī, Sufism did not eclipse the "official" (*rasmī*) fields of Islamic learning (jurisprudence, ḥadīth, theology, exegesis, etiquette), it simply deepened their meaning. He taught jurisprudence in 'Ayn Māḍī (Algeria), Qur'ān exegesis and ḥadīth in Tlemcen (Algeria), Sufi etiquette according to Ibn 'Atā-Allāh's *Kitāb al-ḥikam* in Tunis, and responded to inquiries in Fez that involved all fields of Islamic learning, including poetry and metaphysics in addition to fields already mentioned.

According to Ibn al-Mashrī, among al-Tijānī's miracles was that he could answer any question posed to him to the satisfaction of the petitioner, "as if the divinely guarded tablet (*al-lawḥ al-maḥfūẓ*) was before his eyes."[4] The Moroccan sultan's favored jurist Ḥamdūn b. al-Ḥājj, along with Fez's chief judge 'Abbās b. Kirān, were some of many scholars to consult al-Tijānī for his legal opinions.[5] When the eminent scholar of Tunisia's Zaytūna University, Ibrāhīm al-Riyāḥī (d. 1850) visited al-Tijānī in Fez, he similarly praised his scholarship and remarked, "I prayed the afternoon prayer behind him, and I have never seen one more thorough in his prayer than him, nor so long in prostration and standing, and I was very happy to see such a prayer of the righteous ancestors (*ṣalāt al-salaf al-ṣāliḥ*)."[6] For such early followers, al-Tijānī clearly represented an unflinching religious sincerity and dedication to truth that pervaded all fields of Islamic inquiry. I turn then to an overview of the shaykh's scholarly inquiry and articulation in a variety of classically demarcated fields: jurisprudence (*fiqh*), theology (*'aqīda, kalām*), esotericism (*'ilm al-asrār*), and (Sufi) etiquette (*adab al-sulūk*), gnosis (*ma'rifa*) and spiritual training (*tarbiya*). This overview also tracks the shaykh's movement in time and space in relationship to these subjects of learning. In all of these fields, the broader theme of verification (*taḥqīq*) appears as a central ambition in al-Tijānī's intellectual biography.

Islamic Law

Shaykh al-Tijānī's proficiency in Islamic law, primary sources indicate, was rarely absent from his interactions with students. The Moroccan historian al-Nāṣirī, among others, consistently refers to al-Tijānī with titles such as "jurist" (*faqīh*) and "scholar" (*ʿālim*) along with more predictable titles for a Sufi shaykh, such as "Sufi" (*mutaṣawwuf*) and "gnostic" (*ʿārif*).[7] A good number of al-Tijānī's students were already advanced in their juristic learning, but were no less admiring of the shaykh's knowledge in this field. Al-Tijānī drew from an apparently comprehensive training in jurisprudence of the Mālikī school. He exhibited a propensity for independent scholar reasoning (*ijtihād*) based on, in his opinion, the necessity of an ongoing dialogue between authoritative texts (*naṣṣ*, the Qurʾān and ḥadīth) and legal understanding(*fiqh*).

The town of al-Tijānī's early education, the Algerian oasis of ʿAyn Māḍī, had a reputation from at least the seventeenth century for expertise in the study of Islamic law according to the school of Imam Mālik, especially in the advanced legal text *Mukhtaṣar al-Khalīl*.[8] Al-Tijānī's early studies, following his memorization of the Qurʾān at age seven, consisted of mastering the core texts of the Mālikī curriculum at the time: *Mukhtaṣar al-Akhḍarī*, ʿAbd al-Raḥmān al-Akhḍarī's (d. 1575, Biskra, Algeria) summary of rules relating to prayer and bodily purification; *al-Risāla* of Ibn Abī Zayd al-Qayrawānī (d. 996, Tunis), a comprehensive overview of legal understanding in the Mālikī school; the *Muqaddima* of Ibn Rushd "al-Jadd" (d. 1126, Cordoba), an adaptation of Ibn Saḥnūn's (d. 854, Tunis) *al-Mudawwana* according to the principles of legal theory (*uṣūl*); and the *Mukhtaṣar al-Khalīl* of Khalīl al-Jundī (d. 1365, Cairo), long considered the summation of study in the Mālikī school.[9] Of the last book, al-Tijānī's devotion to learning allegedly made him knowledgeable of the legal understandings of the later chapters before studying them, allowing him to memorize the text quickly.[10] Besides these core texts mentioned in *Jawāhir al-maʿānī* and *al-Jāmiʿ*, there is evidence al-Tijānī also studied a larger corpus of texts on legal precedent and theory, committing to memory works such as *al-Muwaṭṭa* of Mālik b. Anas, *al-Mudawwana al-kubrā* of Ibn Saḥnūn (d. 855, Tunisia), *al-Mukhtaṣar* of Ibn al-Ḥājib (d. 1248), and *al-Tahdhīb fī ikhtiṣār al-Mudawwana* of Khalaf al-Barādhiʿī.[11] While he later voiced criticism of a few opinions that had developed in the Mālikī school, he remained a committed Mālikī. In giving legal opinions, he would often begin with, "It has been established from Mālik, the Imam of our school, may God be pleased with him," or would reference prior juristic consensus (*ijmaʿ*) in the school as binding precedent.[12] The style of Qurʾān recitation in North and West Africa (*warsh*), closely related to the Mālikī school because of its transmission from Mālik's teacher al-Nāfi', is given particular authority in Ḥarāzim's *Jawāhir al-ma'ānī.* It seems the teacher of al-Tijānī's own Qur'ān teacher once dreamed God recited to him the entire Qur'ān in *warsh*, and then said to him, "That is how it was revealed."[13]

Al-Tijānī's own spectrum of legal opinions appears mostly concerned with confirming the foundations of the Sharī'a and Sunni orthopraxy, even in application of his own scholarly legacy. "If you hear something from me," he responded to an inquiry whether false statements would be attributed to him after his death, "weigh it on the scale of the Sharī'a. If it balances, take it. If not, leave it."[14] Concerning so-called Sufis who did not uphold the Sharī'a, the shaykh said simply, "They are the party of Satan."[15] In emphasizing legal obligation in relation to Sufi litanies, he insisted, "The best of litanies (*adhkār*) is the remembrance of God at His command and prohibition."[16] From his early years when his scholarship began attracting visitors from within 'Ayn Māḍī, he was uncomfortable with people kissing his hand.[17] In his later years, he reprimanded some students who bent down to kiss the ground at his feet: "You have disbelieved, so repeat the testimony of faith."[18] Proper understanding and practice of the Sharī'a remained central to al-Tijānī's later teaching. Ibn al-Mashrī recorded al-Tijānī as saying: "The head of knowledge, after the correction of faith (*taṣḥīḥ al-īmān*), is the dedication and approach to God in both form and essence. Then it is learning the legally incumbent acts, including purification, prayer, fasting, and the like. Then a person must learn what he requires of the law in social matters (*mu'āmalāt*) relating to commerce, marriage, and the like."[19] While most of the Tijānī primary sources are admittedly concerned with this approach to God "in essence" through Sufism, there is ample evidence that al-Tijānī did not understand the practice of Sufism to be at the expense of approaching God "in form" through the sacred law. Al-Tijānī clearly exhibited interest in the sacred law. Ibn al-Mashrī, himself trained as a jurist (*faqīh*),[20] attested that the shaykh referenced to him an entire book on Islamic law, "with all of its sections, chapters, and issues," which al-Tijānī had composed in his head, named, "The Book of the Authoritative Text and the Legal Opinion" (*Kitāb al-naṣṣ wa l-fatwā*).[21] Although Ḥarāzim's original copy of the *Jawāhir al-ma'ānī* left with al-Tijānī in Fez did not include sections on al-Tijānī's legal opinions, other versions did include these sections, and they are present in Ibn al-Mashrī's lengthy discussion of al-Tijānī's legal opinions in *al-Jāmi'*. Many of the shaykh's legal rulings are also included in al-Sufyānī's *al-Ifāda al-Aḥmadiyya.*

A recurrent concern for al-Tijānī, evident from primary sources, seemed to be the nonchalance of individual Muslims with the Islamic ritual prayer (*ṣalāt*). He cited the ḥadīth to remind those who delayed their prayers without acceptable cause: "The best of all actions is the prayer in its proper time."[22] Muslims should not rush their prayers and must make at least three distinct glorifications (*tasbīḥ*) in each position of bowing (*rukū'*) and prostration (*sajda*).[23] Extra "Sunnah" prayers (*nawāfil*) could be made up later if missed, especially the supererogatory night prayer (*ṣalāt al-shaf' wa l-witr*). For this latter prayer, al-Tijānī here seemed to follow Abū Ḥanīfa's emphasis on *ṣalāt al-witr*'s compulsory nature, which helped to ensure the acceptance of the five daily ritual prayers.[24] Praying the five prayers, for men to include praying in congregation, became a condition of initiation into the Tijāniyya.[25] Leaving aside the five daily prayers completely was grounds for divorce from one's spouse, even if the negligent spouse was a descendant of the Prophet Muḥammad.[26]

But al-Tijānī was also concerned that legal compendiums had sometimes confused the simple foundations of Islamic law. For example, he blamed unnamed books of (Mālikī) jurisprudence for promoting negligence in ritual purification or ablution (*wuḍū'*) in contradiction to clear injunctions in the Qur'an and ḥadīth. Most Mālikī jurists allowed a person to leave aside making ablution with water if he feared the prayer-time would end, but al-Tijānī strongly disagreed: "The opinion that guarding to the [prayer] time is more important than ritual purity . . . cannot be authenticated, for it contradicts the text (*naṣṣ*)."[27] For al-Tijānī, such practice contravened the Qur'ān verse, "*O you who believe, before you stand for prayer, wash your faces*," and the Prophet's saying, "God does accept the prayer of one who has become unclean (*aḥdatha*) until he makes ablution."[28] Similarly, he disapproved of another juristic opinion allowing a woman to be exempted from proper ablution for prayer during her wedding or honeymoon if she feared disturbing her makeup.[29]

Al-Tijānī used these examples to stress that not everything in the books of jurisprudence was valid. Other invalid interpretations included the permissibility of temporary marriage; of a man's marriage to more than four wives; of the permissibility of pork fat so long as it was devoid of meat; or of female descendants of the Prophet to be automatically exempt from breastfeeding their own children.[30] And while he defended the traditional institution of endowments (*waqf, ḥubus*) by which mosques and schools were usually funded,[31] he rejected the occasional stipulation, often ratified in Islamic courts, that the imam be paid a salary for leading the five daily prayers.[32] Such mistakes in the books of jurisprudence demonstrated that the student required "a scholar or scholars (*ʿulamāʾ*)" possessed of "insight (*baṣīra*) as to the meanings of the Qurʾān and the Sunna" to review with them the accumulated opinions of the legal tradition.[33] In other words, jurisprudence was necessary but could be a dangerous science if pursued without the proper sincerity or if left unverified by the light of true faith. Al-Tijānī thus cautioned students, "Respect the scholars as they are the door to the Law, but abstain from frequenting them so long as they are dominated by their ego-selves."[34]

Legal Methodology

The way al-Tijānī gave legal opinions, with frequent recourse to the Qurʾān and ḥadīth, raises the important question of al-Tijānī's legal methodology (*uṣūl*). In one place, Ibn al-Mashrī appears to suggest that al-Tijānī dispensed entirely with the tradition of legal interpretation: "We have only one rule on which we base our methodology (*uṣūl*), and that is there is no rule (*ḥukm*) except God's rule or that of His Messenger."[35] But as Ibn al-Mashrī himself demonstrates, al-Tijānī often invoked precedent consensus or the opinions of specific scholars in support of various legal opinions. Ibn al-Mashrī thus clarified, "Any statement of the scholars not derived (*mustanad*) from the statement of God or His Messenger is in error."[36] It is tempting to presume that al-Tijānī's frequent visions of the Prophet assisted him in his own *ijtihād*, but such reports are remarkably absent from his legal formulations. Rather, al-Tijānī insisted that the saint (*walī*), no matter the extent of his illumination, cannot alter the Sharīʿa: legal injunctions can only be lifted by prophecy, and prophecy remained sealed with the passing of the Prophet.[37] If the Prophet's appearance to him helped him to better verify legal opinions from the established texts, the shaykh mostly avoided mention of such insight in reminding his students of the appropriate textual source for a given interpretation. Al-Tijānī insisted that interpretation of the Qurʾān and ḥadīth cannot contradict the external (*ẓāhir*) meaning of the text: "It is well known among the verifiers (*muḥaqqiqīn*) that the Qurʾān is not interpreted except by an authenticated narration (*al-khabar al-ṣaḥīḥ*). The interpretation must not depart from its external meaning."[38]

He often appeared unwilling to offer further opinions in the absence of textual support. In response to a question concerning the type of affliction suffered by the Prophet Job (Ayyūb), al-Tijānī said, "The Prophet did not specify, so we cannot do so for the lack of an authentic text" (*li-ʿadam al-naṣṣ*).[39] When he was asked about the meaning of the Qur'ān's reference to a "manifest victory" (*fatḥ mubīn*) and al-Dabbāgh's suggestion in the *Ibrīz* that it meant divine witnessing, al-Tijānī referred students back to the verse's historical context (*sabab al-nuzūl*) of Hudaybiyya permitting the early Muslims to make the pilgrimage. He was otherwise silent on al-Dabbāgh's more mystical interpretation, saying simply, "The meanings of the Qur'ān are wide."[40] Such reference to the text thus was not necessarily meant to shut down inquiry, but also might inspire further exploration. According to Ibn al-Mashrī, he sometimes engaged students in discussion, for example, about the reason (*ʿilla*) of a given injunction in the Qur'ān or ḥadīth.[41] Al-Tijānī's legal methodology can thus be characterized as a heightened reflection on the sources of Islamic law in verification, but not rejection, of the juristic tradition.

Smoking and Slavery

Al-Tijānī's interjection into the world of juristic opinion was based on reaffirming a shared textual tradition, even if certain Muslims neglected the appropriate textual reference or ignored it because of their own inclinations. Al-Tijānī thus voiced strong opinions concerning perceived social ills of his time, in particular concerning tobacco smoking and slavery. When asked about smoking, al-Tijānī stated unequivocally: "Tobacco is forbidden. The reason for its prohibition is the Prophet's words, 'everything that saps the strength is forbidden.' And it among those things that make a person weak."[42] According to al-Sufyānī, he was "stern" in his condemnation, confirming the statement of an earlier scholar that a smoker would die in a bad state if he did not repent.[43] Such statements give the impression that al-Tijānī was relating the Prophet's direct interdiction, but aside from his own legal arguments, publicly al-Tijānī narrated only the account of his Khalwatī shaykh al-Kurdī. A man once asked al-Kurdī about the permissibility of coffee and tobacco. Al-Kurdī told him to come back the next day. That night al-Kurdī saw the Prophet with his companions. Someone came to him with coffee, and he drank some. Another person, "one of the smokers" (*ahl al-dukhān*), tried to enter the gathering, but the Prophet chased him away.[44] This narration, while perhaps suggesting the legislative function of the Prophet's appearance to eighteenth-century scholars, arguably served for al-Tijānī's audience simply to confirm the shaykh's text-based opinion within a broader network of inspired scholarship.

Enslavement was a particularly vexing question in premodern North Africa, mostly due to the possibility that many of the sub-Saharan Africans forced into labor may have already been Muslim at the time of their enslavement.[45] There is no record of al-Tijānī calling for the abolishment of slavery, but he criticized much of the practice as he found it. He openly rebuked political leaders for not restricting enslavement, for enslaving Muslims, and for permitting the unjust treatment of enslaved persons, citing to his companions a narration from the Prophet, "Do not become disbelievers after me by enslaving each other."[46] He was angered to see enslaved persons treated without dignity. Witnessing some without warm clothes in the winter, he cursed those responsible: "May God forbid the owners of these enslaved men from smelling the fragrance of Paradise."[47] On another occasion, on hearing of a man being gifted a slave girl, he sent some students with some money to the owner, saying to them: "Go to the one who was given a servant, and make sure that he is able to care for her. Tell him that he is not to quarrel with any servants. I am her who has been sold, but we are not to be sold. And it is I the manumitted, but we have not (yet) been freed."[48] This was an extraordinary expression of sympathy for the plight of enslaved persons, invoking the common humanity between a descendant of the Prophet and a slave girl. Al-Tijānī was said to have often spent all of his money on manumitting the enslaved,[49] in one day for example freeing fifteen women, in another thirteen men.[50] While still a young man in Algeria, he freed two enslaved women and married both: Mabrūka and Mubāraka, each of whom bore him children and later moved with him to Fez. His close servant (*khādim*), al-Ḥājj Būjamʿa al-Sūdānī ("the black"), who had formerly been enslaved, became the shaykh's close confident and himself experienced the coveted vision of the Prophet.[51]

It is tempting to read al-Tijānī's self-prohibition of processed sugar (*al-sukar al-qālib*) as a particular invective against the transatlantic slave trade at its peak by the turn of the nineteenth century. Sugar was imported to Morocco during this time from Christian Europe.[52] Al-Tijānī claimed, "Processed sugar is forbidden to eat or sell: it has been confirmed to me that it is mixed with blood," and on another occasion, "To me it carries the prohibition of wine."[53] Given the astounding death-rates of enslaved Africans in the Caribbean and other sugar plantations of the European colonies, al-Tijānī's observation of the sugar trade's mixture with human flesh may have been more than metaphorical. In any case, al-Tijānī's prohibition of sugar meant to protect Muslims from the contamination of unverified European production. But there is otherwise no reference in primary sources to the transatlantic slave trade: al-Tijānī's discussion of slavery primarily meant to target the unjust practices of Muslim societies. He may not have openly called for slavery to be abolished, but he clearly observed in his time that Muslims' practice of slavery largely ignored Islamic textual restrictions. He certainly would not have been so vocal in his criticisms if he had felt that other Muslim scholars had already adequately addressed the problem.

Questions of Islamic law and juristic interpretation were never absent in the circles of students who gathered around Aḥmad al-Tijānī. In view of the vibrant legal inquiry pervading Islamic scholarly circles in the eighteenth century, this is not surprising. But such an exploration remains significant given the frequent marginalization of the broader intellectual contributions of Sufi saints.

The Limits of Speculative Theology

Theology, in Islam the discipline charged with giving expression to the doctrine (*ʿaqīda*) of divine oneness (*tawḥīd*), was often a central preoccupation of eighteenth-century scholars. While many castigated the notion of theological argumentation (*ʿilm al-kalām*) based on rational proofs, others embraced reason as necessary for the verification of faith.[54] While al-Tijānī outwardly distanced himself from theological disputation, his concept of reason or exercise of the mind (*ʿaql*) was more complex than a surface reading of sources might suggest. There is no reference in the *Jawāhir al-maʿānī* or *al-Jāmiʿ* to his studying or teaching any book of theology, but he appears to have at least studied the core text of the Ashʿarī creed, the *al-ʿAqīda al-ṣughrā* of Muḥammad al-Sanūsī with a scholar from Sijilmasa during his first visit to Fez around 1758.[55] In any case, Ibn al-Mashrī found his shaykh to be "among the distinguished scholars" (*fuḥūl*) in the science (*kalām*). In his early years, al-Tijānī had been "on the path of the theologians in providing evidence (*adilla*)." After his pilgrimage east, "he returned to providing evidence by transmitted reports (*naql*), not by reason (*ʿaql*), except what accorded with transmitted knowledge."[56] This surprising attestation reveals that renowned Sufi scholars of the period were influenced by broader scholarly currents and explored a variety of Islamic sciences. Their followers certainly perceived that they made useful contributions in fields other than Sufism strictly defined.

The doctrine of divine oneness (*tawḥīd*) was a central preoccupation for al-Tijānī, as it was for other theologians. Al-Tijānī's later teachings on the subject emphasized the limits of the mind in the verification of *tawḥīd*. He was concerned that rational disputation concerning the nature of God's being should not preoccupy the ordinary believer: "As for the *tawḥīd* of the speculative theologians, they have offered a sort of solution for the health of *tawḥīd*, demonstrating what constitutes incapacity, imperfection, or ignorance in the description of the Creator, glorious and exalted is He. They have offered all of this with rational proofs based on what has been firmly established. But these theologians find themselves in great difficulty from the plethora of successive analogies. This type of *tawḥīd* should not occupy a person, due to the abundance of doubt and delirium therein."[57] While rational inquiry may have its place, the veneration of speculative theologians might undermine the simplicity of *tawḥīd* for the common person. Fellow North African Ashʿarī theologians like Muḥammad al-Sanūsī (d. 1490) and Ḥasan al-Yūsī did not exactly obligate the ordinary believer with learning complex rational proofs; al-Yūsī, for example, considered such activity a communal obligation to be undertaken by scholars (*farḍ kifāya*).[58] Al-Tijānī emphasized that no Muslim could be faulted for understanding *tawḥīd* strictly according to transmitted reports: "The truth is that God's covenant with His creation (*ḥujjat Allāh ʿalā khalqihi*) is found in the knowledge reported (*khabar*) from His messengers, peace and blessing upon them, and nothing else."[59]

Following earlier theologians like al-Ghazālī, al-Tijānī blamed the metaphysical pretensions of Hellenistic philosophy for muddying the simplicity of Islam's original *tawḥīd*.

> The reason that the common folk fell into the confusion of the theologians was their coming upon the earlier sciences of philosophy. Philosophy became established in their knowledge as the "science of *tawḥīd*." The truth is that the search for divine knowledge through rational laws and logical demonstrations is the means by which God removed them from the knowledge of the Truth, from drawing near to God, and from the awareness of His majesty.
>
> When this knowledge of philosophy entered their hearts, and they heard this as the discipline of *tawḥīd*, these saddlebags, articulated now in Arabic, changed them from the people of divine favor to those who rejected God the exalted. Generally, all who obtained this science

> leaped into ignorance, while claiming that they had reached the pinnacle of knowledge. But they were far removed from the knowledge of God and the awareness of His majesty.
>
> They expounded to the common folk that whoever did not know their science was as if he knew nothing. The souls of the common folk followed them, inclined towards worldly favor, for they saw how they were exalted in the hearts of the commoners, kings, and princes. On account of following this whirlwind, which differed from the righteous ancestors (*salaf*) without any excuse or restraint, the true knowledge of *tawḥīd* sent with the Messengers was forgotten. Those who sought the *tawḥīd* of the Messengers came to reject the *tawḥīd* of the philosophers as poison for the Sufis and gnostics. And indeed, those who sought the *tawḥīd* of the philosophers became as poison for theology itself.[60]

The obvious reference here is to the Muʿtazilite school beholden to Greek philosophy, briefly established as the official doctrine during the Abbasid Caliphate. Against these perceived sycophant theologians, al-Tijānī credits "Sufi gnostics" (*al-ʿārifūn*) such as Abū Ḥasan al-Ashʿarī (d. 936) and Muḥammad al-Sanūsī, primary formulators of the Ashʿarī school of theology, for taking up the challenge of arguing against the Muʿtazilites.

> As for the interjection into the discipline of theology by gnostics such as al-Ashʿarī and al-Sanūsī and their like, may God be pleased with them, it was only their desire for kindness with the common folk. When it was (argued) that (disputes over) the *tawḥīd* of the Messengers cannot be answered except by the sword, they answered that the commoners could accept the command of God by their own volition if they were given foundational rational proofs (for the correct *tawḥīd*). They saw that this was better than the sword, for the one forced by the sword does not enter the religion except under compulsion and force. This was the reason for their interjection into the science of theology.[61]

Al-Tijānī thus does not eliminate altogether the value of reason in the pursuit of theology, but he suggests the proper use of reason should be used like medicine for a particular illness. Again, in terms similar to al-Ghazālī, al-Tijānī describes the rational theologian, somewhat positively, as one who "devotes his attention to searching for cures, to knowing the sickness, its courses, causes, and remedy."[62]

Elsewhere, al-Tijānī further qualified his critique of reason by elaborating three types of intellects (lordly, comprehensive, and worldly), and four different categories of thoughts (*khawātir*). The highest lordly intellect (*al-ʿaql al-rabbānī*) is described as "an attribute of the spirit (*rūḥ*), before its establishment in the body . . . by which hidden things are discovered, and by which the reality of the truth is known to be true, and the reality of falsehood is known to be false."[63] Thoughts themselves could be inspired by Satan, the ego-self (*nafs*), the angels, or God:

> Satan commands naught but contravening (the divine command), and he does not fixate on only one command, but keeps moving from one matter to the next. Egocentric thoughts command naught but the preoccupation with passionate desires, whether forbidden or permissible, and the escape from what has been commanded or from anything difficult that has been commissioned. These thoughts do not pass away except through struggle (against the self). Angelic thoughts command naught except the good, whether by word or deed. Divine thoughts command naught except for the attachment to God, and the withdrawal from everything except Him.[64]

Al-Tijānī did not object to using the intellect: the mind itself could be purified so that "there is nothing in your mind, nothing in your knowledge, nothing in your imagination, except for God, even for one moment." The act of thinking could be inspired by God, rather than a reflection of the egocentric self.[65] But the rational theologian mostly remained engrossed, not with the larger purpose of knowing God, but with the sickness of rational oppositions, where "as soon as one sickness leaves him, one greater comes to take its place."[66]

The true verification of *tawḥīd* was to be found not in rational disputation, but in direct experience. This tendency toward a necessary "mystical" experience of *tawḥīd* may have been a proclivity of many Ashʿarīs, as the school emphasized God's direct action independent of causality, where God alone sustained every single molecule of creation. Al-Sanūsī's creed suggested that true understanding of the Islamic testimony of faith had to be experienced, and occurred when the utterance had come to "mingle with his flesh and blood."[67] Knowledge of *tawḥīd*, the oneness of the infinite, could be perhaps understood abstractly, but it could not be contained in the finite mind. The rational mind could only articulate what God is not, not what God is. According to al-Tijānī: "The height of attainment and realization in the field of reason (*madār al-ʿaql*) is bound to sense perception, it cannot cross over into God's unseen realm (*al-ghayb al-ilahī*) except by connecting to other than itself in knowledge from prophecy."[68] But beyond the mind, the gnostic, through complete submission to God, could come to experience the divine unity as taught by the Prophets.

> As for the *tawḥīd* of the gnostics, this is the worship of the One God, with contentment and submission to the judgment of the One God. In all of their conditions, they depend only on the One God. They direct their aspirations and their hearts only to the One God. They do not seek to attract good or repel harm except through the One God. They take refuge from their own strength and power in the strength and power of the One God. They have no love or longing except for the One God. Their goal in the beginning, middle, and end of their journey is only for the One God.
>
> All of this is through the dismissal of passion (*hawā*) externally and internally, in both its essence and its traces. The servant is at the remotest distance from the draping of the ego (*nafs*), passion, and Satan. If there should occur to him the slightest inclination towards passion, even the smallest grain or speck of dust, he in fact is unable to testify to the oneness to the One God. He cannot be described as having worshipped the One God. But when the gnostics obtain this sort of [true] *tawḥīd*, they build for it a fortress and come to reside therein. They become drowned in the ocean of Divine satisfaction and submission, knowing from Him that nothing escapes the rule (*ḥukm*) of the One God, the sweetness and the bitterness, the good and the bad. No one has any choice along with Him, for if there were a choice other than His, there would be a god beside Him.
>
> Who has correctly implemented the aforementioned descriptions is at ease with whatever affliction. He sits on the carpet of tranquility and comfort, with a robe of honor that melts away the difficulty, the misfortune of self-direction, in which he was previously engaged. There he sits with God on the carpet of proximity and intimacy. He does not beg for what he finds of provision, gifts, wealth, the fulfillment of all desires. This is from God's might, majesty, and bestowal of honor, for which there is no limit or enumeration.[69]

In other words, the shaykh offers the disposition acquired through self-purification (Sufism) as the remedy for the limits of rational theology.

Al-Tijānī thus agreed with al-Dabbāgh that this "gnostic doctrine of unity" (*tawḥīd al-ʿārifīn*) was that which the Prophet Muḥammad meant to have written on his deathbed:[70] "to be free from the difficulty of defending analogies successively piled up by the theologians. The *tawḥīd* of the gnostics does not cling to analogies."[71] Nonetheless, similar to other Ashʿarī Sufis before him such as al-Nābulusī,[72] al-Tijānī did not articulate this experiential understanding of *tawḥīd* as a fundamental break with the orthodox (Ashʿarī) theology of his day; but rather the logical fulfillment of the space for direct experience indicated by theology.

The Unity of Being

In allowing for the verification of *tawḥīd* through direct experience, al-Tijānī followed earlier scholars like al-Kūrānī and al-Nābulusī in defending the concept of the "unity of being" (*waḥdat al-wujūd*) attributed to Ibn al-ʿArabī. Al-Tijānī explained the relationship between the reality of "being" (*wujūd*) and the multiplicity of creation in a variety of ways, first by suggesting the essential unity of the creation reflected in its creation by One Creator: "The unity of the universe's essence (*ittiḥād dhāt al-ʿālam*) is due to its being all the creation of the One Creator, and [due to] the traces of His names in it. No individual entity in the universe can escape from this decree (*ḥukm*), whatever the diversity of their types."[73] But the creation itself lacked any essential reality. Similarly, a man's hand and eye each had distinct shape and function and could not by itself be called "man," but neither did it have any reality other than the man to whom it belonged.[74] Lacking an essential reality themselves, created entities were but the forms of divine manifestation. According to al-Tijānī: "A parable for the observer is ink. Various letters, words of different types and meanings all give form to ink, but they do not escape their essential reality of being ink . . . if you were to look at the essence of these shapes that form various letters and words, you will see nothing but the ink that has manifested (*tajallā*) in different shapes, while retaining its essence of ink."[75] All of being is thus naught but God's manifestation: "Every world manifests in itself an attribution of the divine presence (*al-ḥaḍrat al-ilahiya*)."[76]

But different manifestations are governed by different rules: "The source of every molecule in existence is an arrangement (*martaba*) belonging to the Real, Glorious and Exalted is He: He manifests (*yatajallā*) in them as He pleases according to His acts (*afʿāl*) and rulings (*aḥkām*)."[77] Here was al-Tijānī's explanation of witnessing divine unity even when confronted with the disbelief (*kufr*) of the non-believers:

> Perfect knowledge is that he (the disbeliever) is to be honored, for this is an arrangement (*martaba*) belonging to the Real, exalted is He, in which God manifests His judgement (*aḥkām*). He is to be honored internally, but disparaged and fought against externally, for that is the ruling of the Sharīʿa (*ḥukm al-sharʿ*) and divine wisdom (*ḥikma*). This matter is perceived by the gnostic only, not from the perspective of the law. But this understanding is referenced by the Prophet's saying, "Do not exalt yourselves over God by (exalting yourselves over) His lands and His servants. Whoever exalts himself over the servants (of God), exalts himself over God, thinking himself greater (than God)." Truly understanding (*taḥqīq*) this ḥadīth is found in what we said before, which is that all created entities are arrangements (*marātib*) belonging to the Real. One must submit to His ruling and what He has established of it in (each of) His creations, (a ruling) not turned back in anything. Legal rulings pertain to a thing's external nature, not its internal. But this is only for the one who is cognizant of the unity of being (*waḥdat al-wujūd*), for he sees both differentiation (*al-faṣl*) and connection (*al-waṣl*). Being is one essence. It is not divided in parts despite the multiplicity of forms and types.[78]

Al-Tijānī's reconciliation of the "oneness of being" with legal responsibility thus returned, as with al-Kūrānī, to the notion of divine manifestation (*tajallī*) and the rulings specific to different manifestations.

The notion of divine manifestation, for the Tijānī tradition as it developed, permitted the witnessing of God in the creation, while affirming God's utter dissimilarity from the creation. Here was the later Tijānī scholar Ibrāhīm Niasse's explanation of divine manifestation in created forms:

> Divine manifestation in creation (*al-tajallī al-ṣūrī*) has three degrees. The lowest of them is what the aspirant honored with arrival sees, when he witnesses the Real Being as the essence of ephemeral being (*al-wujūd al-majāzī*): he sees the divine manifestation in reflection, but he does not witness the mirror, nor the (true) manifestation therein. The middle degree is what the gnostics witness after coming back to their senses (from spiritual intoxication), and with their remaining (after annihilation): they witness the Real in an impossible

> form. As Ibn al-Fāriḍ said, "Beware of rejecting every created form, whatever its frailty or impossible state." The highest degree is what God's Messenger witnessed on the night of ascension. . . . The divine essential being (*al-dhāt*) is absolute being (*al-wujūd al-muṭlaq*), which raises the aspirant above this manifestation in forms, and causes him to arrive to the essential depths (of knowledge). Here there is no reflection, not one manifesting, nor one manifested to. "*The Truth has come and falsehood has perished, surely falsehood is ever perishing*."[79]

In other words, witnessing God in the creation—whatever the strength of that manifestation—should not associate God with that creation: the recipient of manifestation was only an ephemeral mirror, a momentary reflection of divine light, not God Himself. God's essential being was defined as absolute truth, which obliterated all dependence on created forms.

While al-Tijānī appeared to endorse classical notions of *waḥdat al-wujūd*, his emphasis on divine manifestation accented this idea of the creation as the mirror of manifestation, not the manifestation itself.

> Those of weak illumination see the manifestation shining in the mirror, and see nothing else, meaning other than the Real. Such a person, due to the weakness of his illumination, says, "All of the creation is God, and there is nothing else in it." . . . Who has his illumination strengthened witnesses both the mirror and the manifestation therein. And he gives every degree, whether divine or created, its right. One does not veil him from the other.[80]

Nonetheless, al-Tijānī's earlier explanations of *waḥdat al-wujūd* demonstrate the centrality of such understanding for spiritual illumination. Al-Tijānī's words here only meant to remind aspirants of higher forms of illumination, not to dismiss the experience of *waḥdat al-wujūd* altogether. The seeker needed to understand that there was no reality or being except God's being, but he needed to progress further to distinguish the degrees of divinity and creation.

The primary sources of the Tijāniyya are frank in their recognition that the "oneness of being" was a difficult concept to grasp intellectually. But for al-Tijānī, the experience of *waḥdat al-wujūd* was necessary to fully actualize Islam's fundamental doctrine of divine oneness (*tawḥīd*). ʿAlī Ḥarāzim quotes a verse of poetry to explain:

If you should say that you have not committed a sin
The response is that your existence (*wujūd*) is a sin to which no
other can compare.[81]

Shaykh al-Tijānī thus connected the Sufi experience of self-annihilation to the essential realization of *tawḥīd*: "As long as you see that you exist and God exists, so that there are two, where is the oneness (*tawḥīd*)? Oneness only exists if the Oneness is by God, from God, and to God. The servant does not enter in it, nor exit from it. And this is not realized except by way of self-annihilation (*fanāʾ*)."[82] Self-purification was necessary to actualize this *tawḥīd*, as the rational mind could not comprehend the omnipresence of God's essential being (*dhāt*). Al-Tijānī thus insisted that God's "with-ness" (*maʿiyya*) and proximity mentioned in the Qurʾan, "*And He is with you wherever you are*"[83] and "*We are closer to you that your jugular vein*,"[84] referred to God's essence, not only attributes of knowledge or seeing. "There is no way for the rational mind (*al-ʿaql*) to understand the reality of the Real's presence (*maʿiyya*) with everything or His closeness (*qurb*) to everything. For He is with everything in His Essential Being (*bi-dhātihi*) and closer to everything in His Essential Being, in a manner that the mind cannot comprehend."[85] This was the reason, according to al-Tijānī, that the Prophet prohibited the rational contemplation (*tafakkur*) of God's Essence, permitting only the pondering of His creation: "for you will not approximate His grandeur."[86]

The preceding discussion of divine oneness and knowledge demonstrates the close relationship between the actualization (*taḥqīq*) of Islam's core theological principle of *tawḥīd* and the Sufi understanding of the divine being. Al-Tijānī's articulations here were of course elicited by students who posed to him specific questions about the relationship between speculative theology (*kalām*) and divine oneness. What emerges is a clear argument that the truest understanding of *tawḥīd* can only be obtained through the path of self-purification, or Sufism. For al-Tijānī, such actualization of true *tawḥīd* was confirmed in the statements of earlier esteemed scholars. He thus quotes Aḥmad b. Ḥanbal (d. 855, Baghdad) to say, "Idols (*tāghūt*) are anything that occupies a person with other than God, even if for one moment."[87] True *tawḥīd* was thus the essence of Islam: "The secure end," al-Tijānī responded when asked about salvation, "is that we are Muslims. But by God, many of us have not smelled the fragrance of Islam."[88]

The Esoteric Sciences

Aḥmad al-Tijānī had a profound knowledge of the esoteric sciences, a mastery that was likely part of his broader scholarly reputation in Fez.[89] While commoners may have mixed fascination with a certain fear for experts in this field, as attested in Muḥammad al-Ḥāfiẓ's previously mentioned contact with some Moroccan "riffraff," eighteenth-century scholarship largely celebrated such knowledge. Ibn al-Mashrī observed, "As for the discipline of secrets (*fann arbāb al-nawāmīs*), such as the secret of letters, squares, talismans, and other guarded, comprehensive secrets for the good of this world and the next: God singled him out and he had no equal in his age."[90] Tijānī sources confirm that the transmission of the esoteric sciences was often inscribed within eighteenth-century scholarly networks. Ibrāhīm al-Riyāḥī, the later rector of Tunisia's Zaytuna University, thus requested from al-Tijānī, along with his initiation into the Tijāniyya, knowledge of the esoteric sciences for "subjection of spirits (*rūḥāniyya*), men and jinn."[91] But scrutiny of al-Tijānī's internal references to this science demonstrates his application of the lens of "verification" to esotericism, an exploration that appeared to resonate with other scholarly authorities of his age.

Nonetheless, al-Tijānī's public position on the esoteric sciences may have been more restrained than some of his contemporaries, such as Ibn 'Ajība.[92] This sort of nuance may have been a result of the large numbers of followers that began studying with him after his establishment in the scholarly center of Fez in 1798. Similarly, 'Uthmān b. Fūdī (d. 1817) of West Africa's Sokoto Caliphate seems to have been critical of the public misuse of these sciences,[93] while encouraging their use among an initiated elite.[94] In widely circulated letters to disciples, al-Tijānī thus sometimes referred to the esoteric sciences as a "distant mirage" with "little benefit," or even as "sciences of evil."[95] Aside from these published letters, there is evidence that al-Tijānī actively discouraged the esoteric sciences among new initiates. Once a very wealthy man, Maḥmūd al-Tunisī traveled a long distance to visit al-Tijānī in Fez. He asked to be instructed in the arts of *al-kīmiyā'*, here probably including letter science besides just alchemy. Al-Tijānī reproached him: "Get out of this place immediately, do not even spend the night here!" The man went away, purified his intention, and returned to submit himself completely to the shaykh "like a corpse in the hands of its funeral washer" and was granted divine illumination (*fatḥ*) at al-Tijānī's hands.[96] While alchemy was not explicitly beyond the pale of the Islamic esoteric tradition of which al-Tijānī was a master, Sukayrij's account here is meant to emphasize al-Tijānī's positionality as a Sufi shaykh, within a broader Sufi discourse on purity of intention. Interestingly enough, al-Tunisī later developed his own reputation as an esotericist, credited with a number of encounters with the world of spirits: in one instance receiving a special litany from the Jinn Shamharūsh—*Allāhumma yā Laṭīf yā Khabīr*—who had received it from the Prophet Muḥammad.[97]

Al-Tijānī's censure of those shaykhs attracting students by the misuse of the esoteric sciences was nonetheless abrupt. One of his early disciples, Muḥammad al-ʿArabī al-Damrāwī of Tāza (d. 1798), had previously been a disciple of ʿAbd-Allāh b. ʿAzūz (d. 1790, Marrakech), the nephew of Ibn Mubārak al-Lamaṭī—the author of *al-Dhahab al-ibrīz* concerning the teachings of ʿAbd al-ʿAzīz al-Dabbāgh (d. 1719, Fez). Ibn ʿAzūz had apparently gained a reputation for dealings with the jinn and the mastery of esoteric sciences, and perhaps even founded his own subbranch of the Shādhiliyya. When asked about Ibn ʿAzūz, al-Tijānī waited until he heard from the Prophet Muḥammad: "He is the Satan of this [Muslim] community."[98] Perhaps because of Ibn ʿAzūz's training, al-Damrāwī also had a reputation for expertise in this field. "He had complete disposition (*taṣarruf*) with the sciences of talismans (*jadwāl*) and magic squares (*awfāq*)" such that he could obtain whatever he wanted from people. Upon first receiving al-Damrāwī, al-Tijānī told him unambiguously: "Whoever is associated with these matters, definitely he will not obtain illumination (*fatḥ*)." So al-Damrāwī "left all of this behind him at the command of our master," relates the Tijānī historian Aḥmad al-Sukayrij (d. 1944, Marrakech), "and he was granted the grand illumination."[99]

Esotericism was thus a field of significant debate, even among those who practiced these sciences. Tijānī texts make little or no mention of the more famous collections of esoteric sciences, such as Aḥmad al-Būnī's *Shams al-maʿārif al-kubrā*.[100] Ibrāhīm Niasse's *Kāshif al-ilbās* makes a passing reference to al-Būnī as a master of "formulation" (*shakl*) and letter science, before citing Aḥmad Zarrūq's explanation of Ibn al-ʿArabī's censure for diminishing the worshipper's reliance on God earlier mentioned. The person whose knowledge of God's oneness (*tawḥīd*) was not well established could be distracted by secondary causes, such as the appearance of spirits to fulfill his command. Sources mention in this regard that al-Tijānī's father Maḥammad b. Mukhtār, known for his observance of the Sunnah and for teaching ḥadīth and Qur'ān exegesis (*tafsīr*), used to receive visits from spirits (*rūḥāniyyāt*). When they asked him what he wanted, he would tell them, "Leave me alone with God. I have no need for that which I [would have to] depend on other than God."[101] In a lengthy discussion of the esoteric sciences, Aḥmad Sukayrij produced another citation from Zarrūq in apparent summary of the Tijānī opinion: "The sciences of secrets among the letters and names and other things are indeed sciences, but they are an opening not spoken about by their possessors except to assist those with a similar opening, as a benefit to those of truth."[102] Esotericism was a legitimate science, in other words, but only among those who had already obtained divine opening and spiritual illumination.

In the early handwritten "notebook of secrets" (*Kunnāsh al-riḥla*), al-Tijānī transcribed the secrets he obtained in Mecca in 1774 from the elderly Shaykh Aḥmad b. ʿAbdallāh al-Hindī, who died a few days after al-Tijānī's arrival.[103] This text, and the circumstances of its transmission, provides significant insight into al-Tijānī's understanding of the esoteric sciences. The story of al-Tijānī's encounter with al-Hindī, as related in *Jawāhir al-maʿānī*, is as follows. In Mecca, al-Tijānī "sought out the people of goodness and righteousness, of guidance and felicity, as was his custom." Upon hearing of al-Hindī, al-Tijānī requested an audience with him, but was told that the Indian shaykh had confined himself to pious retreat (*khalwa*) for the rest of his life as a condition of the secret divine names he was reciting. Al-Hindī thus communicated with al-Tijānī only by letter and through a designated servant-disciple (*khadīm*), saying to him: "You are the inheritor of my knowledge and secrets, my divine gifts and lights." After writing this to al-Tijānī, al-Hindī informed his servant, "This is the one I've been waiting for: he is my inheritor (*wārith*)." The disciple protested, "But I have been serving you for eighteen years, and now a man comes from the far west, and you tell me that he is your inheritor?" Al-Hindī said that it was not his choice, but a divine command. Were it up to him, he would have given his secrets to his own son who, after all, had been with him longer than the disciple. Al-Hindī said of al-Tijānī: "I have been hoping for him, and drawing near to him in the unseen (*al-ghayb*) in order give him something. God prohibited (its sharing) until its owner should appear." Informing al-Tijānī through letter that he (al-Hindī) would die in twenty days, he implored of al-Tijānī to later share some of the secrets with his own son. After al-Hindī's death on the exact day predicted, al-Tijānī called al-Hindī's son and gave him the specified secrets.[104]

While the *Jawāhir al-maʿānī* relates that al-Tijānī received from al-Hindī "sciences, secrets, wisdom, and lights," and elsewhere "a great secret," nowhere is the content of this transmission elaborated in published sources.[105] A few key pages from al-Tijānī's *Kunnāsh al-riḥla* reference the transmission from al-Hindī: "All that is found in these pages . . . was authorized to us by our shaykh, the righteous guide, our master Aḥmad b. ʿAbd-Allāh al-Hindī, just as his shaykhs gave him authorization. And he wrote me an authorization for all of this."[106] There are certain prayers from al-Hindī that appear to have no previous textual reference, but at least half of al-Tijānī's *Kunnāsh al-riḥla* transcribes sections of two earlier collections of esoteric sciences: al-Ghawth's *Jawāhir al-khams* according to al-Shinnāwī's commentary, and a lesser known Omani text, *Ighāthat al-lahfān fī taskhīr al-amlāk wa l-jān* ("The Fulfillment of Desires in Summoning Angels and Jinn").

Together these texts are distinguished by their authors' situation of esotericism within a broader understanding of orthodox theology. Al-Ghawth's emphasis on worship (*ʿibāda*) and the cosmological significance of the letters (*ḥurūf*) of God's revelation has already been mentioned. ʿUmar b. Masʿūd al-Mundhirī al-Sulayfī (d. 1747, ʿIbrī, Oman), the author of *Ighāthat al-lahfān*, began his work with the warning, "First of all, I advise God's servants to avoid associating partners with God (*shirk*) and to be content with His decree."[107] In other words, a person's relationship with unseen spirits and powers should not undermine the basic foundation of his monotheism (*tawḥīd*). Al-Mundhirī declares in his introduction that he composed the work "when I saw the ignorance and corruption claimed to be knowledge in this science . . . and not one of the scholars (*ʿulamāʾ*) would speak up."[108] He claims his book is meant to clarify "the science at the source of spiritualism (*ʿilm uṣūl al-rūḥāniyya*)" and the "authentic entry points (*abwāb*)" of this knowledge: those "derived from trustworthy books and from gnostic shaykhs, endowed with disposition (*al-mashāyikh al-ʿārifīn al-mutaṣarrifīn*) in creation by the permission of God."[109] He specifically castigates unreliable and misleading texts,[110] but otherwise marshals a host of scholarly authorities to explain the believer's justifiable relationship with the unseen world of spirits. The text thus cites famous Muslim scholars such as Abū Ḥāmid al-Ghazālī, Ibn Ḥajar al-ʿAsqalānī (d. 1499), and Jalāl al-Dīn al-Suyūṭī (d. 1505) in support of this verification of esotericism. Despite their provocative titles, the esotericism of both the *al-Jāwāhir al-khams* and the *Ighāthat al-lahfān* can be defined as a deep reflection on the relationship between God, the words used in a person's supplication, and the spiritual beings that answer prayers by God's direction. There is a clear accent on differentiating between legitimate esoteric inquiries, and those that are beyond the pale of Islamic scholarly activity.

Sacred Words and Spiritual Beings

Al-Tijānī's own understanding of these "sciences of spiritualism" was certainly informed by these earlier articulations, together with his own verification. In his *Kunnāsh al-riḥla*, he copied al-Shinnāwī's explanation of the connection between Arabic letters and the spiritual beings attached to them: "The excellence of every supplication is in its letters and words . . . and the efficacy (*ḥukm*) of the letters is by the efficacy of the angelic names (*al-asmāʾ al-jabarūtiyya*) attached to them."[111] Al-Tijānī would later explain in a letter to disciples: "There are elevated spirits (*arwāḥ*), pure and immaculate, who are in charge of producing results for these secrets, continually occupied with rendering them effective. These spiritual beings have specific procedures, and these procedures are what permit prayers to be answered more quickly than the blink of an eye."[112] Elsewhere, al-Tijānī differentiated between a hierarchy of spiritual beings, whose affective disposition (*taṣrīf*) was linked to specific spheres of divine capacity:

> Know that the saints (*awliyāʾ*) of the Jinn, their sphere (*dawrān*) revolves around the [divine] act, its secret and its light. The angelic spirits (*rūḥāniyyūn*), their sphere revolves around the [divine] name, its secret and light. The sphere of the Angels revolves around the [divine] attributes, their secret and light. As for the human saints, their sphere revolves around the divine essence, its secret and light. Thus, every person should know from where to drink. As for the human, the first station of unveiling he discovers is the rank of the Jinn, and then he ascends until the fourth. May God not prevent us from that.[113]

While a human's potential relationship to God was better and purer than any other creation, a person might also come to understand the effect of God's actions, names, or attributes; all with which a variety of spiritual beings had been commissioned. A consummate esotericist, such as the Prophet Soloman (Sulaymān), might call on the name of a Jinn to perform a particular action "by God's permission" (such as bringing the throne of the Queen of Sheba), or upon the name of an angelic spirit (*rūḥānī*) associated with one of God's ninety-nine names. Al-Tijānī's early *Kunnāsh al-riḥla* thus cites al-Mundhirī's *Ighāthat al-lahfān* in regard to specific supplications used by Prophet Sulaymān and his vizier Aṣif b. Barkhiya to summon and control various Jinn and angelic spirits, including a prayer to discipline an unruly Jinn.[114]

The logic behind the "science of letters" emerges then from a reflection on the relationship between the letters comprising the revealed text and the spiritual world. Al-Tijānī explained further that all enunciated letters are connected to the unseen manifestations, whether the speaker was cognizant of that or not:

> Know that all enunciated letters (*al-ḥurūf al-lafẓiyya*) have their semblances in the world of spirits (*ʿālam al-arwāḥ*). The meaning here is that, with the enunciation of every word, an angel is created who glorifies God the exalted. If you speak a word of good, by this an angel of mercy is created. If you speak a word of evil, by this an angel of punishment is created. If it is God's decree and the speaker repents from the (evil) statement, the angel (of punishment) created from it is held back and turned into an angel of mercy.[115]

Realizing the creation of angelic beings from words spoken would certainly remind a Muslim that all of his actions were under divine scrutiny. Proper sincerity in using these sciences could thus serve to affirm or increase a Muslim's piety and faith, and ultimately his proximity to God. But misuse could also distance a person from God. More generally, al-Tijānī pointed to the existence of spiritual beings as secondary causes (*asbāb*), which God's action animated but of which God remained independent.

The relationship between divine decree and a person's own creative potential, implicit in this meditation on the esoteric sciences, has interesting theological implications concerning the age-old question of free-will and predestination. Al-Tijānī was thus asked how to explain the statement of the Prophet, "Nothing changes destiny except the supplication (*duʿā*)." He replied by making a distinction between fixed destiny (*ḥukm al-qaḍāʾ al-munbiram*) and the decree whose manifestation (*ẓuhūr*) was linked to the appearance of certain conditions. Both were determined in "the guarded tablet" (*al-lawḥ al-maḥfūẓ*), but the latter, should they be tribulations, for example, could be "turned back" (*radd*) through supplication, the giving of charity, or other righteous deeds.[116] Ultimately, al-Tijānī thus redirected the petitioner away from theological speculation concerning decree and individual action, and toward a more general concern with personal piety.

The Greatest Name

As al-Tijānī's rebuke of the improper use of the esoteric sciences confirms, his discussion of this field rendered it wholly subsidiary to Sufi purification and gnosis. Scrutiny of al-Tijānī's inheritance from al-Hindī suggests this notion was also communicated in his earlier initiations: the "greatest secret" from al-Hindī is in fact entirely missing from the *Kunnāsh al-riḥla*. But further reference to al-Hindī is made in al-Tijānī's *Kunnāsh al-maktūm*, another unpublished collection of secrets attributed to al-Tijānī that is transmitted in various forms throughout North and West Africa.[117] This manuscript speaks of God's "greatest name" that was "the name our Shaykh inherited from saintly succor (*ghawth*), the comprehensive unique one (*al-fard al-jāmiʿ*) when he passed away in Mecca."[118] This is undoubtedly a reference to al-Hindī, who is also described in the *Jawāhir al-maʿānī* as the "saintly pole" (*quṭb*) of his time.[119] This name is also likely the "great secret" from al-Hindī alluded to in *Jawāhir al-maʿānī*. Here was al-Tijānī's description in the *Kunnāsh al-maktūm* of this "greatest name" from al-Hindī:

> Whoever desires the greatest sainthood, and arrival to the most exalted of states, let him [say] the greatest name, the letters by which the heavens and the earth were established. It is the guarded, treasured name in truth, which has power over all the other names. Its secret is not obtained except by the permission of one who has permission. For the one who takes it like this, knowing the name, nothing is hidden from him among the affairs of this world or the next. He will become a saint, recipient of spiritual unveilings, provision, success, and God's love.[120]

The text goes on to explain that one recitation of this name is equivalent to all the glorification and praise on the tongues of all created beings, from the beginning of time to the end.[121] Following a lengthy discussion, the text concludes: "And as for the greatest name: it is not written here, but is only (transmitted) from mouth to mouth."[122] Here Sufi initiation clearly takes precedence over the exploration of the letters and names pertaining to the world of spirits: God's greatest name has power over all other names and brings the human out of himself and directly into the presence of the divine essence. Al-Tijānī's exploration of the esoteric sciences thus meant to elaborate on the servant's ultimate dependence on God alone. Whatever his reputation for expertise in esotericism, his general advice to disciples thus remained: "God's servant must not ask for anything except from his Lord, not for one moment, whether in this world or the next."[123]

Walking the Sufi Path

The broader portrait of al-Tijānī's scholarly inquiry permits an alternative framework by which to understand the shaykh's Sufi aspirations from that presented in prior academic accounts. While the vision of the Prophet, the claim to the Seal of Sainthood, the emphasis on God's bounty and worldly involvement are all certainly distinguishing features of the Tijāniyya, primary sources lay more stress on the aspirant's required sincerity on the Sufi path. These accounts present al-Tijānī's own spiritual journey as an ardent quest for the verification and actualization (*taḥqīq*) of Sufism, very similar to the portrayal of his exploration and mastery of other fields of Islamic learning. Due consideration to the tone of these texts provides a window into the content of Sufi exchanges in the 18th century, the nature of the Sufi path as al-Tijānī understood it, and the daily practice of Sufism within the Tijāniyya. Aḥmad al-Tijānī no doubt saw his spiritual path as the fullest realization, rather than the abrogation, of the broader Sufi tradition.

Al-Tijānī embarked on the Sufi path, Tijānī sources tell us, after an early life devoted to external learning and individual asceticism and worship. He began to seek Sufi teachers, "his aspiration being to encounter God's distinguished folk (*al-rijāl*)," during his first trip to Morocco around 1758.[124] He would soon attain initiation into a variety of Sufi orders, including various branches of the Shādhiliyya (Nāṣiriyya, Wazzāniyya), the Qādiriyya, and the Khalwatiyya as previously mentioned. Until his pilgrimage east, al-Tijānī's encounters with the saints of North Africa were relatively short, if intense. He reported expedited initiations (*idhn*) and investitures (*taqdīm*) from a variety of shaykhs, some who also appeared to him in dreams to give him certain prayers.[125] A number of these shaykhs informed him immediately that he would attain "a great station" (*maqam ʿaẓīm*),[126] the station of the paradigmatic North African saint Abū l-Ḥasan al-Shādhilī,[127] or that he was already a "beloved friend of God."[128]

Until his meeting with al-Kurdī in Cairo, al-Tijānī appeared hesitant to submit himself completely to the saints he met in North Africa. The two most eminent shaykhs he met early on in Morocco, al-Ṭayyib al-Wazzānī and Aḥmad al-Ṣaqillī, were both heads of large Sufi communities at the time. Al-Tijānī politely declined an early investiture from al-Wazzānī permitting him to transmit the Wazzāniyya-Jazūliyya path, according to Ḥarāzim, "in order to work on himself."[129] Al-Tijānī elaborated further to Ibn al-Mashrī: "I did not do so (accept the investiture from al-Wazzānī), for I did not understand the spiritual states of the saints. I saw him (only) in the state of the people of the world (*ḥāl ahl al-dunyā*). The same was true for our master Aḥmad al-Ṣaqillī: I did not even say a word to him when I saw his most ordinary appearance. Only later was I informed that he was an axial saint (*quṭb*), may God be pleased with him."[130] This indicates al-Tijānī's initial reserve to Sufism as he found it practiced in Morocco. Such reserve may reflect accounts of the Wazzāniyya's wealth and political involvement in the latter half of the 18th century.[131] But al-Tijānī nonetheless preserved his good opinion of the early saints he met, later attesting to the paradigmatic sainthood of both al-Wazzānī and al-Ṣaqillī.[132] Even after prohibiting followers from visiting the tombs of saints for blessing (*ziyāra al-tabarruk*), al-Tijānī still insisted on treating past saints respectfully, in one case telling disciples not to stretch their feet toward the tomb of Mawlay Idris II, the founding saint of Fez, while praying in his mosque.[133]

Although most of these early initiators died before al-Tijānī's public emergence as a Sufi teacher, Tijānī sources insist on their recognition of something special in the young scholar. Aḥmad al-Ṭawāsh al-Tāzī (d. 1790), an early initiator of al-Tijānī associated with the "path of self-blame" (*Malāmatiyya*) who had predicted for him the attainment of an exalted spiritual station, would later write his former student when al-Tijānī was living in Tlemcen (c. 1780): "By God, you have with us a lofty place. We consider you naught but among the great company of the shaykhs who have taught us: indeed, we are among the least of your disciples if you accept and forgive us."[134] Apparently, the teacher had become the student. For his part, al-Tijānī prayed that salvation be guaranteed for "every one of my masters in knowledge or in the Qur'ān, or in any litany or secret."[135] Al-Tijānī advised his own disciples to maintain a good opinion of all God's saints: "We do not make light of the sanctity of our masters, the friends of God (*awliyā'*), and we are not negligent in exalting them. Exalt the sanctity of the saints (*ḥurmat al-awliyā'*), both living and dead. Whoever exalts their sanctity, God exalts his sanctity. Whoever disparages them, God humiliates him and is angry with him. Do not neglect the sanctity of the saints."[136]

Al-Tijānī's later Sufi training (*tarbiya*) through direct encounters with the Prophet Muḥammad did not lessen his respect for his most significant earlier guide, Maḥmūd al-Kurdī. Al-Tijānī would have been exposed to al-Kurdī's Khalwatī affiliation long before meeting him: first with al-Ṣaqillī and then with the Algerian Maḥammad b. ʿAbd al-Raḥmān al-Azharī (d. 1793), both of whom had been initiated by al-Kurdī's own Shaykh Muḥammad al-Ḥifnī. Ḥarāzim remarks that Ibn ʿAbd al-Raḥmān al-Azharī in particular had "great renown and a large Sufi gathering," and that al-Tijāniyya's first initiation into the Khalwatiyya was at his hands.[137] But al-Kurdī would be his true shaykh. Here is Ḥarāzim's account from al-Tijānī concerning his encounter with al-Kurdī:

> The first time he met him, he [al-Kurdī] said, "You are the beloved of God in this world and the next."
>
> Our master, may God be pleased with him, responded, "From where has this come to you?"
>
> "From God," he answered.
>
> Our master said to him, "I saw you [in a dream] when I was in Tunis, and I said to you, 'My essence is flawed brass (*naḥās*).' And you told me, 'That is true, but I will turn your brass to gold.' "
>
> When he related to him this story, he [al-Kurdī] told him, "It is as you saw." Then after some days, he asked him [al-Tijānī], "What is your aspiration?"
>
> "My aspiration is for the greatest axial sainthood (*al-quṭbāniyya al-ʿuẓmā*)," he responded.
>
> "For you there is much more than that," he said.
>
> He asked, "Is this [station] upon you (*ʿalayk*)?"
>
> "Yes," he said. Then he informed him about himself, and what had befallen him in his journey, the reason for his affiliation with his Shaykh al-Ḥifnī, and the shaykh of his shaykh, our master Muṣṭafā al-Bakrī al-Ṣaddīqī, may God be pleased with them all.[138]

This story emphasizes al-Tijānī's desire for Sufi training or self-transformation at the hands of al-Kurdī. He would later accept the investiture of authority (*taqdīm*) in the Khalwatiyya from him, the order into which al-Tijānī initiated his first disciples in North Africa. The *Jawāhir al-maʿānī* reproduces al-Tijānī's lengthy Khalwatī chain of initiation (*silsila*) through al-Kurdī, al-Ḥifnī, al-Bakrī, and all the way back to the early Sufi figure al-Junayd (d. 910, Baghdad), then of course to ʿAlī b. Abī Ṭālib, and finally to the Prophet Muḥammad.[139] The recent Egyptian Khalwatī publication of al-Kurdī's aphorisms (*al-Risāla fi l-ḥikam*), together with al-Sharqāwī's commentary, remembers the significance of al-Tijānī's affiliation to al-Kurdī: in the introduction al-Tijānī is the first mentioned "among those who took from" al-Kurdī: "The Shaykh of the Tijāniyya Sufi order and the owner (*ṣāhib*) of the well-known (prayer) *Ṣalātal-fātiḥ* . . . before being granted permission for his own Sufi order."[140]

After accomplishing the pilgrimage (1774), Al-Tijānī met his time's other most notable Khalwatī Shaykh, Muḥammad al-Sammān in Medina. Al-Hindī had of course recommended to al-Tijānī that he meet al-Sammān after him, "You will encounter the axial saint (*quṭb*) after me, who will suffice you in my stead."[141] The "sufficiency" here appears to have been the inheritance of certain Sufi prayers and secrets. The prayers al-Tijānī later transmitted from al-Sammān, such as the *Aḥzāb* of al-Shādhilī, the *Dawr al-aʿlā* of Ibn al-ʿArabī, the *waẓifa* of Aḥmad Zarrūq, or the *Dalāʾil al-khayrāt* al-Jazūlī were all prayers previously available in North Africa. The transmission from al-Sammān was clearly out of respect for his ascendant spiritual station. But otherwise, al-Tijānī declined further training from al-Sammān, "having previously entered the companionship (*ṣuḥba*) of Shaykh Maḥmūd."[142] It may be that al-Tijānī was inclined to al-Kurdī's reputed sobriety on the Sufi path, and less to al-Sammān's reputation for ecstatic utterances (*shaṭṭaḥāt*).[143] But it may be that al-Tijānī was simply sensitive to the "highly competitive relations" between various branches of the Khalwatiyya.[144] In any case, al-Sammān told al-Tijānī before the pilgrim returned to al-Kurdī in Egypt that he was to be "the comprehensive pole (*al-quṭb al-jāmiʿ*)."[145]

Etiquette and Self-Purification

This narration of al-Tijānī's encounters with various Sufi masters is meant to underscore the importance of sincerity and proper etiquette on the Sufi path, especially in regard to master-disciple relations, later stressed in the Tijāniyya. Such internal comportment, acquired through Sufi training, was for al-Tijānī the logical corollary of obedience to God through the sacred law.

> Etiquette (*adab*) among the jurists is an expression of righteous deeds (*qiyām*) following what is legally obligatory and the example of the Prophet. These include deeds of excellence and those strongly encouraged pertaining to the (external) states of people, whether while sleeping, awake, eating or drinking, in remembrance and in supplication, and things like this.

> Among the Sufis, etiquette is an expression of all acquired virtue and piety. It is the description of all noble attributes and praiseworthy character traits related to divine adoration and the exaltation of divinity. Whoever gathers such traits in himself becomes refined and well-mannered in the presence of God the Exalted, and in the presence of His messenger, God's peace and blessing upon him. The first (juristic) meaning of etiquette is thus contained within the second.[146]

For al-Tijānī, *adab* on the Sufi path meant a singularity of purpose: acquiring a disposition of "divine adoration and the exaltation of divinity." Having mastered this state, the shaykh allegedly refrained from asking God for anything. According to Ḥarāzim, al-Tijānī said, "I only supplicate (God) with my tongue, my heart remains submitted to (the decree of) God. I do not desire anything, and I do not ask for anything."[147] Of course, such contentment with divine decree only increased God's favor. In explanation, Ibrāhīm Niasse cited God's statement to the Prophet in *ḥadīth qudsī*: "Whoever is too occupied with the Qur'ān and my remembrance from asking anything from Me, I give him more than is given the petitioners."[148] Although al-Tijānī did seek spiritual stations of ultimate proximity to God, he echoed al-Kurdī in warning against asking God for saintly ranks for their own sake. "The perfected saints," al-Tijānī warned, "do not ask for spiritual rank (*maqām*), and they are indistinguishable from others."[149] In explaining different types of "idolatry of purpose" (*shirk al-aghrāḍ*), al-Tijānī thus remonstrated: "Sincerity with the gnostics is to worship God for His own sake alone, anything else is idolatry of purpose."[150]

The state of ultimate contentment with God depended on the enduring Sufi concept of self-purification (*tazkiyat al-nafs*). Although al-Tijānī's teachings deemphasized earlier Sufi understandings of worldly asceticism (*zuhd*) and isolation (*khalwa*), he himself practiced periodic spiritual retreats, restricted his diet, and carried himself with such humility that he could not be distinguished from his students.[151] But he encouraged the cultivation of an internal state of poverty, or dependence on God, over worldly asceticism:

> There are seven jewels of the heart. In the heart there are seven treasuries, each treasury is the location of one of the seven jewels. The first jewel is the jewel of remembrance. The second jewel is that of longing. The third is of love and passion for God. The fourth is the

> jewel of the secret, which is hidden among the mysteries (*ghayb min ghuyūb*) of God the exalted, its identity unknown. The fifth jewel is the jewel of the spirit (*rūḥ*). The sixth is that of gnosis (*maʿrifa*). The seventh is the jewel of poverty (*faqr*). . . . When this (last treasury) is opened in the (heart of the) servant, he witnesses his utter dependence on God and need for Him with each breath.[152]

In other words, this absolute dependence on God was a state that presupposed and transcended the coveted gnosis of Sufi aspiration. Al-Tijānī thus defined Sufi asceticism (*zuhd*) as the purity of the heart from other than God: "When the love of the Holy Essence (*al-dhāt al-muqaddasa*) comes to reside (in the heart), created entities depart and are erased, leaving behind no particularity or trace, and the thought of them no longer leaves any image on the heart."[153]

Despite his insistence that Sufism could be pursued while involved in worldly affairs, al-Tijānī did not mean to compromise the self-purification at the center of Sufi practice. He related an earlier statement of ʿAbd al-Salām b. Mashīsh when asked about the Sufi litany (*wird*) of the gnostic "verifiers" (*muḥaqqiqīn*): "It is the shutting-up of vain desires, and the love of the Guardian Lord."[154] Apparently, some of his disciples trained in jurisprudence once complained to al-Tijānī of the difficulty of this self-purification. His response was firm in defense of classical Sufi teachings:

> You mentioned the difficulty of fettering (*inqiyād*) your carnal self (*nafs*) to God's command, and of persisting in overcoming its unpleasantries. Indeed, this is a general rule God has established in the creation: that whoever should overlook his *nafs* and let it chase after its desires, the path to fulfilling God's command will be made difficult for him. Rather, let him see nothing in his *nafs* except viciousness, disobedience, and refusal of God's command. Who would rectify the screaming tantrums (*aʿwijāj*) of his *nafs*, let him occupy himself with taming (*qamʿ*) his *nafs*, restricting it from the pursuit of its lusts. This is accomplished with persistent withdrawal (*ʿuzla*) from the creation, with silence, with lessening the intake of food, with incrementally increasing the remembrance of God, and with making the heart present to the remembrance (*dhikr*). The heart should be held back from plunging into its habitual distractions with the affairs of the world, held back from indulging in the world and loving it. The heart should be restrained from all volition, choice, planning, and from [seeking]

> information of the creation. Let the heart be bridled with the command of God, free of all anxiety. By persisting in this way, the *nafs* is purified, and it escapes from wickedness to conformity with the command of God. There is no other way than this. "*This is the way of God as it has been in the past, and you will not find any change in the way of God.*"[155]

Pushing further on the necessity of self-purification for obeying God's command, al-Tijānī likened the person mired in his own lusts (*shahwa*) and selfish desires (*hawā*) to one in a state of ritual impurity (*najāsa*). Purifying the internal self was similar to purifying the body for prayer. "This impurity clings stubbornly to his being, so he must endeavor to get rid of the filth from himself. Like this he flees to God, clean and purified. There is no doubt that a person in this state, polluted in filth, has no concern for gaining reward (from God), only for purifying his *nafs*."[156] Self-purification was the necessary prerequisite for sincerity on the path to God, defined here as worshiping God in the denial of all other desire, even for God's reward.

Knowledge of God

The goal of this purification was, as earlier suggested, the confirmation of faith: the direct experience of God's oneness (*tawḥīd*). The aspirant, al-Tijānī warned, should only have two desires: the first for God alone, the second to be the exclusive servant of God. "That all of himself should be exclusively devoted to God, empty from looking elsewhere, completely attached to Him in his secret essence, his spirit, his mind, his soul, his heart: receptive to Him so that not one molecule of his being is a stranger to God the exalted."[157] Al-Tijānī described his own experience of this exclusive devotion to God as follows: "I was pushed forward by a burst from the divine presence. My beginning became my end, my end my beginning. My entirety became my every particle, and my every particle became my entirety. I became Him, and He me, but as becoming of Him, and not as becoming of me. At that moment, if I were asked a million separate questions, I would have given only one answer. Then I became like the niche of light (*miṣbāḥ*)."[158] The specifics of al-Tijānī's proximity to God aside, the experience described here clearly resonates with the long-standing Sufi expression of divine knowledge or direct witnessing. Al-Tijānī described this spiritual witnessing as follows: "Divine witnessing (*maʿāyina*) entails the manifestation of realities without veil or particularity, and with no remaining designation or trace of other or otherness. This is the station of eradication, destruction, annihilation, and the annihilation of annihilation. There is nothing in this station except the direct vision of the Real, in the Real, for (the sake of) the Real, by (means of) the Real. 'Nothing remains except God, nothing besides Him. There is nothing to be added and nothing to be separated.' "[159] Such expressions of self-purification and gnosis (*ma'rifa*) situate the Tijāniyya firmly within traditional notions of gnostic Sufism.

Al-Tijānī also followed earlier Sufis such as al-Ghazālī in specifying that the result of such unveiling was the opening of further knowledge concerning God's manifestations (*tajalliyāt*) through creation, what the West African scholar contemporary to al-Tijānī, Mukhtār al-Kuntī (d. 1811), described as meaning to "see God before everything" in order to "learn from Him about His creation."[160] Al-Tijānī explained this further elaboration of gnosis:

> Then comes true existence, in which one is able to distinguish the degrees on the basis of direct knowledge of their particularities, requirements, and exigencies, and everything to which they are entitled. One will know as well the source for each degree, the reason for its existence, its intended purpose, and the return of its affairs. This is the station of the servant's comprehension of his personal identity and his knowledge of all its secrets and particularities; as well as his knowledge of the divine presence, its grandeur, majesty, exalted attributes, and perfection. And this knowledge of his will be the product of direct experience and indubitable vision.[161]

The fully realized gnostic could thus perceive the true identity of every created entity, based on its essential relationship to God. "Every individual creation has a name among the exalted [divine] names, and this is what sustains its essential identity (*dhātihi*). And each also has a lower name (*ism nāzil*), by which each creation is distinguished from other than it."[162] Chittick summarizes the general concept behind this idea, as earlier articulated by Ibn al-'Arabī: "God breathes out, and while breathing, He speaks . . . Every part of every existent thing is a 'letter' (*ḥarf*) of God . . . who at every instant recreates the cosmos."[163] According to al-Tijānī, the "exalted names" specific to the essences of various created entities were not known except by the perfected saint of the age, who also possessed a divine name "special to himself"; but other names were known by gnostics. Knowledge of these names, whether exalted or lower, permitted the gnostic a divine response from wherever he directed his attention, although his being "overcome with modesty" in God's presence prevented him "from asking his needs by God's names." The gnostic, whose will remained annihilated in God's will, effectively became an instrument of the ongoing divine creative act. "The gnostic becomes a word from among the words of the divine essence (*ḥarfan min ḥurūf al-dhāt*), for he comes to have the power of disposition (*yataṣarraf*) through the divine essence as does the word, although he is not the source of the word."[164] The realized gnostic thus came to see the universe in code, as a manifestation of God's creation through the word; and the gnostic might himself become the word of divine creation for the cosmos re-created every moment.

But such ideas appear mostly as passing mystic references (*ishārāt*) reflective of divine knowledge, rather than a fully developed letter-centric esotericism. According to the contemporary Senegalese scholar, al-Tijānī b. ʿAlī Cisse, reference in the *Jawāhir al-maʿānī* to the "letters of the divine essence" are only a metaphor: "In reality, there is nothing in the presence of the divine essence—no letter, no word, no sound, no color—nothing except effacement and annihilation. Reference to the gnostic as a word among the words of the divine essence is simply an indication of his annihilation in the divine essence."[165] The conclusion (at least for later Tijānīs) seems to be that, while al-Tijānī did not shy from elaborating on the more complex themes of earlier Sufi metaphysics, his more general teachings emphasized the broader Sufi notion of divine knowledge in self-annihilation as the goal of the Sufi path.

The Spiritual Guide

Consistent with classical Sufi understandings, al-Tijānī taught that the self-purification resulting in gnosis could be best attained in the presence of a Sufi master. In explaining the Prophet's advice, "Ask the scholars (*ʿulamāʾ*), mix with the wise (*hukumāʾ*), and keep company with the great ones (*kubarāʾ*)," the shaykh suggested that "the great" were the Sufi shaykhs: "The great one points towards God through the erasure of the *nafs* . . . but companionship cannot happen except with the living (shaykh): the dead do not keep company, they do not speak, they do not mix (with the living)."[166] Elsewhere al-Tijānī was more emphatic:

> Whoever takes refuge with the living people, the special elite of his time, and accompanies them, making them an example and searching for their approval, these succeed in obtaining the overflowing support of God. Whoever turns away from the people of his time, declaring his satisfaction with the words of deceased saints who have gone before, he is marked with exclusion. He is like a person who turned away from the prophet and divine law of his time, declaring his satisfaction with laws of the prophets who came before. He is marked with the stamp of ingratitude (*ṭābiʿ al-kufr*), and the refuge is with God.[167]

Al-Tijānī's encounters with the Prophet Muḥammad thus did not mean to abrogate the Sufi notion of the living "master of spiritual training" (*shaykh al-tarbiya*). Although not legally incumbent, the aspirant's search for such a shaykh was logically necessary, "as the search for water is necessary for the thirsty man."[168] The "truthful aspirant" was thus the one who "exerted effort in seeking the doctor who might end the reason for his sickness, who could point out the medicine necessary for perfect health."[169]

> When the aspirant finds someone matching this description, he must place himself at his disposal without any personal choice or volition, like a corpse in the hands of its ritual washer. He must rely on the shaykh to deliver him from the distress in which he has been immersed, and to transfer him to complete and pure serenity; and this through the contemplation of the divine presence and nothing else. The disciple must purge himself from all other options or desire for anything besides this. . . . In every matter, he (the shaykh) proceeds (as inspired), for the shaykh will only act for the sake of God and with God's help, in order to extract him from the darkness and lust of his lower self.[170]

This description consciously invokes the earlier understanding of shaykh-disciple relations, certainly consistent with the eighteenth-century Khalwatiyya as taught by Muṣṭafā al-Bakrī.

Shaykh al-Tijānī also followed al-Bakrī in emphasizing the exclusive attachment to one shaykh: "Among the greatest conditions of communion between the shaykh and his disciple is that the disciple does not share with anyone else the love for him, the exaltation of him, the seeking of support from him, the complete surrender of his heart to him."[171] Ḥarāzim explained further that the etiquette required of the disciple was to "believe there was no one more complete . . . among the people of his time than his shaykh."[172] This appears to be the most logical context for al-Tijānī's prohibition of disciples visiting non-Tijānī saints for the sake of spiritual blessing, rather than as the expression of "a negative form of *adab*."[173] The overview presented here demonstrates that classical understandings of Sufi *adab* and the shaykh-disciple relationship were at the center of the early Tijāniyya, even if some later Tijānī communities (mis)interpreted the spiritual rank of al-Tijānī as excluding ongoing spiritual training (*tarbiya*) or respect for other saints.

Censure of "False" Sufism

But not all those claiming to be doctors could actually cure the sick. Al-Tijānī reserved some of his strongest censure for such pretenders. Among those Muslims in danger of dying as infidels (*kuffār*), al-Tijānī included those who harmed others, those who fornicated without repentance, those mired in slander, those who lied on behalf of the Prophet, those who lied in their claim to sainthood (*walāya*), and those who announced their ability to guide others without permission.[174] "There is no one God hates more than them on the face of the earth," al-Tijānī said of the scholars who had not purified themselves from self-conceit.[175] Those who followed their own desires while training others were effectively rendering themselves as idols to be worshiped instead of God:

> I advise myself and you with the security (*muḥāfaẓa*) in guarding to the words of the Prophet: "Three things lead to success, and three things lead to ruin. Success is found in the fear (*taqwā*) of God secretly and publicly, the word of truth (spoken) in (both) contentment and anger, and moderation (whether) in (a state of) wealth or poverty. Ruin is found in avarice yielded to, lust followed after, and the self-conceit of a man in his own personal opinion." And his words, "There has never been a god other than Allah more odiously worshipped than a lust pursued."[176]

Satisfaction with the self (*nafs*) and love of leadership, especially when combined with scholarly reputation, represented a form of self-worship. Al-Tijānī warned a young student of Islamic learning: "You must avoid seeking knowledge for the sake of leadership or worldly sustainence, in this is surely found the destruction of this world and the next." In other words, Islamic learning could lead to a form of self-idolatry.

Al-Tijānī's own engagement with Sufism is best described as a search for the essential core of Sufi understanding and practice. Predictably, such "verification" entailed some criticism of existing Sufi practices in late eighteenth-century North Africa. As mentioned previously, al-Tijānī castigated as devils those who misused the esoteric sciences in their false claims to Sufi guidance. When asked whether he, as other shaykhs in Morocco apparently claimed, would be present with his disciples at the interrogation in the grave, he rejected the notion: "The Prophet suffices for my presence with my companions in death and when questioned (in the grave)."[177] If some shaykhs were guilty of false claims, Sufi disciples also exposed their insincerity on the path by frequenting a spectrum of Sufi saints, seeking only worldly blessing rather than spiritual training. Apparently for this reason, al-Tijānī prohibited disciples from visiting (making *ziyāra* to) other (non-Tijānī) saints, and in one case expelled a disciple for visiting the grave of ʿAbd al-Salām b. Mashīsh.[178]

Clearly, the Tijāniyya represents a restriction of the *ziyāra* tradition in North African Sufism. While al-Tijānī himself did not castigate the general practice of visiting graves, a later key source of Tijānī doctrine, ʿUmar Tāl's *al-Rimāḥ*, took up a more explicit critique. To further justify the orthodoxy of Tijānī position on grave visitation within mainstream Sufism, Tāl cites from the earlier Moroccan saint ʿAbd al-ʿAzīz al-Dabbāgh (as recorded in al-Lamaṭī's *Ibrīz*) to condemn those who call on other than God at the graves of saints. Among the "causes of separation from God," Tāl quotes the *Ibrīz* to list "seeking the mediation (*al-tawassul*) of God's righteous saints in order to fulfill wishes: the visitor [to the grave] says, 'I present myself to you, my master so-and-so. For God's sake, fulfill my wish!'" Further separation from God is caused by visiting the graves of saints while the visitor has neglected his own worship of God, such as making the five daily prayers.[179] The Tijāniyya thus situated itself within a longer Sufi discourse of reforming the perceived ignorant practices of some uneducated Muslims, while obviously not rejecting Sufism itself.

By the early 19th century, the Moroccan king Mawlay Sulaymān had himself begun a campaign to purify some of the popular practices of rural Morocco. Among other things, the king criticized the boisterous celebrations of various saints' birthdays (*mawāsim*), the building of domed tombs over graves, and the mixing of genders in Sufi lodges.[180] As a possible Tijānī disciple, Mawlay Sulaymān's actions may have represented al-Tijānī's own opinions. But it is otherwise unclear how far al-Tijānī supported the king's disciplining of rural Sufi leaders in "*la crise maraboutique*." Al-Tijānī did express dissatisfaction with the notion of Sufi gatherings as social events and the public discussion of Sufi sayings without putting these ideas into practice. Hearing of the gatherings in various Sufi lodges (sing. *zāwiya*) in Fez for the "night of power" (*laylat al-qadr*) on the twenty-seventh of Ramadan, al-Tijānī ordered his own *zāwiya* closed on that night to prevent needless social gathering and gender-mixing. Instead, he ordered disciples to pray in their own homes.[181] In another case, he advised disciples to leave praying in mosques where men and women gathered to eat and talk inside.[182] Al-Tijānī also resisted what he considered the insincere perusal of Sufi sayings and collection of Sufi prayers. Instead of moving from one remembrance (*dhikr*) to another, or intellectually contemplating the various statements of Sufi masters, the aspirant should choose one remembrance and one direction to which to devote himself.[183]

Sufi Prayers

The Tijāniyya's relationship with the broader Sufi tradition is perhaps best understood through its incorporation and contribution to the vast spectrum of Sufi liturgical remembrances. Academics may be guilty of a general "scholarly neglect of Sufi prayer texts and recitation"[184]: certainly, devotional prayer manuals provide important insights into the internal aspirations and external influences and connections of and between Sufi communities.[185] Al-Tijānī himself made use of a number of established collections of prayers. In addition to *al-Jawāhir al-khams* and *Ighāthat al-Lahfān* already mentioned, oral tradition records his interest in *Tadhkirat ʾūlā l-albāb*, a prominent collection of healing methods and esoteric sciences by the Syrian physician Dāwud al-Anṭākī (d. 1599, Antioch/Mecca).[186] The Tijāniyya has produced its own body of devotional prayer literature. There is no definitive prayer collection, but prominent publications have included the *Miftāḥ al-saʿāda* of Abū Bakr al-Burūjī (of Guinea, authored in 1963) and the *Aḥzāb wa awrād* of Muḥammad al-Ḥāfiẓ al-Miṣrī (of Egypt, authored in 1972).[187]

A full exposition of the prayers of the Tijāniyya would most certainly require a separate work. Reference to the prayers thought to be distinctive to the Tijāniyya (such as *ṣalāt al-fātiḥ*, *jawharat al-kamāl*, *yaqūṭat al-ḥaqāʾiq*, and *ṣalāt al-ghaybiyya*) are found later in this book. But a representative sampling of al-Tijānī's use of prior Sufi prayers here demonstrates the Tijāniyya's pronounced engagement with the Sufi devotional tradition, as well as its claim to verification of that tradition.

AL-SHĀDHILĪ'S "ORISON OF THE SEA"

By all accounts, the "Orison of the Sea" (*ḥizb al-baḥr*) is one of the more famous prayers in the Islamic world, today used by many Sufis (and some non-Sufis) whatever their order. But the reference to initiation from al-Sammān, mentioned previously, points to al-Tijānī's emphasis on authorization (*idhn*) and tendency to reinvest Sufi rituals with new layers of spiritual power. Later Tijānīs thus interpreted al-Tijānī's continued use of the prayer as a specific Tijānī investiture in a central prayer of the Shādhilī tradition. Here ʿUmar Tāl relates the Tijānī perspective:

> As for the "orison of the sea," God's messenger gave it to the Shaykh of the Sufi path and the divine reality, Abū Ḥasan al-Shādhilī. Then our shaykh and master Aḥmad b. Maḥammad al-Tijānī [also] took it from the Prophet. It is said to contain God's greatest name. Among its special properties is (the reciter's) protection on land and sea, so long as it is taken with authentic permission from one of its guardians (*arbāb*). . . . You might also call it the "Aḥmadan orison" (*ḥizb al-Aḥmadiyya*) . . . since our shaykh Aḥmad al-Tijānī took this *ḥizb* at the Prophet's hand, while in state of wakefulness, so it may (also) be attributed to him.[188]

The Tijāniyya's incorporation of *ḥizb al-baḥr* thus moves from an emphasis on proper initiation from a spiritual master to the prayer's investiture with al-Tijānī's own spiritual station. The later Tijānī tradition undoubtedly came to emphasize its own transmission of the *ḥizb al-baḥr* as being endowed with heightened power. The Tijānī prayer collection *Miftāḥ al-saʿāda* thus warns, "Whoever recites *ḥizb al-baḥr* without authentic permission (from a big shaykh), he is like a person drowning in an ocean with no boat." Al-Tijānī was himself restrictive in granting permission for the prayer, only transmitting it to select companions.[189]

Al-Tijānī's transmission of *ḥizb al-baḥr* to such companions provides further clues as to the intertwined genealogies of prayers thought specific to particular Sufi orders. One of the elite to whom al-Tijānī granted full permission for *ḥizb al-baḥr* was the Tunisian scholar Ibrāhīm al-Riyāḥī, who related from al-Tijānī an additional supplication (*zajr*) to follow *ḥizb al-baḥr*. Among other references, the prayer contains the mysterious non-Arabic words, *aḥmā ḥamītha* [. . .].[190] This name, other Tijānī sources explain, is derived from ancient Syriac, connoting God's majesty and glory.[191]

After providing the basic Arabic equivalent, these sources refer the reader to the relevant explanation of ʿAbd al-ʿAzīz al-Dabbāgh (d. 1719, Fes) in *al-Dhahab al-ibrīz*. In *al-Ibrīz*, al-Dabbāgh is told the story of a disciple who visited the grave of Ibrāhīm al-Dasūqī (d. 1277, Egypt). Al-Dasūqī appeared to the visitor standing next to his grave and taught him a prayer containing the words *aḥmā* [. . .]. Al-Dabbāgh explained:

> No one on the face of the earth today speaks these two phrases . . . in the Syriac language. . . . And in this name is a wondrous secret which no pen and no expression will ever be capable of communicating. . . . The Syriac language is the language of spirits, and the friends of God among the members of the divine "cabinet" (*dīwān*) talk to one another in this language. . . . Every letter of the alphabet in Syriac indicates a self-contained meaning. . . . Whoever knows what each letter stands for . . . ascends to a knowledge of the science of letters. Herein is an awesome science which God has veiled from minds as a mercy unto people lest they be informed of wisdom while in darkness.[192]

The Tijānī version of *ḥizb al-baḥr* thus came to be invested with additional secret names of God composed entirely of mysterious letters. These names were first publicized by the beyond-the-grave appearance of a renowned Egyptian Sufi, and then confirmed by the seventeenth-century Moroccan master al-Dabbāgh, whom (as previously mentioned) al-Tijānī considered the preeminent saint (*quṭb*) of an earlier generation. The Tijāniyya's transmission of *ḥizb al-baḥr* thus means to invoke select treasures of the previous Sufi tradition, along with the infusing of an inherited tradition with new spiritual power.

ZARRŪQ'S "OFFICE"

The "daily office" or "employment" (*waẓīfa*) of the North African Shādhilī saint Aḥmad Zarrūq (d. 1493, Misrata, Libya) is also called "the ark of deliverance for the one who seeks refuge in God" (*safīnat al-najā li-man ʾila-Llāh iltijā*). Zarrūq apparently employed the term *waẓīfa* to avoid the sectarian implications in the terminology of "litany" (*wird*) and "orison" (*ḥizb*),[193] but his encouragement for disciples to recite his *waẓīfa* in their gatherings was no doubt a distinguishing feature of his following.[194] Al-Tijānī's own use of the word *waẓifa* to describe the distinctive congregational remembrance of the Tijāniyya may owe its origin to Zarrūq's earlier use of the term. Zarrūq's *waẓīfa* is a collection of Qurʾān excerpts and supplications of the Prophet. A central refrain of the prayer is the words: "I have sought protection in Him possessed of might and the angelic kingdom (*al-jabarūt*), I have taken refuge in the Lord of the spiritual realm (*al-malakūt*). My reliance is on the One who lives, and never dies. (O God) remove us from harm, for You have power over all things." This prayer appears to invoke the cosmological presences (*jabarūt*, *malakūt*) often used by Sufis to explain the emanation of divinity in the creation. Zarrūq himself spent some time reflecting on its composition, until he had a vision of the Prophet Muḥammad when visiting his tomb in Medina, telling him, "Make this very litany your *waẓīfa*, do not add or subtract a single word from it . . . call it, 'the ark of deliverance for the one who take refuge with God.' "[195] The benefits of the prayer are said to include the guarantee of dying in a state of faith, the beautification and perfection of the spiritual journey, the reward of spending the night in worship, entrance into Paradise hand-in-hand with the Prophet, and the entrustment of seventy thousand angels to pray for the reciter.[196] Al-Tijānī received permission for this prayer from Muḥammad al-Sammān in Medina. It is not included in Muḥammad al-Ḥāfiẓ al-Miṣrī's *Aḥzāb wa awrād*, but it is included in the earlier prayer compilation of Abū Bakr al-Burūjī, as well as other manuscript collections;[197] attesting to its continued use within the Tijāniyya both during and after the time of al-Tijānī.

IBN AL-ʿARABĪ'S "HIGHEST STATION"

Perhaps the most famous prayer attributed to Ibn al-ʿArabī was "the highest station" (*dawr al-aʿlā*), sometimes also called "the orison of protection" (*ḥizb al-wiqāya*). It figured prominently in the Medinan scholarly networks from the sixteenth to eighteenth centuries, transmitted by Ibn al-ʿArabī enthusiasts such as Aḥmad al-Shinnāwī, Aḥmad al-Qushāshī, Ibrāhīm al-Kūrānī, ʿAbd al-Ghanī al-Nābulusī, and Muṣṭafā al-Bakrī, the latter who claimed "direct authorization by him [Ibn al-ʿArabī]."[198] Al-Tijānī's teachers (and al-Bakrī's students) Maḥmūd al-Kurdī and Muḥammad al-Sammān both taught *dawr al-aʿlā*, but Tijānī sources list al-Sammān as al-Tijānī's most elevated initiation.[199] According to another of al-Kurdī's students, Muḥammad al-Dāmūnī (d. 1785, Damun, Palestine), the benefits of the prayer are as follows:

> He need not fear the arrows of war, for he will be victorious, never defeated. He need not fear any kind of enemy, human or jinn. . . . God

> will rip to utter shreds anyone who stands against him. . . . He will be respected and well-liked by all who see him, and they will be unable to endure being away from him. He will be like the sun and the moon among the stars: the heavenly and earthly worlds will love him all his life . . . [the prayer] awakens the heart from the slumber of heedlessness, and helps in sincere repentance and in erasing one's lapses and errors. It elevates one to the highest of stations, in this world and after death.[200]

The prayer is included in all available prayer collections of the Tijāniyya, with special emphasis on its recitation following the afternoon prayer combined with the fifty-sixth chapter of the Qur'an (*sūrat al-wāqiʿa*). Tijānī traditions emphasize the prayer's usefulness in spiritual elevation, protection, and increasing wealth.[201]

JAʿFAR AL-ṢĀDIQ'S "SWORD PRAYER"

The "Orison of the Sword" (*ḥizb al-sayf*) figures perhaps most prominently within both Ḥarāzim's and Tāl's discussion of non-obligatory prayers of the Tijāniyya. The sixteenth-century Indian Shaṭṭarī Sufi Muḥammad al-Ghawth had earlier included the prayer in his widely circulated *al-Jawāhir al-khams*, where it is called "the Yemeni Protection" (*al-ḥirz al-yamānī*), as well as "the Sword Protection." Al-Ghawth claims that it was taught by the Prophet's descendant Jaʿfar al-Ṣādiq (d. 765, Medina Arabia) and that "the shaykhs all over the world" have all directed themselves toward the prayer's recitation.[202] The benefit of this prayer is said to be the equivalent to the fast of Ramadan, to standing in prayer on the "night of power" (*laylat al-qadr*), or to an entire year's worth of worship.[203]

Tijānī sources suggest an alternative transmission to that of al-Ghawth. The devotional collection *Miftāḥ al-saʿāda* sources the prayer to an unidentified Muḥammad al-Tunisī (possibly one of al-Tijānī's earlier initiators in Tunisia) to the Jinn Shamharūsh, who took it directly from the Prophet Muḥammad.[204] Evidently this jinn, allegedly a companion of the Prophet who went on to live at least into the 19th century, appears in a variety of Islamic texts and oral traditions: from adjudicating disputes between men and jinn in Egypt,[205] to transmitting authorizations in Islamic law to Muslim scholars.[206] In any case, al-Tijānī directed his closest disciple ʿAlī Ḥarāzim to seek out Shamharūsh in order to have the blessing of meeting with a companion of the Prophet Muḥammad. Upon meeting him, Shamharūsh transmitted *Ḥizb al-sayf* to Ḥarāzim, telling him that the Prophet had taught him this prayer. Al-Tijānī then confirmed to Ḥarāzim that he had also taken the prayer from Shamharūsh in the same way. The later Tijānī scholar Aḥmad Sukayrij thus insisted that there were two narrations for the prayer within the Tijāniyya: one through *al-Jawāhir al-khams*, and another from Shamharūsh.[207] Given the prayer's wide circulation within Sufi circles contemporary to the Tijāniyya—such as with the community of Aḥmad b. Idrīs in the Middle East,[208] or the West African Qādiriyya of Mukhtār al-Kuntī[209]—such spiritual "verification" both connected the Tijāniyya with earlier Sufi communities and gave its adherents a sense of heightened access to the Prophet's most cherished supplications.

KHIDR'S "TEN-SEVENS"

The "Ten-Sevens" (*al-Musabbaʿāt al-ʿashr*) consist of short chapters of the Qurʾān and prophetic supplications, ten altogether, each recited seven times. Al-Tijānī received this prayer by word of mouth through Maḥmud al-Kurdī in Cairo, who received it by word of mouth from Khiḍr, the guide of Prophet Moses mentioned in the Qurʾān and whom many Muslims consider to be still alive in the unseen world.[210] As the other prayers mentioned in this section, it was among those the Prophet confirmed for al-Tijānī to keep reciting after the establishment of the Tijāniyya.

Al-Kurdī never claimed to be the first recipient of the prayer, only to have had it confirmed by Khiḍr. In fact, Abū Ṭālib al-Makkī (d. 996, Baghdad) referenced the prayer as having first been narrated by Ibrāhīm al-Tīmī, who also claimed Khiḍr gave it to him. It appears it had been recited by followers of the North African Shādhilī Shaykh Muḥammad al-Jazūlī (d. 1465, Marrakesh) from the 15th century, also on the authority of al-Makkī.[211] Al-Tīmī had earlier related to al-Makkī that after getting the prayer from Khiḍr, he then saw the Prophet Muḥammad in the presence of seventy other Prophets, who confirmed to him that the one who recites this prayer would have immense rewards: "He will have all of his major sins forgiven, and God will lift His anger and punishment from him. His [angelic] companion of his left will be ordered to not record his bad deeds for one year. By Him who sent me as a Prophet with the Truth, no one will implement this except whom God has created to be happy, and no one will leave it aside except him whom God has created to be miserable." Following this vision, al-Tīmī did not eat or drink for four months. In relating this narration, ʿUmar Tāl added that he had learned from the "scholars of divine realities" (presumably al-Ghālī in Mecca) the following:

> Whoever persists in reciting it, God the Most High will open for him the doors of goodness and increase, and will extinguish heat and earthly passions, and will provide for him blessing in his religion, his worldly affairs, and in his afterlife, and will illuminate his internal being with lights of happiness, and beautify his external being with the traces of leadership, and bring him wealth in poverty, and ease his difficulty, and facilitate his worldly means, and take away his trouble, and suffice him from every oppressor and envier, and protect him from the evil of the cursed Satan. It contains the Greatest Name. No one's eye falls upon the reciter (of this prayer), except that he loves him. And no one asks for something by it (this prayer), except that he is given what he asks.[212]

After taking the prayer from al-Kurdī, al-Tijānī visited the fellow Khalwatī student of Muṣṭafa al-Bakrī in Medina, Muḥammad al-Sammān, who added to the prayer another supplication to be read three times ("O God, by Your light I found guidance, and by Your grace I have sought assistance"), followed by "*ya Rabbāhu*" three times, and then "*ya Jabbār*" twenty-one times.[213]

Later, al-Tijānī asked the Prophet to confirm the previous narrations concerning the benefit of *al-musabbaʿāt al-ʿashr*. According to Ibn al-Mashrī, al-Tijānī related: "I asked the best of creation (*sayyid al-wujūd*), peace and blessings upon him, concerning the benefit of the 'ten-sevens,' that remembering God with it one time prevented the recording of a year's sins. He told me: 'The benefit and secret of all remembrance is found in the Great Name.'"[214] This somewhat mysterious explanation, presumably referencing God's great or greatest name contained in *al-musabbaʿāt al-ʿashr* as ʿUmar Tāl alludes above, demonstrates that al-Tijānī's verification of previous Sufi prayers sometimes included further exposition. Concerning this same "great name," left unmentioned in the text, al-Tijānī explained: "If one remembers God with the Great Name, God creates a host of Angels from this remembrance, and none can fathom their number except God. Each Angel created from this remembrance, with each one of its tongues, in every [subsequent] blink of the eye, seeks God's forgiveness for the reciter of the Name."[215] In other words, the Tijāniyya's incorporation of the "ten-sevens" both confirmed earlier Sufi narrations and added another layer of divine favor no doubt meant to inspire the aspirant in the prayer's continued use.

SUHRAWARDI'S "IDRĪSĪ NAMES"

The *Jawāhir al-maʿānī* makes reference to another prayer of perceived great value, associated with the Prophet Enoch (Idrīs), but then simply refers readers to a prior textual source: "As for the Idrīsī names (*al-asmāʾ al-Idrīsiyya*), they have great merits and many benefits. Whoever wants should consult the *Kitāb al-jawāhir al-khams* of Sayyidī Muḥammad al-Ghawth, with its commentary by Sayyidī Muḥammad [Aḥmad] al-Shinnāwī, may God be pleased with him. He mentioned their benefit that is beyond limit, and the wonder of wonders."[216] The text in question is of course the famous collection of Sufi prayers and esoteric sciences, *The Book of Five Jewels*, written in India in the 16th century. Although there is no reference to such a prayer in the published version of *al-Jawāhir al-khams*, comparison of the actual text of the prayer from Tāl's *Rimāḥ*, comprising forty-one separate names,[217] with prayers in al-Ghawth's work reveals this to be the "Greatest Names" (*al-asmāʾ al-aʿẓām*) that comprise the second of the book's five "jewels."[218] Each "name" is in fact a short sentence describing God's attributes. The first name, for example, translates as: "Glory to You, there is no god but You: O Lord of all things, Inheritor of all things, Provider of all things, Merciful to all things!" Upon close inspection, much of al-Ghawth's remaining discussion of supplications and angelic names throughout the rest of the book return to these same "greatest names."[219] In other words, al-Tijānī's *al-asmāʾ al-Idrīsiyya* are a central preoccupation of one of the most cherished collections of secret prayers in the Islamic tradition.

There is some mention of an earlier origin for these names. The contemporary Moroccan Tijānī researcher al-Rāḍī Kanūn traces them to the community of ʿUmar Suhrawardī (d. 1234, Baghdād).[220] Suhrawardī, besides being the fountainhead for the Suhrawardiyya Sufi order, also figures prominently in the chain of authorities (*silsila*) for the Khalwatiyya Sufi order into which al-Tijānī had previously been initiated. But al-Tijānī likely received these names from the Indian mystic Aḥmad al-Hindī (d. 1774) while on pilgrimage in Mecca, along with the rest of *al-Jawāhir al-khams*. Al-Ghawth's text does contain intriguing reference to the explanation of past scholars in regard to particular names. Fakhr al-Dīn al-Rāzī (d. 1210, Herat), in his *Sirr al-maktūm fī asrār al-nujūm*, is said to have associated each name with a certain prophet. Such an explanation was also transmitted by ʿAlī Shirāzī,[221] probably the brother of Murād Shāh (d. 1487), an early Naqshbandī Sufi master of Sindh, India. Ibn al-ʿArabī also apparently used these names, authoring an associated supplication for each name.[222] Given their subsequent reference in the *Jawāhir al-maʿānī*, the "Idrīsī names" were evidently among the prayers the Prophet Muḥammad confirmed for al-Tijānī in one of many waking encounters.

As mentioned above, al-Tijānī sometimes encouraged close disciples to explore or verify certain prayers for themselves. In regard to the "Idrīsī Names," it was again ʿAlī Ḥarāzim whom Tijānī sources associate with taking up the challenge. According to narrations collected by Aḥmad Sukayrij, Ḥarāzim met directly with the Prophet Idrīs and took permission for the names from him. This transmission from Idrīs was later confirmed by al-Tijānī for Ḥarāzim.[223] Another Tijānī historian, Muḥammad al-ʿArabī b. Sāʾiḥ (d. 1898, Rabat), further reported from certain "gnostics" (*al-ʿārifūn*) of the Tijāniyya that Ḥarāzim had actually ascended to the "fourth heaven" to meet with the Prophet Idrīs, where he took from him the names.[224] Although these narrations are absent from the core Tijānī sources, they nonetheless appear as the origin for the renaming of the al-Ghawth's "greatest names" as the "Idrīsī names."

The benefits of these names as described in *al-Jawāhir al-khams* are certainly wondrous. For example, recitation of the fifth name, "O Ever-Living, other than Whom there is no life for all time in His kingdom and what comes after," gives life to the dead heart, cures sicknesses, and prolongs a person's life.[225] The nineteenth name, "O Creator of whomever is in the heavens and the earth, to Whom all return," was said to have perfected the external and internal sainthood (*walāya*) of the Prophet's son-in-law ʿAlī b. Abī Ṭālib, and to have secured his knowledge of the Divine essence and attributes (*maʿrifat al-dhāt wa l-ṣifāt*).[226] Its recitation, along with its writing with musk and saffron, will make the location of a missing person apparent to the reciter in his sleep. Or done in an alternative way, will bring "a person" (*shakhṣ*) from the unseen to teach him about hidden matters. Al-Ghawth cautions with this name in particular that the reciter "must remain completely devoted to God and not occupy himself with his own ego or lusts, so that Satan does not intrude upon his work."[227]

As mentioned above, the forty-one "Idrīsī names" are said to be associated with different Prophets: Adam, Noah, Seth, Job, Khiḍr (the guide of Moses), Jesus, Enoch, John the Baptist, and so on. Three names, the thirty-sixth, thirty-seventh, and the fortieth, are linked specifically (*khāṣṣa bih*) to the Prophet Muḥammad. The fortieth name, for example: "is special to our Prophet, upon him blessing and peace, and it was by this supplication that he prayed in the cave of Hirāʾ [where he first received revelation], and the entrusted spirits (*muwakkalāt*) of the name appeared to him in the form of the four caliphs. The Prophet ordered them to remain in these forms and to not depart from them."[228] This intriguing reference suggests a secret alternative spiritual experience of the Prophet during his period of meditation in a cave outside of Mecca, simultaneous to the Qurʾān revelation, which gave him insight into the world of unseen spirits more broadly. The general benefits of this name for the reciter include "the obtainment of desires, the binding of tongues, the manifestation of wonders and strange things (*al-gharāʾib*) of the sciences and wisdom (*al-ʿulūm wa l-ḥikma*)."[229]

Such statements reveal a rich tradition of spiritual exploration and desired verification of which the Tijāniyya, through its incorporation of prayers like the "Idrīsī names," posited itself as heir. The Tijānī tradition thus came to pride itself as having gathered and verified the choicest fruits of the Sufi tradition. As the present-day Shaykh al-Tijānī b. ʿAlī Cissé told an Arab disciple in Morocco, "You will never have to go outside of the Tijāniyya for any secret [prayer]."[230]

Conclusion

This chapter reveals the extent to which al-Tijānī's "verification" (*taḥqīq*) of the Islamic scholarly tradition confirmed, challenged, and elaborated upon certain aspects of the inherited tradition in the 18th century. Of course, al-Tijānī was one of many such scholars of his age pursuing a similar path of scholarly verification, and his conclusions were not always the same as others. Clearly al-Tijānī was mostly associated with spiritual guidance on the Sufi path. But like many other scholars of the 18th century, his scholarly inquiry included jurisprudence, theology, and esotericism. Al-Tijānī did not reject the inherited scholarly tradition, as normally associated with Muḥammad b. ʿAbd al-Wahhāb, for example. But nor was al-Tijānī invested in defending all aspects of the schools of jurisprudence, theology, and Sufism in their historical development, a position more ascribed to Murtaḍa al-Zabīdī. Al-Tijānī confirmed the essential rectitude of traditions of jurisprudence, theology, esotericism, and Sufism, he only meant to remind students of their foundational principles. Jurisprudence was supposed to base its findings on the sacred texts (Qurʾān and ḥadīth) as the source of legislation. In theology, God's oneness (*tawḥīd*) did not require involved rational speculation and was more of an experiential reality, not a matter of confessional disputation. Esotericism could facilitate a person's understanding of the unseen worlds, but it should be taken from verified sources and sublimated to self-purification on the Sufi path. Sufism meant the exclusive devotion to God in the aspiration to attain direct knowledge (*maʿrifa*) of the divine, not communal gatherings around past saints whose people lacked a true living master among them. Al-Tijānī thus did not reject the accumulated practices and understandings of the Islamic scholarly tradition. He meant to subject them to an ongoing process of scholarly verification.

CHAPTER THREE

The Actualization of Humanity on the Muḥammadan Path

After many years in pursuit of knowledge, Aḥmad al-Tijānī came to reside in the Algerian oasis town of Abū Samghūn. There, in 1782, according to Tijānī sources, the Prophet Muḥammad appeared to him, "in a waking state, not dreaming" (*yaqẓatan la manāman*), and bestowed on him his own "Muḥammadan Sufi Path" (*Ṭarīqa Muḥammadiyya*).[1] The shaykh was forty-six years old at the time of this greatest illumination (*al-fatḥ al-akbar*), and the event marked the beginning of what would later be known as the Tijāniyya:

> The Prophet authorized him in this Aḥmadan spiritual path (*al-Ṭarīqa al-Aḥmadiyya*) and chosen way of the Prophet (*al-sīra al-muṣṭafawiyya al-nabawiyya*). God gave him illumination (*fatḥ*) at the Prophet's hands, and the Prophet informed him that he was his educator (*murabbī*) and guarantor, and that nothing arrived to him from God except at the Prophet's hands and mediation.
>
> And the Prophet said to him: "You do not owe any favor to the creation, (even) among the shaykhs of the Sufi path, for I am your means (*wāsiṭa*) and support (*mumidd*) in the (spiritual) actualization (*al-taḥqīq*). Leave aside everything you have taken from the Sufi paths."
>
> And he said to him: "Hold fast to this Path without isolation or withdrawal from the people, until you arrive to the station promised to you. Remain in your current state, without constriction, difficulty, or excessive effort. Leave behind you all other saints."[2]

While these words reveal a decisive claim to al-Tijānī's preeminence within the constellation of Sufi luminaries, the reference to actualization or verification (*taḥqīq*) perhaps best describes the notion of *Ṭarīqa Muḥammadiyya* at work for al-Tijānī. The encounter with the Prophet did not represent a break from the Islamic tradition, but rather was part of a long process of verification and actualization of Islamic knowledge.

The 18th century witnessed the popularization of both the notion of the "Muḥammadan Path" and scholarly inquiries concerned with *taḥqīq*. As previously mentioned, these notions were defined differently in specific contexts, nor were the two concepts always associated with one another. But al-Tijānī's notion of the *Ṭarīqa Muḥammadiyya* arguably drew upon his broader interest in scholarly verification or *taḥqīq*. The Tijānī concept of the "Muḥammadan Path" is best understood as a methodology for the full realization of the human condition, the actualization of humanity (*taḥqīq al-insāniyya*) in the mirror of the Prophet Muḥammad. As the Prophet represented this paradigmatic perfection of the human being, the cherished encounter with him, so formative for the foundation of the Tijāniyya, was the logical result of such human actualization. This chapter thus first considers al-Tijānī's understanding of the human condition as an expression of a Muḥammad-centric "Islamic humanism." I then turn to the controversial subject of encountering the Prophet Muḥammad after his death, a notion necessarily situated within the potentiality of human actualization. In the conclusion to this chapter, I suggest that visionary experience with the Tijāniyya was still largely confined to the realm of saintly miracles. Seeing the Prophet was a method to confirm, verify, or actualize an Islamic religious identity. It was not meant to transcend the foundational sources of Islam.

An Islamic Humanism?

If al-Tijānī's concept of human actualization were to be associated with an "Islamic humanism," it would certainly avoid the European Enlightenment designation of the "rational man," disconnected from God, as his own master of the universe. European colonial conquest in fact used such "humanism" to assign superiority to a white European ideal, and thus as "an excuse for hegemony": justifying the subjection of non-white others as essentially not quite human.[3] This analysis thus explicitly distances itself from attempts to "rationalize" or "humanize" the teachings of the Tijāniyya according to modern standards of (Western) humanism.[4] Exploration of al-Tijānī's understanding of the human condition must not be associated with an apparent political agenda of distinguishing good Muslims (Sufis) from bad Muslims (Wahhabis/terrorists). According to Mamdani's observation of this discursive agenda: "good Muslims are modern, secular, and

Westernized, but bad Muslims are doctrinal, antimodern, and virulent."[5] Indeed, Tijānī leaders have led jihads in West Africa during European colonialism, or opposed Ataturk's secularism in Turkey; while others have been open to relationships with various Western governments.

There is an older concept of humanism that "does not automatically imply an opposition to religion or religious thinking."[6] An Italian renaissance philosopher, Pico della Mirandola (d. 1494, Florence), thus quoted an anonymous Muslim sage to argue for the universal dignity of humankind: "There is nothing more wonderful than Man!"[7] Such wonder was to be actualized through the "purification of the human soul lead[ing] to the true knowledge of God as the ultimate aim and perfection of humanity."[8] Yaḥyā b. ʿAdī, the favored Arab Christian student of the famous Muslim philosopher Abū Naṣr Muḥammad al-Fārābī (d. 950, Damascus) described this humanism that undergirded the religious and cultural diversity of the classical Islamic civilization: "Men are a single tribe, related to one another; humanity (*al-insāniyya*) unites them. The adornment of the divine power is in all of them and in each one of them. . . . Since their souls are one, and love is only in the soul, all of them must then show affection for one another and love one another."[9] Summarizing the thought of Ibn al-ʿArabī on the subject, Vincent Cornell thus concluded of this classical humanism: "To objectify and depersonalize another human being because of ideological or religious differences is to forget that all humans are made up of the same combination of spirit and clay."[10] The useful volume *Humanism in Muslim Culture* introduces the subject of humanism by insisting that it "is only conceivable as a universal concept of humankind in its relationship to the world, implying a set of mutually recognized values, of which the old concept of human dignity is still the most important."[11] The concept of humanism here employed thus invokes this notion of human dignity based on the universal "wonder" of the human being as God's most beloved creation and locus of divine manifestation. ʿAbd al-Ghanī al-Nābulusī had already popularized such an Islamic humanism in the late 17th century, arguing, according to Samer Akkach, that all humans whatever their confessional differences were "none other than God's acts and the traces of His most beautiful names."[12] Reflecting on the "Muhammadan light" that pervades all of creation, al-Tijānī similarly observed, "There is no difference between a believer and an infidel (*kāfir*) in terms of humanity (*fī l-ādamiyy*)."[13]

Muslim scholars often understood the human creation as uniquely capable of divine realization. Modern scriptural rationalism in the Muslim world, in the name of promoting true monotheism, may have deemphasized earlier notions of the human's sacred capacity to realize the Divine. However, earlier Islamic orthodoxy contemplated the relevant Qur'an verse quite literally: "*We will show them Our signs on [all] the horizons and within themselves until it becomes clear to them that He is the Real.*"[14] Abū Ḥāmid al-Ghazālī considered the human being to be the reflection of the divine kingdom: "In the kingdom of man, God's throne is represented by the soul, the archangel by the heart, the chair [footstool] by the brain, the tablet by the treasure chamber of thought. The soul, itself unlocated and indivisible, governs the body as God governs the universe."[15] In his exegesis of the above Qur'ān verse, the twentieth-century Tijānī Shaykh Ibrahim Niasse similarly emphasized this sacred composition of the human being:

> The scholars have named the horizons as the macrocosm (*al-ʿālam al-akbar*) and mankind as the microcosm (*al-ʿālam al-aṣghar*). But the reality is the opposite, for mankind is the macrocosm. Indeed, we find all of the external world enfolded in the being (*jirm*) of this microcosm that is the human being. For the human, the body (*jism*) that contains him is like the divine throne (*ʿarsh*), and his soul (*nafs*) is the footstool (*kursī*). His heart is like the heavenly house around which circumambulate the angels (*al-bayt al-maʿmūr*). His subtle spiritual centers (*laṭāʾif*) are like the gardens of paradise. The strength of his spirit is like the angels.[16]

The human being is thus the most sacred, most wondrous, of God's creations, capable of uniquely perceiving the divine. "I see the seven heavens, the seven earths, and the divine throne inside myself," the *Jawāhir al-maʿānī* cites ʿAbd al-ʿAzīz al-Dabbāgh in explanation, "and what is beyond the throne among the seventy veils, there being within and between each veil seventy thousand years."[17]

The Reality of the Human Condition

Human life, Sufi intellectuals maintained, is not defined simply through the movement of the body, breath in the lungs, or pulse in the veins. This type of life, defined by the "animal" or "vital spirit" (*al-rūḥ al-ḥayawānī*) is also found among animals.[18] Human existence is rather defined by the capacity for knowledge and Divine realization. Only the awakened human being is worthy of being named truly human, and thus the holder of God's vicegerency (*khilāfa*) on earth. According to Aḥmad al-Tijānī:

> The reality of the perfected man (*al-insān al-kāmil*) is that he is a presence (*ḥaḍra*) of perfection embraced in the presence of Divine beauty, which thus enfolds the Divine secret in its entirety. From this wherewithal (*ḥaythiya*), he becomes a deputy (*khalīfa*) for God in the creation. Wherever the Lord is God, (the perfect) man is governor (*ḥākim*) and agent of disposal (*mutaṣṣarif*). Every degree in which the Lord has divinity, man has in this (same degree) a disposal (*taṣarruf*), a judgment (*ḥukm*), and a vicegerency (*khilāfa*), and his judgment is not refused. Because of this secret, God commanded the angels to bow to Adam. And it was this (secret) indicated in words of the Prophet, God's blessing and peace upon him: "Surely God created Adam in His image (*ʿalā ṣūratihi*)."
>
> The true human being is the one who has obtained this degree. As for the one absent from this degree, who has not obtained anything of it, he is only a semblance of humanity: he is not really human. He is like a dead man with no spirit in his body: his appearance is that of a corpse without movement or life. In this death-state of his, all of the special characteristics of humanity are absent from him. These special human characteristics are only found in the living, and the dead have nothing of them.[19]

There is clearly an assumed relationship here between the knowledge of God (*maʿrifa*) and the capacity to become the agent of Divine action. According to Ibrāhīm Niasse, the matter was actually quite simple: "In the sayings of the Prophet, (God says), 'When I love him [a servant], I become him.' This is the door to gnosis."[20] Although Ibn al-ʿArabī and Ṣadr al-Dīn al-Qūnawī (and others) had much earlier developed this idea of humanity's reflection of divine attributes—particularly in relation to the "perfect man" (*al-insān al-kāmil*),[21] al-Tijānī's words accent an undeniable urgency for human actualization. Knowledge of God, and the endowment with the Divine command, activated the "special human characteristics" that separated the dead from the living.

This reference to the special characteristics of humanity (*khawāṣṣ al-insān*) deserves further elaboration. The Sufi tradition formulated myriad ways of understanding the attributes specific to humanity that permit a human's unique relationship to God. Sometimes described as subtle spiritual centers (*laṭāʾif*), the hidden senses (*al-ḥawāss al-bāṭina*), or the internal presences (*ḥaḍarāt*), these are usually named as the following five: internal secret (*sirr*), spirit (*rūḥ*), intellect (*ʿaql*), heart (*qalb*), and the ego-soul (*nafs*).[22] Tijānī texts contain no standardized version of these presences, however, and sometimes they are altered to suit the point being made. The following rendition from the *Jawāhir al-maʿānī* explains how the internal human condition connects a person to God.

> It is said by way of indication (*ishāra*) that God said, "In the body is a cavity (*muḍgha*), and in the cavity, is a heart, and in the heart, is an inner heart (*fuʾād*), and in the inner heart, is an innermost conscience (*ḍamīr*), and in the conscience, is a secret, and the secret is I."
>
> The meaning of "cavity" is cone-shaped flesh, the cavity in which the heart is found. The meaning of heart is the spirit (*rūḥ*) at the level of heart. "And in the heart, is an inner heart." The inner heart is the spirit at the level the serene self (*nafs muṭmaʾinna*).[23] "And in the inner heart is the innermost conscience." The meaning of conscience is the spirit at the level of the pleased soul (*nafs rāḍiya*). "And in the conscience, is a secret." The secret is the spirit at the level of the pleasing soul (*nafs marḍiya*). This is the place where the extinction of extinction (*fanāʾ al-fanāʾ*) is realized. This is the station (*maqām*) of annihilation, eradication, demolition, and destruction, until there is found no source, no trace, no other, and no otherness. At this place (*martaba*), He says, "And in the secret, is I." In this meaning, Ibn al-Fāriḍ, may God be pleased with him, said, "If you should call on me, I am the one to respond."[24]

This rendition of man's inner cosmology appears to consciously undermine overly theorized distinctions between constituent elements of the human being. The larger point is that every human being has been endowed with the ability to know his Creator. The location of this realization appears here as the heart, while the knowledge itself is found with the spirit. But the unveiling of the knowledge latent in the spirit depends of course on the purification of the soul (*nafs*). The reference to the "divine secret" inside man perhaps means to remind a person that God, even if He should manifest in man, is only known by Himself in the absence of otherness.

As the place of realization, al-Tijānī no doubt followed earlier Sufi understandings of the heart as "the mirror of the Divine."[25] With the purification of the heart, all parts of the body come to delight in the worship of God. Al-Tijānī thus commented on Muḥammad al-Buṣayrī's (d. 1294, Alexandria) poetic verse in *al-Hamziya*, "When guidance comes to dwell in a heart, all parts (of the body) are enlivened in worship":

> The guidance coming to dwell in the heart here is the divine assistance which attracts the servant's heart to God the exalted, and holds it back from everything beside God. This assistance is accompanied by (the heart's) being filled with the flood of divine lights. The owner of this heart comes to desire nothing except God the exalted, he has no concern for other than Him. He does not incline to other than God, neither by exaltation, glorification, worship, turning towards, contentment, regard for, intimacy with, or love for. He is completely empty of other than God, and exclusively devoted to Him in his heart. This is the guidance that comes to dwell in the heart, and there is no doubt that when the heart is filled with such lights, the (body's) parts will rejoice in the worship (of God). In other words, all limbs (of the body) will follow the heart, by this raised up for the worship of God the exalted. Burned away from them are all traces of negligence and forgetfulness. Such a person becomes a divine servant, and all his body parts become divine so that he does not move except for the pleasure of God.[26]

This explanation is of course evocative of the Prophet's description of the heart, "In the body is a lump of flesh, if it is good, the whole body is good."[27] Included in the "parts of the body" here is quite obviously the mind itself (as discussed in chapter 2): the purified heart burns away the heedless thoughts from the mind, and the intellect becomes preoccupied of divine or angelic thoughts, rather than devilish or egoistic thoughts.[28] Those whom God "has endowed with love for His Essential Being (*dhāt*)," al-Tijānī summarized, "have no thought (*lā yakhṭir*) in their internal beings except for God the exalted."[29] This purity of the heart's mirror, dependent of course on the self's purification, allowed the individual to perceive the knowledge of God in his own spirit (*rūḥ*).

The Human Spirit (*rūḥ*) and the Inclusiveness of Divine Love

The spirit or soul (*rūḥ*) of every human being, according to Tijānī texts, contains a perfect cognizance of God. Such an idea may be related to the Islamic concept of the innate human disposition (*fiṭra*) of submission to God, but early texts of the Tijāniyya contain little discussion of *fiṭra* by itself. For al-Tijānī, the human spirit (*rūḥ*) is what explains God's "general love" (*al-maḥabba al-ʿāmma*) for all of humanity, including the disbelievers. In responding to a question concerning the nature of God's love, al-Tijānī said:

> All of the worlds are included in this love, even the disbelievers (*kuffār*), for they are His beloveds in the presence of His words, "I loved to be known, so I created the creation and made Myself known to them, and by Me they know Me."[30] Do not imagine that any in creation are excluded from this cognizance (*maʿrifa*). Indeed, all of the souls (*arwāḥ*) have been created with complete cognizance of God the Exalted. Ignorance only occurred to them with their mixture in the material bodies . . . so the ignorance that befell the souls is not intrinsic to them. Knowledge of God the Exalted is that which is intrinsic to them.[31]

The soul or spirit (*rūḥ*), elsewhere defined as "the breath of the Merciful Lord,"[32] bears the trust of divine knowledge and praise and is what animates not only humanity, but the creation at large. Even in their mental denial of God, disbelievers cannot escape the knowledge and praise of God. "The bodies (*ajsām*) of the disbelievers are not ignorant of God," al-Tijānī continued, "for they prostrate to God and praise Him. . . . The Glorious and Exalted said, '*There is nothing that does not glorify His praise.*' And the bodies are among this entirety of creation that glorify God and prostrate to him."[33] In fact, "the spirit of life" animates all of the material creation, so nothing escapes God's worship and praise. When asked about the Qurʾān verse, "*There is no beast except that He has taken it by the forelock, surely my Lord is over the straight path,*"[34] al-Tijānī explained:

> In this sphere, nothing escapes this reality in the entirety of creation, which is either animate or inanimate. And even inanimate things, glory to God, have been dressed with the spirits of life. By this they glorify and sanctify God, and by this they fall prostrate to God the exalted as with everything else, as in the verse, "*Have you not seen that to God prostrate everything in heavens and the earth, along with the sun and the moon?*" By these spirits of life they become cognizant of God, for they would not prostrate or glorify except by their state of knowing God the exalted. But we do not realize this knowledge, prostration, and glorification of theirs. God said, "*There is nothing that does not glorify His praise, but you do not understand their glorification.*"[35]

The forms of all creation have thus been dressed with the spirit of life by which they know and praise God. Human beings, notwithstanding the disbelievers, have been endowed with an immensely more valuable spirit, however: that which carries the "complete cognizance" of God.

This human spirit, according to al-Tijānī, may be said to define the human's "essence" (*ʿayn*); but the veils between the embodied self and the original knowledge of the spirit must be raised to actually "realize" (*adraka*) this humanity. According to al-Tijānī: "Surely the essence of man is his spirit and its identity, nothing else. Indeed, this external body's relationship to the spirit is as the shrouding robe. Man is nothing but the spirit. But in his current state he is veiled from the realization of the reality of his spirit: he does not know or understand this reality, although it is his essence." Realization thus required the removal of this veil obscuring the reality of the spirit, a veil engendered by its coming to dwell in the material body.

> Then when the spirit was settled in the body, it became shrouded in the body's earthly impurity. It became associated with the opposite of its own attribution (*nasab*), which is the utmost purity and light, instead associated with the attribution of the body, which is the utmost darkness and opacity. The spirit then became veiled from the knowledge and gnosis (*al-ʿilm wa l-maʿrifa*) that it contained before its entry into the body. And this veil persists with the spirit from the time of the body's formation. If God wants a servant to arrive to the purity of gnosis, it happens that the veil is raised between a person and what was entrusted to the reality of his spirit in terms of gnosis and knowledge.[36]

The process of realizing one's humanity thus requires the conscious remembrance of his spirit's intrinsic knowledge of God. The shaykh hence understood human identity more explicitly as the realization born of the spirit's insertion into the body. "The reality of man (*ḥaqīqat al-insān*) is the combination of the spirit and the body, and the balance between the two."[37] Elsewhere, al-Tijānī emphasized the realization (*idrāk*) of the spirit's intrinsic knowledge, a realization that then might come to pervade the bodily presence, as the essence of human reality.[38]

> God created the [human] spirit 980,000 years in length, and the same in width. And He left it a long time in His nurturing care, caressing it

> in the tenderness of His kindness, of His graciousness, of the manifest traces of His love for it. And the spirit grew strong in this nurturing care. Then when it tasted the pain of separation, it cried out in complaint, and said, "O my God, my Master and Lord, I cannot endure this separation!" And its Lord said to it, may He be glorified and exalted, "I did not create you to desire yourself, I created you to manifest in you the secret of My oneness (*waḥdāniyya*)."[39]

Realizing the mystery of the spirit's attribution (*nasab*) to the Divine presence and freeing it from its imprisonment in the world of dense bodies, thus defines the purpose of the human creation.[40] The wondrous expanse of the human spirit endowed each individual with the potentiality to obtain full cognizance of the Creator. The realization of this potentiality, the ability to know God, thus defines a person's true human identity.

Human Potentiality

The true honor of humanity is not simply the divine endowment of the spirit (*rūḥ*), but the potentiality of realization to be had in the battle against the self. The ability to control the *nafs* allows a human being to transcend himself and become the conscious agent of divine action and the bearer of divine attributes. Those who do not obtain anything of this potentiality can only be considered a semblance of humanity, since "all of the special characteristics of humanity are absent from him." Consistent with the earlier Sufi teachings of al-Ghazālī and Ibn al-ʿArabī, al-Tijānī emphasized the extraordinary capacity of the human condition.

> The knowledgeable people of God are more complete than the angels. God the Exalted manifests in the bodily presence (*dhāt*) of the gnostic the entirety of the Divine Names and Attributes by which the creation came into being, both common entities and exalted ones. Angels have naught but one Name that God manifests to them, and no more. In all of the creation, there is not one, whether angels or other, in whom God manifests more than one Name. But the Adamic bodily presence encompasses the entirety of existent beings. So in reality, each gnostic contains all of the angels and all of the existent beings, from the heavenly throne to the earthly canopy. He sees all of them in himself, each one individually. If he wanted, he could ascend in the unseen to the guarded tablet (*lawḥ*), and look upon it and examine it within his own

> bodily presence. Such perfection does not belong to any creation except the Adamic being. From such encompassment (*iḥāṭa*), God established the complete and general stewardship (*khilāfa*) [of humanity].[41]

This awesome "encompassment" of the human bodily presence (*dhāt*) defines true human identity as being an authoritative agent (*khalīfa*) of divine will. The battle against the *nafs* is only a struggle to remove the veil clouding a person's true identity, not the essence of this human actualization itself. Becoming the *khalīfa* of God depends on the transformative power of divine love. The shaykh's explanation of this was predictably elicited by his being asked the meaning of God's words in the *ḥadīth qudsī*: "When I love him [a servant], I become his hearing with which he hears, his sight with which he sees, his hand with which he strikes, the foot with which he walks."[42] Al-Tijānī responded:

> The meaning of "until I love him" is as follows. God's love for a servant entails the flood of love upon him from God's holy essential being (*dhāt*). This is the most exalted of favors, and this is where the journey for all travelers ends. Whoever arrives here has all of his worldly and otherworldly needs completed. When He said, "when I love him," He is saying, "I overwhelm him in love of My essential being," to the extent of God's words, "*He loves them, and they love Him*."[43] Were it not for His love for them, they would not have arrived at the love of His essential being.
>
> As for His words, "and when I love him, I become his hearing," till the end of the narration, the meaning is as follows. The servant sees in himself a divine power as if he were the divine sacred essential being, with all of its attributes and names; as if he were He, but he is not He. However, God the Glorious and Exalted has poured on him of the light of His attributes and names in order to raise his station. Thus, he comes to carry what the entirety of the creation cannot carry because of its weight. This is why some of the gnostics have said, "The one for whom is unveiled a grainsworth of divine unity (*tawḥīd*) carries the heavens and the two earths in his eyelashes," because he has been raised to this station by Divine Power. He sees by God, as if his bodily presence (*dhāt*) was the essential being of God the exalted. And he hears by God.
>
> The indication of seeing and hearing by God is that in one glance, he sees all of existence, from the Divine throne to earthly canopy,

with not a single grain hidden from him. He fulfills what is due to each existence, from behind and in front, to the right and left, above and below. He sees all of this in one instant, and he sees existence as a unique jewel of extraordinary apportioning, and (he sees) free of mirrors that would change its states, composition, movement, or color. All of this he sees in one glance, in one instant, in every direction, without mistaking a single grain. The reason for this vision is that eye of the spirit (*rūḥ*) has been opened. If the eye of the spirit should be opened in his bodily presence, all the creations and worlds appear before him, and not one vision is confounded. This is the meaning of seeing by God.

Hearing by God is when a person hears all the enunciations of existence in all of the worlds, with all of their different glorifications and remembrances (of God) in one instant, without obfuscation despite the plethora of enunciations and glorifications. It is as if, for each enunciation, he hears nothing other than it. Audition normally cannot distinguish one voice if there should be many voices all at once. But the comportment (*salk*) demanded of this state is to hear all of the articulations and glorifications of the existent beings without confusion.

"And his hand with which he strikes," is when he strikes by God the exalted, and not by his own power. If God should grant him permission, there is now in this strike the power to kill a million people in one instant, and so on. And this is a divine power.

"And his two feet with which he walks." So like this he can walk across the entirety of the creation with one step. For example, he could put one foot on the earth, and the other foot behind the Lordly throne; but this is in relationship to his spirit, not in relation to his body.

"And his tongue with which he speaks."[44] In this state, he speaks with the speech of the Real, glorious and exalted is He. Like this, he can complete one hundred thousand recitations (of the Qur'ān) in the amount of time the (ordinary) reader can recite the (short) "chapter of sincerity" (*ikhlāṣ*).[45] This is because he becomes endowed with lights and attributes of the Real, and he is not incapacitated from anything. If the light of Divine capacity should flow through him, he can perform in the creation what the minds cannot conceive. He is able to perform deeds in the space of an hour in one place, and perform deeds in another place (at the same time), such as marrying a woman and having twenty children with her, and other things like that. And this

> has happened to many of the saints, for God is not limited by anything in the creation, nor is he bound by customary occurrences. In His unseen are matters that the minds cannot comprehend.[46]

Human identity (*dhāt al-insān*) was thus defined as an act of becoming, the fusion of knowledge in the bodily presence (*dhāt*), a presence that is linked to the material body (*jasad*), but which also transcends it. Such a body was endowed with extraordinary capabilities, although all capacity belonged to God. The only mention in the *Jawāhir al-maʿānī* of al-Tijānī's own capability in this regard was his divulgence to Ḥarāzim that God had allowed him to accomplish many things at once:

> And among his special favors, may God be pleased with him: he told me of himself that he would get through a book while his hand was occupied with the prayer beads, and his tongue was praising (God) until he finished his litany. And his combining between the two did not take away his attention from the other. And he told me also that he could read a book, remember God, delve into other types of knowledge, speak with people, and engage in writing, all in one sitting, all at one time. And no one (action) would occupy him from another.[47]

Such abilities were possible, Tijānī sources suggest, by God's having taken possession of the human identity, "as if his being (*dhāt*) were the being of God." No doubt the later Tijānī scholar al-ʿArabī b. al-Sāʾiḥ had such a saintly miracle in mind in explaining that the paradigmatic saint (*quṭb*) of any time was in fact possessed of 366 bodily presences (*dhāt*), one of which was always in Mecca.[48]

Al-Tijānī further explained this concept of transcending the normal confines of human corporality by telling a story of a shaykh who was able to travel with his spirit in surprising ways. A shaykh and his disciple, al-Tijānī tells ʿAlī Ḥarāzim, were traveling in Iraq. The shaykh fell ill, and the disciple resolved to visit a nearby city to procure medicine for his shaykh. The shaykh advised him not to visit the city, as it was known for its evil inhabitants, but the disciple insisted. Immediately upon entering the city, the disciple was ushered into the presence of the king. To his surprise, the king greeted him like a long-lost brother. Seating him beside him, the king asked how he could help his visitor, and then provided everything requested without delay. Upon the disciple's return, he expressed his surprise to the shaykh, who told him:

> It was I who did all of that for you. When I saw your concern and love for me, and your ardent desire to cure me that motivated your visit to the king, I was afraid your spiritual state would be damaged by his lack of acquaintance with you. So, I transported myself from this place with my spirit (*rūḥ*), transferring my spirit from my body, and I arrived to the king before you. I entered his body, and cloaked his spirit and body. When you entered, it was I who stood up to welcome you. I commanded him, and he was unable to disobey me: I was the spirit and he was the body. Thus, I did for you what you witnessed. It was I who honored you, not him. When you departed, my spirit departed from him and returned to my own body. As for the medicine, I do not need it.[49]

Tijānī disciples no doubt saw in this story a testament to their own shaykh's abilities. There are thus numerous accounts of disciples recognizing the presence of al-Tijānī in a variety of forms. According to oral accounts in Senegal, Ibrāhīm Niasse was once brought before a French colonial administrator in Kaolack. His disciples were afraid, for they knew the Frenchman as a virulent enemy of Muslims, bent on extortion and control. Niasse came back from the meeting smiling, relating, to his surprise, how the Frenchman had welcomed him and agreed to leave him alone. He said that he had witnessed that the spirit of Shaykh Aḥmad al-Tijānī had temporarily taken over the man's body in order to honor Niasse.[50]

While such extraordinary human potentiality defined the true nature of the human condition, it seems this potentiality was meant to actualize rather than distract from the servant's obedience to God. Only in this way does a person really become God's true servant and representative (*khalīfa*) on earth. To emphasis this point, al-Tijānī related the words of ʿAbd al-Qādir al-Jīlānī (d. 1166), "My command (*amr*) is by the command of God, if I should say, 'Be,' it is. Everything is by the command of God, so judge the extent of my power."[51] According to the *Jawāhir al-maʿānī*, the words of the Prophet Muḥammad's son-in-law ʿAlī b. Abī Ṭālib indicate a similar human potentiality: "I am the flash of lightning, the rumble of thunder, the movement of the celestial bodies (*aflāk*)."[52] Al-Tijānī thus repeated an earlier Sufi saying in reference to himself: "I am dressed in (the weightiest of letters) *shīn*; my reach fills where the eye sees; my heart is delight; faraway news comes to me."[53]

The Muḥammadan Reality and Prayer on the Prophet

For al-Tijānī, all human perfection was only the reflection of the Prophet Muḥammad. Sufis of course long located such ideas in foundational Islamic texts. The contemporary of the Prophet Uways al-Qaranī, according to the *Jawāhir al-maʿānī*, thus told other companions of the Prophet, "You have not seen anything of the Prophet except his shadow."[54] The idea of a precedent spiritual reality of the Prophet Muḥammad, or the "Muḥammadan reality" (*al-ḥaqīqa al-Muḥammadiyya*) dates at least to Ibn al-ʿArabī, but probably to earlier Sufis such as Sahl al-Tustarī (d. 896) and Manṣūr al-Hallāj (d. 922). Sufis cited a number of ḥadīth to substantiate the idea, such as the Prophet's words, "The first thing that God created was my spirit," or "I was a Prophet when Adam was between water and clay," or God's inspiration to the Prophet (*ḥadīth qudsī*), "If not for you, I would not have created the spheres (of creation)."[55] While some ḥadīth specialists have contested the authenticity of these narrations, they were widely circulated in premodern Islamic learning and included in such esteemed collections as the sixteenth-century ḥadīth scholar Ibn Ḥajar al-Ḥaythamī's *al-Fatāwa*.[56] In any case, al-Tijānī clearly subscribed to such understandings: "Our master Muḥammad is the first of created beings, and their source. By his blessing they came into being, and by him is their spiritual sustenance."[57] In explaining the words of the prayer *ṣalāt al-fātiḥ*, "the opener of what was closed," al-Tijānī added, "If not for him, God would not have created the creation, and brought them forth from non-existence into existence."[58] Thus: "The Muḥammadan reality is the first creation God brought into being out of nonexistence (*ghayb*), and there was no other creation in the presence of God before it."[59] The Prophet Muḥammad is thus the reason for God's love and mercy to the entire creation: "He it was who opened the closed doors of divine mercy, and he is the cause for their opening for (the rest of) creation. If God had not created our master Muḥammad, He would not have had mercy on any of creation."[60]

The Muḥammadan reality, being the source and sustenance of everything in creation, was thus a reality present in all places and all time. In explaining the verse of al-Buṣayrī's *Hamziyya*, "You are the lantern of every grace, so nothing emerges except from your light of lights," Ḥarāzim recorded al-Tijānī as saying: "He, God's blessing and peace upon him, is possessed of a luminous lantern in the darkness for every existent being in creation, whatever their state of impurity, in all ages. There is no manifestation of light or illumination in any time or place in the universe except that it is from his light and his luminosity. All of existence derives support from his light, God's blessing and peace upon him, without exception."[61] The light of the Prophet thus pervades all being. Al-Tijānī developed this theme of light to explain the relationship between the Muḥammadan reality and the presences or stations of the Prophet's being:

> The station of the Prophet's secret essence (*sirr*) is the Muḥammadan reality, which is pure, divine light. This reality confounds the minds and realizations of all in creation due to its exalted specialty, beyond all comprehension. This is the meaning of his "secret being." Then this Muḥammadan reality was clothed in (other) divine lights, veiled (again) from creation, and called "spirit" (*rūḥ*). Then it descended and was clothed in other divine lights, by reason of which it was called "intellect" (*ʿaql*). Then it descended and was clothed in other divine lights, by which it was (again) veiled and called "heart" (*qalb*). Then it descended and was clothed in other divine lights, by which it was veiled, becoming the reason for being (called) "soul" (*nafs*).[62]

In a similar narration, elsewhere in the *Jawāhir al-maʿānī*, al-Tijānī adds: "After that his noble body (*jasad*) appeared."[63] As the Prophet's being contained the entire creation, later Tijānī scholars expounded on the relationship between the Prophet's being and the cosmological presences of creation. Ibrāhīm Niasse explained:

> The cosmological presences (*ḥaḍarāt*) manifested themselves in the best of creation (*sayyid al-wujūd*), thus becoming his five presences: his secret essence (*sirr*), his spirit (*rūḥ*), his intellect (*ʿaql*), his heart (*qalb*), and his soul (*nafs*). The "realm of effacement in the divine essence" (*hāhūt*) became manifest in his secret essence. The "realm of manifestation of divine attributes" (*lāhūt*) became manifest in his spirit. The "realm of angels and spirits" (*jabarūt*) became manifest in his intellect. The "realm of the heavens and divine command" (*malakūt*) became manifest in his heart. The "material world" (*nāsūt*) became manifest in his soul. And this is the meaning of God's prayer (*ṣalāt*) on him, and it is the meaning of (the name) Muḥammad, servant of God (*ʿAbdallāh*).[64]

In this way, God's prayer on the Prophet—referenced in the Qurʾān, *Surely God and His angels send prayer on the Prophet*[65]—may be considered the origin of all creation, and certainly the reason for the pervasion of the

Muḥammadan being in all places. The Prophet was not only with every molecule in creation, but he was closer to them than themselves. Asked to explain the Qur'ān verse, "*The Prophet is closer to the believers than their own selves*,"[66] al-Tijānī responded: "The Prophet has a mastery (*istīlā'*) over all degrees and individual entities, with judgment and command in each of them, in every countenance, and in every expression. The degrees include the individual creations in all of their substances, identities, molecules, and forms. Every entity marked by individualization has a degree (*martaba*) with the Real, so each is a degree of divinity. In this manner, the Prophet is closer to every one of them than their own selves."[67] Such articulations demonstrate the multiple ways al-Tijānī understood the Muḥammadan spiritual presence: an unseen secret reality, an all-pervasive light manifesting in different ways, and a discernible presence closer to every created being than their own selves.

The *Ṭarīqa Muḥammadiyya*, for Tijānīs, was the means of accessing this spiritual reality of the Prophet. Although later Tijānī scholars elaborated many other reasons for calling the Tijāniyya the *Ṭarīqa Muḥammadiyya*,[68] arguably the practical definition revolved around the centering of Sufi devotion on the "prayer on the Prophet" (*ṣalāt ʿalā l-nabī*). "I have been prohibited," al-Tijānī told followers, "from seeking God by any of His names, and commanded to devote myself to Him with only *ṣalāt al-fātiḥ*," or the "prayer of opening" dedicated to the Prophet central to the Tijāniyya.[69] Later Tijānī texts thus elaborated that the prayer on the Prophet, particularly *ṣalāt al-fātiḥ*, was the primary means of spiritual training (*tarbiya*) in the Tijāniyya. The nineteenth-century Moroccan Tijānī Muḥammad Akansūs thus quoted Aḥmad Zarrūq to say, "I saw the doors to God as they were about to close, and the only ones that remained open were those of saying blessings on the Prophet Muḥammad."[70] According to Seesemann's useful summary of the nineteenth-century Mauritanian scholar Ibn Anbūja, "*ṣalāt al-fātiḥ* alone is sufficient to traverse the various stages of the mystic journey, because the Prophet had given the guarantee that everybody who recited the formula according to the conditions (*shurūṭ*) would eventually attain illumination and experience rapture (*jadhb*)."[71]

For Tijānīs, then, the *Ṭarīqa Muḥammadiyya* was the path of offering prayers on the Prophet. An early disciple of al-Tijānī, Muḥammad al-Damrāwī, described the spiritual concentration on the Prophet associated with the prayer on the Prophet in the *Ṭarīqa Muḥammadiyya* in a remarkably similar way to the prior articulations of al-ʿUjaymī and al-Sammān:

"The result (desired) from plenty of prayers on the Prophet is that the one invoking the prayer comes to emulate God's command. He does this while venerating the Prophet, God's blessing and peace upon him, and thus finds love in it [his obedience]. Thereby, some of the Prophet's beautiful attributes become present in him, and he comes to behold his noble form as if he were (being held) between his two hands."[72] In other words, the prayer on the Prophet was the means by which to take delight in the worship of God and best reflect the Prophet's perfection. Al-Tijānī elaborated on this concept through a prayer he claimed to have received directly from the Prophet called "the ruby of realities" (*yaqūtat al-ḥaqāʾiq*). He explained the following in reference to the lines, "O God, make him (the Prophet) our spirit and the secret of our worship. Make our love for him a power by which [we] are assisted in venerating him. O God, make our veneration of him the life of our hearts, by which we stand and are assisted in remembering him, and in remembering his Lord":

> His being, God's peace and blessing upon him, is the spirit of everything in the universe, and there is no existence for anything without him, even for the non-believers. A second (higher) degree of his being the spirit for all created things is something not common to all, but special to some. This second degree is the spirituality (*rūḥāniyya*) of all gnostics, truthful ones, saintly poles, prophets, messengers, and any brought close (to God). This spirituality of his is that by which they stand in the presence of God the Exalted, fulfilling His rights and perfecting their comportment (*adab*) with Him. It is that by which they obtain effacement in the eye of the gathering (*ʿayn al-jamʿ*), by which they drown in the oceans of oneness. In this station, they are to God, by God, in God, from God, and for God; unblemished by other or otherness. There is nothing in the entirety of their senses, suppositions, imaginations, remunerations, or perceptions except God the Exalted, the One. There is no thought that occurs to them other than God in this station. The heart like this can be described as the sanctified house (*al-bayt al-muḥarram*) into which God has forbidden anything else from entering. This steadfastness of theirs is (a gift) from God because of the Prophet's spirituality in them.[73]

This explanation is significant, as it demonstrates that the ultimate goal of this form of concentration on the Prophet's essential reality is not the worship of the Prophet, but rather the more perfect worship of God.[74] Al-Tijānī encouraged the recitation of the prayer *yaqūtat al-ḥaqāʾiq* specifically for the actualization of true monotheism (*tawḥīd*): "Whoever recites this prayer twice in the morning and twice in the evening will have all of his sins forgiven, large and small, whatever their extent; and no delusion will befall him in (his understanding of) divine oneness (*tawḥīd*)."[75] For al-Tijānī, the *Ṭarīqa Muḥammadiyya* did not replace annihilation (*fanāʾ*) in God with annihilation in the Prophet.[76] Rather, connection to the spiritual reality of the Prophet was the means to attain annihilation in God, the means by which to better worship God.

The understanding of the Prophet's enduring spiritual presence presupposes the idea that the Prophet is possessed of a life beyond the grave, a notion summarized most clearly by the Egyptian scholar Jalāl al-Dīn al-Suyūṭī (d. 1505).[77] Fritz Meier summarized "orthodox" opinion on the subject by the 16th century, expressed by al-Suyūṭī, as suggesting that: "Muḥammad is alive in the spirit and the body, that he moves about freely and travels wherever he wishes on the earth and in the supernatural world (*malakūt*), that he still looks as he was before death, but that he eludes the external eye like the angels and is only visible to those for whom God lifts the veil by means of special grace. And the latter do not then simply see a likeness but they behold the Prophet himself."[78] Al-Tijānī clearly held as self-evident this understanding of the Prophet as a perceivable presence in both spirit and body. In explanation of the Prophet's saying, "God returns my soul to me to return the greeting" of one who offered prayer upon him, al-Tijānī said:

> The Prophet, God's blessing and peace upon him, is alive in his grave in his noble bodily presence (*bi-dhātihi al-sharīfa*), as he was in the worldly abode. But his spirit (*rūḥ*) is always in the Holy Presence, for all eternity. The meaning of his life in the grave is that the spirit extends, by its light, to the body from the Holy Presence. And this is the same with the life of the gnostics (in their graves). . . . And the meaning of his life in his grave is that the spirit reaches the body in the grave by its light from the holy presence.[79]

Both body and spirit of the Prophet were alive. While the Prophet's body remained in his grave, divine light, as al-Tijānī's earlier statement above indicates, clothed his being in different veils: sometimes as spirit, sometimes as intellect, sometimes as heart, sometimes as the material world, and sometimes as bodily form. Perhaps for this reason, al-Tijānī recommended another prayer he received directly from the Prophet, "the jewel of perfection" (*jawharat al-kamāl*), describing the Prophet as "the brilliant light filling all places of existence": "One recitation is equivalent to three times all the creations' glorification of God. Whoever reads it seven times or more, the spirit of the Prophet is present with him . . . who persists in reading it seven times before sleeping . . . will see the Prophet (in his dream)."[80] In other words, the Prophet's divine light could be perceived as present in both spirit and bodily form. But the ability to perceive him depended on the purity of the perceiver, facilitated by the transformative power of the "prayer on the Prophet." Seeing the Prophet was a natural result of the actualization of an individual's human potentiality, the realization of the light and gnosis in his own spirit as the reflection of the Muḥammadan reality.

The Vision of the Prophet and Disciple Verification

In explaining the verse of the Qur'ān, "At every moment, He [God] is involved in an affair,"[81] Aḥmad al-Tijānī (d. 1815, Fez) related to students the following story:

> It is said that (Aḥmad) al-Rifāʿī,[82] may God be pleased with him, was once teaching in his learning circle. Someone whom he did not know asked him, "What is the meaning of *At every moment, He is involved in an affair*?" He became perplexed and did not know how to respond, so he said nothing. That night in his sleep, he saw the Prophet, and he asked him about the verse. He said to him, "Affairs that He causes to appear, not that are presented to Him." When he returned to teaching the next day, the same man came to ask him again. So he told him, "Affairs that He causes to appear, not that are presented to Him." The man responded, "May God's blessing and peace be upon (the Prophet) the one who said that." And it was then made known (to al-Rifāʿī) that the petitioner was Khiḍr.[83]

The immediate context for this discussion is the explanation of God's unique oneness (*aḥadiyya*), such that no matter in creation is independent of God's fashioning. The shaykh nonetheless integrated reference to past visionary experience in an explanation of orthodox Sunni theology (*ʿaqīda*). The implication was clear: the Prophet Muḥammad has been intimately involved in the intellectual development of the Muslim world since his disappearance from the earthly abode in the 7th century.

It is difficult to exaggerate the importance of visionary experience for the foundation of the Tijāniyya Sufi order. For al-Tijānī, the denial of this ability to learn directly from the Prophet was an undervaluation of the Prophet's rank.

> Know that the Prophet used to impose general rules on the general populace (*al-ʿāma*) during his lifetime. Thus, when he declared something unlawful, it became unlawful for everyone. When he prescribed something, he prescribed it for everyone. This was the case for all the manifest rulings of the sacred law.
>
> In addition to all of these general rulings, he used to instruct the elite (*al-khāṣṣa*) with special knowledge (*khāṣṣa*), and he used to single out certain of his companions and not others for certain affairs. This is something well-known and thoroughly recorded in the traditional reports concerning him.
>
> When he was transferred to the abode of the Hereafter, the situation was therefore the same as it had been during his life in this world. He had begun to entrust to his community the special command for the elite, but without modification of the general command given to everyone. Modification of the general command ceased with his death, while the flood of his grace (*fayḍahu*) persisted in providing the special command to the elite.
>
> Whoever imagines that all of his support for his community came to an end with his death, as in the case of other dead men, he is ignorant of the Prophet's rank. He is guilty of treating him indecently, and he is therefore in danger of dying as an unbeliever if he does not repent of his deluded conviction.[84]

Al-Tijānī's articulation of the Prophet's spiritual reality was clearly not meant as an abstract theorization: the description of this reality was necessary to properly respect the rank of the Prophet. The denial of the Prophet's enduring support to his community, indeed to the universe at large, was a serious concern.

Al-Tijānī's encounters with the Prophet, in his "noble bodily form" (*al-dhāt al-sharīfa*), thus appear in Tijānī sources as the logical conclusion of the Sufi tradition's long-standing understanding of the "Muḥammadan reality" and the actualization of true knowledge. The later Tijānī scholar ʿUmar Tāl quoted from the explanation of al-Dabbāgh in *al-Ibrīz* to explain the spiritual implications of seeing the Prophet:

> If a person should obtain the witnessing of the Prophet's bodily presence (*dhāt*) in a waking state, he will have obtained security from the wiles of Satan. For he will have met with the [embodiment of] God's mercy, our master and prophet Muḥammad. His meeting with the Prophet's noble bodily presence (*al-dhāt al-sharīfa*) is the cause for his true knowledge, by the Real, Glorious is He, and his witnessing of God's eternal divine essence. This is because he finds the Prophet's noble bodily presence disappearing in the Real, enraptured in witnessing God. By the blessing of [witnessing] the Prophet's noble bodily presence, the saint remains devoted to the Real, and ascends in the knowledge of God bit by bit. He will then acquire the [complete] witnessing [of God], the secrets of gnosis, and lights of divine love.[85]

After al-Tijānī's waking encounter with the Prophet, disciples claimed they learned from him "what we had not heard before in regard to the (Islamic) sciences and the secrets."[86] Perhaps most significantly for disciples, affiliation to the Tijāniyya appeared to provide them with a procedure for direct access to the spiritual being of the Prophet, verified through their own respective experiences.

The role of visionary experience in the foundation of the Tijāniyya Sufi order, though perhaps marked by certain historical distinction, certainly was not unprecedented. The vision of the Prophet Muḥammad has played a surprisingly significant role in providing guidance and inspiration to the Muslim community from the time of the Prophet's passing to the present day.[87] According to Ignaz Goldziher: "It is no uncommon thing in Islamic literature to find both theological doubts and questions of practical controversy solved by the decision of the Prophet, who appears in a dream . . . decisions which extend as well to isolated cases affecting individuals, as to matters affecting the interests of the community at large."[88] Such decisions related to the appearance of the Prophet include reconciliation between feuding companions after the Prophet's death,[89] political tolerance toward Christians,[90] the Muslim conquest of Spain,[91] the foundation of the Ashʿarī theological school,[92] matters pertaining to the ritual prayer,[93] sobriety in Sufi practice,[94] or the emphasis on loving the Prophet: "He that loves God must have loved me."[95] Here is an example from the wider Islamic scholarly tradition, related in this case by the ḥadīth scholar, theologian, and Shāfiʿī jurist Ibn Ḥajar Haythamī (d. 1566, Mecca): "It is related that a saint attended a session directed by a jurist. While the latter was citing a hadith, the saint interrupted him: 'This *ḥadīth* is false.' The jurist then asked him, 'Where did you get that?' and the saint replied: 'The Prophet is here and he is standing before you! He says that he never uttered these words!' At that moment, the jurist had an unveiling and [he also] saw the Prophet."[96] This possibility of verifying knowledge through seeing the Prophet was, according to al-Haythamī, "among the graces bestowed to saints as confirmed by al-Ghazālī, Bārazī, al-Tāj al-Subkī, al-ʿAfīf al-Yāfiʿī among the Shāfiʿīs, and Qurṭūbī and Ibn Abī Jamra for the Mālikīs." In other words, it was an accepted occurrence within orthodox Sunni scholarship at least by the 16th century. Such visions perhaps reflected "a more general epistemological suspicion of written knowledge" among Muslim scholars, but some of the most accomplished visionaries—such as ʿAbd al-Ghanī al-Nābulusī and Shāh Walī-Allāh—were also some of Islam's most prodigious writers.[97] Aside from Suyūṭī's opinions mentioned above, there were several important expositions of encountering the Prophet by Islamic scholars before al-Tijānī.[98] An early defense of the Tijāniyya from Mauritania foregrounded the justification for seeing the Prophet and sourced the verification of the practice to the "greatest of scholars": famous Sufis like al-Ghazālī and Ibn al-ʿArabī as well as the Mālikī author of *al-Madkhal*, Ibn al-Ḥājj al-ʿAbdarī al-Fāsī (d.1336, Cairo), and the Egyptian Shāfiʿī scholar Jalāl al-Dīn al-Suyūṭī (d. 1505).[99]

Visionary encounters with the Prophet, whether experienced by al-Tijānī or his close disciples, played a variety of functions in the foundation of the Tijāniyya. They served as sources for special prayers, provided testimony to the blessing of the Tijāniyya, and communicated teachings from the Prophet to al-Tijānī, to be shared with his students. Tijānī sources provide intimate details about these experiences of al-Tijānī and of several important disciples. There is often no reference to whether an encounter (*liqāʾ*) or witnessing (*ruʾyā*) occurred in a waking or dreaming state. According to the early Tijānī text, *al-Jaysh al-kafīl*, the experiences of the Prophet's companions are enough to prove that witnessing the unseen world, such as angels or the spirits of the Prophets, while in a waking state is a verifiable reality. Here al-Shinjīṭī refers to the famous ḥadīth where the Angel Gabriel appeared to the Prophet in the company of his companions to "teach them their religion." "In denying the vision, the veiled ones say, 'The spirit is part of the celestial world, and celestial is not perceived by [those in] the earthly [realm]' . . . but did not the Prophet's companions see the Angel

Gabriel with their own eyes in while in this earthly abode?"[100] Clearly the Tijānī understanding followed that of al-Ghazālī and Ibn al-ʿArabī, that higher forms of spiritual unveiling allowed a person to perceive the unseen in a waking state the same way others did in their sleep. According to Ibn al-ʿArabī, "The person who undergoes unveiling sees while he is awake what the dreamer sees while he is asleep."[101] Ḥarāzim observed that al-Tijānī rarely distinguished between dreaming and waking visions: "His sleeping became like his waking . . . these states of the distinguished folk are due to the victory of their spirit (*rūḥ*) over the bodily presence (*dhāt*), for the spirit is purity at its source."[102] As demonstrated later on, Ḥarāzim and other disciples also experienced similar states.

The Visionary Experiences of Aḥmad al-Tijānī

There is no doubt that Aḥmad al-Tijānī's own visionary experiences inspired disciples to both follow him and to experience visionary realization themselves. The most cherished vision was of course the encounter with the Prophet Muḥammad, but such experiences could also include meeting other Prophets, past saints, angels, or perceiving special prayers written on sheets of light. Sources speak to al-Tijānī's visionary experience in four broad categories: guidance in worldly affairs, instruction in religious or spiritual knowledge, reception of special prayers or invocations, and assurances of saintly rank. This latter topic is the subject of chapter 4.

Sufism necessarily stressed the aspirant's emptiness of worldly concerns in order to attain spiritual perfection. Al-Tijānī insisted, "As for the one connected to the divine presence, his state does not permit him to be occupied with [anything] other than God."[103] Visionary experience as it relates to worldly affairs thus ideally manifested the Sufi's desire to remember God in the process of his unavoidable involvement in the world. Exploration of this type of visionary experience provides interesting insight into the particular worldly challenges a Sufi may have faced in the process of occupying himself only with God.

The most obvious quandary al-Tijānī faced was the matter of wealth or worldly provision. Early in his life, al-Tijānī had a visionary encounter with Prophet Moses (Mūsā), where he asked him about his nephew Korah (Qārūn) who turned his back on God because he had acquired immense wealth.

> I saw our master Moses, in the form of our Prophet (*ʿalā nabīnā*) upon him blessing and peace, and I said to him, "We have heard that Qārūn saw the place where you wrote the Greatest Name (of God) that you threw into the sea to reveal the grave of our master Joseph (Yūsuf), upon him peace. (It is said that) Qārūn took the Greatest Name from that place where you wrote it, and that he would cast it over the locations of (buried) treasures, so that they appeared to him. From this he obtained immense wealth." Moses said to me, "Yes (it is true)." So I asked him, "Does the knowledgeable one of God have a choice between wealth and poverty (*al-fiʿl wa l-tark*)?" He said to me, "Yes indeed, if he has obtained such a spiritual station."[104]

Later in his life, al-Tijānī did indeed become wealthy—so much so that the daily amount he gave in charity was considered one of his saintly miracles (*karāmāt*).[105] Nonetheless, he was reportedly scrupulous about the sources of his income. He only accepted the lodging the Moroccan sultan provided for him after the Prophet appeared to him and gave him permission to accept it, provided the shaykh gave away in charity what he would have paid for the house.[106]

Al-Tijānī's visionary experiences thus played an important role in his day-to-day affairs, although he was sometimes hesitant to seek guidance on worldly matters directly. ʿAlī Ḥarāzim, himself no stranger to visions of the Prophet, nonetheless remarked with obvious admiration: "The Prophet guaranteed for him whatever he asked, even with regards to worldly affairs."[107] But al-Tijānī was apparently shy to ask the Prophet directly about such concerns, and often requested Ḥarāzim to serve as an intermediary. As Aḥmad Sukayrij explained: "The greatest of the unique Muḥammadans (*al-afrād al-Muḥammadiyūn*) employed intermediaries between themselves and the Prophet in order to ask him what they wanted. They were unable to address him directly due to the intensity of their modesty (*ḥayāʾ*) before him, and their absorption in his beauty when meeting him. They would forget themselves and all of their needs in his presence."[108] In this way, al-Tijānī once asked Ḥarāzim to petition the Prophet to leave Fez and relocate to Syria due to the hostility of some of the city's scholars to the new Sufi order.[109] Here was the Prophet's response for Ḥarāzim to relay to al-Tijānī:

> As for the response that you requested from me, I say to you: I know of this matter that has preoccupied your heart concerning residence

> in the lands of the East, and the state of constriction and apprehension visited upon you by your residence in the West (*al-Maghrib*). But I inform you truthfully with something contrary to what you have heard from the mouths of people: know that the leaders and princes of the people of the East have no Islam, no religion, no honor (*ʿahd*) and no covenant (*mīthāq*). Corruption has prevailed in all of their lands: including open wine drinking, fornication, and appropriation of peoples' wealth. And if they do not desist contravening the Real, His religion, and His messenger, surely God will give the Christians victory over them.[110]

The Prophet thus ordered al-Tijānī to stay in Fez and to appreciate the security and blessing with which he was surrounded. Visionary experience clearly played an important role in al-Tijānī's worldly movements.

Like other Muslim scholars before him, al-Tijānī's visionary experience sometimes helped him answer questions pertaining to Islamic law or religious knowledge more broadly. For example, the Prophet appeared to him to allay obsessive juristic doubts over the purity of water used for ritual ablution.[111] On another occasion, there was a question concerning the ruling on giving the alms tax (*zakat*) to an unjust, oppressive ruler. The Prophet cursed such rulers, but told al-Tijānī not to withhold the tax from them.[112] Al-Tijānī's more significant independent legal judgments (*ijtihād*) were sometimes influenced by visions of the Prophet. The shaykh advised followers, contrary to the Mālikī legal school that most of them followed, to recite the *basmala* ("In the Name of God . . .") out loud before the rest of the Qur'ān's opening chapter when the ritual prayer was to be recited. The adoption of the Shāfiʿī opinion in this matter was because, according to what the Prophet told him, there was a secret name of God contained in the *basmala* and what followed.[113]

The Prophet's visionary intervention in al-Tijānī's use of Sufi prayers was remarkably thorough. Al-Tijānī explained this to his followers by saying, "We do not make any remembrance except that God's Messenger has arranged it for us."[114] This statement comprehended the wide range of Sufi prayers, some of which were explored in chapter 2, that al-Tijānī integrated into the practice of his new order from prior initiations.[115] The most central prayer of the Tijāniyya, the "Prayer of Opening" (*ṣalāt al-fātiḥ*), was sourced to the sixteenth-century Egyptian saint Muḥammad al-Bakrī through the obscure seventeenth-century Shādhilī prayer collection, the "Bosom Rose" (*wardat al-juyūb*). Al-Bakrī allegedly was given the prayer by an angel on a sheet of light after spending "a long time in devotion to God, asking Him for the best way to invoke blessings on the Prophet, in which was found the reward and secret of all invocations."[116] Al-Tijānī told Ḥarāzim:

> I was preoccupied with reciting the "Prayer of Opening what was Closed" (*ṣalāt al-fātiḥ limā ughliq*) when traveling to Tlemcen on the way back from pilgrimage, due to what I saw of its merit. As mentioned in the "Bosom Rose" (*Wardat al-juyūb*), one recitation is equivalent to six hundred thousand of any other invocation (of blessing on the Prophet). The author of *Wardat al-juyūb* said that its composer was Muḥammad al-Bakrī al-Ṣiddīqī of Egypt. This saintly pole (*quṭb*) said, "Truly, whoever recites the 'Prayer of Opening' once and does not enter Paradise, let him hold its author accountable before God."[117]

The narration continues that al-Tijānī then left *ṣalāt al-fātiḥ* for another invocation of blessing on the Prophet, only to have the Prophet appear to him and command him to return to it, saying "No one has invoked blessing on me with anything better than *ṣalāt al-fātiḥ*."[118] The Prophet informed him of its ultimate merit: "one recitation of it is equal to all the glorification of God that has ever occurred in the creation, every remembrance, and every supplication, large or small, and to the Qur'ān six thousand times, as the Qur'ān is included among the remembrances." The later Moroccan Tijānī scholar Muḥammad al-Naẓīfī's four-volume commentary on *ṣalāt al-fātiḥ* summarized the shaykh's dispersed statements on the subject to say that the best of all merits of the prayer was that the reciter would "die in the religion of Islam,"[119] and that *ṣalāt al-fātiḥ* was the "secret of all prayers on the Prophet," and thus equal in reward to 600,000 times any other invocation of blessing.[120] According to al-Tijānī, the Prophet was aware of *ṣalāt al-fātiḥ* during his life, but he did not share it with his companions (*ṣaḥāba*)—although they received the reward of *ṣalāt al-fātiḥ* together with the reward of all good deeds of the Muslims who came after them. The Prophet knew that "its appearance would not come in their time, so did not mention it to them . . . for God, knowing the weakness of the people of this time [of al-Tijānī], and the burden of distraction and corruption upon them, had mercy on them, and bestowed on them abundant reward for a simple good deed."[121]

Al-Tijānī insisted that this extraordinary merit was only for those who recited the prayer with permission from him or his inheritors, and who had certain faith that it was God's own prayer on the Prophet.[122] Unlike other earlier prayers, the Prophet's visionary confirmation to al-Tijānī of *ṣalāt al-fātiḥ* may have rescued it from relative obscurity. As mentioned in chapter 1, the Egyptian Khalwatiyya seems to remember al-Tijānī as the "owner" (*ṣāḥib*) of the prayer. The contemporary popularity of *ṣalāt al-fātiḥ* outside of the Tijāniyya (in the Shādhiliyya, Naqshbandiyya, or Murīdiyya) usually can be traced to contact with the Tijāniyya, where a Tijānī shaykh might transmit the prayer to a non-Tijānī scholarly peer. The famous Moroccan scholar Muḥammad b. Jaʿfar al-Kattānī (d. 1927), for example, opened every lecture with the recitation of *ṣalāt al-fātiḥ*.[123] He traced his authorization to do so from his teacher in the Islamic sciences, the Tijānī shaykh Aḥmad al-Bannānī (d. 1889), "the highest scholar of his time" in Fez, who gave permission to al-Kattānī in the prayer despite his student's lack of formal initiation into the Tijāniyya.[124] Indeed, there is no record of Sufi communities prior to al-Tijānī paying much attention to the prayer, notwithstanding those associated directly with al-Bakrī, such as the scholar-saints of Timbuktu earlier mentioned. Al-Tijānī himself claimed, "There is no one on the face of the earth that is able to grant permission in this (*ṣalāt al-fātiḥ*) except me, or one who has entered among my companions in the *ṭarīqa*."[125]

There were of course other prayers the Prophet allegedly gave to al-Tijānī that were entirely unknown to the previous Sufi tradition. The most famous of these was the "Jewel of Perfection" (*Jawharat al-kamāl*), which when recited a certain number of times brought immense reward: "the Prophet will love him with a special love, and he will not die until he becomes one of the saints."[126] Two other prayers al-Tijānī obtained directly from the Prophet included the aforementioned "Ruby of Realities" (*Yaqūtat al-ḥaqāʾiq*), and the "Invocation of the Unseen concerning the Aḥmadan Reality" (*ṣalāt al-ghaybiyya fī l-ḥaqīqa al-Aḥmadiyya*). According to the *Jawāhir al-maʿānī*: "Our master the Messenger of God, blessing and peace upon him, granted these prayers from his noble flooding grace (*min fayḍihi l-sharīf*) in a state of wakefulness to our Shaykh Abū l-ʿAbbās (Aḥmad al-Tijānī)."[127] More precisely, the prayers are attributed to a divine inspiration (*waḥy*) delivered to al-Tijānī in the presence of the Prophet. Concerning *ṣalāt al-ghaybiyya*, al-Tijānī explained, "It is so named because it emerged from the unseen (*al-ghayb*): it was not composed by anyone."[128] Such accounts suggest that al-Tijānī continually reminded his disciples that it was the Prophet himself who had arranged their Sufi practices.

The intensity of al-Tijānī's waking encounter in Abū Samghūn that served as the foundation for the Tijāniyya was such that later Tijānīs sometimes considered the Prophet Muḥammad as the real shaykh of their Sufi path. ʿUmar Tāl thus suggested that al-Tijānī's path was the *Ṭarīqa Muḥammadiyya* because the Prophet was the true "guarantor" for al-Tijānī's disciples: "He is their guarantor (*al-ḍāmin*), and the patron of their affair in a special way. Every one of them [Tijānīs] has written between his eyes the seal of the Prophet, 'Muḥammad the Messenger of God,' and on his heart and back, 'Muḥammad the son of ʿAbdallāh.' And on his head is a crown of light, on which is written, 'The *Ṭarīqa Tijāniyya*, founded on the Muḥammadan reality.' "[129] Indeed, after al-Tijānī illumination at the Prophet's hands, Tijānī sources claim that the Prophet kept the shaykh constant company. According to Ibn al-Mashrī, "He informed me that (Muhammad) the master of existence never departs from him at any time, and this is the greatest of all miracles."[130] A later source explains: "Among the graces with which God honored him was the waking vision of the Prophet, continuously and ever, so that it was never absent from him for the twinkling of an eye. And he was honored with being able to ask the Prophet anything and seeking counsel from him in small and weighty matters. And he underwent training at his hands. This is the highest of all graces granted to the people of knowledge."[131] This claim appears more subtly in the *Jawāhir al-maʿānī*. When asked about the statement of Abū l-ʿAbbās al-Mursī (d. 1287, Alexandria), the inheritor of the Abū l-Ḥasan al-Shādhilī, "Were the Prophet to be veiled from me for the blink of eye, I would cease to count myself among the Muslims," Ḥarāzim reports al-Tijānī's response: "This specialty was not only for al-Mursī, but it belongs to the 'pole of poles' (*quṭb al-aqṭāb*) in each time. Since his occupying the chair of axial sainthood (*quṭbāniyya*), there is never a veil between him and God's Messenger. Indeed, since the majesty of God's Messenger appeared in the presence of witnessing from the presence of the unseen, the eye of the 'pole of poles' has taken up residence in witnessing him. He is not veiled from him for a moment."[132] As the next chapter discusses, the *quṭb al-aqṭāb* was among the saintly positions of which the Prophet assured al-Tijānī. The intriguing reference to the enduring reality of *quṭbāniyya* perpetually gazing at the Prophet emphasizes the position's persistent reality in creation, and perhaps a distinctive doctrinal contribution of the Tijāniyya to the concept.

In any case, by the time ʿAlī Ḥarāzim finished writing the *Jawāhir al-maʿānī* in 1798, al-Tijānī had taken to concealing these visionary encounters, along with his saintly miracles (*karāmāt*) more generally.[133] After narrating a number of visions of the shaykh, Ḥarāzim explained, "He had numerous visions, but these were the ones for which I was present in the beginning of his affair. As for now, he does not mention any of them, except very rarely . . . these days, praise to God, the Prophet (simply) informs him of his spiritual station (*maqām*), and God's covenant in it."[134]

The Visionary Experiences of al-Tijānī's Disciples

Several close disciples of Aḥmad al-Tijānī played important roles in elaborating the distinction of their shaykh and of the new Sufi order he transmitted. There is no doubt that several of these disciples had their own unique personalities and reputations for saintliness, perhaps only rivaled among their saintly peers by al-Tijānī himself. Once, a future disciple, ʿAlī Amlās, entered the Tijānī *zāwiya* in Fez. Upon seeing him, al-Tijānī said, "I saw that man among the council of saints (*dīwān al-awliyāʾ*), but I do not know his name." After initiation in the Tijāniyya, al-Tijānī remarked that Amlās had reached a spiritual station only attained by three saints every thousand years. Even so, when Amlās was presumptuous enough to don al-Tijānī's turban when visiting him in his house, he experienced such intense divine manifestation (*tajallā*), that he stood "with his eyes bulging out of his head from the secret that it had contained," and became ill for some time.[135] Adnani reads these sorts of interchanges as an early challenge or testing of al-Tijānī's spiritual claims by prominent disciples, many of whom had already developed their own saintly reputations; thus representing a series of "difficulties encountered by disciples disorientated by the rank of Ahmad al-Tijānī."[136] This may have been partially true: disciples clearly sought to verify al-Tijānī's claims for themselves. But disciple articulations appear to stress not only their successful verification of these claims, but also the opportunity these claims provided for their further, personal spiritual realization. This opportunity explains, in my opinion, Adnani's second identified tension in the early Tijāniyya: that between various elite disciples of al-Tijānī who competed for proximity with the shaykh.[137] Noteworthy here is not that people tested and disagreed with each other within the context of Sufi realization—human beings are after all human beings—but that such controversies were reconciled into a cohesive narrative of positive spiritual verification and actualization. The visionary experience of disciples in fact became a key means of the Tijāniyya's popularization. This section focuses on two such prominent disciples but first considers the general contours of disciples' visions and spiritual experiences.

Disciples appear in sources first of all as earnest seekers of their own spiritual realization. The ability to meet the Prophet was certainly a primary source of attraction to the new order. The Tunisian scholar Ibrāhīm al-Riyāhī (d. 1850) made his first request upon entering the Tijāniyya at the hand of ʿAlī Ḥarāzim in 1802, "the continuous vision of the Prophet, God's blessing and peace upon him, without doubt or confusion."[138] After his establishment in Fez, even the Moroccan sultan Mawlay Sulaymān (d. 1822) sought out al-Tijānī in order to meet the Prophet.[139] After becoming al-Tijānī's disciple, the imam at the mosque of Mawlay Idrīs, Muḥammad b. Aḥmad al-Sanūsī (d. 1841), used to periodically become quiet while teaching the ḥadīth collection of al-Bukhārī. When asked why, he said that at those times the Prophet would appear to him, and he would become silent in the awe of the Prophet's presence.[140] Another scholarly disciple in Fez, Aḥmad Bannīs, was cured from a grave illness after seeing al-Tijānī in the presence of the Prophet.[141] Another close disciple, ʿAbd al-Wahhāb b. Aḥmar, saw al-Tijānī after his passing with the Prophet in the Tijānī *zāwiya*, saying to him, "Here you are, and here is your Prophet."[142] Tijānī sources claim that the Prophet appeared to al-Tijānī to tell him of his love for all of al-Tijānī's disciples, as earlier mentioned. Muḥammad al-Ghālī, himself a descendant of the Prophet, reportedly heard directly from the Prophet after becoming a disciple of al-Tijānī, "You are the son of the beloved, and you have taken the *ṭarīqa* of the beloved."[143] In another instance, the Prophet allegedly guaranteed complete gnosis and grand illumination for ten of al-Tijānī's most elite disciples.[144]

Several disciples testified to their love of al-Tijānī through their own saintly miracles. Ibn al-Mashrī, known in Tijānī sources as "the jurist" (*al-faqīh*), once was riding through the desert and passed the tomb of a non-Tijānī saint. The hooves of his horse sank in the sand, and he was unable to pass until he called out to the saint in his tomb, "By God, if you do not free my horse, I will complain about you to the Shaykh whose power of disposition is in you."[145] ʿAlī al-Tamāsīnī (d. 1844), the shaykh's designated successor after his death, used to visit al-Tijānī in Fez, teleporting himself from eastern Algeria with "one step." Al-Tijānī reprimanded him: "If you desire connection to me for the sake of God, do not come to me except by the external rules of the common folk."[146] Prohibited from visiting his shaykh so quickly, al-Tamāsīnī resorted to teleporting gifts to al-Tijānī. Once fresh dates appeared on the shaykh's prayer rug in front of a congregation. At his disciples' surprise, al-Tijānī said, "This is the doing of that man, the joker (*bahlūl*)," meaning al-Tamāsīnī, who was in Algeria at the time. When the shaykh later saw his disciple, he asked him, "What got into you?" He said, "My master, please forgive me. At the time, I was in my garden, and a servant brought me fresh dates. They pleased me greatly when I saw them, and I wanted them to arrive to you still fresh. This idea overcame me, so I threw them to you." Once again, al-Tijānī reminded al-Tamāsīnī to refrain from such open miracles.[147]

Other disciple experiences communicated lasting understandings to subsequent followers of the Tijāniyya. Muḥammad al-Ghālī (d. 1829, Mecca), the later initiator of ʿUmar Tāl in Medina Arabia, once saw al-Tijānī in a dream after his passing. He said to his shaykh, "My master, you have gone away and left us." Al-Tijānī told him, "I am not absent from you, nor have I left you. I have only been transferred from the earthly abode to an abode of lights."[148] Indeed, al-Tijānī had told another student Aḥmad Kallā Bannānī while he was still alive, "My disciple (*ṣāḥibī*) is never absent from me for the blinking of an eye."[149] Later Tijānī scholars were no doubt influenced by such narrations in their general conclusion, "This is among the saintly miracles of our master, that his spiritual energy (*himma*) is with the disciple wherever he is."[150] But it was the disciples' ability to meet the Prophet directly that helped popularize the Tijāniyya. Such capacity is best demonstrated by two of al-Tijānī's disciples: Muḥammad al-Damrāwī and ʿAlī Ḥarāzim.

Muḥammad b. al-ʿArabī al-Tāzī al-Damrāwī

The end of the second volume of Ḥarāzim's *Jawāhir al-maʿānī* contains an intriguing account of one disciple, the Algerian Muḥammad b. al-ʿArabī al-Damrāwī (d. 1798), who used to experience the waking vision of the Prophet Muhammad twenty-four times every day. The Prophet came to al-Damrāwī and recited for him a poem, told him to memorize the verses and recite them to al-Tijānī. Included in the poem were the following verses:

> By the truth of the truth you see God's reality . . .
> Drown yourself in the sea of Divine oneness, and you will see
> His oneness
> Veils will be lifted until you see what is not real by its opposite.

Later the Prophet came again to al-Damrāwī to provide an explanation: "Listen to what I tell you, and memorize what you hear from me concerning these verses I previously ordered you to memorize. Write their meaning with certainty, and give it to al-Tijānī. Tell him . . ." What follows is a lengthy explanation, interspersed with the sort of exhortations a master would give his disciple: "Tell him to exert effort in worship and contravening his carnal self (*nafs*)." Or, "Tell him that the people of divine manifestation (*ahl al-tajallā*) are those who inherit my spiritual station (*maqām*)."[151]

This intriguing account suggests that disciples participated alongside the shaykh in visionary experience. Such participation meant that disciples sometimes assisted the shaykh in the realization of knowledge, or least served as the means by which al-Tijānī learned from the Prophet. It seems that al-Tijānī's space for spiritual retreat in Abī Samghūn was divided in two, one room for al-Tijānī and another for al-Damrāwī.[152] On one occasion, the Prophet told al-Tijānī to visit al-Damrāwī and treat him kindly, as "he has a right upon you."[153] But the commendation was mutual. Once al-Damrāwī expressed his love for al-Tijānī to the Prophet. The Prophet revealed to him, "If not for this love of yours for al-Tijānī, you never would have seen me."[154]

Al-Damrāwī's visionary experiences in fact mirrored those of al-Tijānī in many ways. His visions similarly provided him with guidance, knowledge, prayers, and insight into spiritual stations. Despite his young age, he was considered al-Tijānī's inheritor (*khalīfa*), to whom al-Tijānī sometimes sent his disciples to learn from. On one occasion, al-Tijānī sent his companion al-Ḥājj Musaqqam to al-Damrāwī. Musaqqam's horse died on the way, but then al-Damrāwī sent a spirit (*rūḥānī*) at his command to enter the horse and bring it back to life. When Musaqqam reached his destination, al-Damrāwī called the spirit out and the horse collapsed.[155] Clearly, al-Damrāwī might have asserted his own claim to sainthood and gathered about him his own circle of students had he so desired.

Otherwise, al-Damrāwī's own story was quite different from al-Tijānī's.[156] He did not have a scholarly training. Before finding al-Tijānī, he was affiliated to a branch of the Shādhiliyya passing through Ibn ʿAzūz, a famous esotericist from Marrakech whom al-Tijānī famously labeled "the Satan of this [Muslim] community" for his misuse of talismans and other occult sciences. After obtaining illumination at al-Tijānī's hands, al-Damrāwī's beautiful countenance became the talk of ʿAyn Māḍī, the birthplace of al-Tijānī where he had come to reside. Some of the townsmen, rivals to the Tijānī family,[157] eventually could no longer bear their wives' incessant admiration for al-Damrāwī, so they murdered him. It was only after his death that ʿAlī Ḥarāzim became known as al-Tijānī's *khalīfa*, and himself played an increasing role as visionary intermediary between al-Tijānī and the Prophet.

Al-Damrāwī is perhaps best known in the Tijāniyya for having received special prayers from the Prophet in his various waking encounters. Among those who knew him best was Ibn al-Mashrī, who testified: "When he became illuminated by the greatest treasure, the waking encounter with the master of all nations, our master Muḥammad, God's blessing and peace upon him and his family, there emerged from him strange secrets and wondrous methods, such that intellects were astounded."[158] The context for Ibn al-Mashrī's description was namely al-Damrāwī's drafting of the prayer, *Yāqūtat al-maḥtāj fī ṣalāt ʿalā ṣāḥib al-miʿrāj* ("The Ruby of Necessity in the Prayer on the Master of Ascension").[159] This prayer on the Prophet is essentially a collection of different invocations of blessing on the Prophet arranged according to the letters of the Arabic alphabet. By way of example, one stanza reads: "O God, send blessings and peace on our master and prophet and patron Muḥammad, and upon the family of our master Muḥammad; for every tear that falls from every eye, furrowing the cheeks in fear of God."[160] According to Ibn al-Mashrī, al-Damrāwī recorded the prayer at the Prophet's dictation, with ease and in beautiful Arabic without reference to any book, despite al-Damrāwī's own lack of book-learning. "I knew him since he was young," Ibn al-Mashrī remarked, "and I know that he was not acquainted with the craft of writing or the arrangement of words. So I learned that he was taught from the ocean of overflowing grace."[161] Ibn al-Mashrī would later compose a commentary on this prayer, called *al-Sirāj al-wahhāj*.[162] When asked about the prayer's merit, al-Damrāwī simply related what the Prophet told him about it: "Pass it to the believers for them to read it, and encourage them to do so, for they will derive benefit from it if God wills." But later al-Damrāwī added, "Whoever persists in reading it, he is guaranteed without doubt to see the Prophet either in a dream or while awake."[163]

Another prayer of the Tijāniyya sourced to al-Damrāwī was the secret "Circle of Lights" (*Dawr al-anwār*), the transmission of which was apparently restricted to the elite of the shaykh's companions. The content of this prayer is not contained in published sources. Aḥmad Sukayrij only refers to the prayer cryptically:

> Praise to God, I happened upon a great treasure in his [al-Damrāwī's] blessed handwriting. It was a letter he wrote to our master [al-Tijānī],

> may God be pleased with him. In it, he informed him that he had received authorization from the Prophet in a secret among secrets: the "circle of lights" that no one would obtain unless God had foreordained he would be one of the chosen. He mentioned to him some of the great specialties of this prayer, and matters that should not be written here unless delusional imbeciles should come upon it.[164]

Elsewhere Sukayrij emphasized that the Prophet commanded al-Damrāwī "to provide it [*dawr al-anwār*] to our master (al-Tijānī), along with its explanation."[165] Sukayrij makes clear he himself had the prayer. There is also evidence of the prayer's continued transmission among select followers of Ibrāhīm Niasse (d. 1975, Senegal).[166] While neither the "Ruby of Necessity" or the "Circle of Lights" were among the foundational prayers of the Tijāniyya, al-Damrāwī certainly represented the disciple's potential to receive his own prayers through visionary experience. The fact that al-Tijānī readily received these prayers from disciples demonstrates his cultivation of spiritual experience as a participatory medium shared between shaykh and disciple.

There is also indication that the knowledge al-Damrāwī received from visions was incorporated into the Tijānī tradition. Once al-Damrāwī was asked whether animals will enter Paradise or just humans. He related: "I was perplexed by their question, and knew not how to answer. Then I met the Prophet and I asked him about this. He informed me that some would indeed enter Paradise, they being the animals of the prophets, messengers, and saints, and the animals that died in jihad, and those ridden in the pilgrimage, and others like this who died in the way of God."[167] In any case, continued the Prophet to al-Damrāwī, this Paradise was not like the Paradise for those of intellect, but was filled with lush meadows and other things loved by animals. Al-Damrāwī described this encounter in a letter to al-Tijānī; and the later Tijānī tradition narrated al-Damrāwī's experience as part of its primary sources.

ʿAlī Ḥarāzim al-Barrāda

Similar to al-Damrāwī, ʿAlī Ḥarāzim's visionary experience played an important role in the elaboration of the practice and doctrine of the Tijāniyya. Most significantly, Ḥarāzim also served as an occasional intermediary between the Prophet and al-Tijānī. According to the *Mashāhid*, al-Tijānī entrusted him with posing certain difficult questions to the Prophet, in addition to the more mundane queries mentioned above. Examples of such questions included the relationship between the divine names and the angels connected to them, or whether or not the reward for the utterance of the angels created from a human's recitation of the prayer *ṣalāt al-fātiḥ* was awarded to the reciter in addition to the reward he received for his own recitation. The Prophet's answer in this latter case was that God created the angels at the moment of the prayer's recitation, without any other reason. The reciter received this reward even after death, since the angels created at his recitation continued to invoke blessings on the Prophet until the end of time.[168]

ʿAlī Ḥarāzim's *Mashāhid* contains more everyday details of the close relationship between the Prophet and al-Tijānī. As mentioned above, Tijānī sources conceptualize al-Tijānī's use of Ḥarāzim as an intermediary with the Prophet as being due to al-Tijānī's respect for the Prophet, and his being shy to query him about trivial matters. The contemporary shaykh al-Tijānī Cissé further explained that the Prophet used Ḥarāzim as an intermediary as a further grace to al-Tijānī, just as God had used the Angel Gabriel as an intermediary with the Prophet to facilitate communication without the weight of direct manifestation, "even though God can certainly speak with the Prophet directly."[169] In any case, the *Mashāhid* chronicles the Prophet's guidance to al-Tijānī in all manner of affairs, from warning specific disciples from talking too much,[170] to encouragement for the construction of the main Tijānī lodge (*zāwiya*),[171] to advice on when and where to travel (such as the Prophet's prohibition of moving to Syria as mentioned above). Much of the Prophet's worldly advice to al-Tijānī was bracketed by a warning concerning the corruption of the age. Al-Tijānī should avoid unnecessary talk, for example, because "evil has gained sovereignty (*istawā*) over this age (*zamān*), and oppression and injustice have proliferated."[172]

These passages appear to reveal an intimate shaykh-disciple relationship that existed between the Prophet and al-Tijānī through visionary experience, in this case witnessed by al-Tijānī's own disciple Ḥarāzim. For example, the Prophet had apparently become aware of an unbearable heat in al-Tijānī's body as a result of certain litanies. Ḥarāzim related to al-Tijānī:

> I was reciting my litany (*wird*) in the middle of the night after performing two prayer cycles, and he [the Prophet] came and said to me: "O ʿAlī, tell your shaykh and your teacher that we have come to know

> by touch (*lams*) of the heat that has overwhelmed (*fāḍat*) him in a great flood, so that he has come to fear destruction. But that is a result of the recitation [of God's greatest name] that he has been reciting. Surely with this recitation the heat will increase beyond what he has previously experienced."[173]

Here al-Tijānī's human frailty was on display: his body suffered from the weight of God's secret "greatest name" to the point he feared the recitation might destroy him. The Prophet encouraged him to continue nonetheless. The Tunisian scholar Ibrāhīm al-Riyāḥī would later tell of a related experience of Ḥarāzim himself. After leaving Fez for his last trip to the Ḥijāz, Ḥarāzim came to stay with al-Riyāḥī in Tunis. He told al-Riyāḥī not to enter his room until he had finished his remembrance. After some time, al-Riyāḥī became worried and entered to find no one there. After some time, Ḥarāzim came out of the locked room and explained, "When a gnostic recites the greatest name (of God), he dissolves (*yadhūb*), and when he finishes, he returns as he was."[174] In other words, Ḥarāzim apparently experienced a similar intense manifestation through God's greatest name that overwhelmed his physical condition.

But the heat in al-Tijānī's body, according to the *Mashāhid*, had a further secret beyond God's greatest name. In another vision with the Prophet, Ḥarāzim related to al-Tijānī the underlying reason for the heat:

> Know, my master, that I saw the Prophet, God's blessing and peace upon him, sitting on your right side on the couch. He smiled at you and his light emerged from his honorable breast and pervaded your whole body and every hair of your head. He said, "O ʿAlī, tell your master and your shaykh that he has been complaining for some time about the increasing heat [in his body]. But I advise him to be patient. I have not revealed to him the truth of the matter, but I will do so now. . . . Say to him, 'Have I not informed you time after time that I do not depart from you for the blink of an eye? And if I do not separate myself from you, and my light is always with me, never separating from me, then my light is the permanent state of your bodily presence (*dhāt*). It will never pass, and will remain for all eternity. And know that my light is always increasing and ascending. This heat will always increase due to the intensity of my light's inhabitation (*ḥulūl nūrī*) of your bodily presence.' "[175]

The shaykh experienced heat in his body (*jism*) because the Prophet's light had come to dwell inside his bodily presence (*dhāt*). This passage of course speaks to the notion of knowledge as light coming to inhabit the human presence. The nature of true human actualization is here revealed as the inhabitation of the Prophet's light inside an individual, an inhabitation that burned away the self's impurities.

Ḥarāzim's visions are meant to serve as witness to the extraordinary intimacy between the Prophet and al-Tijānī. This intimacy included certain expressions of human fallibility. Al-Tijānī thus confided that he had earlier sometimes felt distracted during his remembrance of God. Ḥarāzim included in the *Mashāhid* a letter he found from al-Tijānī. Al-Tijānī wrote: "I expressed my regret to God and His Messenger, God's blessing and peace upon him, that I was unable to make my heart present in all of the litanies the Messenger had ordered me to persist in reciting."[176] The Prophet told him to focus on two particular acts of worship: two extra prayer cycles and reciting a special prayer of glorification called "the key of axial sainthood" (*miftāḥ al-quṭbāniyya*). Al-Tijānī wrote: "I supplicated (God) by the grace and generosity of God's Messenger, until the Prophet said to me that, with the performance of these two prayer cycles and the glorification, I would obtain the station of the 'Pole of poles' and the 'greatest of unique ones' (*al-fardāniyya al-ʿuẓmā*). Even if my performance was only by the recitation of my tongue and devoid of the presence of heart, I would nonetheless obtain the aforementioned goal."[176] This rare passage, together with the reference to bodily constraint above, reveal the very human concerns of al-Tijānī even as he ascended through the greatest of spiritual stations. Of course, such accounts invoke a certain human vulnerability common to Islamic sainthood. The Prophet in fact communicates his warning in this regard to al-Tijānī through Ḥarāzim, "You know that no servant [of God] is infallible (*maʿṣūm*). Even if he is among the elect, or has the highest of spiritual ranks, he is not infallible."[177] But to fairly contextualize Ḥarāzim's inclusion of such passages, these accounts should be read in dialogue with others pointing to al-Tijānī's exemplary conduct and spiritual focus. For Tijānī disciples, the momentary lack of presence in al-Tijānī's remembrance was the result of his absorption in God, not ordinary negligence. As Ibrāhīm Niasse quotes al-Wāsitī (d. 932) to say, "Those who remember His remembrance are more heedless than those who forget His remembrance, for the remembrance is other than He."[178]

The *Mashāhid* is thus an invaluable resource for the examination of notions of spiritual authority at the foundation of the Tijāniyya. Aside from containing disciple testimony to al-Tijānī's spiritual claims, the work models shaykh-disciple relations that remain the core practice of any Sufi community. Most explicitly, ʿAlī Ḥarāzim demonstrates the importance of disciple experience in the formation of such communities. On several occasions, the Prophet interceded with al-Tijānī on behalf of Ḥarāzim. For example, the Prophet appeared to Ḥarāzim and ordered him to tell al-Tijānī the following: "We have commanded the servant (*khadīm*) ʿAlī Ḥarāzim to act by our command on your behalf . . . and I have told you more than once that he is from me, and I am from him. He is under my protection and guardianship, and this is a grace from God and a pre-eternal divine decree. Also, he is the intermediary for you in [dispensing] all that comes to you from God and from me. You must honor him when he comes to you, even though he is your servant and your disciple."[179] The disciple's role as an active participant in the reception and elaboration of a new Sufi order is here advanced by the Prophet himself. Elsewhere the Prophet informs al-Tijānī, "O Aḥmad, know that we have given permission to the servant ʿAlī Ḥarāzim in all three degrees of [the prayer] 'the opener of what was closed' (*salat al-fatih lima ughlaq*): its apparent degree, its hidden degree, and the hidden of hidden degrees. In each of these three degrees his permission is comprehensive and everlasting."[180] The remarkably pervasive presence of the Prophet in the life of al-Tijānī and his disciples is difficult to miss. Here the Prophet sometimes took on the role of initiator of the shaykh's own disciples; and in some cases, used them to initiate the shaykh. In the *Mashāhid*, ʿAlī Ḥarāzim attests that he found "an old paper" on which al-Tijānī had written, as if to remind himself: "My path is the *Ṭarīqa Muḥammadiyya*, given to me by the Prophet, from him to me. And my disciples are his disciples."[181] According to the twentieth-century Moroccan Tijānī scholar, al-Aḥsan al-Baʿqīlī (d. 1949), the direct connection to the Prophet was among the conditions of the Tijāniyya: "Whoever enters this path and is veiled from him for even one breath, he should repent to God, knowing that he left a condition of the *ṭarīqa*."[182] While this exaggeration was probably not taken literally by most Tijānīs, there is no doubt such direct connection to the Prophet has remained a central preoccupation for many within the Tijāniyya.

Conclusion

Analysis of human potentiality and visionary experience at the foundation of the Tijāniyya lends itself to provocative conclusions concerning realization of the human condition. For Tijānīs, the Tijāniyya is the fullest actualization of *Ṭarīqa Muḥammadiyya*: it owes its entire existence to the direct intervention of the Prophet Muḥammad in visionary encounters. This chapter has demonstrated that disciples, not only al-Tijānī himself, played formative roles in testifying to the reality of this new Sufi order through their own visionary experiences. Al-Tijānī and key disciples such as al-Damrāwī and Ḥarāzim were recipients of special knowledge, poetic verses, advice, warnings, and special prayers that the Prophet often ordered them to exchange with each other. Sometimes the Prophet interceded between the shaykh and specific disciples. Indeed, the Prophet once appeared to al-Tijānī to order him to reconcile with a disciple whom he distanced, and to promote him as a lieutenant (*muqaddam*) of the Tijāniyya.[183] Al-Tijānī's *Ṭarīqa Muḥammadiyya* was thus most explicitly a methodology of *taḥqīq*: both in terms of human actualization and spiritual verification. Significantly, both the shaykh and his disciples participated in this path of verification.

The visionary experience alluded to here was clearly not limited to the Tijāniyya, but rather unfolds within an apparent popularization of "true visions" in the seventeenth and eighteenth centuries. According to ʿAbd al-Ghanī al-Nābulusī's magisterial work on dreams and visions, *Taʿṭīr al-anām*, the Prophet once said in hadith, "Whoever does not believe in the true vision (*al-ruʾyā al-ṣāliḥa*) does not believe in God and the last day."[184] When Muṣṭafā al-Bakrī (the shaykh of Maḥmūd al-Kurdī, who earlier initiated al-Tijānī into the Khalwatiyya order) received spiritual authorization from al-Nābulusī in a vision and later sought to confirm with his teacher in person, al-Nābulusī reprimanded him: "I gave you permission. I gave you permission. The two worlds are one."[185]

However, visionary experience in Sufism, the Tijāniyya notwithstanding, was still largely confined to the realm of saintly miracles (*karāmāt*). In other words, such experiences did not take the place of learning from living teachers, and they certainly could not justify the contravening of the sacred law. The Tijāniyya laid particular emphasis on hiding miracles, and al-Tijānī was widely cited as saying, "An act of righteousness is better than one thousand miraculous fetes."[186] Elsewhere al-Tijānī defined the best of saintly miracles as the saint's continuous increase in "gnosis, love, and divine proximity."[187] The later renowned Tijānī shaykh Ibrāhīm Niasse thus emphasized to disciples, "The one who experiences visions is not better than the one who does not."[188] Elsewhere Niasse articulated remarkably similar sentiments to those of al-Ḥasan al-Yūsī concerning visionary experience earlier cited, writing: "These visions that are counted among glad tidings (*mubashshirāt*) are considered in secret, for they do not change the external rules, as is well known in the established sacred law (*sharīʿa*)."[189] In another letter, Niasse was more emphatic: "We [Tijānīs] are the Malāmatī masters, and we are concerned with concealing spiritual stations (*maqāmāt*) and leaving aside saintly miracles (*karāmāt*). Whoever has a vocation is occupied in it, and whoever has work is busy with it. We do not make claims to any special merit or peculiarity. We are not concerned with contravening normality or gaining information by spiritual unveiling, for all of this is but the menstruation of saints (*ḥayḍ al-rijāl*)."[190] The notion that the saint cannot avoid miracles but must hide them was well established in the prior Sufi tradition,[191] and indeed at the foundation of the Tijāniyya. Al-Tijānī and his close disciples mostly exchanged accounts of their visionary experiences in personal correspondence. When meetings with the Prophet were made public, these were normally at the express command of the Prophet himself. Similarly, the Prophet later commanded al-Tijānī to stay silent about his unceasing visionary encounters with the Prophet.[192]

There seems little benefit then in comparisons of visionary experience between various Sufi saints, except to recognize certain trends and elaborations over time. The appearance of the Prophet at the foundation of the Tijāniyya may have been distinctive in terms of frequency and intimacy expressed, but it was not unprecedented. Visionary experiences are more valuable for the insights they provide into notions of saintly authority within a given Sufi community, and especially the relationship between shaykh and disciple. Visionary experience for the early Tijānī community demonstrates the surprising accent on individual human actualization for both al-Tijānī and his disciples. Notions of saintly authority, formulation of Sufi litanies, and religious and worldly knowledge were all articulated in dialogue between the founding shaykh and his close students.

This chapter has argued that visionary experience was the result of a more general discourse on human actualization, which may be described as a version of "Islamic humanism" as it referenced a universal human condition. Indeed, ʿUmar Tāl's central Tijānī text *al-Rimāḥ* admits of non-Muslims being capable of miracles such as walking on water and seeing the unseen.[193] It is an intriguing coincidence to find this notion of an Islamic humanism, which invoked a common humanity between Muslims and non-Muslims, articulated on the very eve of the Muslim world's political eclipse and occupation by non-Muslim Europe. It may be that such an orientation allowed many Muslims to live peacefully and actually spread Islam under colonial occupation, emphasizing shared discourses of justice and human dignity over religious exclusivism. As Ibrāhīm Niasse would remark at the end of French colonialism in West Africa: "A believer can live for a long time with those of no faith, but he will not last long with the unjust."[194] The present-day scholar al-Tijānī b. ʿAlī Cissé explained his understanding of the Tijānī perspective, "Islam is a religion of virtue and reconciliation toward the whole of the human race . . . the religion of Islam is a religion of tolerance and mercy that encompasses the entirety of humankind," and this through the realization of a "higher humanity" in emulation of the Prophet Muḥammad.[195] Islamic humanism, though based in the idealized potentiality of the human creation, also could be seen as a practical orientation that might facilitate peaceful interaction between Muslims and non-Muslims. The argument here is not that Muslims of "realized human potentiality" never go to war or never disagree with others. Reichmuth points out that "respect for human dignity" cannot be prescribed "by legal or political means" but "remains bound to the credibility and reliability of human relations, and even more to their mutuality."[196] The breakdown of human relations, as with instances of mutual respect and cooperation, is an apparent historical inevitability. The eighteenth-century articulation of an Islamic humanism is all the more noteworthy *because* it came at a time of immense political and social uncertainty.

CHAPTER FOUR

The Seal of Muḥammadan Sainthood and Hidden Pole

Toward the end of his life, some visitors asked Shaykh Aḥmad al-Tijānī, "If your companions have been given what has not been given the greatest axial saints (*aqṭāb*), where does that leave you?" He responded, "I am nothing but a poor man (*miskīn*)."[1] As a manifestation of divine favor rather than individual merit, Islamic sainthood never set itself in opposition to human frailty. Claims to high spiritual rank are thus not inconsistent with the humility inseparable from the human condition, reflecting divine bestowal rather than personal ascription. "The meaning of *miskīn*," al-Tijānī explained, "is contained in the Prophet's words, 'O God, raise me among the needy (*iḥyanī miskīnan*).' It is the locus of God's gaze in His creation."[2] As the focus of divine "gaze," the saint and his claims were not to be taken lightly. Al-Tijānī warned his contemporaries: "We do not take the sanctity (*ḥurma*) of our saintly masters lightly, and we are not negligent in venerating them. Whoever venerates the sanctity of the saints, both alive and dead, God will exalt his own sanctity. Whoever disparages them, God humiliates him and is angry with him. We do not overlook the sanctity of the saints."[3] Al-Tijānī's own assertions of paradigmatic sainthood must be read in this context: although they were meant as an expression of divine grace rather than personal merit, they were also meant to be taken seriously. And as the visitors' question reveals above, such expressions foregrounded the spiritual aspiration of disciples. Al-Tijānī's claim to be the "Seal of Saints"—the most perfected saint from the beginning till the end of time—did reference an elaborate saintly hierarchy, but in the end, it defined itself mostly in terms of what it provided to aspirants on the new "Muḥammadan Way."

The spiritual claims that emerge from within various Sufi traditions cannot simply be dismissed as individual hagiography. Islamic sainthood was a profoundly participatory medium in which disciples and lay affiliates invested their own aspirations for divine proximity, salvation, and even worldly reputation. Al-Tijānī's alleged saintly rank has no doubt become a key identity marker for millions of Tijānī Muslims. Moreover, the complexity of al-Tijānī's claim cannot be understood as a simple vulgarization of earlier Sufi thought from the "golden age" of Ibn al-'Arabī. As a significant crystallization of eighteenth-century intellectual vibrancy, the Tijāniyya certainly represents the fruition of a highly developed saintly cosmology.

Shaykh al-Tijānī was not the first to claim to be the Seal of the Saints, but he may have been the last to put forth the claim with such coherency.[4] He consciously drew on earlier articulations of perfected sainthood, especially the understandings of Ibn al-'Arabī, but went further in emphasizing the saintly seal's unequaled vicegerency from the Prophet Muḥammad. To explain the seal's intimate proximity to the Prophet, al-Tijānī developed the concept of the "Hidden Pole" (*al-quṭb al-maktūm*) as a spiritual station beyond that previously articulated in the Sufi tradition. While al-Tijānī's own statements were of course formative to these ideas, later Tijānī scholars also played important roles in explaining such claims to wider audiences. Al-Tijānī's perceived spiritual rank certainly appealed to adherents of the Tijāniyya, but this rank was immediately translated into specific benefits to Tijānī disciples more broadly. This chapter considers precedent understandings, al-Tijānī's own claims, the understandings of later scholars, and the assurances offered disciples in order to understand the meaning of sealed sainthood within the Tijāniyya.

The Saintly Seal in Earlier Sufism

Paradigmatic sainthood has been a consistent theme within most Sufi orders, even those, like the Shādhiliyya, Naqshbandiyya, and Qādiriyya, whose primary sources do not normally mention the notion of a "Seal of Saints." Over the centuries in any case, the concept of the seal became widespread enough among prominent Sufi intellectuals for Ibrāhīm Niasse to claim that the Muslim community was "united on its existence."[5] Invocations of the concept normally revolved around a few key thinkers such as Ḥakīm al-Tirmidhī, Ibn al-'Arabī, Muḥammad Wafā, and 'Abd al-Wahhāb al-Sha'rānī. The writings of these earlier scholars explored certain central themes that Tijānī sources would also develop: intercession, knowledge, relationship to Prophecy, and divergent understandings of the word "seal." Tijānī sources regularly reference such earlier expositions.

Ḥakīm al-Tirmidhī (d. 905–910), a Sufi and hadīth scholar from central Asia, was the first to leave a written description of the "Seal of Saints." Al-Tirmidhī said he had smelled the perfume of this spiritual position, but made no definitive claim to the rank himself.[6] As a ḥadīth scholar, he did not publicly associate himself with any notable circle of Sufis and attempted to conceal his writing on the subject,[7] no doubt anticipating the censure of those who might misinterpret his text as claiming equality between saints and prophets. After writing the *Kitāb sīrat al-awliyā'*, he allegedly threw the book in the sea (according to some Tijānī narrations), only to have it later wash up on a distant shore.[8] In any case, al-Tirmidhī's ideas would later become the starting point for discussion of the concept.

The Seal of Saints, in al-Tirmidhī's rendering, is distinguished by ultimate sincerity on the path of the Prophet Muḥammad. God bestows on him this station, "the highest rank of the friends of God," as a gift "from the treasuries of [sincere] exertion (*sa'ī*)." Al-Tirmidhī explained: "There are three sorts of treasuries: the treasuries of saintly favor, the treasuries of exertion for this leading Imam, and the treasuries of proximity to the Prophets, upon them peace."[9] In other words, God favored him (to treat the second of the treasuries first) by "sealing" his personal exertion, by guarding him from his own carnal soul (*nafs*) and from the devil. "The life of this Friend of God follows the path of Muhammad. He is purified and then refined. Then Friendship with God is bestowed on him, then his Friendship with God is sealed so that the carnal soul and the Enemy may not have access to what he has been honored with."[10] He is the "Seal of Saints" first of all because God has sealed, or guarded, his purity from his own *nafs*. Such refinement results in singular proximity to the Prophet Muḥammad, causing him to carry the weight of God's praise: "He is the trustee of the list of saints and their leader. He upholds the praise of his Lord, in the presence of God's messenger. The Messenger takes pride in him in this station, and God extols him with His Name in this rank. He becomes the delight of the Messenger's eye."[11] The treasury of "proximity to the Prophets" is sealed with this rank. The Seal of Saints is the most beloved of the Prophet, and thus the leader of all saints in the presence of God. As such, the seal comes forth on the Day of Judgment as the saintly exemplar against whom all other saints are evaluated for the favors they were given.

> Then God will send a Friend whom He has chosen and elected, whom He has drawn unto Him and made close, and He will bestow on him everything He bestowed upon the [other] friends but He will distinguish him with the seal of Friendship with God (*khātim al-walāya*). And he will be God's proof against all the other Friends on the Day of Judgement. By means of this Seal, he will possess the sincerity of Friendship with God the same way that Muḥammad possesses the sincerity of Prophethood. The Enemy [Satan] will not speak to him and the carnal soul will not find the means to seize its share of the Friendship with God. . . . The Station of Intercession will be set up for him and he will praise his Lord with such praise and commend Him with such commendation that the Friends of God will recognize his superiority over them with regard to knowledge of God.[12]

The Seal of Saints thus "seals" a third treasury, that of "saintly favor." These themes of self-purification, proximity to the Prophet, and the exemplary repository of saintly favor, are themes that also define paradigmatic sainthood within the Tijānīyya many centuries later.

The "Greatest Shaykh" (*shaykh al-akbar*) Muḥyī l-Dīn Ibn al-ʿArabī further developed the concept of the Seal of Saints and apparently claimed the title for himself.[13] Scholars such as Chodkiewicz have done remarkable work in untangling Ibn al-ʿArabī's statements on the subject, but the fact remains that the relevant primary source material can be read in a variety of ways. Ibn al-ʿArabī himself famously admitted, "We are the people whose books should be forbidden to outsiders."[14] His writings nonetheless made notable contributions to the concept, later emphasized by the Tijānī tradition. Above all, Ibn al-ʿArabī emphasized the saintly seal's guardianship of the "house of sainthood," the seal's knowledge of God, his spiritual reality pre-existent to the creation of physical bodies, and multiple definitions of the "Seal of Saints."

The Seal of Sainthood, for Ibn al-ʿArabī, is first of all the fullest expression of sainthood. This saint guards God's bestowal of sainthood similar to the exemplary proof of sincerity in al-Tirmidhī's rendering. According to Ibn al-ʿArabī: "If the house were without a seal, the thief would come unexpectedly and kill the child. Verify this, oh my brother, by considering him who protects the house of sainthood."[15] Thus protected from the carnal soul's attempted theft, or self-ascription of divinity, the Seal of Saints is the greatest of all Friends of God: there is no saint "who is not subordinate to him."[16] His light was created before the creation of physical forms: "The Seal of the Saints was a saint when Adam was still between water and mud, whereas the other saints only became saints when they fulfilled the conditions of sainthood."[17] He is not the last saint before the end of time, but his understanding of God is unrivaled: "The Seal is not called the Seal because of the moment in which he appears, but because he is the person who most completely realizes the station of direct vision."[18] In other words, he most fully actualizes the knowledge of God (*maʿrifat Allāh*): "The Seal of Muḥammadan Sainthood is the most knowledgeable of created beings on the subject of God."[19]

The "Seal of Muḥammadan Sainthood" is distinguished, according to Ibn al-ʿArabī, from the "Seal of General Sainthood," namely the Prophet Jesus. Ibn al-ʿArabī also mentions the existence of a third seal, "the Seal of [Adam's] children," the last of the human race to be born in China.[20] Later scholars would further develop the concept of multiple saintly seals, but it was Ibn al-ʿArabī's expansion of the concept that no doubt inspired later formulations. Although Ibn al-ʿArabī claimed in his magisterial *Futūḥāt al-Makkiya*, "I am without doubt, the Seal of Sainthood,"[21] the same text contains an intriguing passage referring to the seal of Muhammadan Sainthood as other than himself. He claims to have met this seal in Fez, Morocco, and that he was an Arab, "one of the noblest in lineage and power." Ibn al-ʿArabī continues, "I saw the sign which is exclusive to him and which God has hidden away in him from the eyes of His servants, but which He revealed to me in the town of Fez in order that I might perceive in him the presence of the Seal of Sainthood." He goes on to say that God would test him "by exposing him to the criticism of people."[22] Chodkiewicz reads Ibn al-ʿArabī's claim to be the seal in preference to this strange encounter in Fez and holds Ibn al-ʿArabī's claim to the title as irrefutable.[23] However, Chodkiewicz's assertion that Ibn al-ʿArabī's meeting with the seal in Fez came before his own claim to the position is impossible to prove, as both narrations appear in the same text (*Futuḥāt*). Tijānī scholars were not alone in believing, despite their profound respect for the "Greatest Shaykh," that Ibn al-ʿArabī's claim to be the Seal of Saints was relative to his time, or that the unique Seal of Saints was other than him.

Sufi scholars from the fourteenth to seventeenth centuries who mentioned the Seal of Saints made significant contributions to the topic, but most agreed that the title did not exclusively belong to Ibn al-ʿArabī.[24] The eastern commentator on Ibn al-ʿArabī's work, ʿAbd al-Razzāq al-Qāshānī (or Kāshānī, d. 1330, Samarqand) wrote that the Seal of Saints was "the person through whom the welfare of this world and the next is attained to perfection," but that this position was relegated to the savior at the end of time: "He is the rightly guided one, the *Mahdi*, the one who is promised at the end of time."[25] Muḥammad Wafā' (d. 1363, Cairo), originally of the Shādhilī Sufi order but whose son 'Alī (d. 1405) formalized and added to his father's teachings as the Wafā'iyya order, gave an alternative elaboration, and claimed the title for himself. Muḥammad Wafā' saw himself as "Seal of the age,"[26] a reflection of Muḥammad as the perfect human: "The human secret and the silent reality appear in every secret, and are included in every knowledge which has neither been known nor taught until the Seal of sainthood; and the fixing from all the tidings are deposited in trust with him; and faces turn to him from all directions."[27] 'Alī Wafā' thus explained that the Seal of Saints "exists thanks to the Seal of Prophets." Wafā' further added to Ibn al-'Arabī's notion of multiple ways in which the term "Seal of Saints" could be used and insisted that the Prophet's son-in-law 'Alī b. Abī Ṭālib was also a saintly seal. But he nonetheless upheld his father's claim to be the "greatest saintly seal."[28]

The Egyptian scholar 'Abd al-Wahhāb al-Sha'rānī (d. 1565, Cairo), one of Ibn al-'Arabī's foremost "later advocates,"[29] reconciled the competing claims of Ibn al-'Arabī and the Wafā'iyya by suggesting that each age was graced by a Seal of Saints: "Many men of sincere spirituality have claimed to occupy this office of Seal. It seems to me that at every epoch there is a Seal."[30] Al-Sha'rānī avoided the apparent contradictions in Ibn al-'Arabī's writings on the subject by criticizing those Sufis who studied the works of Ibn al-'Arabī instead of engaging in devotional acts: only the accomplished gnostic should read such writings.[31]

It may be that the paradigmatic sainthood claimed by other saints, such as that by the Indian Naqshbandī master Aḥmad Sirhindī (d. 1624), was akin to Ibn al-'Arabī's concept of the Seal of Saints.[32] Otherwise, Sirhindī seems to insist that the paradigmatic sainthood claimed by the likes of 'Abd al-Qādir al-Jilānī (and Ibn al-'Arabī by extension) applies to the people of his time, not all times.[33] Similarly, the North African Shādhiliyya-Jazūliyya, by the sixteenth century, articulated a notion of paradigmatic sainthood, the axial "bell saint" (*al-jaras*), that fully reflected Muḥammad as the Perfect Human. According to Vincent Cornell, Muḥammad al-Jazūlī (d. 1465, Marrakesh) saw himself the Perfect Human (*al-insān al-kāmil*), whose grasp encompassed all Muslim scholars.[34] Although they do not use the words "Seal of Saints," both Sirhindī and al-Jazūlī appear to suggest that their own ranks were above any previous saint.

The scholarly networks from the late seventeenth to eighteenth centuries were likewise not unfamiliar with the concept of the Seal of Saints. Ibrāhīm al-Kurānī's teacher Aḥmad al-Qushāshī held that the Seal of Saints was a "divine level" or station in which "we have lived."[35] The twentieth-century Moroccan scholar Idrīs al-ʿIrāqī thus included al-Qushāshī—along with Ibn al-ʿArabī, ʿAlī Wafā, and Muḥammad al-Jazūlī—among those who had claimed the position of Seal of Saints prior to al-Tijānī.[36] But the larger point was that many scholars had previously believed that the rank was not restricted to Ibn al-ʿArabī. ʿAbd al-Ghanī al-Nābulusī apparently followed al-Shaʿrānī in believing that every age possessed a "Seal of Saints": "He is the Seal of Saints," al-Nābulusī said of Ibn al-ʿArabī, "in his time." And like al-Qushāshī, al-Nābulusī, as attested by his grandson Kamāl al-Dīn al-Ghazzī, seems to have claimed the rank for himself.[37] According to al-Nābulusī's biographer Elizabeth Sirriyeh, "ʿAbd al-Ghanī considered himself as a new Seal of Saints."[38] There is no doubt that claims of paradigmatic sainthood proliferated in a variety of forms in the eighteenth century, as in previous ages. The Indian mystic and poet Mir Dard thus claimed that his father Nāṣir ʿAndalīb, who was said to receive the *Ṭarīqa Muḥammadiyya* in a waking encounter with the Prophet's grandson Ḥasan b. ʿAlī, was "the First of the Muḥammadans, and the top-rose of the bouquet."[39] Muḥammad al-Sammān considered his own Shaykh Muṣṭafa al-Bakrī as the "Seal of Sainthood," and some of al-Sammān's own followers claimed the position for al-Sammān himself, although the claim cannot be substantiated in al-Sammān's own words.[40] The mystical utterances (*shaṭaḥāt*) attributed to al-Sammān may be, according to Muthalib, an expression of absorption in the Muhammadan presence: thus, "I am Muḥammad whom you seek," and "I am the pure light; other saints are enlightened by my light."[41] In any case, al-Sammān clearly articulated a version of paradigmatic sainthood similar to that of Ibn al-ʿArabī, al-Nābulusī, and ʿAndalīb. The dominant opinion within eighteenth-century *Ṭarīqa Muḥammadiyya* networks thus appears to have been that Ibn al-ʿArabī's claim to be the Seal of Saints was not exclusive of future claims.

The notion of the Seal of Saints was widespread enough by the eighteenth century for the Indian scholar resident in Cairo, Murtaḍā al-Zabīdī (d. 1791), to include some commentary on the concept: "The Seal according to the people of divine reality is the one by whom is sealed Muḥammadan sainthood. The other type of Seal is he who seals general sainthood."[42] This general definition clearly echoes that given by Ibn al-ʿArabī, but it permits of claims to the title after Ibn al-ʿArabī, especially as Zabīdī forwards no precise claim that the title belonged to Ibn al-ʿArabī. The West African Qādirī scholar ʿUthmān b. Fūdī (d. 1817) thus used the vocabulary liberally in verse: "We have been sealed with his [the Prophet's] honor between the two worlds. We are completely dissolved from devotion to [the] Prophet Muḥammad."[43] Ibn Fūdī's grandson ʿAbd al-Qādir b. Muṣṭafa ("Dan Tafa"), perhaps articulating the consensus of Ibn Fūdī's community in following the opinion of al-Qāshānī above, nonetheless held that the true identity of the Seal of Saints was none other than the Mahdi (Ibn Fūdī did not consider himself to be the ultimate Mahdi[44]). Dan Tafa thus declared himself party to secrets "which none will disclose except the Muḥammadan Seal, the Mahdi, upon him peace."[45]

Another West African shaykh of the Qādiriyya (who claimed to be Ibn Fūdī's master on the Sufi path[46]), Mukhtār al-Kuntī, believed otherwise. Al-Kuntī was cited in his son's *al-Ṭarāʾif wa l-talāʾid fī dhikr al-shaykhayn al-wālida wa l-wālid* to say that the Seal of Muḥammadan sainthood (who was other than the Mahdi) would appear in his own time, the twelfth century after the Hijrah, or end of the eighteenth century: "In it [this century] there will appear the Seal of Saints, just as in his [the Prophet's] century there appeared the Seal of Prophets." Al-Kuntī added that this seal's companions would be like the Prophet's companions in remaining steadfast with the truth, but that where the Prophet's companions "believed in God alone and fought the misguided nations," the saintly seal's companions would "fight the carnal self (*nafs*), lust, and Satan in the greater holy war (*jihād al-akbar*)."[47] Tijānī scholars believed al-Kuntī, who appears never to have claimed to be the Seal of Saints himself, was speaking about none other than Aḥmad al-Tijānī. Even if many remained affiliated to al-Kuntī's legacy, his publicly circulated prediction no doubt played an important role in the reception of the Tijāniyya south of Morocco.

Aḥmad al-Tijānī as Seal of the Saints

According to his own testimony, Aḥmad al-Tijānī did not seek the position of "Seal of Saints," nor even of "axial sainthood" (*quṭbāniyya*) prior to his own illumination.[48] But he would have inevitably been exposed to the idea given its wide circulation, and there is evidence of a more direct exposure from his own travel notebook penned during or soon after his trip to Egypt and the Hijāz in 1774–75. Al-Tijānī copied down the response to a question concerning the hidden hierarchy of saints (*rijāl al-ghayb*), contained in a letter of a certain Yemeni scholar in the Hijāz considered fondly in the original text, the aforementioned Aḥmad Sālim b. Aḥmad Shaykhān Bā-ʿAlawī.[49] Sālim Bā-ʿAlawī wrote that there are fourteen "guarded ones" at any given time acting on behalf of the Prophets: one axial pole (*quṭb*), two imams, four "stakes" (*awtād*), and seven saintly "substitutes" (*abdāl*). The pole, imams, and stakes all act as deputies on behalf of four prophets: Idrīs, Jesus, Ilyās, and Khiḍr. Jesus is the seal of "general" sainthood, and after his return to earth near the end of time, there will be no saint after him. The seven *abdāl* are deputies on behalf of seven respective prophets: Ibrāhīm, Mūsā, Hārūn, Idrīs, Yūsuf, Īsā, and Adam. Bā-ʿAlawī later follows Ibn al-ʿArabī more closely, suggesting that there are forty other saints "on the heart" of Nūḥ at any given time, and three hundred on the heart of Adam: when one of them dies, he is replaced by another.[50] The text specifies the particular realms (sky, earth, sea, etc.) each rank is entrusted with guarding (*ḥifẓ*), the inner names (ʿAbdallah, ʿAbd al-Malik, ʿAbd al-Rabb, etc.) corresponding to each position. Next Bā-ʿAlawī writes: "The Seal (*al-khatim*) is the one, not in each time, by whom God seals special sainthood (*al-walāya al-khāṣṣa*), and he is the 'greatest shaykh.'"[51] This would first appear to be a reference to Ibn al-ʿArabī, but elsewhere Bā-ʿAlawī refers to the title *al-shaykh al-akbar* interchangeably with *al-khatim* as a saintly rank, in addition to other ranks such as the singular savior saint (*ghawth*) of each age, for example.[52] The text further elaborates a number of different saintly ranks under the seal and suggests that a supplicant can hope for God's response to his prayers through knowledge of this hidden saintly hierarchy.[53] Sukayrij quotes this same Bā-ʿAlawī, this time recorded in al-Muḥibbī's (d. 1699) *Khulāṣat al-athar*, "The Special Seal (*al-khatmiyya al-khāṣṣa*) is a divine rank that descends on anyone to whom it belongs when their time and age appears, and it is never interrupted until there is no one on the face of the earth saying the name of God."[54] Bā-ʿAlawī's opinions cannot be taken as representative of al-Tijānī's later understanding, but it does demonstrate al-Tijānī's broad interest in the hidden hierarchy of saints with specific reference to the "Seal of Saints," here described as a position beyond that of the singular, axial saint (*quṭb*, *ghawth*) of any given time, but not exclusive to Ibn al-ʿArabī.

The Tijāniyya quickly synthesized previous opinions about the saintly seal. There are actually four persons to whom this title could be applied,

Ibrāhīm Niasse later summarized: the seal of the age alive at any given time, the Mahdi, the seal of general sainthood (Jesus), and the "greatest seal" on the heart of the Prophet Muḥammad.

> As for the Greatest Seal, he is the Seal of Muḥammadan Sainthood, unique in all time. There can only be one after the time of the Prophet by whom God seals Muḥammadan sainthood in the unseen . . . the meaning of this station (*maqām*) is that no one, whether before or after, will appear with such saintly perfection, for he is the greatest seal on heart of the seal of prophets . . . among his signs is that he has come to actualize the spiritual experiences of all the saints. He is then distinguished from them by his own experience (*wijd*), just as the Seal of Prophets actualized the experiences of all prophets, and then was distinguished from them.[55]

For the Tijānī tradition, then, the opinions of Ibn al-ʿArabī, ʿAbd al-Wahhāb al-Shaʿrānī, Aḥmad al-Qushāshī, and ʿUthmān b. Fūdī were not mutually exclusive. Al-Tijānī also echoed Muḥammad Wafāʾ's consideration for ʿAli b. Abī Tālib as a type of seal, saying that he was unique among the Prophet's companions because of his knowledge of a greatest name of God special to him, a name that guaranteed axial sainthood (*quṭbāniyya*), and which was also revealed to Ibn al-ʿArabī, ʿAbd al-Qādir al-Jilānī, and al-Tijānī himself.[56] But clearly, the Tijāniyya followed most closely the articulations of Ibn al-ʿArabī about the exclusive "greatest seal," unique in all times and other than Jesus or the Mahdi.

Tijānī sources usually leave statements concerning al-Tijānī's rank in the mouth of the Prophet Muḥammad himself, through a variety of encounters with al-Tijānī. In other instances, al-Tijānī responded to the specific questions of disciples. Sometimes, significant understandings from the spiritual experiences of disciples were presented to al-Tijānī and confirmed by him, thus making their way into the primary sources of the Tijāniyya. Taken together, two themes emerge from the exposition of the Seal of Saints in Tijānī sources: the seal's unrivaled connection to the Prophet Muḥammad, and the ability of this saintly rank to benefit his followers.

"All shaykhs take from me," declared al-Tijānī, "from the time of the [Prophet's] companions until the resurrection." When asked how this could be possible when uttered by a man living thirteenth centuries after the Prophet, the shaykh extended his middle and index fingers joined together and said of the Prophet: "His noble spirit (*rūḥ*) and mine are like this.

From the beginning of creation, his noble spirit has given assistance to the messengers and prophets, and my spirit has given assistance to the poles, saints and gnostics."[57] The Seal of Saints is defined first of all, then, by proximity to the Prophet Muḥammad. In an encounter with ʿAlī Ḥarāzim, the Prophet gave a message for Ḥarāzim to relay to al-Tijānī: "Tell him that his station (*maqām*) is my station, and his state (*ḥāl*) is my state, and his degree (*martaba*) is my degree. Whoever harms him, harms me. And who disputes with him, disputes with me. And whoever disputes with me has picked a fight with me. And whoever fights me, God declares war on him."[58] Remarkable here is the jealous love of the Prophet for al-Tijānī. The Prophet thus warned him, "All the creation is an enemy to you because what we have given you."[59] But unlike the writings of Ibn al-ʿArabi, there is no ambiguity in Tijānī sources that this spiritual position is below that of Prophecy.[60] The Prophet tells al-Tijānī directly: "There is no spiritual station above yours except that of Prophecy."[61] In some instances, al-Tijānī further gave preference to the Prophet's companions over any other saints: "From Adam until the resurrection, no one has obtained our station except the [Prophet's] companions, indeed from before Adam."[62] Al-Tijānī defended the precedent rank of the Prophet's companions over all other saints on more than one occasion, in one case supporting his pronouncement with reference to the ḥadīth, "God has chosen my companions over all the worlds, except for the prophets and messengers." Al-Tijānī concluded, "Our good deeds compared to theirs is as the crawling louse compared to the flying bird."[63] From textual sources, it remains unclear whether al-Tijānī endorsed al-Dabbāgh's opinion (earlier referenced) that constant visions of the Prophet granted a later Muslim the same rank as the companions.[64]

Tijānī sources return frequently to the special relationship between the Prophet and al-Tijānī as the primary explanation of the shaykh's rank. Ibn al-Mashrī commented on al-Tijānī's claim to be the "Hidden Pole" (*al-quṭb al-maktūm*): "[It means that] no one has witnessed the reality of the station specific to him, except God the Exalted, and the master of existence [the Prophet Muḥammad], God's blessing and peace upon him."[65] Based on the Prophet's response to al-Tijānī's query about Ibn al-ʿArabī's knowledge of the *al-quṭb al-maktūm*, ʿAlī Ḥarāzim similarly summarized the Prophet's response: "The Prophet hid it [al-Tijānī's identity] from all of creation and he took exclusive possession of information concerning this *quṭb* and his position, his ascendancy, his proximity to God, and his time, his state, the station specific to him. For he is in the Prophet's hand and he did not show the specialty of this greatest inheritor to anyone."[66] By the time al-Tijānī had obtained the position of Seal of Saints and Hidden Pole—according to Tijānī sources—he had been ordered by the Prophet to keep quiet about his station.[67] But the Prophet's love for the shaykh still finds written expression in an encounter with Ḥarāzim, where the Prophet tells Ḥarāzim to inform al-Tijānī of the Prophet's direct address to the shaykh: "You are the imam over every axial saint (*quṭb*) in creation."[68] For Tijānī disciples, such direct dictations from the Prophet are unrivaled testimony to al-Tijānī's spiritual ascendancy beyond any other claimant to the position of Seal of Saints. Al-Tijānī said definitively to his disciple Muḥammad al-Ghālī, "The master of existence [the Prophet Muḥammad] informed me that I am the Hidden Pole, from him, by word of mouth, while awake, not while dreaming."[69] As explained below, the Hidden Pole for al-Tijānī was in fact a saintly rank that assumed and was superior, or perhaps interior, to the Seal of Saints.

Since the concept of the Hidden Pole (*al-quṭb al-maktūm*) is an apparently unique contribution of al-Tijānī to prior discussions of the unseen hierarchy of saints, the concept deserves further exploration. The Hidden Pole is first of all a rank that presumes attainment of two other ranks: the Pole of Poles (*quṭb al-aqṭāb*) and the Seal of Saints. For al-Tijānī, the Pole of Poles is similar to prior conceptions of paradigmatic sainthood at any given time. In the *Jawāhir al-maʿānī*, ʿAlī Ḥarāzim includes a supplication (*duʿāʾ*) transcribed from al-Tijānī's own handwriting to describe this position. In a prayer to which the Prophet guaranteed acceptance (according to Ḥarāzim's relation of al-Tijānī's handwritten notes on this document), al-Tijānī asked:

> O God, I ask that you make my station (*maqām*) as pole, unique saint, succor, deputized inheritor, and gathering point be unrivaled in magnitude; so that in comparison to it all other poles, unique saints, succors, inheritors, gathering points, gnostics, lovers, beloveds, seekers, and enraptured ones—all melt away and vanish. And [I ask] that you put my illumination (*fatḥ*) in them, with every glance and blink of the eye, to the extent that the "Night of Power" (*laylat al-qadr*) supersedes other nights, indeed increased by one thousand raised to the tenth power . . . [I ask] that you make me in this axial sainthood the singular pole (*quṭb*), the unique saint (*fard*), the comprehensive succor (*al-ghawth al-jāmiʿ*), the greatest inheritor (*al-khalīfa al-aʿẓam*), whose assistance (*madad*) is from God's messenger, peace and blessing upon him, without any

> intermediary: Your deputy (*nā'ib*) and his deputy in all the worlds, with complete, unlimited, general and perfected power of disposition (*taṣarruf*) in all these worlds; obtained from our master Muḥammad and from [the four caliphs:] Abū Bakr, 'Umar, 'Uthmān, 'Alī, [and from the four archangels:], Raphael, Gabriel, Michael, and Azrael.[70]

Such a notion of paradigmatic sainthood (*quṭbāniyya*), stressing unrivaled spiritual rank, disposition (*taṣarruf*) in the creation, and assistance (*madad*) in all beings' worship of God, invokes classical notions of *quṭbāniyya*. These allusions to the *quṭb*'s abilities, remembering similar descriptions of full human actualization from the previous chapter, are no less arresting in what is meant to represent al-Tijānī's firsthand experience. In the *Mashāhid*, 'Alī Ḥarāzim bears witness to his shaykh's apparent attainment of this position, before dawn on a Sunday, the twelfth of Muḥarram 1214 (16 June 1799):

> The station of the greatest inheritance (*maqām al-khilāfa al-uẓmā*) descended upon him, and this was bestowed on the Mount Arafat right before dawn. My master (al-Tijānī) took me by the hand, and after walking a few steps we were on the aforementioned mountain. There was no one with the Shaykh except [me] his inheritor (*khalīfa*). Then a green light descended from the presence of the Real, like the bright morning light, until it came to rest on his head like a turban. This (turban of light) has remained on his head until now: a sign of the station special to him.[71]

Putting the miracle of al-Tijānī taking Ḥarāzim by the hand aside for a moment—folding space to walk from Fez to a mountain outside of Mecca in a few steps—what is remarkable here is the ability of Ḥarāzim to share in al-Tijānī's experience.

Since this investiture comes prior to al-Tijānī's claim to be the Seal of Saints and Hidden Pole, it apparently refers to the shaykh's attainment of the station, Pole of Poles, the greatest inheritor (*khalīfa*) of the Prophet on earth at any given time. But here al-Tijānī seemed to avoid Ibn al-'Arabī's (and Aḥmad Bā-'Alawī's) more complex linking of the paradigmatic "saving" saint (*al-quṭb al-ghawth*) to one of four prophets: Enoch, Elijah, Jesus, or Khiḍr; who in turn receive from the Prophet Muḥammad.[72] The above supplication suggests that al-Tijānī connected the paradigmatic saint directly to the Prophet Muḥammad, but perhaps more precisely the axial saint accesses the prophetic assistance through the seal of Muḥammadan sainthood and the Hidden Pole. Ibrāhīm Niasse observed the difference between Ibn al-ʿArabī's version and that of al-Tijānī as follows: "The venerable Imam al-Ḥātimī, despite the depth of his experience in the science of gnosis, was not aware of the Hidden Presence through which the saintly pole derives support. He mentioned that the pole's support comes from the spirituality of the (four) prophets. In fact, the saintly savior-pole receives support (from the Prophet) through the ocean of the greatest assistance, that of the Hidden Pole and renowned Seal of Muḥammadan Sainthood."[73] As these distinct stations quickly became folded together for al-Tijānī, his more general conclusion concerning paradigmatic sainthood's unmediated link to the Prophet may indeed define a significant departure from Ibn al-ʿArabī's conception. Al-Tijānī thus related the Prophet's words to him: "The Pole of poles receives from God a complete manifestation (*tajallā*) encompassing all other manifestations. He receives from God the Greatest Name, and everything contained therein. He receives from God the Prophet's assistance (*madad*) without any intermediary. And God puts the assistance for all saints in his hands."[74] This narration of the Prophet's own description of paradigmatic sainthood is thus consistent with the tendency of eighteenth-century scholars to define sainthood in terms of spiritual proximity to the Prophet. The result in this case includes the knowledge of God's manifestations and divine assistance to all saints of his time. At one point, al-Tijānī thus requested of the Prophet to be granted intercession for all those alive during his own lifetime. With the Prophet's guarantee for that, al-Tijānī was also informed that the same had been granted to previous axial saints such as al-Tuhāmī b. Muḥammad al-Wazzānī of the Shādhiliyya.[75]

A month after al-Tijānī's Muḥarram investiture on Mount Arafat, ʿAlī Ḥarāzim related a further experience associated with his shaykh's attainment to the position of Seal of Saints and Hidden Pole. This experience, dated Monday 18 Ṣafar 1214 (22 July 1799), adds to the articulation of paradigmatic sainthood in Tijānī sources in its emphasis on this saintly rank's uniqueness from the beginning to the end of time. But otherwise, the shaykh's attainment of sainthood's highest rank is normally explained by al-Tijānī's testimony to Muḥammad al-Ghālī earlier mentioned: "The master of existence (Muḥammad) informed me that I am, from him, the Hidden Pole, in a waking state, by word of mouth, not dreaming."[76] Ḥarāzim's rather lengthy account seems to be the central narrative of Ḥarāzim's

Mashāhid and certainly provides greater context for such statements found elsewhere. The eighteenth of Ṣafar continues to be celebrated in Tijānī communities around the world as the "Night of the Hidden Pole" (*laylat al-katmiyya*).[77] Once again, Ḥarāzim narrates his experience in the company of al-Tijānī, here quoted at length for its significance:

> The earth became waves like those of a great sea, and I lost (sight of) the earth. Then the Muḥammadan reality became manifest, and the most fragrant light (of the Prophet) became fixed (in form). He was sitting on a great throne (*kursī*) in the middle of the sea, and you (al-Tijānī) were standing before him. This great sea was purer (*abyaḍ*) than milk, so pure that the eyes rejoiced, and sweeter than anything in existence. All of the Prophets, Messengers, and axial saints (*aqṭāb*) were encompassed by the Muḥammadan reality. The sea surged with great waves but all those mentioned stood in the middle of the sea as if they stood on land, firmly rooted and still. Then a great column descended from the presence of God the mighty and exalted, and with it, angels purer than milk, similar to the column itself, connected as it was to the Muhammadan reality, the water of which was pure, the rainwater like the sea. . . . (The column and angels) descended upon all those standing in the presence of the Muḥammadan reality. In the first row were the Messengers and Prophets, and behind them were the axial saints and the leaders among the unique ones (*afrād*). (And in this row) was our shaykh and the sinful servant (Ḥarāzim), standing in the presence of the Muḥammadan reality and our masters Abū Bakr, purely distinguished, and ʿUmar the differentiator, awesome in luminous presence, and ʿUthmān, modest and grave, and ʿAlī, knowledgeable and perfected. Then in our shaykh's hand was an enormous banner that enveloped everyone in the gathering. And its purity was like the purity of the sea's water that had descended from the presence of the Lord . . .
>
> I asked one of those close to me, I know not whom out of bashfulness . . . "What is the reason for the gathering of so many honorable and lordly masters?" He said, "The reason for this gathering is your shaykh." I asked, "But for what reason?" He said, "For what you are witnessing." I asked, "What am I witnessing?" He said, "The descent of the greatest rank and most majestic inheritance (*khilāfa*) . . . on behalf of God and His Messenger, the great unlimited inheritance. . . .

> There is no one in this gathering who has not obtained the greatest great name (of God) special to the station of Messengership and deputyship. . . ." Then I saw that everyone at the gathering had written on his being (*ʿalā dhātihi*) the Greatest Name . . .
>
> He (the Prophet) said, "O Aḥmad, praise to God, He has selected you for the greatest inheritance that no one, but you, has ever obtained, you must praise God for that. . . . No one, but you, has obtained this from me since God created the creation, and brought beings forth from non-existence to existence. I call all in existence to witness that I am the guarantor of your affair, the secret of your spirit and divine intimacy. I am witness over you until the (final) meeting with your Lord. The secret of your divine reality (*sirr ḥaqīqatik al-rabbāniyya*) never separates from me. . . ."
>
> And he (the Prophet) said . . . "I bear the support (*amdād*) that the entirety of God's servants cannot bear; and from the ocean of my power, this assistance (*amdād*) comes to you. From my support (*madad*), you receive acceptance and happiness. But there is no pride for you for this greatest station (*maqām*), this hidden, sealed and mysterious secret that none of the creation has (ever) obtained. O Aḥmad! You are the greatest beloved, the purest friend (*khalīl*), the most famous deputy (*khalīfa*). You are my beloved, and my love, sincerely and truthfully. You are from me, and I am from you, and there is no intermediary between you and me. Know that whoever loves you, I become like the spirit to his body, and this is obtained from me as the bodily presence (*dhāt*) obtains from the true, pre-eternal spirit. O Aḥmad, you are the Divine treasure. O Aḥmad, you are the Lordly secret. O Aḥmad, you are the mysterious secret. O Aḥmad, you are the unlimited deputy (*khalīfa*) over all the ranks. . . . Peace to you from me with a thousand greetings in every instant. Surely, I am never absent from you for the blinking of an eye, externally and internally."[78]

This vision represents several key features of the Seal of Saints and Hidden Pole as understood by al-Tijānī and his companions. The most significant aspects of Tijānī understandings here include the notion of unprecedented proximity to the Prophet, and the continued accent on humility despite the loftiness of al-Tijānī's spiritual rank. For Tijānīs, such unambiguous statements of the Prophet clearly supersede the claims of earlier saints.

Significantly, these words also hint that al-Tijānī's unrivaled intimacy with the Prophet is an invitation for disciples to become closer to the Prophet's spiritual reality.

Before exploring this proximity to the Prophet, it is useful to note that Ḥarāzim was not alone in his spiritual verification of al-Tijānī's claims. In one letter, al-Damrāwī wrote to al-Tijānī that he had come to perceive of a spiritual rank (*maqām*) between prophecy and axial sainthood (*quṭbāniyya*). He wanted to ask for this rank for himself, but the Prophet told him it was not for him, but for his shaykh, Aḥmad al-Tijānī. In relating his experience to al-Tijānī, al-Damrāwī added that he perceived God had "expanded the tongue" of the shaykh so that one utterance of his was greater than seventy years of remembrance of the most elite Sufis (including al-Damrāwī).[79] Similarly, Ibn al-Mashrī related a vision witnessing the Prophet leading the dawn prayer, followed by the other prophets in the first rank, followed in the second rank by the first four caliphs of Islam (Abū Bakr, ʿUmar, ʿUthmān, ʿAlī) along with al-Tijānī. After finishing the prayer, the Angel Gabriel descended "between the hands of the Prophet" and called out in a voice like thunder, "Congratulations, and congratulations again are due to those who enter the *Ṭarīqa Tijāniyya*."[80] Such examples of disciple verification of their shaykh's claim to be the Seal of Saints were formative for the understanding of later Tijānīs.

The saintly seal was conceived in the Tijāniyya as an antecedent reality, emerging from the Muḥammadan reality from the beginning of time. The seal has an unmediated relationship with the Prophet Muḥammad, but is relegated to a rank below prophecy. Other than the prophets, none but the Seal of Saints receives from the Muḥammadan reality directly: he, alone among the saints, swims in the ocean of prophecy despite his not being a prophet. According to al-Tijānī: "As for the salt-water ocean, those who drink from it drink nothing but salt. The exceptions are the fish, which drink sweet water. This is due to their station from God, on account of His wisdom. Surely, if they were to drink salt water, they would die."[81] In other words, the Seal of Saints drinks the sweet water of sainthood from the salt-water of prophecy: if other than the saintly seal were to drink from this ocean, he would die (or claim prophecy falsely). All other saints receive their favors from the Muḥammadan reality through the seal, who effectively render its water sweet for them to drink. This assistance (*madad*) from the seal was hidden from all in creation except the Prophet, however. Thus the seal was also the Hidden Pole: "The Hidden Pole is the intermediary between the Prophets, upon them peace and blessing, and the saints. The saints are unable to themselves receive the overflowing grace (*fayḍ*) from the Prophet except through the (other) Prophets *and* through him (the Hidden Pole). His assistance (from the Prophet) is special to him, for he receives from him without any intermediary prophet. Indeed, he drinks directly from the presence of the Prophet, along with the other Prophets."[82] This statement suggests that a saint might actually believe, as Ibn al-ʿArabī described, that he or she receives divine favor through the reality of a particular prophet. While that is partially true, al-Tijānī insists on the added mediation of the Hidden Pole, through whose hands all saints receive from the prophets. The Muḥammadan reality remains the source of both prophecy and sainthood, but the Hidden Pole, alone among the saints, drinks directly from the sea of prophecy. "Nothing arrives to you," the Prophet told al-Tijānī, "except by my hand."[83] All other saints in turn drink sainthood from the sea of the saintly seal: "No saint drinks or gives to drink except from our sea, from the beginning of the world until the resurrection."[84] Ibrāhīm Niasse often invoked this statement: "He is the confluence of the saints and their ocean, such that no saint drinks or quenches another's thirst except from his ocean."[85]

The notion that the reality of the Hidden Pole mediates between the Muḥammadan reality and the saints is expanded further elsewhere: Tijānīs have often referred to their shaykh simply as "the renowned isthmus" (*al-barzakh al-maʿlūm*). Al-Tijānī expanded on the position of the Hidden Pole as follows:

> The Hidden Pole receives an interior divine manifestation similar to that received by the prophets. The Real, Glorious is He, manifests to him in every moment one hundred thousand (divine) manifestations. Each manifestation contains the like of one hundred thousand divine manifestations for the denizens of paradise, or more. [. . .] He also bears the gathering of everything given to all the worlds from the divine flux, except for the Prophets, and all the worlds derive support from him. He is the intermediary between them [the creation] and the Muḥammadan reality, upon him blessing and peace, excepting the Prophets. They derive support from the Prophet without any intermediary. The Hidden Pole possesses a position before the Muḥammadan reality that no one else possesses among the greatest of saints.[86]

This passage seems to suggest that the Hidden Pole mediates not only between the saints and the prophetic presence, but also between the entire creation and the Prophet. This is partially explained by complete human actualization as encompassing all of creation, as elaborated in the previous chapter. Al-Tijānī was careful to position the Hidden Pole (and thus all saintly ranks) as below the station of prophecy, and (at least publicly) below the Prophet's own companions. But the Hidden Pole's assistance, through the Muḥammadan reality, to "all the worlds" remains a remarkable claim. Al-Tijānī may have found further explanation controversial, and in one letter avoided further articulation: "We have a degree in the presence of God that has been forbidden to mention."[87]

The second remarkable articulation in Ḥarāzim's above account of al-Tijānī's investiture as Seal of the Saints and Hidden Pole is the accent on humility: "there is no pride for you in this greatest station." Al-Tijānī, like others present at the assembly, is animated by God's greatest name (*ism ʿaẓam*) inscribed in his bodily presence (*dhāt*), perhaps a further explanation of al-Tijānī's reference to the gnostic as "a letter among the letters of the divine essence" mentioned in chapter 2. The saintly hierarchy, Ḥarāzim's vision means to remind us, is definitively God's decree not the result of individual human efforts. But the accent on humility actually invokes a stern warning concerning those who would belittle al-Tijānī's claims: al-Tijānī's spiritual station is nothing but a further manifestation of the Prophet's perfection. The Prophet assures al-Tijānī that he is never absent from him, that their souls were joined from the beginning of creation, that he is the secret of the saintly seal as a divine reality. The Prophet's own saintly perfection is the hidden essence of al-Tijānī's own being. Whoever disparages the shaykh for his claims in fact slanders the divine assistance of the Prophet himself and distances himself from the Prophet: "Whoever disparages you," the Prophet told al-Tijānī, "will die as an unbeliever (*kāfir*), unless he is of my family (*ahl al-bayt*)."[88] A similar narration adds, "Even if he performed jihad or hajj, whoever tries to harm the Shaykh or find blame in him, the Prophet is angry with him so that even his prayer on the Prophet is not recorded for him, nor does he benefit from it."[89] The true power and reality of al-Tijānī's station thus appears in his effacement of his own identity: the saintly seal is the inscription of God's greatest name in the most complete saintly reflection of the Prophet.

Al-Tijānī and Previous Claims to Paradigmatic Sainthood

Tijānī scholars, beginning with al-Tijānī himself, clearly had to confront the rival claims of saints such as Ibn al-ʿArabī and ʿAbd al-Qādir al-Jilānī. Usually, al-Tijānī only publicly articulated his own claim when pressed by petitioners about the rank of other saints. Reacting to al-Jilānī's statement, "My feet are on the neck of every saint," al-Tijānī responded: "These two feet of mine are on the neck of every saint of God most high, from the beginning of creation till the resurrection. He (al-Jilānī) meant by saying, 'My feet are on the neck of every saint of God': the saints of his time only."[90] Once when al-Tijānī returned from praying the Friday prayer, he suddenly declared, "Praise be to God who gave me just now the rank of Shaykh ʿAbd al-Qādir al-Jilānī, and increased (for me) from what He gave him by forty degrees."[91] It appears that for many in his immediate Moroccan audience, the seventeenth-century Shādhilī master Muḥammad b. al-Nāṣir was the most familiar paradigmatic saint or *quṭb*. Once a Nāṣirī Sufi came to al-Tijānī to request initiation into the Tijānīyya. Al-Tijānī told him, "Staying with it [the Nāṣiriyya] will suffice you." When the man insisted, al-Tijānī told him of his path's condition to leave all other Sufi litanies, but the man expressed his fear of Ibn al-Nāṣir's jealousy. Al-Tijānī responded, "If Ibn al-Nāṣir were here, and I said to him, 'leave it aside [his *wird*],' he would have no other choice but to do so."[92]

According to primary sources, al-Tijānī posed questions concerning the rank of previous saints to the Prophet directly: "Among all saints, who had the highest rank?" The Prophet responded, "The ranks of ʿAbd al-Qādir [al-Jilānī] and [Ibn al-ʿArabī] al-Ḥatimī were higher than all other saints."[93] As mentioned, al-Tijānī later explained that al-Jilānī and Ibn al-ʿArabī had both attained the rank of the Prophet's son-in-law ʿAlī b. Abī Ṭālib, due to their shared inheritance (along with al-Tijānī) of a special name of God reserved for those who would realize axial sainthood (*quṭbāniyya*).[94] In other instances, the Prophet's explanation of al-Tijānī's rank form part of the Prophet's response to al-Tijānī's questions about Ibn al-ʿArabī and al-Jilānī in particular.[95] The Prophet thus assured al-Tijānī that no other saint had fully witnessed the station of Hidden Pole, as mentioned above: "you are the Imam over every *quṭb* in this luminous creation." Clearly referencing such earlier statements, al-Tijānī later explained the position of the Hidden Pole as follows: "A pulpit (*minbar*) of light will be given to me on the Day of Resurrection, and someone will call out so that all in the station of questioning (*al-mawqif*) will hear, 'O people gathered in the place of questioning, this is your Imam from whom you derived assistance in the world, without any of you being aware.'"[96] In other words, the Hidden Pole was a rank of which even the greatest saints had been previously unaware. Ibn al-Mashrī summarized simply: "No one has seen the reality of the station specific to him, except for God the exalted and (Muḥammad) the master of existence, God's blessing and peace upon him."[97]

Tijānī sources thus admit that Ibn al-ʿArabī had made an exclusivist claim to be the Seal of Saints, but suggest two qualifications. The first is that the Seal of Saints is in reality bound to the position of the Hidden Pole: the lack of having claimed the second meant that Ibn al-ʿArabī was not the fullest actualization of the first. This was reflected in Ibn al-ʿArabī's understanding of an individual saint's direct draught from a spirit of a Prophet: he had not perceived the enduring mediation of the Hidden Pole, as that was a position kept hidden from him. The second qualification was that Ibn al-ʿArabī's claim to be the Seal of Saints was a claim he later retracted, and that he later perceived "on the unseen" that the position belonged to other than him. Here ʿUmar Tāl cites al-Shaʿrānī's report of ʿAlī al-Khawāṣṣ's explanation of Ibn al-ʿArabī's claim:

> While he was in that state [of claiming to be the seal], he heard a divine voice calling out, "It is not as you suppose and hope. It belongs to a saint near the end of time, and there is no saint so honored in God's presence than he." Then he (Ibn al-ʿArabī) said, "I submit all affairs to the creator and fashioner. Long did I preoccupy my spiritual vision in the unseen, trying to discover him, his rank, his name, the name of his land and place, and the nature of his spiritual state. But God did not reveal anything of this, and I was unable to even perceive his [the seal's] fragrance."[98]

This explanation seems to best explain how al-Tijānī, and certainly the later Tijānī tradition, reconciled the enduring respect for Ibn al-ʿArabī while making a definitive claim to the position of Seal of Saints and Hidden Pole.

Later Tijānī scholars expounded further on the implications of al-Tijānī's claim, quite obviously in dialogue with the competing claims of both earlier and contemporary saints. One of the most coherent explanations was that of the nineteenth-century Mauritanian scholar residing in the Sudan, Muḥammad b. al-Mukhtār al-Shinqīṭī (d. 1882), who was asked how to harmonize the divergent claims of Ibn al-ʿArabī, ʿAlī al-Khawāṣṣ, and others concerning the identity of the Seal of Saints.[99] Al-Shinqīṭī responded that there was no contradictions between any of these statements: Ibn al-ʿArabī learned that the position did not belong to him, then he was veiled from it, then later allowed to encounter al-Tijānī's reality in Fez. The claim of al-Khawāṣṣ could be explained by the manifestation of the Prophet in his being, similar to the experiences of Abū Bakr al-Shiblī (d. 946, Baghdad), and ʿAbd al-Karīm al-Jīlī (d. 1424, Baghdad) in relation to his shaykh of the Qādiriyya order, Ismaʿīl al-Jabartī (d. 1405), the latter who said, "I saw our master Muḥammad in the form of my master Ismāʿīl al-Jabartī." Alternatively, the claims to being the Seal of Saints by others besides al-Tijānī—here al-Shinqīṭī mentions Ibn al-ʿArabī, Muḥammad al-Wafā, ʿAlī al-Khawāṣṣ, and Muḥammad al-Mirghānī (d. 1853, the student to Aḥmad b. Idrīs)—could be explained by "the appearance of al-Tijānī's spirituality in the mirror of their essential beings (*dhāt*)."[100] Similarly did Aḥmad b. Idrīs (d. 1837), according to al-Shinqīṭī, first claim to be the Mahdī "because he obtained the manifestation of the Mahdī's spirituality in the mirror of his essential being," but then later renounced the title.[101] Al-Tijānī's statements about his rank are the most coherent of any claimant, al-Shinqīṭī concludes, nor did any other saint fulfill Ibn al-ʿArabī's description of the seal's appearance in Fez (in the *Futūḥāt al-makkiyya*): no one besides al-Tijānī claimed to be the Seal of Saints in Fez.[102]

Ibrāhīm Niasse laid particular emphasis on al-Tijānī's spiritual experience and unrivaled gnosis as evidence for his being the Seal of Saints. According to Niasse (as mentioned previously), "he has come to actualize the spiritual experience of all saints." Niasse emphasized the point in his poetic eulogies of al-Tijānī:

> The reality of second secret of existence, a [divine] creation
> The seal of the unique saints (*afrād*), then named further
>
> Given illumination in the holy presence,
> The cup-bearer of quenching gnosis.
>
> By my life, this Shaykh is the spring (*ʿayn*) of sainthood
> Absolute purity bursting forth from the spring of prophecy.[103]

This "quenching gnosis" brought by al-Tijānī was largely to be experienced rather than expressed in books. In his earlier allusion to the Seal of Saints, al-Tirmidhī had suggested a certain number of esoteric questions to which the seal would be able to respond. While Ibn al-ʿArabī had endeavored to respond to these questions, Niasse rejoined that al-Tijānī did not publicize some knowledge out of etiquette (*adab*) with God. He points out that Tirmidhī said the seal would know the answers to his questions, not that it would be appropriate for him to share his knowledge of such matters.[104] But in reflecting on al-Tijānī's position as Seal of the Saints in assisting disciples to attain gnosis, Niasse interpreted the established Tijānī saying, "The end of the axial saints (*aqṭāb*) are the beginning of companions of Shaykh al-Tijānī," to mean that the true followers of al-Tijānī would come to realize a higher degree of gnosis than earlier saintly communities: "I have not seen in the earlier generations knowledge except of the first degree (of gnosis)."[105] Niasse thus urged disciples, "You must speak about the matter of the Tijānī Seal among the beloveds, for it is better than all other litanies, especially during Ramadan."[106]

Tijānī scholars thus reconciled the competing claims of diverse saints, without (from their perspective) denying any saint's particular relationship to God. It is not surprising, then, to find West African scholars like al-Shinqīṭī and Niasse both authenticating the saintly articulations of contemporaries, such as al-Mirghānī or Aḥmad Bamba,[107] while demonstrating (for Tijānīs) the superior rank of al-Tijānī. A similar methodology is employed by contemporary Tijānī scholars when apprised of various more recent claims. A book describing Shādhilī saints of Morocco contains a narration of an early twentieth-century Sufi from Tangier, Muḥammad b. al-Ṣaddīq (d. 1935), who had a vision of al-Tijānī in the presence of the Prophet while visiting the Tijānī *zāwiya* in Fez. He asked al-Tijānī, "Is it true what your followers claim, that you are the Seal of Saints?" al-Tijānī reportedly responded to him, "You are also the Seal (*khatm*)."[108] Ibrāhīm Niasse had of course suggested, following earlier Tijānī understandings, that any saint who realized perfect sainthood could be called a "Seal," but only "for his own designated time."[109] But in this case, the present-day Shaykh al-Tijānī Cissé, after nodding to the wider definition of the term *khatm*, simply said, "That is only his [al-Ṣaddīq's] claim (to sainthood). As for the true identity of the unique Seal of Saints, that is only Shaykh Aḥmad al-Tijānī."[110] In other words, Tijānī disciples believed their shaykh's claims to be of unrivaled coherence, capable of making relative sense of and respecting other claims, while preserving the uniqueness of al-Tijānī's saintly rank.

Disciple Actualization and Spiritual Rank

The history of North African Sufism is replete with the assurances saints gave their followers. The founder of the Wazzāniyya ʿAbdallāh al-Sharīf (d. 1678), the most popular branch of the Shādhiliyya in eighteenth-century Morocco into which al-Tijānī had earlier been initiated, told disciples, "I asked Him (God) that whoever entered my house and memorized my *dhikr* would be saved from Hell on the Last Day of Judgment. He granted me all that, thanks to Him."[111] Ibn al-Mashrī's *Rawḍ al-muḥibb* reflects on some of these claims popular in North Africa at the time, most particularly the similar assurances of ʿAbd al-Qādir al-Jilānī (d. 1166) and Mawlay Tuhāmī (d. 1715) that whoever saw him, and who saw someone who saw him, up to seven degrees removed, would enter Paradise.[112] The foundation of the Tijāniyya thus clearly emerged from a discursive space where promises of salvation to disciples were quite common. While al-Tijānī's claims in this regard undoubtedly meant to go beyond earlier assurances in keeping with his claim to ascendant saintly rank, he also cautioned disciples, perhaps paradoxically, against relying on such assurances to abrogate the enduringly essential jihad against the *nafs*, or to feel themselves safe from God's punishment.

Tijānī primary sources contain elaborate discussion of the excellences (*faḍāʾil*) of initiation into the Tijāniyya. There is a pronounced claim that such assurances transcend the promises given to any other saint. Al-Tijānī asserted, "No one among the distinguished saints (*rijāl*) is able to cause all of his companions to enter Paradise, without accounting or punishment, except I alone."[113] Ibn al-Mashrī considered the similar statements of al-Jilānī and Tuhāmī above, then explained the distinction specific to al-Tijānī, "It has not been reported from one of them the lack of accounting for their companions, or for one who saw them, as our Shaykh has mentioned."[114] In other words, the Tijāniyya not only offered Paradise, but exemption from "accounting" (*ḥisāb*) on the Day of Judgment. ʿUmar Tāl explained this was because God would have mercy on the shaykh's companions "from the treasuries of His grace (*faḍl*), not on account of their good deeds."[115] This was specifically meant to endure beyond the shaykh's lifetime. Ibn al-Mashrī thus relates the Prophet's words to al-Tijānī: "Whomever you grant permission and he gives to another, it is as if he took from you directly, and I am the guarantor for all of them."[116] Al-Tijānī thus remarked of the Qurʾān verse, "*A goodly portion of the later generations*," whom God would save as *"companions of the right"* (*aṣḥāb al-yamīn*): "The goodly portion from later times are our companions."[117] Elsewhere he added, "No one will enter Paradise before our companions except the companions of the Prophet."[118] The initiate's parents, spouses, and offspring would also enter Paradise "without accounting or punishment," so long as they did not become an enemy to the shaykh.[119] Al-Tijānī insisted such assurances to disciples were only a partial insight into the blessing of joining his path: "What we have mentioned of blessing of this *ṭarīqa* compared to what is hidden is like a drop in the ocean."[120]

Indeed, Paradise was not the only assurance al-Tijānī gave to disciples. He said, for example, that his companions would be granted one hundred thousand times the credit for good deeds relative to other Muslims.[121] He further promised sincere disciples the attainment of sainthood: "As for the grace (*faḍl*) upon his followers, may God be pleased with him, the master of existence, peace be upon him, informed him that anyone who loves him is beloved to the Prophet, and will not die until he becomes a saint (*walī*)."[122] The Prophet was thus said to have promised him that all who took his litany would enter Paradise along with the shaykh in "the first company," to reside in "the heights of Paradise (*'iliyyīn*) in the company of the Prophet."[123] The saintly rank of al-Tijānī's true disciples was higher than earlier axial saints: "The greatest poles (*aqṭāb*) of this (Muslim) community do not realize the rank of my companions," said al-Tijānī, "and we have been given this despite the disdain of the doubters."[124] "If the greatest of poles came to know what has been given to our companions, they would cry to God and say, 'Our Lord! You have given us nothing.'"[125] This divine grace was to be allegedly realized whatever the state of the Tijānī aspirant. Once a jurist (*faqīh*) criticized a disciple of al-Tijānī for apparently being distracted in the mosque, "You people (Tijānīs) fill the mosques with your bodies, but not with your hearts." When informed, al-Tijānī responded, "You people (al-Tijānī's companions) are the beloved and accepted ones (in God's presence), in whatever state (*ḥāla*) you are."[126]

There is good evidence that disciples strove to actualize this promise of divine selection and spiritual rank. As mentioned in chapter 3, the Prophet promised ten of al-Tijānī's disciples "grand illuminion" (*al-fatḥ al-akbar*), normally associated with the highest of saintly ranks; al-Damrāwī only saw the position of the saintly seal above that of his own; and 'Alī Amlās attained a rank only reached by three people every thousand years. 'Alī Tamāsīnī was said to have become the axial saint (*quṭb*), or the highest saint on earth after the passing of al-Tijānī in 1815.[127] At one point, ʿAlī Ḥarāzim wrote to al-Tijānī to request from him the spiritual rank (*maqām*) of Ibn al-ʿArabī: "I did not ask for the *maqām* of Ibn al-ʿArabī until I came to know and verify that your *maqām* is above his own." Al-Tijānī wrote back to guarantee for Ḥarāzim the gnosis (*maʿrifa*) from the *maqam* of Ibn al-ʿArabī, but that the earlier saint's singular rank (*quṭbāniyya*) was only for God to decree.[128] Nonetheless, al-Tijānī later wrote in his authorization (*ijāza*) to Ḥarāzim: "He has come to stand in our station, as a replacement for us, on behalf of our spirit and our holy rank. He stands for us in our presence and our absence, in our life and after our death. Whoever takes from him is as if he took from us directly without any difference. Whoever exalts him, exalts us. Whoever respects him, respects us. Whoever obeys him, obeys us, and who obeys us, obeys God and His Messenger."[129] In other words, Ḥarāzim had come as close as possible to the station of the Seal of Saints, so that there was no spiritual rank in between his own and that of al-Tijānī himself. Elsewhere, al-Tijānī insisted that he had not given this complete inheritance (*khilāfa*) to anyone except for Ḥarāzim, a bestowal he had granted by the command of the Prophet.[130] The later Moroccan Tijānī scholar Aḥmad Sukayrij suggested that this *khilāfa* of Ḥarāzim was a rank open to other Tijānī luminaries after the passing of Ḥarāzim.[131] But more generally, Tijānī adherents were probably encouraged in their spiritual aspirations by the shaykh's promise, "There is a group among our companions such that, if the great poles gathered together, they would not equal one drop in the ocean of one of them."[132]

While al-Tijānī's spiritual rank meant to inspire the zeal of disciples, it also seemed possessed of a unique exclusivity or singular majesty (*jalāl*), perhaps evocative of ʿAlī Wafā's earlier description of the Seal of Saints: "The appearance of the saints in the time of their Seal is like the appearance of the stars along with the sun."[133] Primary sources speak briefly of a short-lived conflict between partisans of two elite disciples, ʿAlī Ḥarāzim and Ibn al-Mashrī; both of whom had spent years in the company of al-Tijānī and had written their own compilations of the shaykh's teachings. Rather than openly siding with one side or the other, al-Tijānī's response was, "My companions are one. Who would know me, knows me alone."[134] The lesson seems to have been that aspiration for spiritual rank should not distract the disciple from sincerity in his commitment to the Sufi shaykh, particularly when one's shaykh was the Seal of Saints.

Perhaps even before claiming the highest rank of Saintly Seal and Hidden Pole, al-Tijānī called together his elite disciples who had obtained divine gnosis and "the station of God's answering their prayers (*taṣarruf*), and the ability to provide spiritual training (*tarbiya*) to the creation." He warned them, "Whomever God has granted illumination among my disciples, and remains in the place where I am, he should fear his own destruction (*halāk*) . . . this is from God, and I have no choice in the matter."[135] In other words, al-Tijānī's saintly rank might undermine the achievements of others unless they were vigilant in their sincerity or moved elsewhere. Apparently, not all of these disciples wanted to leave their shaykh: rather than leave al-Tijānī, Muḥammad b. al-Nāṣir, oral traditions in Fez recount, accepted al-Tijānī's personal warning to him that he would die in obscurity if he did not leave. To this day, his grave in Fez is allegedly found in a place where no one visits due to the repulsive odors of the surrounding neighborhood.[136] The twentieth-century Senegalese shaykh Ibrāhīm Niasse did what he could to avoid spending the night in Fez out of respect for al-Tijānī's saintly rank, perhaps because of his own claim to axial sainthood (*quṭbāniyya*). This practice is maintained by the current imam of Niasse's community, Shaykh al-Tijānī Cissé, who explained cryptically when pressed, "There is a certain secret, which if you possess it, you cannot spend the night in Fez."[137] Together, such narrations reveal the way in which later saints within the Tijāniyya served to reinforce the precedent claims of al-Tijānī, rather than to challenge or supersede them, even while they made their own spiritual claims.

While the assurances of the Tijāniyya may go beyond the claims of other Sufi communities, they were certainly articulated in dialogue with them. Tijānī sources admitted, for example, the virtue for any Sufi disciple in exalting his shaykh beyond any other. Al-Tijānī thus advised Sufi disciples in general: "Let the disciple be with his shaykh as if he were with the Prophet, exalting him, loving him, seeking his spiritual support, and removing other than him from his heart." Al-Tijānī continued: "Every shaykh from among God's elect has an audience or presence (*ḥaḍra*) with God that he does not share with anyone else. If a light should be revealed to a person from this presence, and he should attribute it to other than this presence, the light will return back to its original location."[138] Any illumination the disciple perceived in himself was thus a light granted him from or through the presence of his shaykh. In a letter to fellow disciples, ʿAlī Ḥarāzim emphasized that, while one should not disparage other saints, "It is necessary for a person to exalt his shaykh over others in order to benefit from him." Proper manners with one's shaykh, according to Ḥarāzim's understanding of the broader Sufi tradition, meant that the "disciple does not see anyone in creation better than his shaykh, nor does he see anything in creation except his shaykh and himself."[139]

Nonetheless, al-Tijānī's uncompromising claim to be the Seal of Saints invariably posited the Tijāniyya with a degree of qualitative distinction. In some cases, al-Tijānī went so far as to suggest the "abrogation" of other Sufi orders with the appearance of the Tijāniyya: "Our path abrogates (*tansakh*) all other paths, rendering them ineffective; and no path enters into our path."[140] But the more widely cited statement, "Our seal (*tābiʿ*) descends over all seals, and no seal will descend over ours,"[141] may best articulate al-Tijānī's continued respect for existing Sufi paths while asserting the specialty of the Tijāniyya. After all, according to al-Tijānī, "The paths of the saints all return to one source, which is their connection to him (the Prophet)."[142] The twentieth-century Egyptian Tijānī shaykh Muḥammad al-Ḥāfiẓ al-Miṣrī (d. 1978) commented that the abrogated path only referred to those Sufi orders that allowed aspirants to leave aside practicing the litany (*wird*) upon which that order was founded.[143] Ibrāhīm Niasse emphasized the centrality of spiritual training (*tarbiya*). For him, the abrogation of a Sufi order meant its inability to persist in providing followers with the knowledge (*maʿrifa*) of God: "And perhaps the other spiritual paths have been abrogated, since not one of them is maintained by someone capable of providing spiritual training (*tarbiya*)."[144] In other words, the validity of a Sufi path depended on its continued ability to fulfill its purpose. These explanations thus reflect al-Tijānī's notion that the Tijāniyya was the purest Sufi path because of its direct connection to the Prophet. "Our path is a path of pure grace, a gift from him (the Prophet) to me," al-Tijānī said: "Our seal (*tābiʿ*) is the Muḥammadan seal, and it descends on all who take our litany (*wird*)." Such statements were certainly a challenge to the existing Sufi tradition. But given al-Tijānī's evident respect for preexisting Sufi saints and incorporation of their teachings, his own statements certainly did not call for the abolishment of non-Tijānī Sufism. Rather, al-Tijānī meant to reinvigorate the essence of Sufi practice as a methodology of providing direct access to God and His Prophet.

The Tijāniyya made specific claims about its ability to connect followers to the enduring spirituality of the Prophet. Al-Tijānī related the relevant words of the Prophet to him as follows: "You are among those guaranteed safety, and all those who love you are safe. You are my beloved, and whoever loves you is my beloved. Your disciples are my disciples. Your followers are my followers. Your companions are my companions. Anyone who takes your litany is liberated from the Fire."[145] Disciples were thus assured of being the special loved ones of the Prophet, so that "Whoever harms them, harms the Prophet."[146] Al-Tijānī's warning in this regard was directed more internally to his own followers than externally: "The Prophet said to me, 'Tell your companions not to harm each other, for whoever harms them, harms me.'"[147] This is apparently explained by the Prophet's words to al-Tijānī cited above: "Whoever loves you, I become like the spirit to his body."[148] Al-Tijānī no doubt hoped aspirants would thus actualize the Qur'ān verse, "*The Prophet is closer to the believers than their own selves.*"[149]

In publicizing the Prophet's extraordinary assurances to his disciples, al-Tijānī obviously had to maintain a delicate balance with orthodox Islamic understandings of divine reward and punishment. Such dynamic tension is evident in the Prophet's own teachings, it must be admitted, at the foundations of Islam. The Prophet Muḥammad's assurance of Paradise to anyone who once uttered the Islamic testimony of faith,[150] was tempered with statements like, "No one will enter the Fire (of Hell) who has a speck of faith in his heart, and no one will enter Paradise who has a speck of pride in his heart."[151] Similarly, al-Tijānī warned disciples against pride and complacency on the spiritual path. Specifically, the aspirant should never feel himself safe from God's misguidance: "All that we have mentioned in this path will surely be realized so long as we are made safe from God's misguidance (*makr*). For even the Prophets never felt themselves secure from God's misguidance, despite their exalted worth and elevated rank. '*No one feels secure from God's misguidance except those in loss.*'"[152] Guidance is God's gift alone: "The (divine) conductor of felicity steers a man to this presence, and the divine misdirector (*ṣārif*) beguiles others from it,"[153] al-Tijānī explained.

Tijānī texts thus demonstrate an apparently well-developed understanding of the "misguidance of God" (*makr Allāh*). The *Jawāhir al-ma'ānī* describes God's misdirection from the path of felicity as a process of successive veiling as a result of disobeying God:

> Let a person not take our litany (*wird*) and, having heard what it contains concerning the entrance to Paradise without accounting,

> punishment or harm from disobedience, then cast his carnal self (*nafs*) into disobeying God, taking what he heard as a protection from God's punishment in his disobedience. Whoever does that, God clothes his heart in our hatred until he disparages us. And if he should disparage us, God causes him to die as a disbeliever. I warn you from disobeying God and (to be fearful) of His punishment. Whomever God has judged to be in sin—and the servant (of God) is not infallible—let him not approach us unless he does so in tears, his heart fearful of God's punishment.[154]

Disobedience certainly included external violation of the sacred law (*sharīʿa*), but it more generally included any act of turning away from God, externally or internally. Al-Tijānī related: "The Imam of the Sufi path, al-Junayd, may God be pleased with him, said, 'A person could have a thousand years of worship accepted with God, but then he turns away for one moment. What he loses in that one moment is more than what he gained in a thousand years.'"[155] Such passages emphasizing the fear of God within the Tijāniyya are no less arresting than earlier citations concerning God's favor. In balancing between hope and fear of God, al-Tijānī returned to an apparently classical Islamic definition of true faith:

> Faith has two wings like a bird. One wing is the fear (of God), which causes the heart to lament in fear of (God's) threatened punishment. The Prophet said, "The believer sees his sins as having placed him beneath a mountain, and he fears lest it fall on top of him. The hypocrite considers his sins as (inconsequential) flies passing before his nose." The other wing is the hope in God, glorious and exalted: that He might forgive him, and not punish him nor cause him tribulation in his faith. The one who has only hope (in God) without fear feels himself secure, and feeling oneself secure from God is the source of disbelief (*ʿayn al-kufr*). The one who has only fear (of God) becomes desperately hopeless of God, and despair of God is (also) the source of disbelief.[156]

The Tijānī aspirant should thus be inspired by the promises of the Tijāniyya concerning Paradise and sainthood, his hopes raised in God's mercy. But the heightened awareness of God's capacity to misguide the insincere should also give new urgency to his fear of God. After all, feeling safe from God's punishment was a form of pride. The Mauritanian-Sudanese

Muḥammad b. al-Mukhtār al-Shinqīṭī thus explained al-Tijānī's teaching in this regard: "Part of pride is thinking that any blessing you have is because you deserve it."[157] A person's affiliation to the Tijāniyya, or to any path of guidance, was God's action, and not a source for individual pride over others. Indeed, such arrogance constituted an act of turning away from God, subjecting a person to God's further misguidance.

These warnings evidently responded to tensions within al-Tijānī's early community. Clearly, some affiliates understood their connection to the Tijāniyya as an occasional association as permitted in other Sufi gatherings. The Prophet warned al-Tijānī that whoever took his litany but then left it would be "licensed with destruction in this world and the next."[158] Elsewhere al-Tijānī admitted of different degrees of association between a shaykh and his disciples: "He has three circles (of disciples): those far, those near, and those in the middle. When a disciple enters into the circle of proximity, it is said to him, 'If you go against me after today, you will die as a disbeliever.'"[159] The conditions he placed on those whom he initiated, such as practicing the litany until death, certainly meant to exempt more general associates from the heightened promise and warning al-Tijānī articulated as specific to the Tijāniyya.

Even still, there is evidence of the shaykh's disappointment with unnamed disciples. The Prophet came to Ḥarāzim to apprise him of a certain disciple who was taking the shaykh's words out of context and distorting them for his own purposes, "in order to eat of the world," telling Ḥarāzim to tell al-Tijānī: "You and I have nothing to do with him and what he is doing. All the dissension (*fitna*) stirred up against you here (Fez), and in the desert, is because of him and from him. He persists in mixing with those filled with hatred, elaborating to them what is with you. I detest that and all types of dissension."[160] This chilling rebuke points to an enduring discourse within the Tijāniyya about the dangers, for the initiated or even elite disciple, of willfully disregarding al-Tijānī's balance between hope and fear, between the external orthodoxy and divine reality. Assurances were to be made among an audience who could read them in the context of true faith, which meant not feeling safe from divine misguidance and punishment. Disciples who publicized the claims of the Tijāniyya in inappropriate contexts perhaps meant to attract other initiates for their own selfish purposes, not for the purpose of connecting others to God. Ibrāhīm Niasse picked up on this theme in later generations, warning Tijānī disciples: "You must avoid in the (Tijānī) path those who are slaves of (their own) desires . . . they are the enemies of God and His Messenger."[161] Internal Tijānī histories tend to silence such internal dissension. But their lingering traces indicate that the balance between fear and hope was not always an easy one to maintain, especially in the absence of the physical presence of the shaykh or his completed inheritors. It became clear even during al-Tijānī's lifetime, then, that not all who dressed themselves in the name of the Tijāniyya represented the shaykh's teachings. But Tijānī sources seem reconciled to the fact that al-Tijānī's claims would inevitably incite jealous enmity. The shaykh related the Prophet's warning to him, partially mentioned above: "All people are your enemies and the enemies of your companions, due to the rank bestowed on you . . . so hold back your tongue."[162]

Conclusion

The foundation of the Tijāniyya, especially from its establishment in Fez in 1798, was marked by insistent claims of saintly authority. Such expressions emerged from a long Sufi tradition of elaborating a hidden hierarchy of saints. Al-Tijānī developed these ideas further and may have asserted a new position altogether. Nearly synonymous with the Seal of Saints, the Hidden Pole was a further perfection of saintly proximity to the enduring spirituality of the Prophet Muḥammad, such that no one in creation was apprised of his reality except the Prophet. Despite such lofty claims, Tijānī tradition apparently meant to hold to earlier ideas of spiritual humility before God, and the idea of saintly rank as nothing other than a reflection of God's favor to the Prophet. "Whoever loves me for the sake of God and His Messenger, let him love me," al-Tijānī said: "Whoever loves me for another reason, I am only a blind man distributing (goods), but I have nothing myself."[163]

Those who took directly from the Hidden Pole, thus the affiliates to the new *Ṭarīqa Muḥammadiyya*, perceived themselves as participating in an unprecedented saintly authority that offered individual aspirants both salvation and saintly rank. Such claims inevitably led to external jealousy and internal tensions, especially when disciples did not live up to the required comportment on the Sufi path. But the shaykh's underlying emphasis on combining fear and hope in God provided an enduring legibility to the Tijāniyya within traditional Sufism and orthodox Islamic theology. Accusations that al-Tijānī had "superseded" Islam with his claim to be the Seal of Saints or his promises of salvation, whether made by non-Tijāni detractors or academics,[164] rely on a (sometimes unintentional) selective reading of primary sources. Interestingly, Tijānī sources also accuse insincere Tijānī associates of similar misreadings. Invariably, lost in this noise is the manner in which saintly authority and salvation was understood and transmitted by most Tijānī disciples, and certainly by al-Tijānī himself. The exposition presented here, based on a wide array of primary sources, hopes to contextualize claims to saintly authority within a broader reading of al-Tijānī's teaching, and within a larger discourse of saintly claims contemporary to the emergence of the Tijāniyya. Such a contextualized understanding of saintly authority in one of the world's largest Sufi orders is long overdue.

It is certainly not an academic's place to evaluate the competing claims of Muslim saints. But the lack of serious consideration to al-Tijānī's claims to saintly rank has been a gaping hole in academic research on Sufism, albeit understandable for the difficulty in external access to all relevant sources. As this chapter has demonstrated, al-Tijānī articulated a well-developed understanding of the hidden saintly hierarchy, made a coherent claim to occupy the highest position as the Seal of Saints in dialogue with previous claims, and formulated an apparently new expression of paradigmatic sainthood surrounding the notion of the "Hidden Pole." Given the popularity of the Tijāniyya throughout the Muslim world, al-Tijānī's claim to be the Seal of Saints is arguably upheld by as many Muslims today as is the competing claim of any other saint.

CHAPTER FIVE

Abundant Blessing in an Age of Corruption

GOD THE GLORIFIED AND EXALTED knows the weakness of the people of this time," Aḥmad al-Tijānī said of the late eighteenth-century Muslim world, "so He had mercy on them, and gave them abundant good for small (good) deeds."[1] This statement was meant to allude to the need for powerful Sufi prayers in an age of corruption, but it more generally characterizes al-Tijānī's understanding of the historical context within which the Tijāniyya was taking shape. The Sufi aspirant could not avoid entanglement in a world increasingly distant from divine guidance. There was no choice but to "Walk on the way of the people of your time,"[2] al-Tijānī cautioned disciples. The solution was not to withdraw from the world, but rather for individuals to become instruments of God's bountiful grace (*faḍl Allāh*), even as traditional Muslim institutions and societies were appearing to crumble around them. Such an understanding may not have specifically referenced the impending European colonial occupation of Muslim societies, but it certainly facilitated the survival and even spread of Islamic learning and identity when Muslim political regimes where eclipsed by European powers. This chapter considers al-Tijānī's understanding of the corruption of the age in the context of broader discourses of late eighteenth-century reformism. As some of this understanding was connected to concern for an apparently fast-approaching end of times, some reference is made here to eschatology within the Tijāniyya. Lastly, this chapter discusses al-Tijānī's central emphasis on God's grace as the individual's only logical escape from the distress decreed for his age.

The Corruption of the Age and the Turks in Algeria

Aḥmad al-Tijānī, like many of his time, made frequent reference to the perceived corruption and sinfulness of the age. It is tempting to suggest that at least some of these references, like the shaykh's self-prohibition of sugar, responded to a changing global balance of political and economic power toward non-Muslim European powers. But the discourse on corruption seems to have been mostly directed internally at Muslim societies. As previously mentioned, the Prophet advised al-Tijānī not to emigrate East as the rulers of those lands "had ceased to be good Muslims" on account of alcohol consumption and unjust expropriation of wealth. While much of al-Tijānī's censure of perceived corruption may indeed have been directed at the Ottomans, particularly the Ottoman government of Algiers, the shaykh was more concerned with the spread of corruption in the individual souls of Muslims.

The Algeria in which Aḥmad al-Tijānī came of age had technically been an Ottoman province since the sixteenth century. By the mid-seventeenth century, however, Ottoman elites in the provincial capital of Algiers, hoping to reassert their Turkish identity and gain favor with a sultan apparently disinterested in Algeria, came to increasingly isolate themselves from the local population.[3] Muslim scholars (*ʿulamāʾ*) close to Algiers were subject to intense surveillance, and those of perceived dangerous influence over local populations were often executed, exiled, or purposefully impoverished.[4] The traditional independence of inland oases like ʿAyn Māḍī, where al-Tijānī was born, was threatened by augmented taxes imposed to supplement a decline in tolls exacted on Mediterranean shipping.[5] The Ottomans in Algiers imposed an annual tribute on ʿAyn Māḍī in 1785 and sent the first in a series of armed forces to collect the tax from the town in 1788.[6] Newly established Sufi orders in the rural interior felt particularly targeted by such policies, and the Turks laid siege to Algerian centers of the Raḥmaniyya (Khalwatiyya) and Darqawiyya (Shādhiliyya), in addition to the Tijāniyya in ʿAyn Māḍī.[7] The Bey had Ibn ʿAbd al-Raḥmān al-Azharī (al-Tijānī's first initiator into the Khalwatiyya) imprisoned in Algiers and later plotted to have al-Azharī's corpse stolen from its tomb in Kabyles and brought to Algiers, apparently to avoid the concentration of the Raḥmāniyya in a rural area outside of their control.[8] The combination of being disconnected from the local population, the marginalization of urban scholarship, and the forced expropriation of the wealth of inland oases no doubt contributed to the perception of some that, in Algeria "the Turks enjoyed little Islamic justification for their rule."[9] For their perceived unjust shedding of blood, theft of wealth, and general privileging of their own legislation over the Sharīʿa, al-Tijānī gave his opinion of the Turks in Algeria: "Their rulers are infidels" (*ḥukkāmuhum kuffār*).[10]

Tijānī sources contain only fleeting references to al-Tijānī's personal conflicts with the Turkish authorities in Algeria, but external sources provide suggestive details. The earlier narratives of Abun-Nasr and Adnani, focusing on al-Tijānī's alleged expulsion from Algeria, rely almost exclusively on accounts from the Moroccan historian Abū l-Qāsim al-Zayānī (d. 1833). Al-Zayānī's rendition has al-Tijānī being accused of practicing alchemy, of collecting around him the "dregs of the Berbers and the Arabs," and of being imprisoned and then expelled first from Tlemcen by the Turkish Bey in Algeria, Muḥammad b. ʿUthmān (d. 1791), and then from Abī Samghūn by the Bey's son who had become the governor of Oran.[11] But the authenticity of al-Zayānī's narration with regard to al-Tijānī is highly doubtful, suggests the more recent Moroccan historian Aḥmad al-Azmī. Neither French nor Algerian accounts written during the period mention any such imprisonment or expulsion: it is highly unlikely the action of the Turkish Bey in Algiers or prince in Oran against a religious notable would have escaped the notice of observers who reported on Algeria's internal developments more closely than did al-Zayānī.[12] Indeed, it seems al-Zayānī had developed a reputation for spreading lies and slander, even in Moroccan circles. According to the central Moroccan biographical dictionary of the period, *Salwat al-anfās*: "He (al-Zayānī) was possessed of impetuosity (*ḥidda*), and his tongue neither remained (in his mouth) nor sowed (good). This finally led him to disparage the great saints, and we seek refuge in God from that."[13] Al-Azmī believes al-Zayānī's animosity to al-Tijānī caused him to accept dubious narrations or even to fabricate them: al-Zayānī may have been jealous of Sultan Mawlay Sulaymān's reception of al-Tijānī in Fez, and he probably considered al-Tijānī a "Wahhābī" for his restriction of grave visitation.[14] If true, such clear biases undermine not only al-Zayānī's credibility, but also the credibility of subsequent narratives that exclusively rely on his account.

Two other nineteenth-century historical accounts do reference al-Tijānī's dislike for the Turkish government in Algeria but do not contain al-Zayānī's likely fabricated stories of imprisonment and expulsion. The Algerian historian Muḥammad b. ʿAbd al-Qādir al-Jazāʾirī (writing in 1842) states that al-Tijānī's move to Fez was voluntary, but that he did indeed hope to escape the perceived injustice of the Turks: "When his affair [the spread of the Tijāniyya] became public in the country, he feared the government's treachery. So he moved with his family and children to Fez in the time of Mawlay Sulaymān."[15] Similarly, the Moroccan history of Aḥmad al-Nāṣirī cites a letter that al-Tijānī sent to Mawlay Sulaymān upon his arrival in Fez in 1798, informing him that he had come fleeing the oppression of the Turks and seeking protection from them with the Prophet's family (*ahl al-bayt*). Al-Nāṣirī's version makes reference to the Turkish Bey's "harassment" of al-Tijānī in Tlemcen and his son's "menacing" of him in Abī Samghūn, suggesting al-Tijānī's move to Morocco was not unwarranted. In any case, "when he [the sultan] saw his character and his mastery of the knowledge disciplines, he welcomed him, believed in him and gave him a house to consider his own."[16]

There is ample evidence from internal sources that al-Tijānī was not fond of Turkish rule in Algeria, but he cautioned against open rebellion. Sometime in the late 1780s, the shaykh asked the Prophet to protect his followers and their wealth from the Bey Muḥammad b. ʿUthmān, and from a political leader of Tlemcen named Sulaymān, as well as from "all oppressors, thieves, and usurpers."[17] Presumably on behalf of followers from Algeria, the shaykh asked the Prophet in one encounter: "What about the alms-tax (*zakāt*) taken by the unjust rulers among the Muslims by force, is that permissible for them?" The Prophet responded, "Did I not command them (Muslims) to obey them?" The shaykh said, "You said to them, 'Anyone who can give it [*zakāt*] to other than them, without meeting harm [should do so].'" The Prophet said, "Give it [to the unjust], but upon them is God's curse."[18] The Turkish Bey's siege of ʿAyn Māḍī in 1788 was likely the context for this dialogue. Sometime between 1785 and 1798, the shaykh's disciples in ʿAyn Māḍī wrote to al-Tijānī, apparently asking permission to embark on armed rebellion against Algiers: they wanted to know whether they had to obey the Bey, and if al-Tijānī could send them gunpowder and bullets. The shaykh first expressed his regret for not visiting ʿAyn Māḍī due to the "plethora of enemies" along the way, but then cautioned: "As for the matter of the Bey with you, hear my full advice offered as a father to his son. If you would put my advice into practice, hasten to him in his land. Give him what you can of money, and do not fight him. There is no good for you in fighting him. . . . Do not contemplate anything except that which will rectify relations between yourselves and the Bey."[19] Al-Tijānī thus tried to stave off open revolt against the Turkish regime in Algiers. But there is no doubt the shaykh's opinion of the Algerian Turks soured further after his establishment in Fez.

When Turkish authorities executed, apparently without cause, one of his disciples in Tlemcen in 1805, Aḥmad al-Baghdādī al-Turkī, al-Tijānī "became furious with the actions of the Algerian government and their brutal transgression." He prayed out loud, "May God cause it [Algeria] to be closed off from them, as Andalusia was closed off."[20] Tijānī disciples no doubt saw the French conquest of Algiers in 1830 as the fulfillment of their shaykh's prayer. Probably al-Tijānī could be included among a wider range of eighteenth-century scholars who were primarily concerned with "tyrants who oppress Muslims."[21] But neither al-Tijānī nor the later Tijāniyya extended the censure of the Ottoman government beyond Algeria: al-Tijānī had been on friendly terms with the Turkish government in Tunis, and later Tijānī scholars were welcomed by the Ottoman sultan in Istanbul.[22]

Rather than the predictable corruption of government elite, al-Tijānī's primary concern was the corruption of Muslim societies. In the letter to ʿAyn Māḍī cited above, al-Tijānī went on to suggest that the injustice of the Bey was God's punishment for the sinfulness of Muslims in the Algerian desert. "I inform you that the following has been unveiled to me from the secret of the unseen, of which neither you nor we knew before: God the glorious and exalted has decreed, from His wisdom, that all among His creation among the people of the desert . . . will suffer punishment on account of their disobedience and lack of repentance, and for the public spread of injustice and abominations in every locale . . . '*Who has done an atom's weight of evil will see it.*' "[23] Al-Tijānī may have been referring to specific perceived injustices, such as the alliance of a rival confederation with the Turks against the Tijāniyya in ʿAyn Māḍī, or the harassment and later murder of his primary representative in the city Muḥammad al-Damrāwī.[24] But al-Tijānī seemed more broadly concerned with the sinfulness of his age: the spread of slander, fighting between Muslims, and open violation of the Sharīʿa. The shaykh's secret collection of prayers, *Kunnāsh al-aṣfar*, thus lists many prayers based on Qurʾān verses that, for example, guide the heedless one toward obedience, promote reconciliation between people, separate people who do wrong together, or cure addiction to wine drinking or fornication.[25]

On the one hand, al-Tijānī's warning about preoccupation with the lower world of sin and lust had a certain timeless quality reflective of earlier Sufi masters. He wrote disciples in Morocco: "You must have patience with God's command in what occurs among calamities and trials. The world is the abode of troubles (*fitan*). Its calamities are like waves of the sea. God only sent down the children of Adam into the world to encounter its troubles and calamities. No one among the children of Adam can expect to escape from this so long as he remains in the world. . . . Take comfort that, if calamity or trial should be visited upon you, it was for this reason that the world [was] created and fashioned."[26] A righteous life might protect a person from some of the world's problems, but obviously not all. Al-Tijānī's delimitation of sin invoked long-standing Islamic understandings: fornication, slander, missing prayer times without just cause, misappropriation of wealth, eating (or drinking) forbidden things, or disparaging the Prophet's companions. For the spiritually elite (*al-khawāṣṣ*), sin included not giving witness to God's blessing (*ʿadam shuhūd al-minna*) or being ungrateful for God's favors.[27]

On the other hand, al-Tijānī saw his own time as unparalleled in its sinfulness. "No one in this time has an ability to separate himself from sins," al-Tijānī warned disciples, "for they fall on mankind like heavy rain."[28] Aside from general advice to avoid sin to the best of one's ability, key supplications al-Tijānī offered to disciples provide insight into his understanding of the individual's condition in such a time. Al-Tijānī advised disciples to say three times every day: "O God, your forgiveness is wider than my sins, and your mercy is a greater hope for me than my deeds." In the same letter, speaking of the sinfulness of the age, the shaykh advised disciples with another prayer: "O God, I beg forgiveness for what I have repented from but then returned to. I seek forgiveness for every promise I made, but then failed to keep. I seek forgiveness for every deed I intended for your sake alone, but then mixed with what was not for You. I seek forgiveness for every blessing You bestowed on me, but which I used in disobeying You."[29] In other words, al-Tijānī encouraged disciples to at least recognize how the people of their time had mixed negligence and insincerity in all of their actions; repenting from sin but then returning, using God's blessing for disobeying God. "The people of this time are like chickens, provided for without obtaining any understanding or concern for whence they came, or for whither they are going."[30]

Aḥmad al-Tijānī perceived his time, perhaps now often understood as the dawn of the modern age, as one in which people had begun to worship themselves instead of God. This entailed nothing less than the desacralization of the world. According to al-Tijānī: "The regular order of existence has been disrupted by the will of the Real, something no one can deny. Now, the only concern for every individual is the pursuit of his selfish interests and carnal desires, in total disregard of the divine presence, and of the duties and properties he ought to fulfill."[31] In a letter meant for all disciples earlier cited, al-Tijānī thus quoted a ḥadīth censuring "the self-conceit of a man in his own personal opinion," and the "lust pursued" as the idol "most odiously worshipped."[32] While the warning against following the desires of the lower self was certainly a long tradition in Sufism, these citations seem to indicate an understanding of heightened egocentrism.

Such self-worship meant wise people should avoid stirring up the evil of others' carnal selves by all means necessary. Here al-Tijānī's advice tends toward an active passivism rather than open confrontation. Although parts of this letter have already been referenced above, this significant address to "the entirety of disciples" is included here at length:

> I advise myself and you with the security (*muḥāfiẓa*) in guarding to the words of the Prophet: "Three things lead to success, and three things lead to ruin. Success is found in the fear (*taqwā*) of God secretly and publicly, the word of truth (spoken) in (both) contentment and anger, and moderation (whether) in (a state of) wealth or poverty. Ruin is found in avarice yielded to, lust followed after, and the self-conceit of a man in his own personal opinion." And his words, "There has never been a god other than God more odiously worshipped than a lust pursued." And his words, "Do not wish to meet the enemy, and ask God for safety (*ʿāfiya*). And if you should meet them (the enemy) then have patience."
>
> And this was related in the context of jihad, fighting against the non-believers. The statement is more appropriate (*munqalib*), in this time, to overlooking the evil of mankind. The one who wishes in his heart to stir up evil among men, God gives them power over him and he has no defense against them. The servant should rather ask God for safety from the awakening of men's evil and tribulation. And if such evil should be aroused against him, let him not be the cause for it.
>
> The best way, demanded by knowledge, is to meet them in the face of their evil with the best of character (*iḥsān*). If he cannot do this, then let him pardon and forgive them in order to extinguish the fire of tribulation. If he cannot do this, then let him have patience with the unfolding of the Divine decree, and let not their offenses provoke him. And if the flames of their evil should set him ablaze, then let him defend himself with what is better in gentleness and conciliation. If he should not arrive to this, then he must escape if he can and flee from his abode. And if obstacles should prevent his escape, then let

> him fight with restraint to minimize the harm. He does this externally, but secretly he increases his humility before God and supplicates that their evil should be lifted from him. And he persists in this until God grants him felicity. [. . .]
>
> This way (of pardoning) that we have mentioned: all of the creation needs it in this time. Who persists in following this program (*minhāj*) finds happiness in this world and the next. But who deviates from this, God entrusts him to his own carnal soul (*nafs*), and he will set out to meet the evils with (only) his own strength and delusion. Sooner or later, this is a most ruinous destruction.[33]

This important letter does not go so far as to abrogate armed jihad (and later Tijānīs did take up arms), but it clearly describes an age of inescapable tribulation in which forceful confrontation only fanned the flames of enmity.

Indeed, the remarkable spread of the Tijāniyya in Algeria is inexplicable without appreciating al-Tijānī's accent on friendly relations with government and local communities alike, prior to his establishment in Fez. Prominent representatives (*muqaddams)* hailed from all over Algeria, from the Sharīf ʿAlī al-Tamāsīnī in the southeastern oasis of Tamāsīn,[34] to ʿAbd al-Qādir al-Mashrafī in the northeastern town of Arrīs,[35] to Muḥammad b. al-Tabbāl al-Qasanṭīnī in the northeastern city of Constantine,[36] to Muhammad b. Ḥirzallāh al-Zakīzkī[37] and Muḥammad b. al-Dāwdī al-Aḥlāfī in the southcentral city of al-Aghwāṭ,[38] to Aḥmad al-Tuwātī and Muḥammad al-Fuḍayl al-Tuwātī in the southern oasis of Tuwāt,[39] to Ibn al-Mashrī in the western province of Tlemcen,[40] to Muḥammad b. al-ʿAbbās al-Samghūnī in the southwestern oasis of Abī Samghūn,[41] to Muḥammad al-Māzirī in the northwestern town of Mazer,[42] to Imam ʿAbd al-Jabbār of Chellala just south of Algiers,[43] to the aforementioned Aḥmad al-Turkī in Algiers.[44] Such Algerian disciples appear in Tijānī sources as scholarly exemplars, possessed of noble lineage and wealth: certainly not the "dregs of the Arabs" as al-Zayyānī claimed. Al-Tamāsīnī, for example, was a wealthy date farmer and scholar. Al-Māzirī was a prominent jurist, a descendant of the famous jurist and ḥadīth scholar Muḥammad al-Tamīmī al-Māzirī (d. 1141). Several of his disciples from Aghwāṭ were known for their scholarly credentials. Aside from the aforementioned Aḥlāfī, the jurist Aḥmad b. Ismāʿīl had such beautiful Qurʾān recitation (*tajwīd*) that the Prophet appeared to another scholar to say, "Tell Aḥmad b. Ismāʿīl to raise his voice when reciting the Qur'ān!"[45] Al-Tijānī's disciple Saḥnūn b. al-Ḥājj al-Aghwāṭī got his name because his explanation of Islamic law was thought equal only to the legendary Mālikī scholar Saḥnūn al-Tanukhi (d. 784, Tunis).[46] The Tijāniyya was certainly thriving in Algeria well before al-Tijānī's emigration to Fez. The shaykh's trusted disciple Maḥmūd al-Tunisī regularly toured Algeria collecting large amounts of money, both from al-Tijānī's farms and from gifts from disciples, which he brought to the shaykh in Fez.[47] This financial independence no doubt impressed his Moroccan hosts. While al-Tijānī may have left Algeria to escape the Turks, his Algerian followers provided the foundation that facilitated the growth of the Tijāniyya in Fez and throughout Morocco and North Africa.

The Tijāniyya's spread south of the Sahara is normally associated with the affiliation of several Mauritanian scholars—such as 'Abd al-Raḥman, Muḥammad al-Ḥāfiẓ, and the "Imam and judge of his people" Muḥammad al-Ṭālib Jadd al-Shinqīṭī—with al-Tijānī in Fez.[48] But the earlier spread of the order in southern Algeria, especially the region of Tuwāt of long-standing importance in the trans-Saharan trade routes, undoubtedly provided another pathway. Recent research has proven the importance of Tuwāt as a point of diffusion for Nāṣiriyya into the Sahara in the early eighteenth century.[49] As previously mentioned, members of Mukhtār al-Kuntī's West African Qādiriyya were also present in Tuwāt from the late eighteenth century.[50] By the mid-eighteenth century, the region had developed its own version of the Nāṣiriyya, the "Rekkāniyya" associated with the teachings of Mawlāy 'Abdallāh and his son 'Abd al-Mālik (d. 1793)—the latter described in a contemporary source as the paradigmatic saint (*quṭb*) of this time—in the Tuwāt oasis of Reggane.[51] It seems Tuwātī scholars such as Mawlay 'Abd al-Mālik, according to the *Fatḥ al-shakūr*, had developed a fearsome reputation for the subjection (*taskhīr*) of creation and "penetrating supplications."[52] While in Abū Samghūn, al-Tijānī wrote a letter to one of Tuwāt's most renowned saints, Muḥammad b. al-Fuḍayl, from the people of Takrārīn of Western Tuwāt, asking for certain "secrets" (*asrār*). Ibn al-Fuḍayl refused to respond, desiring to meet al-Tijānī in person. Al-Tijānī guessed his intention and visited him, on which occasion Ibn al-Fuḍayl "left his own Sufi path to take advantage of this Muḥammadan way."[53] It was likely on this trip, or on al-Tijānī's subsequent visit to Tuwāt while he was living in Fez, that other Tuwātī scholars were initiated into the order. The aforementioned Aḥmad al-Tuwātī, known for the "speedy response of his supplications," authored the influential prayer *ḥizb al-mughnī* to be recited after *ḥizb al-sayf*, an addition included in Tijānī prayer manuals to the present day.[54] The Tijāniyya was thus in early dialogue with preexisting Saharan scholarship through its establishment in Algeria, and its successful spread throughout the Sahara and was likely already assured before al-Tijānī's establishment in Fez. Indeed, the Tijāniyya achieved remarkable success in both urban and rural spaces in Algeria itself, a fact that serves to qualify (or perhaps explain) the alleged enmity between the Turks in Algeria and the nascent Tijāniyya. The shaykh's apparent distrust of the Ottoman government in Algiers is best understood as a perception of a more general decline in Islamic morality.

Scholasticism and Disciple Realization in Fez

Aḥmad al-Tijānī and an entourage of his close followers and family, according to the *Jawāhir al-maʿānī*, "left the desert" and after a twenty-day journey, arrived in Fez, Morocco, in September, 1798.[55] It is unclear whether al-Tijānī's entrance into Fez attracted the immediate attention of Mawlay Sulaymān. Tijānī sources do not mention the alleged letter al-Tijānī sent to the Moroccan king requesting asylum,[56] and al-Tijānī's entourage first stayed with the family of ʿAlī Ḥarāzim al-Barrāda, whose father maintained a large house in Fez.[57] The twentieth-century Moroccan scholar Idrīs al-ʿIrāqī (d. 2009) insisted on an oral tradition passed from the family of al-Tijānī's disciple Ṭayyib al-Sufyānī that the shaykh did not meet the sultan until a year after entering Fez.[58] The scholarly establishment did, however, take immediate notice: likely al-Tijānī's reputation had preceded him. At least one of the city's scholars, "the consummate scholar" (*ʿallāma*) of Arabic, jurisprudence, and ḥadīth, ʿAbd al-Wāḥid al-Fāsī al-Fihrī (d. 1799), who composed poetry in al-Tijānī's honor, had become affiliated with the shaykh before his 1798 settlement.[59] A group of learned men, including the likes of the two jurists Idrīs al-Bakrāwī and Muḥammad Laḥlū, came out to welcome al-Tijānī before his entrance into the city. Laḥlū had heard of al-Tijānī from his teacher al-Bakrāwī and "ardently desired to meet him." Al-Tijānī said of him upon meeting him, "He is among our companions" and instructed him to lead the prayer. The shaykh visited Laḥlū in his home, and after curing his mother from paralysis, effected his family's affiliation to the Tijāniyya.[60]

Another scholar to recognize al-Tijānī early on was the aforementioned Mauritanian ḥadīth scholar resident in Fez, ʿAbd al-Raḥmān al-Shinqīṭī, who had earlier studied under Ṣāliḥ al-Fullānī in Medina, Arabia, and who attracted "all the nobles of the age to Fez just to be present in his learning sessions." Soon after his arrival in Fez, al-Tijānī entered the grand mosque in upper Fez, where al-Shinqīṭī sat teaching a large group of students. Al-Shinqīṭī waited until al-Tijānī had greeted the mosque in prayer, then interrupted his lesson to tell his students, "Get up! Let us seek blessing from this Shaykh." Al-Shinqīṭī then went to sit with al-Tijānī and asked him a number of questions. After returning to his lecture, his students asked, "O Sīdī, we did not take you as a shaykh, lowering our gaze from all others, until we were certain there was no one more knowledgeable than you in the Maghreb. But you stood up for this man from the desert . . . you asked him questions and listened to his answers." Al-Shinqīṭī responded, "Be quiet, my child. By God, other than whom there is no god, there is no one on the face of the earth more knowledgeable than him."[61] Indeed, it was this testimony of al-Shinqīṭī, as referenced earlier, that ultimately persuaded his countryman Muḥammad al-Ḥāfiẓ to later visit al-Tijānī inFez.

Such early scholars were not alone, and very quickly others came to take notice of al-Tijānī. After his arrival in Fez and while still a guest of the Barrāda family, the shaykh took to teaching in a nearby mosque, and soon large crowds of students began to gather for his lessons.[62] Within a few months, al-Tijānī's scholarly reputation had become the subject of discussion in the sultan's prestigious "council of scholars." This council was dominated by three scholars in particular: the elder shaykh of the sultan's court, ʿAbd al-Qādir b. Shaqrūn; the leading Qurʾān scholar at Fez's Qarawiyīn University, al-Ṭayyib b. Kīrān; and the leading Mālikī jurist of the city, Ḥamdūn b. al-Ḥājj. All three had earlier taught Sultan Sulaymān the Islamic sciences and had been recently appointed to the council in the sultan's attempt to revive the scholarly heritage of Fez, following a devastating plague in which many of the earlier scholars had died. Apparently, when al-Tijānī's name was first brought up in the presence of the sultan, Ibn Kīrān began to disparage the shaykh, "perhaps fearing he would undermine his position of prominence with the Sultan."[63] This led the elder Shaqrūn, in fact Ibn Kīrān's earlier teacher, to break his customary silence and to remind the assembly of al-Tijānī's reputed knowledge and virtue. The result was that the sultan decided to invite al-Tijānī for an audience with the council, with the sultan himself present, to make a more informed judgment.[64]

Two mutually supportive accounts of what happened at the council are related in Sukayrij's *Kashf al-ḥijāb* and *Rafʿ al-niqāb*, both on the authority of scholars who had been appointed by the sultan and were present during al-Tijānī's first appearance at the council: ʿAbbās al-Sharāybī, a student of Ibn Kīrān, and al-ʿAbbās b. Muḥammad b. Kīrān (d. 1855), who had studied with Ḥamdūn b. al-Ḥājj, who would accompany the sultan's delegation to the Hijaz in 1811, and who would later become the chief judge (*qāḍī*) of Meknes.[65] Here is the account of al-Sharāybī, who would later take the Tijāniyya, as related to Aḥmad ʿAbdallāwī (1815–1910) and then to Sukayrij:

> That day, we had come to discussing the explanation of the Qurʾān chapter "Mankind" (*sūrat al-nās*). Ibn Kīrān began, as was his custom in the presence of the King in that august assembly, due to his reputation in the formal and interpretive sciences (*al-ʿilm al-ẓāhir wa ʿilm al-maʿqūl*). He started and finished, thinking that no one possessed as much knowledge as he. And some of those present conceded as much. Then the King turned to the Shaykh (al-Tijānī), may God be pleased with him, and asked, "What does the Shaykh say about these verses?"
>
> Then our master began speaking about the noble verses, from transmitted reports (*manqūl*) and interpretation (*maʿqūl*) in ways that astonished the minds. Then our master addressed a matter that Shaykh al-Ṭayyib b. Kīrān, thinking that his achievement was unmatched, had exaggerated beyond all bounds: "What this exegete (Ibn Kīrān) has mentioned is not correct, and is not supported by those of sound hearts (*dhawī l-albāb*)."
>
> Shaykh al-Ṭayyib responded, "So you would raise objections against us, on the basis of what so-and-so among the Qur'ān interpreters have said?" And he went on like this at length.
>
> Our master said to him in this assiduous gathering, "The floor does not belong to you, so do not be like those weighed down (with themselves). You were not commissioned to hold (the floor) yourself. The word belongs rather those who interpret the Qurʾān."
>
> Then our master explained the correct interpretation with transmitted and logical evidence, until the truth was revealed in every aspect. And the truth was clear, and the falsehood dissipated. And he settled with certainty (*bi l-taḥqīq*) every controversy. Everyone in the assembly said, "By God, that is the evident truth." And all of this was seen and heard by the King. Then the assembly dispersed, and profuse gratitude for our master was on the tongue of every participant.
>
> Afterward, the King addressed those who remained with him: "(Now) you know the rank (*maqām*) of Sīdī Aḥmad al-Tijānī, and his

> splendor in external knowledge. As for his esoteric knowledge (*ʿilm al-bāṭin*), he is the father, mother, and offspring of that knowledge. So, what do you say?"
>
> They said, "By God, his word is true. He clarified the truth, free from falsehood. He made clear what is correct for anyone who can see." From that moment, Shaykh al-Ṭayyib harbored resentment in himself, may God forgive him and us.[66]

This account, useful despite the lack of external corroboration from non-Tijānī sources, points to several significant details concerning al-Tijānī's appearance in Fez. The first is that al-Tijānī capably demonstrated his knowledge in the external science of Qurʾān interpretation (*tafsīr*), no doubt drawing on his many years teaching *tafsīr* in Algeria where he reportedly "limited himself to the circumstances of revelation (*aṣbāb al-nuzūl*) for the Qurʾān verses, and their relevant issues and legal implications."[67] In other words, al-Tijānī bested Fez's most established *tafsīr* authority in his own field, pointing out Ibn Kīrān's contradiction of earlier Qurʾān exegetes. This mastery of *tafsīr* remained a salient feature of al-Tijānī's reputation. Muḥammad al-Sanūsī related that he studied the Qurʾān with al-Tijānī in Fez despite never having taken the Tijāniyya: "I learned from him, and I took the Qurʾān from him, and he told me that he had taken it from the Prophet, asleep and awake. And he excelled in following his example in all actions, and he honored me by letting me take the Qurʾān from him, by this noble *sanad*, after he had taken it from him."[68] Clearly, al-Tijānī's subsequent appointment to the sultan's council of scholars would not have been possible without such wide recognition of al-Tijānī's scholarly credentials. The "eldest shaykh in the Sultan's court" Ibn Shaqrūn (d. 1804) did not take the Tijāniyya, but he began frequenting al-Tijānī and took from him "gnosis and secrets."[69] According to the Moroccan historian Aḥmad al-ʿIrāqī's recently published biography of Ibn Shaqrūn, "He had a relationship of love and truthfulness with Shaykh Aḥmad al-Tijānī. He used to meet with him, but he did not take the oath of his *ṭarīqa*, [simply] taking refuge in his good pleasure, and accepting his emulation of the Prophet."[70] The aforementioned ʿAbbās b. Kīrān, who later did take the Tijāniyya, consulted al-Tijānī for various questions of jurisprudence, such as the permissibility of a mosque hosting a second Friday prayer after that led by the designated imam.[71] Abun-Nasr's suggestion that al-Tijānī wanted to "ban all religious learning" thus seems altogether unsubstantiated.[72] Al-Tijānī did not obligate all initiates to become scholars, but he certainly stressed learning for laity as well as the elite. His advice to a father concerned about his son's education was practical: "Teach him what you can of the Qur'ān, teach him how to read and write, and teach him a trade by which he can support himself."[73]

Al-Tijānī's first appearance at the sultan's scholarly council thus demonstrates his appeal to Morocco's learned elite. Many scholars, apparently impressed by his erudition, began to make their own inquiries into al-Tijānī's spiritual claims. Al-Sharāybī's subsequent affiliation with the Tijāniyya, despite earlier apprenticeship with al-Ṭayyib b. Kīrān, was occasioned by a dream the night after witnessing al-Tijānī's performance in the council. He saw himself talking about al-Tijānī with "some of God's people (*ahl Allāh*)," about what had transpired with Ibn Kīrān. One of them said to him concerning al-Tijānī, "O my brother, did you not hear the words of God (in the Qur'ān)? *O you who believe, do not be like those who insulted Moses. God rendered him innocent of their allegations, and he is highly honored in the presence of God.*"[74]

Another jurist, Muḥammad b. Faqīra from Meknes, came to visit al-Tijānī in the company of some "distinguished scholars" (*akābir*), one of whom came to ask the shaykh to pray for children as he had none. Ibn Faqīra gave al-Tijānī one silver dirham, while the other scholar gave him forty gold riyals as a gift. The shaykh took the dirham in his hand, looked at it, put it in his pocket, and turned back to his house. The other scholar called after him, "Take what is yours!" The shaykh stopped and said to him, "This (dirham) is for the sake of a pious visitation (*ziyāra*). But (as for you) take back your property, for we are not in the business of selling children." Ibn Faqīra was evidently impressed with al-Tijānī's sincerity and asked the shaykh for initiation into the Tijāniyya.[75]

Well-known scholars in Fez who took the Tijāniyya included not only the previously mentioned al-Sharāybī, ʿAbbās b. Kīrān, Muḥammad Laḥlū, ʿAbd al-Waḥid al-Fāsī, and ʿAbd al-Raḥmān al-Shinqīṭī, but also the imam of central Mawlay Idrīs mosque Muḥammad b. Aḥmad al-Sanūsī (d. 1841),[76] several members of the scholarly Bannīs family,[77] the jurist Aḥmad b. Maḥammad al-Bannānī,[78] the wealthy scholar al-Ṭayyib al-Sufyānī (d. 1843),[79] and the city's chief jurist Ḥamdūn b. al-Ḥājj (d. 1817). Al-Sufyānī, who later authored the important Tijānī text *al-Ifāda al-Aḥmadiyya*, was a prominent *sharīf* and representative of the Wazzāniyya order in Fez, who also taught the traditional Islamic sciences. He encountered al-Barrāda's

Jawāhir al-maʿānī with a fellow Moroccan Maḥammad b. ʿAbd al-Wāḥid al-Bannānī al-Maṣrī while visiting Egypt on the way to Ḥajj and resolved to visit al-Tijānī on his return to Fez. When he came to al-Tijānī, the shaykh told him, "I have been your spiritual trainer and guarantor since before your mother gave birth to you," and proceeded to inform him of the reason for certain scars on his head only known to his mother.[80] Aḥmad al-Bannānī initially resisted following his friend al-Sufyānī, believing himself to be of superior learning and spiritual rank to al-Tijānī. Finally, he visited al-Tijānī and heard from him "one secret word" that he considered more valuable than "a world full of gold" and found himself unable to sleep until he returned and took the Tijāniyya. Al-Bannānī was known to have a photographic memory, and al-Tijānī frequently discussed with him interpretations of the Qur'ān and ḥadīth.[81]

Ḥamdūn b. al-Ḥājj was the "official jurist" of Mawlay's Sulaymān's court,[82] who had been endowed by the king with "the special chair" of ḥadīth instruction at Qarawiyīn in Fez.[83] Like Ibn Shaqrūn and Ibn Kīrān, with whom he had studied some of the Islamic sciences, Ibn al-Ḥājj had earlier been sent by Sultan Muḥammad (r. 1757–90) to teach the future Sultan Sulaymān in Sijilmasa.[84] Mawlay Sulaymān had developed a high opinion of him: "I (Mawlay Sulaymān) bear witness that this writer (Ibn al-Ḥājj) is the literary scholar (*adīb*) of his time, the likes of whom is not found in the Maghreb or in the lands of Egypt."[85] Al-Kattānī testified to Ibn al-Ḥājj's scholarship: "He perfected the application of legal reasoning (*ijtihād*) in both specific and general matters, he was the guardian of the pens of old in the field of 'deriving the source' (*instinbāṭ*)."[86] Ibn al-Ḥājj's student ʿAbd al-Qādir al-Kūhan testified that his teacher "was among those who had mastered all disciplines of knowledge . . . especially Qur'ān exegesis, Prophetic narrations, and Sufism based on the Qur'ān and the Sunnah."[87] Aside from Ibn Kīrān and other Moroccan scholars, Ibn al-Ḥājj had authorization (*ijāza*) from the likes of Murtaḍā al-Zabīdī in Egypt, whom he had met while on pilgrimage. The sultan appointed him the "overseer of virtue" (*muḥtasab*) of Fez, a position he held for three years (1804–7). He otherwise maintained an intense schedule of teaching at the main centers of learning in Fez: he taught prophetic traditions (from *Ṣaḥīḥ al-Bukhārī*) in the mosque of Mawlay Idrīs after the dawn prayer; and then spent the rest of his day at the Qarawiyīn mosque-university teaching Islamic law (from the *Mukhtaṣar Sīdī Khalīl*) from mid-morning to the noon prayer, Arabic rhetoric (from *Takhlīs al-miftāḥ*) between the noon and afternoon prayer, and then Qur'ān exegesis (*tafsīr*) from the afternoon prayer until the night prayer.[88] He was also the most famous poet of the sultan's court, and in one poem praised Mawlay Sulaymān as the "Harūn al-Rashīd" of his time.[89] He also wrote books on logic, theology, exegesis, and prophetic traditions and biography; although his son Muḥammad al-Ṭālib's seminal commentary (*ḥāshiya*) on Ibn 'Āshir's *Murshid al-mu'īn* would be become more famous than Ibn al-Ḥājj's own writings.[90]

After meeting al-Tijānī in Algeria on the way back from his pilgrimage (1790–91),[91] Ḥamdūn b. al-Ḥājj became one of the shaykh's closest disciples. He frequented al-Tijānī upon his settlement in Fez, "paying no mind" to those who criticized the shaykh. Despite being unable to attend the congregational remembrance (*waẓīfa*) in the Tijānī *zāwiya* due to his teaching schedule, he came to al-Tijānī's house to pose questions related to the Islamic sciences "seeking further knowledge," and to take from him "secrets and gnosis."[92] Ibn al-Ḥājj's own letters demonstrate a depth of Sufi understanding, and his son Ṭālib attested to his father's attainment of spiritual illumination (*fatḥ*); among his last words being, "All of you listen to these words, for you will not find them in any book."[93] In one letter, providing explanation of the Qur'ān "chapter of sincerity" (*sūrat al-ikhlāṣ*), Ibn al-Ḥājj wrote: "The Prophet's statement, 'God is singular (*witr*), and He loves the singular,' means [that God loves] the heart singularly devoted to Him. Divine proximity with this Name [the One] means that you do not see anything in this world or the next except Him, and that you do not turn to other than Him. Like this you will achieve actualization, and you will become unique in your time, in your age, among humankind."[94] Ibn al-Ḥājj thus hinted at the notion of a saintly hierarchy, as well as the orthodoxy of the concept of *waḥdat al-wujūd*. Later in the same letter, Ibn al-Ḥājj cited Ibn al-'Arabī and then concluded with the statement of Abū Ḥasan al-Shādhilī, "We do not see the creation; but if we must, we see them only as minute particles of smoke disappearing into the air."[95]

If Ibn al-Ḥājj's opinions can be taken as representative of scholarly culture in late eighteenth-century Morocco, there appear to have been few ideological barriers for the nascent Tijāniyya's establishment there. For his part, Ibn al-Ḥājj did not allow his own renown to veil him from attesting to al-Tijānī's claimed spiritual rank. He once followed a blind man in prayer just because he saw him sitting with al-Tijānī, saying "I would pray behind anyone who sits with him."[96] Among his almost four thousand lines of extant poetry are several dedicated to the shaykh:

I commend you to the resplendent, luminous moon
Abū l-ʿAbbās, I mean Aḥmad al-Tijānī
The sun of mastery, the axis (*quṭb*) of the sphere of guidance
The full moon of felicity, the star of spiritual excellence
The sea of generosity, our elucidator of heavenly wisdom
Like rare gems in a necklace or crown
The best of imams who has been granted ascension
With righteous deeds. So be not among the negligent.[97]

For his part, al-Tijānī had high consideration for his scholarly disciple, attesting in a letter, "He is surely the master of the scholars of his time. I ask that God record him among the felicitous, and that the creation not harm him."[98] The larger point here, then, was that among the three leading scholars of the sultan's court—Ibn Shaqrūn, Ibn Kīrān, and Ḥamdūn b. al-Ḥājj—one was sympathetic to al-Tijānī, one was opposed to him, and the last undoubtedly became his disciple.

This account is based mostly on sources internal to the Tijāniyya, and thus is not beyond dispute. But it is also corroborated by external sources such as *Salwat al-anfās* and others, none of which dispute that al-Tijānī was welcomed by an important cross section of the scholarly establishment in Fez, and that he was appointed to the prestigious scholarly council of the sultan. The idea that there was an intractable broad "hostility of the population in Fez towards him [al-Tijānī],"[99] or that the Tijāniyya depended on royal patronage "to settle permanently in the Moroccan capital,"[100] have thus been exaggerated in later academic accounts. With many of the city's reputable scholars impressed with al-Tijānī or formally initiated into the new *ṭarīqa*, the shaykh had clearly made an impression in North Africa's most significant center of Islamic learning. There is no doubt such popularity would have further infuriated those who opposed him, such as Ibn Kīrān and al-Zayānī, and al-Tijānī's onetime desire to leave Fez, which the Prophet warned him against, was probably a response to the obstinacy of such scholars.[101] But such critics were the minority. In one narration, al-Tijānī credits "the saints of the Maghreb" who "refusing that they should lose their protection, gathered together and interceded with the Prophet that he should remain" in Morocco despite his desire to move to Syria.[102] In other words, a majority of scholars wanted al-Tijānī to stay in Fez. Like other Sufis of his age, al-Tijānī certainly had little patience for what he considered the "venal scholars" (*al-ʿulamāʾ al-sūʾ*), who would be the first killed on the return of the Mahdī toward the end of time: "When the Sultan of Truth comes, he will gather the scholars in the cold and kill them all at once."[103] But such controversy surrounding al-Tijānī's settlement in Fez was clearly a product of his appeal. The enmity of certain scholarly elites perhaps was a result of their feeling undermined and even isolated by a significant cross section of their peers, who broke ranks with the likes of Ibn Kīrān and joined al-Tijānī.

The affiliation of the Moroccan sultan Mawlay Sulaymān to the Tijāniyya remains contested, with Tijānī sources claiming his submission to al-Tijānī and external (mainly from the Nāṣiriyya order) claiming he remained loyal to the Nāṣiriyya-Shādhiliyya as had his father.[104] But there is no doubt the sultan welcomed al-Tijānī in Fez, invited him to his scholarly council, furnished him a large house, and offered him assistance in constructing the *zāwiya*. There is no evidence, however, that the sultan paid him a salary as some later Moroccan historians claimed.[105] In fact, Mawlay Sulaymān appears to have tested al-Tijānī with money, once offering him two thousand riyals to help build the *zāwiya*. After al-Tijānī returned it to him, saying "Its affair is undertaken by God," the sultan admitted his intention had only been to know whether al-Tijānī was among those who desired this world or those working for the afterlife.[106] While the gift of a house, known as the "House of Mirrors," was significant, it seems the house had a reputation for being haunted with jinn and no one could stay there very long: the house may have been another of the sultan's tests to see if al-Tijānī was spiritually strong enough to drive out the jinn.[107] In any case, al-Tijānī at first refused the house until he received permission from the Prophet to stay there, but on the condition that he distribute in charity what he would have paid for the house.[108] And although the sultan did invite him to his council, his turning to him suddenly to explain the Qur'ān in front of the kingdom's most learned scholars was as much a test as an opportunity. Clearly, al-Tijānī's reputation had reached the sultan prior or soon after his establishment in Fez, and the sultan was evidently interested in making his own assessment.

The sultan's last test for al-Tijānī was to ask the shaykh to allow him to see the Prophet in a waking state. According to Sukayrij, Mawlay Sulaymān had heard that al-Tijānī had his Sharifian status confirmed by the Prophet, and he also wanted to hear from the Prophet of his own descent from the Prophet. But secondarily, the sultan wanted to verify the shaykh's saintly claims, "so that his soul could find tranquility in that, and not turn to what his enemies said."[109] The shaykh—who communicated through the sultan's trusted servant[110]—first refused, saying, "I fear you cannot bear it." But after the sultan kept insisting, he gave him some remembrances (*adhkār*) to recite alone in his room. When the sultan began the invocations, he was seized with a great awe and bewilderment and sent a message pleading with al-Tijānī to be present at the occasion. The shaykh obliged.

> When they both began the remembrance, the place where they were became illuminated and filled with the Muḥammadan lights. The sultan became astonished when this happened, and he became absent from his senses. After some time, he regained consciousness, and found our master's hand on his chest. When he opened his eyes, our master said to him, "Do not be concerned, the Prophet has guaranteed for you such-and-such." The Sultan said, "May God reward you. You said I could not bear it, but I allowed my ego (*nafs*) to insinuate otherwise, until I saw (the truth of what you said) with my own eyes."[111]

According to Tijānī sources, the sultan had by this point come to attest to al-Tijānī's scholarship, sincerity, and now his direct connection to the prophetic presence so important for articulations of sainthood by the eighteenth century. Tijānī sources insist that the sultan's discipleship to the shaykh was the logical conclusion of this period of examination. Sukayrij reproduces an exchange of letters between the two that seem to indicate such a relationship did exist. In one letter, al-Tijānī warns the sultan to hide the secret prayers he had given him and encourages him to be a righteous king: "God will ask you about His trust, and what you did with it, so be careful that God does not find you neglectful or to have taken His affair lightly . . . and I commend to you the underprivileged of the creation, for they are the locus of God's gaze in His creation, and to the extent that you provide for them will your rank be raised in the presence of God."[112] In another letter, al-Tijānī tells the sultan that the Prophet had appeared to him and said, "Write a letter to my son Sulaymān . . . and say to him that there is nothing on the face of the earth greater in merit or more exalted in consideration than this (Tijānī) litany (*wird*) that I have given you."[113] Sukayrij claims to have come upon a letter in the sultan's handwriting that he believes was written in response to al-Tijānī's letters:

> The replacement (*ʿiwaḍ*) of our parents, our master, our shaykh, our Muḥammadan exemplar, Abū l-ʿAbbās Sīdī Aḥmad. . . . Your most

> blessed lines have reached us, and we praise God for His favor on us. . . . May God establish us in the presence of God's Messenger, by your grace. As for this matter, I should not allow myself to leave its performance. . . . What I strive for is the dedication to God, my Lord, in the purification of my heart; and that He remove me from everything that prevents me from gazing upon His Noble Countenance; and that he place me in the rank of those drawn near, by the grace of God's Messenger. So this (prayer for me) is incumbent on you, for you know that in my righteousness is found the righteousness of those with whom I am entrusted, and in my corruption is their corruption. The prayer for me is the prayer for everyone.[114]

Moroccan historians external to the Tijāniyya have yet to dispute the authenticity of this exchange of letters.[115] Mansour's insistence that the sultan remained committed to the Nāṣiriyya depends simply on ignoring the accounts from Tijānī sources and relying on a single authorization (*ijāza*) the sultan gave, allegedly transmitting the Nāsiriyya.[116] Tijānī sources, read in dialogue with the sultan's welcoming of al-Tijānī in Fez and the open association of many leading scholars, viziers, and the sultan's son Mawlay Abd al-Salām,[117] make a convincing case that the sultan did indeed join the Tijāniyya.

At the very least, the sultan's respect for al-Tijānī demonstrably extended beyond the shaykh's supposed utility in the sultan's political and religious reforms. Several academic accounts explain Mawlay Sulaymān's evident regard for al-Tijānī as politically or ideologically motivated: that the Tijāniyya alone "remained loyal to the Sultan" in his alleged war against the rural Moroccan Sufi orders,[118] or that the "hostility of al-Tijānī to saint worship and the celebration of *mawāsims* was certainly appreciated by Mawlay Sulaymān."[119] These accounts suggest that Mawlay Sulaymān was secretly influenced by Wahhabism, that he was bent on government centralization like other modernizers of his time in Egypt and the Ottoman Empire, and that the sultan saw the Tijāniyya as a reformist "neo-Sufi" order to be employed in attacking other Sufi orders.[120] It may be true, as al-Nāṣirī has it, that al-Tijānī's de-emphasis of saintly grave visitations (*ziyāra*), to be conducted only "within the confines of the law," may have accorded with the sultan's warning against "over-glorification of the saints."[121] But al-Tijānī in fact encouraged glorifying the sanctity of the saints (as cited earlier)—"whoever exalts them is exalted by God"—and restricted *ziyāra* out of concern for his disciples' spiritual support (*madad*) from the Prophet, rather than any rejection of tomb visitation itself. Nor did Mawlay Sulaymān prohibit grave visitation or reject the miracles of the saints.[122] For his part, the sultan maintained his support of the Sufi tradition more broadly, saying, "I only deny the innovations that have occurred in some of the orders, I do not deny the Sufi orders."[123] Furthermore, the sultan was not opposed to the political or religious independence of the diverse Sufi orders. He seemed more concerned that some Sufi centers be considered exempt from the universal justice of the Sharīʿa: "The role of the *zāwiya*," he remarked in his conflict with some of the rural Sufi centers, "is to serve as a refuge for the oppressed and not for the oppressor."[124] For his part, al-Tijānī defended the primary target of state modernization elsewhere in the Muslim world: the inalienable endowments (*waqf*, *ḥubus*) of religious institutions. He confirmed the inviolability of the ancient Qarawiyīn endowment, declaring, "The inalienable property (*aḥbās*) of Qarawiyīn is forbidden (for other than what it has been designated)."[125] While certain Moroccan orders did come to oppose Mawlay Sulaymān,[126] the sultan's broader reputation among scholarly Sufis, both inside and outside of Morocco, remained intact. The son of West Africa's most important shaykh of the Qādiriyya, Muḥammad b. al-Mukhtār al-Kuntī, offered Mawlay Sulaymān as an exemplar of righteous Muslim kingship in advising the Sokoto Caliphate of ʿUthmān b. Fūdī.[127]

The sultan's mild reforms, and the Tijāniyya's association with them, must be understood within a Moroccan context, rather than a supposed association with neo-Sufism or Wahhabism. The idea that Sufism must conform to the Sharīʿa was a very old idea in North Africa,[128] and certainly stressed by the Nāṣiriyya. The sultan did not require the Tijāniyya to make that argument. While the ḥadīth collection of Aḥmad b. Ḥanbal (of the Ḥanbalī school associated with Wahhabism) and the *tafsīr* of Ibn Kathīr (the student of Ibn Taymiyya, also appropriated by Wahhabism) were increasingly circulated in late eighteenth-century Morocco,[129] the sultan insisted on a traditional North African curriculum. For Islamic law, he emphasized the centrality of classical works of Mālikī jurisprudence, such as the *Mukhtaṣar* of Sīdī Khalīl (on which the sultan authored his own commentary), the *Risāla* of Ibn Abī Zayd al-Qayrawānī, and the *Murshid al-muʿīn* of Ibn ʿĀshir.[130] The latter book also contains a summary of Ashʿarī theology that was rejected by Wahhabis. He instructed Ibn Kīrān to include Sufi classics like the *Iḥyā ʿulūm al-dīn* of Abū Ḥāmid al-Ghazālī and the *Dalā'il al-khayrāt* of Muḥammad al-Jazūlī as part of the core curriculum at Fez's Qarawiyīn University.[131]

The sultan certainly attempted to limit tobacco smoking, music, female singers, and the mixing of genders, especially at the festivals commemorating various Sufi saints.[132] But he was "vigorous" in celebrating the birthday (*mawlid*) of the Prophet, and he enjoyed listening to traditional Moroccan musical instruments such as the stringed lute (*oud*);[133] both practices prohibited by the Wahhābīs. As previously mentioned, al-Tijānī ordered his own *zāwiya* closed on the "Night of Power" during Ramadan to prevent the unnecessary mixing of men and women and exaggerated festivities that would distract people from worship. But he encouraged his followers to celebrate the *mawlid*, and also enjoyed listening to the *oud*, even during the month of Ramadan.[134] One of al-Tijānī's disciples, a blind musician named ʿAbd al-Ḥaqq al-Jabbārī, was renowned for his expertise on the stringed *rabāb*: "He was welcome among the [Tijānī] brethren and the beloveds, and their happiness was not complete in any celebration except with his presence, because of his knowledge of the art of music, by which the spirits moved in their bodily lanterns."[135] These were hardly the type of practices that the contemporary Wahhābī movement in Arabia would have condoned.

Mawlay Sulaymān's delegation to the Saudi king Medina in 1811, aimed at securing the safe passage of Moroccan pilgrims during the Ḥajj, stopped far short of endorsing the Wahhābī agenda. The delegation included the prince Mawlay Ibrāhīm b. Sulaymān and the jurist ʿAbbās b. Kīrān (recently initiated into the Tijāniyya) and presented to the Saudi king a poem of Ḥamdūn b. al-Ḥājj, probably commissioned by Mawlay Sulaymān himself. This poem, which alone was allegedly what "protected the Moroccan pilgrims from the wrath of the Wahhābīs,"[136] praised the Saudi king for "disallowing senseless killing and plundering,"[137] perhaps subtly demanding that the Wahhabis respect these same standards of decency. Ibn al-Ḥājj continued, "God forbade us from any wrangling in our faith" and abruptly warned the Wahhābīs even while commending their campaign against excessive ornamentation of graves: "No one is allowed to use the sword against another Muslim except in the case of apostasy. . . we therefore advise you not to erase one innovation (*bidʿa*) with another."[138] Even such backhanded compliments were too much for al-Zayānī, who claimed that Ḥamdūn b. al-Ḥājj had converted to Wahhabism.[139] In their rush to reassure the Moroccan delegation of their orthodoxy, Wahhābī scholars told their

Moroccan counterparts that they considered the Prophet alive in his grave, that they only prohibited *ziyāra* to those who "ask the dead rather than God for favors," that they agreed with Imam Mālik concerning God's attributes as described in the Qur'ān, and that they did not deny the notion of sainthood.[140] King Sa'ūd granted the Moroccans safe passage during the Ḥajj, and in fact Moroccans were the only Muslims permitted to make the pilgrimage from 1811 until 1818 when the Egyptian army liberated the Hijaz.[141]

Rather than an endorsement of Wahhabism as this delegation is sometimes portrayed, the Moroccans had won an important ideological victory over the Wahhābīs. They had secured safe passage for Moroccan Ḥajj pilgrims and forced the Wahhabis to retreat, at least publicly, from most of the doctrinal aberrations with which the rest of the Muslim world had come to associate them. A contemporary Moroccan court poet probably best captured the Moroccan perspective: "The Maghreb prides itself over the East for its religiosity."[142] If the Tijāniyya did not openly castigate Wahhabism, at least at first,[143] it was not due to any alleged affinity between Moroccan reformism and Wahhabism. Whatever al-Tijānī's personal opinion on the Wahhābīs, he no doubt observed that two of his close students, Ḥamdūn b. al-Ḥājj and 'Abbās b. Kīrān, had played central roles in securing assurances of orthodox belief and civil behavior from the Wahhābīs, all with the backing of a sultan who was likely also a Tijānī. This 1811 "Tijānī delegation" may very well represent an early attempt to doctrinally discipline the Wahhābī movement.

In summary, Shaykh al-Tijānī's 1798 establishment in Fez was a noteworthy event in the intellectual history of Morocco. Despite the rejection of a few noteworthy figures, a significant cross section of the scholarly establishment—from jurists, to imams, to notable public teachers—alternatively became affiliated with him before his arrival in Fez, quickly took the *ṭarīqa* after his settlement, broke ranks with earlier scholarly authorities to join him, or respectfully frequented him for learning despite not taking the Tijāniyya. The sultan's support, likely including his affiliation with the Tijāniyya directly, followed a series of (sometimes public) tests of al-Tijānī's scholarship, sincerity, and sainthood. The shaykh's emphasis on the balance between the law and Sufism, and overall sobriety in mysticism,[144] coincided with the sultan's censure of certain aspects of popular Islam in Morocco. But neither the shaykh nor the sultan endorsed the extremist reform programs associated with Wahhabism of the same period. They no doubt saw themselves, along with the North African scholarly establishment more broadly, as superiors in both comportment and Islamic learning to the Wahhābīs of the East.

The Way of Gratitude

The distinctiveness of the Tijāniyya, and thus the basis for its appeal (and controversy) in North Africa and elsewhere, has often been associated with an accent on God's grace or bounty (*faḍl*), despite the perceived corruption of the age. For detractors, this emphasis licensed individual sinfulness and linked the dispensation of divine grace to a hidden hierarchy of saints in a manner approximating polytheism (*shirk*).[145] For the founder of the Tijāniyya, access to God's grace was ensured through gratitude (*shukr*), a disposition that warded off divine punishment and singled out servants for the favor of divine proximity and sainthood. The polemics surrounding the Tijāniyya in this matter deserve a separate discussion that cannot be justly treated here. But often obscured in these debates is the way al-Tijānī, and probably a majority of his later followers, contextualized extraordinary expressions of divine favor within a discourse on gratitude to God. It was this emphasis on gratitude that ultimately best captures al-Tijānī's idealized realization of Muslim identity in a time of perceived unprecedented corruption.

Gratitude to God was a popular subject among Sufi scholars long before the eighteenth century. Abū Ḥāmid al-Ghazālī, as referenced by the early Mauritanian Tijānī text *Mīzāb al-raḥma*, differentiated between three types of gratitude: the gratitude for the gift, the gratitude for the giver (God), and the highest form of gratitude, which was to use the gift to seek ever increased proximity to the Giver: "to go out in service of the King and bear the toil of the journey in His service, obtaining the rank of proximity to the King."[146] Spiritual rank was important only as an expression of such proximity, for according to Junayd, "Gratitude is to not see yourself as worthy of the favor."[147] Gratitude thus included knowledge (*ʿilm*), spiritual state (*ḥāl*), and action (*ʿamal*), and therefore, according to the Tijānī scholar Ibn Anbūja (d. 1867), gathered together all three stations of the religion—submission (*islām*), faith (*īmān*), excellence (*iḥsān*)—and the nine related steps of the Sufi path (*sulūk*): repentance, steadfastness, wariness, truthfulness, sincerity, serenity, witnessing, observation, and gnosis.[148] According to William Chittick, Ibn al-ʿArabī differentiated between the servant who was occasionally thankful (*shākir*) and the one who went "to great lengths" or who had actualized a state of being continuously grateful (*shakūr*). Ibn al-ʿArabī associated God's increase to the thankful servant ("*If you are grateful, I will increase you*"[149]) with the continued act of creating him in a human form rendering thanks to God: "He has brought the entity of thanksgiving into existence and made its configuration an embodied form, glorifying and mentioning God."[150] In other words, the fullest realization (*taḥqīq*) of gratitude could be manifested in the human creation—"asking nothing except for its Lord"[151]—and its ability to achieve increasing stations of proximity to God, as a result of God's favor rather than the servant's merit.

Much of al-Tijānī's public teaching returned to the concept of gratitude. According to ʿAlī Ḥarāzim, "He reminded people of their Lord's favor to them, and of what He had bestowed upon them and with what He had entrusted them. By this, he guided them to the love of God the Glorious."[152] Al-Tijānī taught that faith itself was the greatest of divine gifts:

> He explained that faith (*īmān*) in God and His messenger was among the hidden favors always with the servant, and that by it [faith], God was granting him assistance in each moment among moments, and holding him tight with each [stray] thought among thoughts, and not permitting Satan—ever desiring his corruption—to have power over him . . . [he said] "If mankind were to sense this great favor (*niʿma*) and gain awareness of it, he would be drowned in the happiness with God, and he would surrender himself to love and adoration with the Generous Benefactor and Great Patron Lord."[153]

Elsewhere, the shaykh explained the Qur'ān verse, "*Why would God punish you if you are thankful and have faith in Him?*" to say simply, "Faith is happiness with the [divine] blessing."[154] At first glance, this public teaching appears to miss the earlier Sufi tradition's more lengthy reflection on the difference between divine favor and the divine, with Ibn al-ʿArabī in fact suggesting that "blessings are a greater veil over God than trials."[155] But al-Tijānī urged students to witness nothing else but God in the creation, whether in blessing or trial: "The servant must know his Lord, and see nothing but His beneficence and mercy . . . he must not ask for anything except for his Lord, with utmost sincerity, expecting no favor in this world or the next."[156] Al-Tijānī was in reality suggesting that faith is defined by giving thanks for the blessing of faith itself.

The favor of recognizing God's favor, for al-Tijānī, is what distinguishes the generality of humanity (*al-ʿām*) from the elite (*al-khāṣṣ*). Gratitude was thus the best way of entering the divine presence. According to *Jawāhir al-maʿānī*:

> All of mankind is drowned in the ocean of [divine] favor (*al-niʿam*), but they do not give thanks: "*How few of My servants are thankful (shukūr).*"[157] If God wants good for a servant, He makes him among the select few of His servants who are aware of the favor upon him, and inspires him with gratitude. If God added no more than this, the servant would be among the elite. All people are favored, but the distinguished are those who bear witness to that. Gratitude is the greatest door to God, and His straightest path. That is why Satan sits on its way to obstruct the believers from it.[158]

Divine selection thus was only the result of the servant's gratitude, which was itself a divine bestowal. According to ʿAlī Ḥarāzim: "If someone complained to him [al-Tijānī] about his lower self (*nafs*), mentioning his evil state and his ugly actions, he pulled him (*jadhabahu*) away from looking at that, and toward gazing on God's mercy, causing him to know that God shows mercy without any reason. Then he would mention the supplication of al-Shādhilī, 'If we are not worthy of reaching Your mercy, surely Your mercy is worthy of reaching us.' "[159] Al-Tijānī thus certainly meant for this discourse on gratitude and divine favor to contextualize his own spiritual claims. As mentioned previously, the Prophet Muḥammad warned al-Tijānī that no saint was infallible (*maʿṣūm*) and that there was no pride (*fakhr*) for him in his saintly rank; and the Prophet obligated him with performance of the prayer for gratitude (*ṣalāt al-shukr*) after his own spiritual attainment.[160] One of al-Tijānī's close disciples, Muḥammad b. Nāṣir al-ʿAlawī, thus equated the notion of spiritual rank in the Tijāniyya with "the path of self-blame" or *Malāmatiyya*[161]: "They do not make any claim, and they have no distinguishing feature from their people. The one who has a vocation is involved in his vocation. The one who has work is involved in his work. All the while, some of them possess divine disposition in the creation, with their states but not by their distinguishing features or natural proclivities. Without doubt, they are the *Malāmatī* masters, whose chief is Abū Bakr al-Ṣiddīq."[162] While al-Tijānī's claims to spiritual rank undoubtedly remained a source of controversy for non-Tijānī Muslims, it is worthwhile to recognize that (from a Tijānī perspective) the notion of gratitude for God's favors certainly motivated such claims, rather than personal boastfulness. After his establishment in Fez and attainment of the station of the

"Hidden Pole," the Prophet appeared to ʿAlī Ḥarāzim to tell al-Tijānī, after warning him that "all of the creation has become enemies to you and your companions because of that rank you have obtained": "Hold back your tongue and stay in your house until God brings ease. . . . Although we ordered you before to speak [openly] and recite [of God's favors], now that the rank has descended upon you, you must stay in this state: not mixing with the creation nor speaking about the glorious affairs, hiding the divine realities as a means to prevent harm (to others). We have only commanded you thus out of mercy and sympathy towards you."[163] According to Tijānī sources then, al-Tijānī only spoke of his rank by direct order of the Prophet, otherwise he remained silent. Tijānī disciples have not always heeded this warning against speaking openly about the saintly rank of their shaykh where it would cause controversy. Nonetheless, discussion of saintly rank within the Tijāniyya was meant to be situated within a discourse on gratitude for divine favor, it was not meant to contradict, for al-Tijānī himself, the "Malāmatī" disposition of humility and self-blame.

While the concept of gratitude was very old in Sufism, it is difficult to miss al-Tijānī's increased sense of urgency. For him, gratitude's emphasis on God's action despite the servant's incapacity rendered it the sole remaining path to God in an age of unprecedented corruption:

> The closest of doors to God in this time is the door of gratitude (*shukr*), and who does not enter by the door of gratitude in this time does not enter. For the ego-selves (*nufūs*) have become thick, meaning that spiritual discipline (*riyāḍa*) and worshipful obedience (*ṭāʿa*) has no effect on them, nor does self-accounting or rebuke restrain them. But if the souls are drowned in happiness with [divine] favor, they absent themselves from these [exercises] entirely, traversing the distance that separates them [from God]. And you will find all promises in God's revelation associated with gratitude: *If they are grateful, We will increase them.*[164]

The "path of gratitude" was thus uniquely suited to a perceived new age of history. The shaykh, as attested earlier, certainly emphasized classical Sufi notions of self-purification. The point here is simply that arrival in God's presence was God's action, not the result of the servant's efforts. While this had certainly always been the case for Sufis, the stubbornness of human souls had come to exceed all bounds and to expose as fraudulent all pretension to the asceticism of old.

Gratitude in Practice

Many of the disciples that gathered around al-Tijānī articulated coherent understandings of the "Way of Gratitude." ʿAbdallāh al-Yamanī, among those from Abū Samghūn "drowned in the ocean" of al-Tijānī, described the Tijāniyya: "The way of the Shaykh is the way of gratitude (*shukr*). Among the obligations of gratitude is contented submission to Him who decrees, secretly and openly."[165] Mawlay Sulaymān's minister Muḥammad Akansūs (d. 1877, Marrakesh), himself one of Morocco's most famous jurists and man of letters of the nineteenth century, described his affiliation to the Tijāniyya:

> The reason for my entering this Muḥammadan Tijānī path is that when I was in Fez, I heard what God had promised the people of this *ṭarīqa* by way of divine bounty (*faḍl*), on the tongue of its Imam, reported from the master of creation. And indeed, it is a path of pure grace. When God made known the incapacity of the people of the age in remaining completely steadfast like the righteous forefathers (*al-salaf al-ṣāliḥ*) in the times of righteousness (*fī l-zaman al-ṣāliḥ*), He brought forth by His grace and generosity this Muḥammadan way (*al-ṭarīqa al-Muḥammadiyya*), which is the path of bountiful grace (*ṭarīqat al-faḍl*) in this corrupt age, so that God may assist those whom He wills among the people of happiness.[166]

Such statements attest to the manner in which the Tijāniyya was received among its followers in North Africa. Gratitude meant contentment with God's decree, to "walk on the way of the people of your time," as al-Tijānī himself encouraged.[167] The path of gratitude allowed Muslims continued access to God's bountiful grace, despite their lack of righteous steadfastness (*istiqāma*) affecting all people in an "age of corruption."

Several accounts attest to al-Tijānī's emphasis on the facility of the Sufi path in the context of the increased distraction of Muslims in his time. He remarked to a student who asked him to pray for him to be steadfast, "May God accept you by his bountiful grace and good pleasure," explaining, "The one who desires to remain steadfast in this time is like a person wanting to build a ladder up to heaven."[168] Elsewhere, he related this idea to the inability of Sufi aspirants to make *sulūk*, or to travel the way to God through self-exertion: "The one who desires to make *sulūk* in this time is like one entrusted to slaughter himself with his own hand."[169] The solution that al-Tijānī offered aspirants was simply to be grateful that God had guided them to the path of felicity.[170]

Becoming a Tijānī did not require any major adjustment to the ordinary Muslim's way of life. Close disciples attested to al-Tijānī's private asceticism: he normally ate one meal a day consisting of vegetables and couscous, refused to eat sugar, and maintained a rigorous routine of prayer and remembrance late at night and early in the morning.[171] But he placed great emphasis on making visitors welcome, commissioning one servant to buy only the best food to serve his guests.[172] He apparently considered feeding people an act of worship: "The blessing (*baraka*) of feeding people is like the blessing of prayer in the mosque (*al-ṣalāt fī makānihā*)."[173] The renowned disciple Muḥammad b. al-Nāṣir later admitted that he first started visiting al-Tijānī because of the abundance of food with him, and al-Tijānī's ability to "give him more than he could imagine, so that his heart grew to love him."[174]

The shaykh was reputed to be of such beautiful appearance—"luminous (even) in his elder years," attired in the finest of clothes—that Mawlay Sulaymān bought a house overlooking al-Tijānī's road to the *zāwiya* just to look at him walking to the mosque.[175] The elder scholar Ibn Shaqrūn, on his deathbed, asked ʿAlī Ḥarāzim to write al-Tijānī: "He asks you to return to him for the sake of God just so that he may look upon you."[176] Sitting with the shaykh engendered a forceful love in his disciples, "No one came upon him suddenly except that he was in awe of him, and no one spent time with him except that he was endowed with love of him."[177] Such companionship was itself the best spiritual training (*tarbiya*): "Those who sit with him forget the material world, and achieve certainty of God and contentment with His blessings."[178] As *tarbiya*, such physical proximity was not without its tests. When he found the son of ʿAlī Ḥarāzim to have momentarily neglected proper manners in his presence, apparently by sitting with his legs extended, he warned him: "You must put etiquette (*adab*) into practice while sitting in the presence of the shaykhs. Even if I am lenient with you, the spiritual rank does not tolerate poor etiquette in its presence."[179] Even in cases of discipline, students apparently found al-Tijānī lenient, approachable, and possessed of exemplary hospitality. Whatever elaborate rituals of spiritual training that may have existed in the earlier Sufi tradition, *tarbiya* in the nascent Tijāniyya mostly meant spending time in the shaykh's presence. And apparently, that was something many people liked to do.

Such approachability extended to those of lower social standing and to women. Al-Tijānī's critique on enslavement was mentioned previously. Several formerly enslaved persons achieved high reputations within the Tijāniyya. The "black man" al-Ḥājj Būjamʿa, who after his manumission voluntarily became a servant in the shaykh's household, experienced "grand illumination" (*al-fatḥ al-akbar*) so that he often saw the Prophet Muḥammad. With al-Tijānī's permission, he regularly recited al-Jazūlī's *Dalāʾil al-khayrāt* in a neighboring mosque, and on one occasion saw the Prophet afterward revealing to him the "Seal of Prophecy" on his back. The Prophet said to him, "You are among those who have seen Muḥammad in truth."[180]

Several women played prominent roles in the early Tijāniyya. The "enraptured saint" (*majdhūba*) Ṣāfiyya Labbāda (d. 1785), consulted by eminent scholars such as al-Tāwudī b. Sūda, predicted the establishment of the Tijānī *zāwiya* in the exact place it was later built in Fez. All six of her sons later took the Tijāniyya. She also had a widely circulated dream that reflected al-Tijānī's own understanding of the "corruption of the age" and was later transmitted in Tijānī sources: "I saw last night three angels descend from heaven and remain on earth until dawn. One of them took modesty and ascended back with it. Another took blessing (*baraka*) and ascended back with it. The third tried to take back the Qurʾān, but he was unable, so he left it and ascended back."[181] Another female saint of Fez was Lallā Mannāna (d. 1815), who "had a firm grounding in the science of unveiling (*al-mukāshāfa*)." She was often consulted by Mawlay Sulaymān and some of Fez's most eminent scholars. On one occasion, she dreamed that the sultan was asking to speak with her, but when she came to find him she found in his stead Shaykh al-Tijānī among a large crowd of people. When the jurist Aḥmad al-Bannānī later came to ask her if he should take the Tijāniyya, she told him before hearing his question, "Accept my advice and take from him [al-Tijānī], for he is the Sultan." Al-Tijānī credited her presence in Fez with averting an affliction from the city, and sent disciples to consult with her.[182]

Al-Tijānī's evident approachability included a certain sociability sometimes overlooked in studies of Sufi communities. Despite the shaykh's assiduous religious practice, several accounts attest to his ability to hide the extent of his pious devotions as one of his saintly miracles.[183] After all, the power of the Tijānī litany was conceived as a type of short-cut to the lengthy exertions of past Sufi practices. The later Moroccan Tijānī scholar al-Ḥusayn al-Ifrānī thus advised the Tijānī disciple: "Upon completing his litany (*wird*), he should remain motionless and quiet. He should be present to the meaning of the remembrance, letting it engage his heart, drawing near to the remembrance's inspiration (*wārid al-dhikr*). His desire is for the source of inspiration (not the inspiration itself). Let him drown his entire existence in this one glance (into the unseen), for he will be inundated in this one moment with more than he can obtain in thirty years of struggle and spiritual exertion (*riyāḍa*)."[184] In any case, the result was that disciples often found their shaykh available for their instruction and companionship. Once a visitor was surprised to find al-Tijānī sitting with his companions late into the night during Ramadan, instead of alone making prayers. The shaykh responded, "God gives us and our companions one hundred thousand times (the reward) of others, even while we sleep."[185] On another occasion, al-Tijānī consoled the scholarly disciple Muḥammad Laḥlū, who could not make extra worship while he was sick, "Any of my companions who was making a remembrance but then became sick, God grants him an angel who makes it for him."[186] Despite the voluminous prayer collections associated with the Tijāniyya, disciples came to find in the new order an opportunity for sociability, facility, and immense reward that they found attractive.

The Tijāniyya, as a "way of gratitude," did not require disciples to remove themselves from worldly occupations and social involvement. Al-Tijānī commanded disciples to perform the ritual prayer with the rest of the Muslim community, even in the case of ideological differences.[187] The shaykh was himself reputedly possessed of great wealth, such that the immense sums he regularly distributed in charity were considered evidence of his Muḥammadan blessing (*al-baraka al-Muḥammadiyya*) and among his saintly miracles (*karāmāt*).[188] But he cautioned some disciples against giving away all of their wealth, unless their faith in God be shaken.[189] While he praised the disposition of poverty (*faqr*), he discouraged mendicancy. His advice for parents to teach their children a craft to support themselves, not only Islamic learning, was mentioned previously. Upon finding a young person remaining in the *zāwiya* after taking the Tijānī litany, he gave the advice directly: "Go poor one (*miskīn*), learn a craft while you are still young."[190] Nor did he favor monasticism: "Whoever wants to take his wealth with him to the next world and not leave anything behind, let him have plenty of children and spend on them."[191] Such fundamentals of sociability—frequenting mosques, charitable giving, gainful employment, and family life—no doubt put socially involved new recruits at ease.

Akansūs's association of the Tijāniyya with "abundant grace" meant to invoke the immense rewards al-Tijānī promised disciples. Much of this reward is associated with the prayer of blessing on the Prophet Muḥammad, "the prayer of the opener" (*ṣalāt al-fātiḥ*), considered multiple times better than any other form of prayer on the Prophet. But al-Tijānī, in statements often ignored by anti-Tijānī polemics, considered the Qur'ān enduringly precedent to *ṣalāt al-fātiḥ*, saying "The Qur'ān is the best remembrance."[192] The larger point was that the discourse on the power of the Qur'ān or the invocation of blessing on the Prophet would have had a broad resonance in Muslim societies. Here was al-Tijānī's testimony concerning the reward of the Qur'ān's opening chapter, *al-Fātiḥa*: "The Messenger of God informed me that every recitation of *al-Fātiḥa* has the reward of reciting the entire Qur'ān. I asked him, 'Some reports have reached me that whoever recites *al-Fātiḥa* once attains the reward of every praise that all of God's creation has ever praised Him with in all the world.' He replied, 'In *al-Fātiḥa* is more than that. He who recites it is given the reward of each of its letters and the letters of the whole Qur'ān. Each letter has the reward of seven palaces and seven *houris*.'"[193] In reference to *al-Fātiḥa*, al-Tijānī initiated disciples in a secret "greatest name" of God contained in it, declaring that this name was itself worth six thousand times the reward of *ṣalāt al-fātiḥ*.[194] While these statements certainly attracted later controversies in non-Sufi circles, scholars like Akansūs no doubt saw this emphasis on the immense reward of simple prayers as a foundation of the "way of gratitude." New affiliates to the Tijāniyya, then, found the "abundant grace" of the new order to be really a deeper appreciation of the Islamic tradition they already knew.

Conclusion

"God knows," al-Tijānī said in the statement cited in the beginning of this chapter, "the weakness of the people of this time, and their confusion and corruption, so He had mercy on them, and gave them abundant good for a simple deed."[195] This idea most certainly corresponded with a general malaise in the Muslim world in the late eighteenth and early nineteenth centuries. Jonathan Katz thus speaks of a global "anxiety by some Muslims over the spiritual health of their community in the early nineteenth century," which made many receptive to the circulation of accounts of visionary meetings with the Prophet Muḥammad.[196] But the concept of abundant grace within the Tijāniyya is best contextualized in a historical understanding of corruption in late eighteenth-century North Africa. For the early Tijāniyya, corruption was sometimes associated with the Turkish government in Algiers, but more often it meant to explain the waning religious zeal and distraction of Muslims from concern with the divine reality. The solution al-Tijānī offered was the saving grace of paradigmatic sainthood, which opened for Muslims direct access to God's bountiful love overflowing on the Muḥammadan presence. While this saintly personalization of grace raised eyebrows in its own time, the wholesale rejection of such ideas in later Salafī-Wahhābī circles was largely absent in North Africa in the late eighteenth and early nineteenth centuries. Shaykh al-Tijānī was not an intellectual easily overlooked by the scholarly establishment of his day, and his claims attracted a significant cross section of the Muslim population—scholars, government elite, businessmen, women, and commoners alike—in both Algeria and Morocco.

In late eighteenth-and early nineteenth-century North Africa, the spiritual disposition of gratitude (*shukr*) for divine favor meant to hold open the door of bountiful grace in a perceived age of corruption. *Shukr* thus became the means of actualizing the highest promises of Sufi sainthood, whatever the inevitable shortcomings of human beings. In the emphasis on social engagement, and upholding basic Islamic rituals like attending the mosque and reciting the Qur'ān, gratitude meant to cultivate a certain humility and appreciation for the wider Muslim community. If gratitude meant the realization (*taḥqīq*) of divine favor, it also meant the actualization of the Tijānī's basic religious identity as a Muslim. Indeed, I once observed an Arab ask the present-day Senegalese shaykh al-Tijānī Cisse, what was the benefit of initiation into the Tijāniyya? The shaykh responded with just a few words, "What we want from the Tijāniyya is just to become better Muslims."[197]

Conclusion

THE CENTRAL ARGUMENT of this book has been that late eighteenth-century Islamic scholarship—informed by an emphasis on actualization, realization, or verification (*taḥqīq*) in all fields of religious learning—deepened and sustained individual Muslim religious identities at a time of immense political and social uncertainty. Such *taḥqīq* did not depend on the support of rulers, nor even was it theoretically constrained by the lack of Muslim political sovereignty or an inability to maintain an "abode of Islam" separately from an "abode of infidelity." This religious actualization was led by a loose network of remarkable scholars, who saw themselves as the fruition (and masters) of a long tradition of Islamic scholarship rather than its pale reflection. Significantly, these scholar-saints represented mediums of participatory learning and verification, whereby ordinary Muslims were invited to more fully realize their own religious identities.

Reappraisals of eighteenth-century scholarship often have been pervaded by later frameworks that fail to comprehend the broader intellectual trends of the period and the holistic contributions of some of its most notable scholars. Such ahistorical questions include whether a particular scholar was urban or rural, wrote books or gave lectures, fought in jihad or acquiesced to colonial rule, was primarily a jurist or a Sufi, followed the early forefathers of Islam (*al-salaf*) or supported the traditional religious institutions that had developed by the medieval period. Aḥmad al-Tijānī, for example, located himself at the center of urban scholarship in North Africa (Fez), but his wealth and influence was assured in rural Algeria. He wrote little, but he supervised the production of a number of useful disciple-authored primary sources and orally commented on the Qurʾān and literary classics like the Ibn ʿAṭā-Allāh's *al-Ḥikam* and al-Buṣayrī's *Hamziyya*. He censured corrupt political rulers, but tried to restrain his followers from armed confrontation. He was well versed in both Islamic law and Sufi literature. He believed that no scholar had license to contradict the established example of the Prophet or an authenticated textual proof, but he upheld the overall sincerity and validity of the traditional schools of jurisprudence, theology, and Sufism. Indeed, such artificial dichotomies imposed on the eighteenth century reflect later preoccupations. As Nile Green observes: "As the nineteenth century progressed, what had begun as an early modern pattern of legally minded Sufi reformism gradually divorced itself from its Sufi origins under the pressures of colonialism to become a movement of vehemently anti-Sufi reform presenting Sufis as the principal obstacle rather than the means to a renewal of the faith."[1] It is indisputable that the most influential scholars of the late eighteenth century—men like Aḥmad al-Dardīr, Murtaḍā al-Zabīdī, and Muḥammad al-Shawkānī in the Middle East; Shāh Walī-Allāh and Mir Dard in India; ʿUthmān b. Fūdī and Mukhtār al-Kuntī in West Africa; and Muḥammad al-Sanūsī and Aḥmad al-Tijānī in North Africa—were all part of a loose network of Islamic scholars who sought to verify and revive the basic foundations of both Islamic law and Sufism. This does not mean these scholars all had the same opinions on the legal schools or belonged to the same "Muḥammadan Path." It means they were participants in a vibrant Islamic scholarly tradition that, far from being eclipsed, was bearing some of its sweetest fruits in the eighteenth century. These fruits emerged in central fields like legal methodology, ḥadīth criticism, theology, and Sufism as well as in other fields that constituted legitimate objects of inquiry in the eighteenth century, such as the esoteric sciences. Aḥmad al-Tijānī's mark on later Islamic intellectual history has been primarily as the founder of the Tijāniyya, today one of the world's most widespread Sufi orders. But his emergence as a prominent Muslim scholar within the vibrant eighteenth century would not have been possible without demonstrated scholarly capacity in a variety of fields of Islamic learning.

Unfortunately, it has been the pale reflections of eighteenth-century Islamic scholarship that have received the most air time. The broad ḥadīth learning and rigorous Sufism of Muḥammad Ḥayāt al-Sindī was apparently lost on his one-time student Muḥammad b. ʿAbd al-Wahhāb.[2] The emphasis on scholarly reasoning (*ijtihād*) and personal Sufi purification in the teachings of Shāh Walī-Allāh may have been forgotten in the millenarian expectations of the followers of the Indian jihadist Sayyid Aḥmad Shahīd Barelwi (d. 1831), who was a student of Walī-Allāh's son ʿAbd al-ʿAzīz.[3] The emphasis on the ego's purification under a legitimate shaykh as taught by Muḥammad al-Sammān was evidently ignored by a later affiliate of the Sammāniyya in the Sudan, Muḥammad Aḥmad, the "Sudanese

Mahdi," who broke with his Sammānī Sufi shaykh before founding his own Mahdist community.[4] Ahmad Dallal observes the following of Ibn 'Abd al-Wahhāb's marginality to eighteenth-century scholarship, despite the common perception that "Wahhabism was a prototype of eighteenth-century thought and movements": "Far from the tolerant and sophisticated thought of the vast majority of eighteenth-century thinkers, Ibn 'Abd al-Wahhāb provides a grim and narrow theory of unbelief, which fails to link the creedal to the political or the social, or to generate a meaningful discourse that could justify its perpetuation as a legitimate theoretical reading of Islam."[5] Indeed, it may be that "the stance against *takfīr* was the main unifying feature of the reformers of the eighteenth century."[6] Al-Tijānī's observation of the common humanity of both Muslims and non-Muslims thus speaks to a more mainstream, broad ethical concern for social harmony in the eighteenth-century Muslim world. The larger point here is that a more recent generation of researchers have already done much to look beyond the Ibn 'Abd al-Wahhāb's and unpack the more profound thinkers of the eighteenth century. It is hoped this exploration of Aḥmad al-Tijānī's intellectual contributions add something to that ongoing effort.

In understanding the emergence of the Tijāniyya, I have laid some emphasis on broader scholarly currents throughout the Islamic world in the eighteenth century. Aḥmad al-Tijānī's thought resonated with intellectual discourses surrounding ḥadīth, Qur'ān exegesis, legal methodology, theology, and the notion of "Muḥammadan Sufism." In suggesting that the notion of *taḥqīq*, verification and actualization, is a useful framework for understanding this broader intellectual inquiry, I am arguing that al-Tijānī shared similar preoccupations with the scholars of his age, not that he always arrived at the same conclusions. For the founder of the Tijāniyya, the fullest realization of Islamic identity in a time of perceived instability and corruption depended on the actualization of individual human potentiality in the mirror of prophetic light and guidance. This included an interrogation of the textual sources of Islam; it also meant an internal purification to permit direct connection with the living spiritual presence of the Prophet Muḥammad. Both processes depended on the continued availability of scholarly exemplars: the jurists who was "the door to the law," and the Sufi guide who had obtained complete effacement in the light of the Prophet, "not veiled from him for a moment."[7] Such ideas were certainly legible within eighteenth-century scholarly discourses, but al-Tijānī no doubt saw his own actualization of them as their fullest realization, beyond that of his contemporaries.

North Africa in the late eighteenth century provided the historical context that gave immediate meaning to al-Tijānī's teachings. But Algeria and Morocco were also fluid discursive spaces. The names of scholars and texts from the Middle East, India, and Sudanic Africa circulated among intellectuals in North Africa; just as the respective scholarly accomplishments of North Africans circulated elsewhere. Aside from the intellectual tradition of North Africa, al-Tijānī's own scholarly influences included intellectuals from India (al-Ghawth's *al-Jawāhir al-khams* through al-Hindī in Mecca), Yemen (Bā-ʿAlawī in al-Shinnāwī's commentary on *al-Jawāhir al-khams*), Oman (al-Mundhirī's *Ighāthat al-Lahfān*), Arabia (through al-Sammān), Egypt (through al-Kurdī), the Sahara (through scholars from Tuwāt), and sub-Saharan Africa (largely through al-Dabbāgh's teacher from Bornu in *al-Ibrīz*).

This fluidity of North Africa as an intellectual space helps to explain the rapid spread of the Tijāniyya in other parts of the Muslim world, particularly in sub-Saharan Africa, following the death of al-Tijānī in Fez in 1815. As I argued in chapter 1, the Tijāniyya was largely welcomed in West Africa because the region's scholarship, from Timbuktu and beyond, had already anticipated many of the central ideas at the heart of the Tijāniyya, and indeed had long been part of the intellectual exchange that gave rise to eighteenth-century scholarly vibrancy. From the vision of the Prophet, paradigmatic sainthood, *ijtihād* outside and within the Mālikī legal school, the notion of a Muḥammadan Path as the essence of Sufism, to the exploration and verification of the esoteric sciences: all were ideas that readily circulated among West African scholars by the eighteenth century. The Tijāniyya may have been a new Sufi order for West African Muslims, but it was one that mostly resonated with their own preexisting scholarly discourses. Such resonance, rather than an allegedly shared heterodoxy of the Tijāniyya and African Islam, accounts for the observed popularity of the order in sub-Saharan Africa. As one writer concludes, "Ahmad al-Tijānī is without doubt the greatest saintly figure in African Islam."[8]

But the spread of the Tijāniyya has not been limited to North and West Africa. Significant communities developed around Tijānī scholars, possessed of their own saintly reputations, in Egypt, Sudan, and Ethiopia, from the early twentieth century.[9] The famous Egyptian Tijānī scholar Muḥammad al-Ḥāfiẓ b. ʿAbd al-Laṭīf (d. 1978) was a prominent figure in the transmission of ḥadīth in the mid-twentieth-century, and his journal *Ṭarīq al-Ḥaqq* ("The Path of Truth") was widely read by Arabic-speaking "traditionalists."[10] Among al-Ḥāfiẓ's admirers was the popular Egyptian preacher Muḥammad al-Shaʿrāwī (d. 1998), who may have also taken the Tijāniyya.[11] Tijānī activists in Turkey gained notoriety for resisting the Turkish state's ban on the Islamic call to prayer in the mid-twentieth century.[12] In Eastern European countries such as Albania, the Tijāniyya similarly became popular among Muslims resisting state appropriation of religious identities; and the former chief mufti of Albania—Ḥāfiẓ Ṣabrī Koçi (d. 2004)—openly identified with the Tijāniyya.[13] The order has maintained a presence in Palestine, claiming among its ranks the famous anti-zionist leader ʿIzz al-Dīn al-Qassām (d. 1935).[14] The Tijāniyya has been established in Arabia since the migration of Alfa Hāshim (d. 1931), the nephew of ʿUmar Tāl, to Medina in the early twentieth century.[15] Students of Hāshim popularized the Tijāniyya in East Asia, particularly Indonesia; and the former Indonesian president Susilo Yudhoyono was allegedly an initiate of the order.[16] The Tijāniyya today also commands a following in English-speaking Muslim minority communities, such as the United States, the United Kingdom, and South Africa.[17] While the majority of Tijānīs in the world are no doubt from sub-Saharan Africa, the Tijāniyya has no less of a global reach than older orders such as the Qādiriyya or Naqshbandiyya, or any other global Muslim network for that matter.

If the Tijāniyya's most visible constituency today is from West Africa, this is certainly due to the charisma and intellectual accomplishments of later Tijānī scholars like ʿUmar Tāl, Mālik Sy, and Ibrāhīm Niasse. It is difficult to verify Ḥasan Cisse's claim in a 2007 "World Tijānī Conference" (Fez, Morocco) that 80 percent of all Tijānīs in the world now trace their affiliation to the Tijāniyya through Niasse. But clearly a majority, certainly in West Africa, seem to have accepted that Aḥmad al-Tijānī's prediction of a great "flood" within the Tijāniyya applies to Niasse's mission: "A flood (*fayḍa*) will come upon my companions, and people will enter our Sufi path in large numbers."[18] Tijānīs outside of West Africa have had to contend with the fact that their Sufi order is largely represented by a black African leadership on the world stage.[19] The Royal Jordanian Institute's annual ranking of the "500 Most Influential Muslims" recognizes Niasse's grandson and imam in Medina-Baye (Senegal), Shaykh al-Tijānī Cisse, as the leading Tijānī scholar alive today (and sometimes as the world's most influential Sufi leader), consistently ranked within the top 20 "most influential Muslims" in the world.[20] Such notoriety, together with the devotion of many West African Tijānīs to their more immediate initiators, has occasioned some misunderstandings, particularly among Tijānīs who do not recognize Niasse's claim to the *fayḍa*. These latter accuse disciples of Niasse of substituting love for al-Tijānī with love for Niasse.[21] But the Tijāniyya—despite occasional public disagreements of Tijānī scholars[22]—has so far remained free from the branching normal to other Sufi orders, where followers of later authorities come to practice alternative sets of litanies. Later Tijānīs mostly seem to have recalled the Prophet's alleged words to al-Tijānī, "Whenever you authorize someone, and he gives it to others, it is as if they have received from you personally (*mushāfahatan*), and I am a guarantor for them."[23] Niasse's own claim to authority within the Tijāniyya was thus quite straightforward: "Our affiliation and link today are with Shaykh al-Tijānī, the Seal of Saints, without intermediary, since he is always present with us."[24]

While the success of West African scholars within the Tijāniyya was certainly due to their accomplishments, the circumstances of late colonialization and decolonization in North Africa increasingly marginalized Tijānī scholars there from having the mainstream appeal that was afforded their West African counterparts. The Tijāniyya in Algeria became associated with French colonial collaboration in the nationalist rhetoric from the 1930s. This may have been unfair. An exchange of letters, only discovered in 1997, between al-Tijānī's son Muḥammad al-Ḥabīb (d. 1853) and the Qādirī saint and anti-French jihadist ʿAbd al-Qādir al-Jazāʾirī references their reconciliation based on the discovery of French spies who had hoped to ensure the disunity of Algeria's Sufi orders.[25] In any case, other branches of the Tijāniyya in Algeria remained at odds with French occupation.[26] But the French exile of al-Ḥabīb's eldest son ʿAmmār al-Tijānī to Bordeaux, and subsequent close surveillance of ʿAyn Māḍī after his return (in the company of his French wife Aurélie Picard), gave the Tijāniyya in Algeria little option other than accommodation.[27]

In Morocco, the Tijāniyya went from being the most popular Sufi order in the 1940s—with prolific scholars like Aḥmad Sukayrij (d. 1944), al-Aḥsan al-Baʿqīlī (d. 1948), Muḥammad al-Naẓīfī (d. 1951), and Muḥammad al-Ḥajūjī (d. 1952)—to being largely eclipsed; with a large segment of the Moroccan population having little knowledge of the Tijāniyya, many believing al-Tijānī was actually from Senegal.[28] This was apparently due to French insistence on supporting the descendants of al-Tijānī in Algeria, rather than Moroccan scholars, to claim leadership of the Tijāniyya in Morocco. Several of al-Tijānī's descendants from ʿAyn Māḍī arrived in Fez after the establishment of the French protectorate of Morocco in 1912. Their later designation by the French and Moroccan monarchy as the sole representatives of the Tijāniyya in Morocco resulted in the gradual eclipse of public Tijānī scholars from the 1940s.[29]

Indeed, the scholarly activity in the main Tijānī center in Fez, as attested by an Egyptian visitor in 1937, stands in stark contrast to the *zāwiya* of later days. The Egyptian Tijānī scholar Muḥammad al-Ḥāfiẓ wrote to his peers in the Middle East that the Fez *zāwiya* maintained the following teaching schedule. After the dawn prayer and the subsequent congregational Sufi remembrance (*waẓīfa*), "one of the most famous scholars of Fez, distinguished in both rational and transmitted knowledge" Muḥammad b. ʿAbdallāh taught from *al-Shifāʾ* of Qāḍī Iyāḍ (d. 1149, Marrakesh), concerning the life and miracles of the Prophet. After that, those present in the *zāwiya* read one-thirtieth of the entire Qurʾān "in one voice." Before the midday prayer, the "distinguished jurist" al-Ḥasan Mazzūr taught from *al-Shamāʾil al-Muḥammadiyya* of Muḥammad al-Tirmidhī (d. 892, Uzbekistan), a collection of ḥadīth describing the habits and appearance of the Prophet. After the midday prayer, those in the *zāwiya* read another thirtieth section of the Qurʾān. Following the afternoon prayer, the Tijānīs read this same section once more, stayed gathered for the congregational remembrance (*waẓīfa*), and then made their individual litanies.[30] At this time, Qurʾān recitation and the classics of Islamic scholarship were seminal activities in the *zāwiya*. Today, individual worship in the Fez *zāwiya* is only punctuated by a number of al-Tijānī's descendants on individual cushions, available to make supplications on behalf of visitors, and to receive their gifts (*hadiya*) when offered.[31] On asked to explain the Tijāniyya's current lack of scholarly reputation in Morocco, the late Shaykh Ḥasan Cissé confirmed this contrast between earlier scholarly efforts and the contemporary routinization of saintly charisma: "That is because the scholars of the *ṭarīqa* are no longer visible."[32]

West African scholars have been able to emerge as global representatives of the Tijāniyya because al-Tijānī's own descendants, unlike in many other Sufi orders, have been unable or unwilling to advance a convincing claim for inherited leadership (*khilāfa*). Al-Tijānī entrusted ʿAlī Ḥarāzim, rather than his own sons, as his deputy (*khalīfa*) during his own lifetime. When Ḥarāzim died, al-Tijānī did not appoint another such deputy, but did surrender his sons into the care of a close disciple ʿAlī Tamāsīnī, instructing him to take al-Tijānī's sons out of Fez and back to the desert: "My sons are not suited except for the desert, there they will live and be happy."[33] While the Prophet had evidently guaranteed that both of al-Tijānī's sons would obtain the experiential knowledge of God (*maʿrifa*),[34] these sons avoided claims of further investiture in the Tijāniyya. Of al-Tijānī's thirteen disciples granted unlimited authorization (*ijāza muṭlaqa*) in the Tijāniyya as listed by Idrīs al-ʿIrāqī (d. 2009, Rabat), neither of al-Tijānī's sons are listed.[35] Once, the son of ʿAlī Ḥarāzim, Abū Yaʿzā (who had the *ijāza muṭlaqa* from al-Tijānī's disciples Muḥammad al-Ghālī and Maḥammad Bannānī al-Miṣrī), wrote to al-Tijānī's son Muḥammad al-Ḥabīb to request an additional *ijāza* for the blessing of taking from al-Ḥabīb. Al-Ḥabīb wrote back from ʿAyn Māḍī, "As for us, we do not have permission to grant full authorization, or to give the litanies."[36] The designation of al-Tijānī's eldest living descendant in ʿAyn Māḍī, currently ʿAlī Bilʿarābī al-Tijānī, to be the "comprehensive leader" (*al-khalīfa al-ʿām*) of the Tijāniyya[37] seems to be received more as a claim to seniority among al-Tijānī's descendants than a claim to overall leadership of the order. Once a disciple came to the Senegalese imam al-Tijānī b. ʿAlī Cisse in Dakar to relate a dream, "I saw you telling me that Shaykh Aḥmad al-Tijānī, following his death, did not entrust anyone with leadership (*mā kallafa aḥadan*) except Shaykh Ibrāhīm Niasse, Saydi ʿAlī Cisse, and Sayyidī ʿAlī's sons [Ḥasan, al-Tijānī, and Muḥammad al-Māḥī]." The imam responded simply, "That is the truth."[38] Clearly, this was not a public claim to overall leadership of the Tijāniyya, and perhaps similar understandings exist among the followings of Tijānī shaykhs elsewhere. The point is simply that claims to overall leadership in the Tijāniyya are not limited to the descendants of al-Tijānī or to North African scholars, but are sometimes voiced, especially in the community of Ibrāhīm Niasse, by West African shaykhs as well.

The continued spread of the Tijāniyya points to the enduring resonance of the intellectual vibrancy of the eighteenth-century Islamic world. Despite the success of the Tijāniyya in West Africa, the order cannot be considered only an "African *ṭarīqa*." It is today found all over the Muslim world, including among minority Muslim populations in the West. There has perhaps even been a revival of interest in the order in North Africa.[39] Earlier academic explanations of the Tijāniyya's popularity—that it fought colonial rule or took advantage of it, that it provided mystical assurances to those denied the benefits of modernization, or that it somehow corresponded to the alleged messianic tendencies of African Islam—are increasingly unsatisfying. As a particular crystallization of eighteenth-century thought, the Tijāniyya continues to advance several apparently appealing notions that circulated widely at the "dawn of modernity." These ideas, as outlined in this book, include the notion that each human being is endowed with an extraordinary spiritual potentiality, that Islamic scholarship and Muslim identity require learned verification and personal realization, that the prophetic presence is an enduringly accessible reality, and that the perceived corruption of rulers and Muslim societies is not an obstacle to accessing divine grace. From the perspective of followers of the Tijāniyya, then, the eighteenth century may appear as a sort of bridge between the Islamic tradition and the modern age. Scholars such as Aḥmad al-Tijānī saw themselves as verifying the essential truths of the inherited Muslim intellectual legacy and bequeathing it again to subsequent generations. Such scholars no doubt hoped that later Muslims, despite living in an age of insecurity and corruption, would find in their efforts a revived appreciation and connection to the beauty of Islam.

Full *taḥqīq*—verifying the foundations of legal judgments through lengthy study or actualizing the full potential of the human condition through Sufi practice—was certainly an ideal that only a few elite realized. Moreover, the potential for religious actualization was not the only cause for the Tijāniyya's spread. Moroccan social and political elites in the early nineteenth century were no doubt encouraged to join the Tijāniyya by the presence of notable Tijānīs among the bureaucratic and business elite. Muslim scholars in Tunisia perceived the Tijāniyya favorably as a result of the reputation of Ibrāhīm al-Riyāḥī, who became Zaytuna University's leading scholar. Political, social, and intellectual critics of established, perceived corrupt hierarchies of nineteenth-century Mali probably welcomed the confrontation of the new Muslim-Tijānī community of ʿUmar Tāl with the elite of Masina and Timbuktu. The sense of belonging, cohesion, and stability offered by Tijānī communities in the context of French colonial occupation, associated with Mālik Sy and ʿAbdallāh Niasse (d. 1922) in early twentieth-century Senegambia, certainly furthered the reputation of the Tijāniyya. The idea of more "democratic" access to elite knowledge within the spiritual "flood" of Ibrāhīm Niasse no doubt attracted new groups of youth, women, and new Muslim converts to the Tijāniyya. These various historically contingent explanations for the Tijāniyya's later spread are not unimportant, but neither are they exclusive of affiliates' underlying desire for the deepening of their religious identities.

The Tijāniyya continues to spread, then, because followers find in it a means of actualizing their religious identities. *Taḥqīq* was not an ideal restricted to the scholarly elite. Not only did al-Tijānī emphasize the incumbency of human realization to order to be truly alive, he invited all Muslims to realize sainthood. The alleged promise of the Prophet to al-Tijānī is no doubt as appealing today as it was in the late eighteenth century: "Whoever loves you is my beloved. Your disciples are my disciples. Your followers are my followers. Your companions are my companions."[40] While certainly controversial among some, many Muslims appear to find in the teachings of al-Tijānī the promise of illumination at the hands of the Prophet, according to the Prophet's alleged words to al-Tijānī at the foundation of the Tijāniyya: "I am your means and support in *al-taḥqīq*," in religious actualization and spiritual realization. The Tijāniyya was thus perceived as a means for becoming a true Muslim and a true human being.

NOTES

Introduction: The Tijāniyya and the Verification of Islamic Knowledge

1. Ḥarāzim, *Jawāhir al-maʿānī*, 2: 143.

2. Aḥmad al-Tijānī, letter to Muḥammad b. ʿAbdallāh al-Tilmasānī; in Sukayrij, *Kashf al-ḥijāb*, 654; al-Tijānī, *Mukhtārāt min rasāʾil al-shaykh*, 185–186.

3. Wehr, *Dictionary of Modern Written Arabic*, 191.

4. Todd, *Sufi Doctrine of Man*, 91–92.

5. Chittick, "The Quran and Sufism," 1738.

6. Ḥarāzim, *Jawāhir al-maʿānī*, 1: 93–94.

7. Ḥarāzim, *Jawāhir al-maʿānī*, 1: 108.

8. Green, *Sufism*, 4.

9. Wright, *Living Knowledge in West African Islam*, 171–173.

10. Al-Sufyānī, *Ifāda*, 110.

11. Ḥarāzim, *Jawāhir al-maʿānī*, 1: 153.

12. Voll, "Hadith Scholars and Tariqahs," 264.

13. Dallal, *Islam without Europe*, 18.

14. El-Rouayheb, *Islamic Intellectual History in the Seventeenth Century*, 28, 235–236.

15. This tripartite epistemological division was earlier articulated by Abū Ḥāmid al-Ghazālī (d. 1111). See Abū Ḥāmid al-Ghazālī, "The Elaboration of the Marvels of the Heart," in Renard, *Knowledge of God in Classical Sufism*, 306–307.

16. This latter aspect stressing an "elevated" hadith chain, was, Voll believes, particularly stressed in the eighteenth century. See Voll, "ʿAbdallah ibn Salim al-Basri and 18th Century Hadith Scholarship," 366.

17. El-Rouayheb, *Islamic Intellectual History in the Seventeenth Century*, 28.

18. Dallal, *Islam without Europe*, 18, 281.

19. El-Rouayheb, *Islamic Intellectual History in the Seventeenth Century*, 235.

20. Voll, "al-Basri and 18th-Century Hadith Scholarship," 356.

21. Voll, "Linking Groups in the Networks of Eighteenth-Century Revivalist Scholars," 71.

22. Dallal, *Islam without Europe*, 63.

23. Seesemann, "A New Dawn for Sufism?" 280.

24. His father Maḥammad's name is an alternate spelling of Muḥammad. Al-Tijānī

was attributed status as *sharīf*, a descendant of the Prophet through the legendary founder of Islamic Morocco, Mawlay Idris, and then through Ḥasan b. ʿAlī Abī Ṭālib. In one waking encounter of al-Tijānī with the Prophet, he confirmed al-Tijānī's descent from him: "Verily, you are my son" (repeated three times). See Ḥarāzim, *Jawāhir al-maʿānī*, 1: 42.

25. Ḥarāzim, *Jawāhir al-maʿānī*, 1: 49.

26. This *wird* consists of asking God's forgiveness (*istighfār*), invoking blessing on the Prophet (*ṣalāt ʿalā l-nabī*), and declaring the oneness of God (*tahlīl*). Al-Tijānī laid particular emphasis on invoking blessing on the Prophet, specifically invocations such as the "Prayer of Opening" (*ṣalāt al-fātiḥ*) and the "Jewel of Perfection" (*jawharat al-kamāl*). See al-Ḥāfiẓ al-Miṣrī, *Aḥzāb wa awrād.*

27. Al-Kattānī, *Salwat al-anfās*, 1: 248.

28. George Drague, *Esquisse d'histoire religieuse du Maroc* (1951), cited in Berriane, *Ahmad al-Tijânî de Fès*, 60. The 1939 French colonial study Drague references considered separate branches of the Shādhiliyya (Wazzāniyya, Nāṣiriyya, Darqawiyya, etc.) as separate orders, but the Tijāniyya clearly had significant presence, with numerous aspirants and zāwiyas in all major Moroccan towns. Despite its provocative title, Berriane's work is not actually about "Ahmad Tijânî de Fès," but rather a mostly contemporary anthropological study of the Tijānī zāwiya in Fez.

29. The contemporary popularity of the Tijāniyya owes much to the remarkable career of Niasse, who claimed to embody the "flood" of divine gnosis predicted by al-Tijānī. See Seesemann, *The Divine Flood*; Wright, *Living Knowledge in West African Islam.*

30. For more on the global presence of the Tijāniyya despite, or perhaps inspired by, its contemporary West African leadership, see Wright, "Afropolitan Sufism."

31. Aḥmad al-Tijānī, cited in Niasse, *Jawāhir al-rasāʾil*, 1: 19.

32. Abun-Nasr, *The Tijāniyya*, 14.

33. Triaud, "La Tijâniyya, une confrérie musulmane pas comes les autres?" 15–17. Triaud's footnote for the latter comment, that "implantations" outside of Africa are only "traces," is simply false. See Wright, "Afropolitan Sufism."

34. Wright, *On the Path of the Prophet* (2005, 2015); Wright, *Sur la voie du Prophète.* The original master's thesis by the same title as the 2005 publication was submitted to the Department of Arabic Studies, American University in Cairo (2003).

35. For a history of order written in Arabic, see al-Azmī, *al-Ṭarīqa al-Tijāniyya.* Al-Azmī provides some important insights concerning eighteenth-century politics in the Maghreb, related later in this book, but he mostly narrates a superficial biography of the shaykh from Tijānī sources with little consideration of al-Tijānī's intellectual contributions in dialogue with broader eighteenth-century scholarship.

36. El-Adnani, *La Tijâniyya.*

37. El-Adnani, *La Tijâniyya*, 226.

38. Knysh, *Sufism*, 164.

39. Ḥarāzim, *Jawāhir al-maʿānī.* Bernd Ratke, Rvanne Mbaye, and Rāḍī Kanūn read

al-Barrāda, but many others omit the *shadda* (double consonant) on the "r." Most published versions of the *Jawāhir* read *fī fayḍ* in the title instead of *fī fuyūḍ*, but this work gives preference to the 2011 publication of Tijānī Cissé (see below), which reads *fuyūḍ*.

40. Al-Qādirī, *Kitāb al-maqṣad*. I am grateful to Harvard's Widener Library for providing me access to the copy of this text in their collection.

41. Abun-Nasr, *The Tijaniyya*, 24. El-Adnani echoes Abun-Nasr: "The composition of his work and the presentation of the *Jawāhir* is faithful to the *Kitāb al-maqṣad* to the point of plagiarism." El-Adnani, *La Tijaniyya*, 102.

42. This is based on my own comparison between the two texts conducted in the Harvard Widener reading room in the summer of 2019. I did not find evidence for Abun-Nasr's general or more specific claims, for example that Ḥarāzim had borrowed al-Qādirī's chapter headings. See Abun-Nasr, *The Tijaniyya*, 24.

43. This was a point made by the Moroccoan Tijānī historian Aḥmad Sukayrij, who authored a book to defend Ḥarāzim's work. See Sukayrij, *Tījān al-ghawānī fī sharḥ Jawāhir al-maʿānī*, 66–82.

44. For more on this debate, see Abun-Nasr, *The Tijāniyya*, 24–25.

45. Ḥarāzim, *Jawāhir al-maʿānī*, 1: 64. This statement of the Prophet appears to complicate Seesemann's theory that the *Jawāhir al-maʿānī* was originally written as a "secret compilation of Sufi teachings" (Seesemann, "New Dawn for Sufism," 285–286); but this perhaps could be reconciled if the statement "the saints after you" is understood to mean that the *Jawāhir al-maʿānī* should only be read by such elite saints (*al-khāṣṣ*), and not the "common folk" (*al-ʿām*).

46. Al-Sufyānī, *al-Ifāda*, 65.

47. This was mostly a claim made by the Nigerian Tijānī scholar Ibrāhīm Ṣāliḥ. See Seesemann, "The Takfīr Debate," 52.

48. Ḥarāzim, *Jawāhir al-maʿānī* (ed. Rāḍī Kanūn, 2012), 41–72. Other significant manuscripts of the *Jawāhir al-maʿānī* mentioned by Kanūn include a version in the handwriting of Muḥammad al-Akansūs and Muḥammad al-ʿArabī b. Sāʾiḥ.

49. Ibrāhīm Niasse, handwritten testimony photocopied in the introduction, Ḥarāzim, *Jawāhir al-maʿānī*, 5–6. Both Shaykh Ḥasan and Shaykh Tijānī Cissé allowed me to see the original manuscript on which this publication was based and also provided me with photocopies of the manuscript earlier in Shaykh Ḥasan's possession (1982–2008) and now with Shaykh Tijānī Cissé. A common prior publication was ʿAlī Ḥarāzim al-Barrāda, *Jawāhir al-maʿānī wa bulūgh al-amānī fī fayḍ Sayyidī Abī l-ʿAbbās al-Tijānī* (Beirut: Dār al-Fikr, 2001), which included the shaykh's answers to various questions on Islamic law, not found in the "Kaolack" manuscript, but which omitted a short chapter on his miracles (*karāmāt*) included in the Kaolack version.

50. This was the testimony of Bashīr al-Tijānī to ʿAbdallāh Niasse, recorded by Ibrāhīm Niasse and included in the beginning of al-Tijānī Cissé's 2011 publication. Kanūn's discussion does not otherwise identify the original manuscript al-Tijānī kept with him in Fez after Ḥarāzim's departure.

51. Ḥarāzim, *Jawāhir al-maʿānī*, 1: 10.

52. Some manuscript experts, such as Faissal al-Hafian of the Institute of Arabic Manuscripts of the Arab League in Egypt, have thus become critical of recent published editions that draw from different manuscript copies of the same text but fail to reproduce any one of the original texts. Al-Hafian argues that such editors in fact produce an entirely new text. Faissal al-Hafian, "The Culture of Comparing Heritage Texts: A New View" (Conference paper, *Symposium on Living Arabic-Script Manuscript Cultures*, University College London in Qatar, April 15–16, 2019).

53. Ibn al-Mashrī, *Rawḍ al-muḥibb*. The date of authorship was undoubtedly before al-Tijānī's establishment in Fez in 1798. Kanūn's introduction to the work reproduces a letter from al-Sā'iḥī dated 1206 A.H. (1792) referring to various pages (*awrāq*) of the *Rawḍ al-muḥibb*.

54. Ibn al-Mashrī, *al-Jāmi'*. Manuscript copies of the *Jāmi'* were also referenced by Abun-Nasr and El-Adnani. "Ibn Mashrī," rather than the more popular pronunciation in West Africa "Ibn Mishrī," is the version Kanūn believes to be more authentic. Some writers in French (such as El-Adnani and Samba Diallo) used "Ibn Muchri."

55. Al-'Alawī, *Ifādat al-Tijānī bi-mā laysa fī kitāb Jawāhir al-ma'ānī*.

56. Al-Sufyānī, *al-Ifāda*.

57. Ḥarāzim, *Kitāb al-irshādāt*.

58. Sukayrij, *Kashf al-ḥijāb*.

59. Sukayrij, *Raf' al-niqāb*.

60. Al-Tijānī, *Mukhtārāt min rasā'il al-shaykh*. This work was edited by Muḥammad al-Kabīr b. Aḥmad b. Muḥammad al-Kabīr al-Tijānī.

61. Tāl, *Rimāḥ*.

62. Ibn al-Sā'iḥ, *Bughyat al-mustafīd*.

63. Niasse, *Kāshif al-ilbās*.

64. Al-Tijānī, *Kunnāsh al-riḥla* (M.S., Personal Archive of Shaykh Tijānī Cissé, Medina-Baye Kaolack, Senegal). The manuscript itself is untitled. The authenticity of this text is attested to by Muḥammad b. al-Mashrī's handwritten statements on the margins, the oral testimony of Shaykh Tijānī Cissé upon letting me view the text, and al-Rāḍī Kanūn's judgment on a copy of the text in his possession. For the latter, see Kanūn in Ibn al-Mashrī, *Rawḍ al-muḥibb*, fn. 1, 54.

65. Ḥarāzim, *al-Mashāhid*. This manuscript is in the handwriting of 'Alī Cissé, who writes that he copied the original manuscript in the handwriting of 'Ali Ḥarāzim at the command of Ibrāhīm Niasse in the year 1938.

66. Two in particular have been useful, both of which claim to be transcriptions of al-Tijānī's secret prayers. The first is a typed manuscript of 112 pages, the *Kunnāsh al-aṣfar al-maktūm*; the second is the 137-page *Kunnāsh al-maktūm al-makhzūn* in the handwriting of 'Alī Cissé. Most of my interviews with Shaykh Tijānī Cissé on the subject of these manuscripts, as well as their viewing in his personal archive, took place in Medina-Baye during successive research trips from 2014–2016.

67. Al-Zayānī, *al-Tarjumāna al-kubrā*; al-Nāṣirī, *al-Istiqṣā*; al-Kattānī, *Salwat al-anfās*.

68. This also appears to have been the realization of the Moroccan researcher Aḥmad al-Azmī, see *al-Ṭarīqa al-Tijāniyya*, 1: 28–32, 99–112.

69. Ḥasan b. ʿAlī Cissé, interview with author, Medina-Baye Kaolack, Senegal, August 1997.

70. For example, Andrea Brigaglia observes an "authentic boom of Islamic literature" in Northern Nigeria as a result of the Tijāniyya's spread in the twentieth century. See Brigaglia, "Sufi Revival and Islamic Literacy," 105. The same phenomenon could be observed in Mauritania and Mali in the nineteenth century and in Senegambia in the twentieth century.

71. I took part in an earlier initiative led by Rüdiger Seesemann (initially hosted by Northwestern's Institute for the Study of Islamic Thought in Africa and funded by the Ford Foundation), as yet incomplete, that hopes to produce an exhaustive catalogue of Tijānī literature.

72. Seesemann, *Divine Flood*, 143.

73. Wright, *Living Knowledge in West African Islam*, 92.

Chapter One: Sufism and Islamic Intellectual Developments in the Eighteenth Century

1. Marsot, "Political and Economic Functions of the ʿUlamāʾ," 133.

2. Dallal, *Islam without Europe*, 63.

3. Robinson, *Paths of Accommodation*, 53; Low, "Empire and the Hajj," 269–290.

4. These three disciplines that define the core of Islamic intellectual history are derived from the three stations of the religion (*maqāmāt al-din*)—submission (*Islām*), faith (*Imān*), and spiritual excellence (*Iḥsān*—mentioned in ḥadīth. See Murata and Chittick, *Vision of Islam*, xxv–xxiv.

5. Dallal, *Islam without Europe*, 18–19.

6. Loimeier, "Is There Something Like 'Protestant Islam'?" 242–243.

7. This was the testimony of the early Wahhābī king Saʿūd b. ʿAbd al-Azīz to Mawlay Sulaymān's delegation of Moroccan scholars in 1811. See Mansour, *Morocco in the Reign of Mawlay Sulayman*, 142–143.

8. Ibn ʿAbd al-Wahhāb, *al-Rasāʾil al-shakhṣiyya*, 256. Citation from the electronic copy is available from the Qatar National Library.

9. Wright, *Living Knowledge in West African Islam*, 6–15.

10. John Voll, email communication with author, May 25, 2018.

11. The Nāṣiriyya castigated the early Darqawiyya for alleged "animal sacrifice, singing, and dancing." See Gutelius, "Sufi Networks and the Social Contexts," 30. But such accusations were probably unfounded. Ibn ʿAjība's accounts of initiation into the early Darqawiyya make no reference to these practices, although his Darqawi shaykh required him to beg in the souq and to carry garbage "hoping to attain pure sincerity and psychic death (*qatl al-nafs*)." See Michon, *Autobiography of a Moroccan Sufi*, 92–93.

12. Hammoudi, "Sainteté, pouvoir et société," 619. For more on the scholarly legacy of the Nāṣiriyya, see Ahmed, "Desert Scholarship," 103–108.

13. Gutelius, "Sufi Networks," 19.

14. Gutelius, "The Path Is Easy and the Benefits Large," 32.

15. Gutelius, "Sufi Networks," 34.

16. El-Rouayheb, *Islamic Intellectual History in the Seventeenth Century*, 211, 351.

17. Al-Yūsī, *Discourses*, 299.

18. Reichmuth, *World of Murtaḍā al-Zabīdī*, 32–33, 74, 189. The initiation was at the hands of Muḥammad b. al-Ṭayyib al-Fāsī (d. 1757), a Moroccan scholar resident in Medina. Al-Zabīdī's guest (and ḥadīth student) in Cairo was the head of the Nāṣiriyya in the late eighteenth century, Muḥammad b. ʿAbd al-Salām (d. 1823), who would later transmit to Muḥammad al-Sanūsī, founder of the Sanūsiyya order. Despite the common al-Nāṣirī ascription, al-Zabīdī disagreed with al-Yūsī on the status of rational logic (*manṭiq*) in the Islamic sciences. See El-Rouayheb, *Islamic Intellectual History*, 135.

19. It did spread to Algeria, where it was known as the Ṭayyibiyya. See Mansour, "Wazzāniyya."

20. See Mansour, *Morocco in the Reign of Mawlay Sulayman*, 165.

21. The Jazūliyya is sometimes also called the Dalāʾiliyya on account of Muḥammad al-Jazūlī's (d. 1465, Marrakesh) famous prayer on the Prophet Muḥammad, *Dalāʾil al-khayrāt*. For key aspects of the Jazūliyya mentioned here, see Cornell, *Realm of the Saint*, 157, 210–211.

22. Cornell, *Realm of the Saint*, 227.

23. Mansour, 'Sharifian Sufism," 72, 78.

24. Mansour, "Wazzān." In his related entry, "Wazzāniyya," Mansour cites a French report claiming that half of all Moroccans were affiliated to the Wazzāniyya by the nineteenth century, a figure Mansour admits is "impossible to verify."

25. Ḥarāzim, *Jawāhir al-maʿānī*, 1: 54.

26. Ḥarazim, *Jawāhir al-maʿānī*, 1: 54.

27. Ibn al-Mashrī, *Rawḍ al-muḥibb*, 45.

28. Mansour, "Wazzāniyya."

29. Al-Sufyānī, *Al-Ifāda*, 77.

30. Ibn al-Mashrī, *Rawḍ al-muḥibb*, 47–48. For supplemental details on al-Tuzānī, see al-Rāḍī Kanūn's commentary in fn. 2, 47.

31. Ḥarāzim, *Jawāhir al-maʿānī*, 1: 55. Al-Tijānī cultivated multiple initiations in the *Dalāʾil al-khayrāt*. His servant Būjamʿa al-Sūdānī persisted in reciting the prayer in a mosque close to the shaykh's house in Fez, on one occasion seeing the Prophet as a result. See Sukayrij, *Kashf al-ḥijāb*, 336–337.

32. In addition to the *Dalāʾil al-khayrāt*, these include the *Aḥzāb* of al-Shādhilī (especially *ḥizb al-baḥr* and *ḥizb al-kabīr*) and the *waẓifa* of Aḥmad Zarrūq (d. 1493, Libya). See Ḥarāzim, *Jawāhir al-maʿānī*, 2: 91.

33. Al-Lamaṭī, *Pure Gold*.

34. A letter from al-Tijānī to a grandson of al-Dabbāgh, who had entered the

Tijāniyya, praised al-Dabbāgh as "the arrived axial saint and the perfect succor (*ghawth*)." Sukayrij, *Kashf al-ḥijāb*, 630.

35. Radtke and O'Kane, "Translator's Introduction," in al-Lamaṭī, *Pure Gold*, xx.

36. Al-Lamaṭī, *Pure Gold*, 130, 137.

37. Al-Lamaṭī, *Pure Gold*, 133.

38. Al-Lamaṭī, *Pure Gold*, 135.

39. Al-Lamaṭī, *Pure Gold*, 132–133.

40. Bobboyi, "Abd Allah al-Barnawi," 115–124.

41. Al-Yamanī was an ascription of lineage, not birth, as he was apparently born near Sinnar in modern-day Sudan. See Norris, *Sufi Mystics of the Niger Desert*, 1.

42. Al-Kattānī, *Salwat al-anfās*, 2: 480.

43. Aḥmad al-Ḥalabī, *Rīḥān al-qulūb*; cited in Bobboyi, "Abd Allah al-Barnawi," 115–124.

44. Muḥammad al-Qādirī, *Nashr al-Mathānī*; in Muḥibbī, *Mawsūʿat aʿlām*, 4: 1593–1597.

45. Muḥammad al-Qādirī, *Nashr al-Mathānī*; in al-Muḥibbī, *Mawsūʿat aʿlām*, 4: 1593-1597; Aḥmad al-Ḥalabī, *Rīḥān al-qulūb*; cited in Bobboyi, "Abd Allah al-Barnawi," 115–124.

46. Al-Kattānī, *Salwat al-anfās*, 2: 478–479.

47. This was according to Muhammad Bello b. ʿUthmān b. Fūdī, and also in Aḥmad b. Uways's *Qudwā*. See Norris, *Sufi Mystics*, 129.

48. Norris, *Sufi Mystics of the Niger Desert*, n. 30, 76. An intriguing reference in the *Qudwā* to a "Muhammad al-Shannawi" (perhaps Ahmad al-Shinnawi? See Norris, *Sufi Mystics*, 66) may indicate the later Maḥmūdiyya's connection with the Middle Eastern Shaṭṭariyya tradition as transmitted from Muhammad al-Ghawth by Ahmad al-Shinnawi to Ibrāhīm al-Kūrānī in Medina in the seventeenth century.

49. Norris, *Sufi Mystics*, 70.

50. Norris, *Sufi Mystics*, 66.

51. Norris, *Sufi Mystics*, 7.

52. The notion of the *Ṭarīqa Muḥammadiyya* had in fact appeared in Morocco in the sixteenth century with the teachings of Muḥammad al-Ghazwānī of the Jazūliyya-Shādhiliyya. See Cornell, *Realm of the Saint*, 219.

53. Al-Kattānī, *Salwat al-anfās*, 1: 404.

54. Reichmuth, *World of Murtaḍā al-Zabīdī*, 273.

55. Mukhtār al-Kuntī, *Kitāb al-minna*, cited in Moos, "The Literary Works of Shaykh Sīdī Al-Mukhtār Al-Kuntī," 78.

56. Hunwick, *Timbuktu and the Songhay Empire*; Wise (ed.), *Timbuktu Chronicles*.

57. This despite its desecration during the 2012 invasion of the city by the "Islamist" Ansar al-Din group. Extremists forced open a certain door to Sidi Yahya's mausoleum, which legend in the city held would not be opened till the end of time. See "Definiant Mali Islamists pursue wrecking of Timbuktu," Reuters, 2 July 2012.

https://www.reuters.com/article/us-mali-crisis/defiant-mali-islamists-pursue-wrecking-of-timbuktu-idUSBRE8610JQ20120702.

58. Hunwick, *Timbuktu and the Songhay Empire*, 40.

59. Levtzion, "Islam in the Bilad al-Sudan to 1800," 73. Levtzion is here quoting from the *Taʾrīkh al-fattāsh.*

60. According to al-Saʿadī: "Of them [the Aqit] the gnostic, the qutb Sidi Muhammad al-Bakri said: 'Ahmad is a friend of God, and Mahmud is a friend of God, as is Abd Allah." See Hunwick, *Timbuktu and the Songhay Empire*, 43.

61. Hunwick, *Timbuktu and the Songhay Empire*, 61, 76. It is not always clear from the text whether al-Bakrī actually traveled the long distance to Timbuktu by ordinary means or simply appeared in the city at will.

62. Levtzion, "Eighteenth-Century Sufi Brotherhoods," 154.

63. Winter, *Society and Religion in Early Ottoman Egypt*, 170.

64. Hunwick, *Timbuktu and the Songhay Empire*, 43, 87.

65. Concerning al-Bakrī's wealth, see Winter, *Society and Religion*, 170; concerning his endorsement of Mālikī texts despite his Shāfiʿī affiliation, see Hunwick, *Timbuktu and the Songhay Empire*, 76; concerning his spiritual unveiling, see Ḥarāzim, *Jawāhir al-maʿānī*, 1: 164.

66. *Shuhūdiyya lā wujūdiyya.* El-Rouayheb considers this a "remarkable anticipation" of Ahmad Sirhindi's later position. See El-Rouayheb, *Islamic Intellectual History in the Seventeenth Century*, 244.

67. Al-Nabulusī named this work *al-Laṭāʾif al-unsiyya ʿala naẓm al-ʿAqīda al-sanūsiyya.* See Reichmuth, "Islamic Education in Sub-Saharan Africa," 428.

68. For al-Nabulusī's influential work on the subject, see al-Nabulusī, *al-Ḥadīqa al-nadiyya sharḥ al-Ṭarīqa al-Muḥammadiyya.*

69. An important summary of Kashnāwī's life and work can be found in chapter 4 of Dahlia Gubara's fascinating dissertation, "Al-Azhar and the Orders of Knowledge."

70. Gubara, "Al-Azhar and the Orders of Knowledge," 259–260.

71. According to Van Dalen, "By the end of the seventeenth century, most jurists in the centres of the Middle East as well as the Maghrib, and certainly most Maliki jurists, had come to the conclusion that smoking tobacco was allowed." See Van Dalen, *Doubt, Scholarship and Society in 17th-Century Central Sudanic Africa*, 166.

72. For al-Tijānī's uncompromising stance against tobacco, see al-Sufyānī, *al-Ifāda*, 84; and the later discussion in chapter 2.

73. Al-Kashnāwī, *Durr al-manẓūm*, cited in Gubara, "Al-Azhar and the Orders of Knowledge," 319.

74. Gubara, "Al-Azhar and the Orders of Knowledge," 323.

75. Gubara, "Al-Azhar and the Orders of Knowledge," 330–333.

76. Gubara, "Al-Azhar and the Orders of Knowledge," 247–248.

77. Ahmed, *West African Ulama*, 92.

78. Ahmed, *West African Ulama*, 95.

79. Ahmed, *West African Ulama*, 96. Ahmed claims that al-Fullānī was "introduced

to the Sammāniyya tariqa and maybe to other turuq, though he was not formally initiated into a Sufi order."

80. This phrase appears in the subtitle of al-Fullānī's most important work, *Iqāẓ himam ūlī l-abṣār.* See Hunwick, "Ṣāliḥ al-Fullānī," 139–154; Ahmed, *West African Ulama*, 94.

81. Al-Kattānī, *Ṣalwat*, 3: 469–470.

82. Ahmed, *West African Ulama*, 95; for al-Tijānī's discussion of the centrality of *naṣṣ* in legal opinions, see Ibn Mishri, *al-Jāmiʿ*, 879.

83. Levtzion, "Islam in the Bilad al-Sudan to 1800," 72.

84. Muḥibbī, *Mawsūʿat aʿlām*, 10: 3706–3707.

85. Reichmuth, *The World of Murtaḍa al-Zabīdī*, 190–191. Certainly, comparison of the secret notebooks (*Kunnāsh*) of al-Kuntī and al-Tijānī demonstrate certain similarities in use of secret divine names. This appraisal is based on comparison of *Kunnāsh* attributed to al-Tijānī with the *Fawāʾid nūrāniyya* attributed to al-Kuntī's son Muḥammad b. al-Mukhtār al-Kuntī. I thank Ariela Marcus-Sells for providing me a copy of this manuscript from Morocco's al-Maktaba al-Ḥasaniyya. For more on the Kuntī lineage's use of the esoteric sciences, see Marcus-Sells, "Science, Sorcery, and Secrets," 432–464.

86. Ḥarāzim, *Jawāhir al-maʿānī*, 1: 59.

87. For a representative sample of this literature, see Voll, "Muḥammad Ḥayya al-Sindī and Muḥammad ibn 'Abd al-Wahhab," 32–39; Dallal, "The Origins and Objectives of Islamic Revivalist Thought," 341–359; Nafi, "Taṣawwuf and Reform," 307–355.

88. El-Rouayheb, *Islamic Intellectual History*, 51.

89. Saʿīd ʿAbd al-Fattāḥ, "Muqaddimat al-muḥaqqiq," in al-Kūrānī, *Rasāʾil fī waḥdat al-wujūd*, 29.

90. Bashir Nafi, "Taṣawwuf and Reform in Pre-Modern Islamic Culture," 343.

91. Al-Kūrānī, *Iʿmāl al-fikr.*

92. El-Rouayheb, *Islamic Intellectual History*, 332.

93. Dallal, *Islam without Europe*, 116–117. Dallal does not mention that Shawkānī's reference to Ibrāhīm al-Kurdī, the student of Aḥmad b. Muḥammad al-Madanī, could have been none other than Ibrāhīm al-Kūrānī (al-Kurdī), the student of Aḥmad al-Madanī, known as Aḥmad al-Qushāshī (one of al-Kūrānī's Sufi initiators). See Voll, "The Mizjaji Family in Yemen," 76, for specific reference to Shawkānī's link to al-Kūrānī in the study of ḥadīth.

94. El-Rouayheb, *Islamic Intellectual History*, 345.

95. El-Rouayheb, *Islamic Intellectual History*, 328.

96. Ibrāhīm al-Kūrānī, *Maṭlaʿ al-jūd fī taḥqīq al-tanzīh fī waḥdat al-wujūd* and *Jalāʾ al-naẓr fī baqāʾ al-tanzīh maʿa l-tajallī fī l-ṣūr*, in al-Kūrānī, *Rasāʾil fī waḥdat al-wujūd*, 38–173, 175–191. The collection appears to have been published by a disciple of the contemporary Egyptian Tijānī shaykh Ṣalāḥ al-Dīn al-Tijānī, to whom the edition is dedicated. These texts appear to have missed El-Rouayheb's analysis, although most of the key ideas also appear in al-Kūrānī's seventy-five-page *Itḥāf al-dhakī* on which

El-Rouayheb focused for his involved discussion of *waḥdat al-wujūd*. El-Rouayheb doubts the authenticity of *Maṭla' al-jūd*'s (the first and longest component of the *Rasā'il* collection) attribution to al-Kūrānī (interview with author, Harvard University, June 2019). Sa'īd 'Abd al-Fattāḥ nonetheless claims to base his edition on a forty-eight-page manuscript in the Azhar library, "in the handwriting of the author [al-Kūrānī], and it is a beautiful copy" (*Rasā'il fī waḥdat al-wujūd*, 35). He admits that up to eight pages appear to have been added to the manuscript later, but he declares they are nonetheless attributable to al-Kūrānī "without doubt." While I am incapable of declaring either side more accurate than the other, it appears that 'Abd al-Fattāḥ anticipated El-Rouayheb's doubts, while El-Rouayheb did not have a chance to consider or dispute 'Abd al-Fattāḥ's authentication. This analysis thus considers the *Maṭla' al-jūd* authentic, at least as an authentic source for understanding how the later Tijānī tradition received Kūrānī's teachings.

97. Al-Kūrānī, *Maṭla' al-jūd*, in *Rasā'il fī waḥdat al-wujūd*, 53, 57.

98. Al-Kūrānī, *Maṭla' al-jūd*, in *Rasā'il fī waḥdat al-wujūd*, 57.

99. Al-Kūrānī, *Maṭla' al-jūd*, in *Rasā'il fī waḥdat al-wujūd*, 69.

100. Al-Kūrānī, *Maṭla' al-jūd*, in *Rasā'il fī waḥdat al-wujūd*, 59.

101. Al-Kūrānī, *Maṭla' al-jūd*, in *Rasā'il fī waḥdat al-wujūd*, 83. The text adds that such rules and effects here refer to (and result in) the multiplicity of created forms. But the reference to *aḥkām* was nonetheless intentional, as Kūrānī thought it "imperative that one not deviate from the Quran and the Sunnah." See El-Rouayheb, 321.

102. Al-Kūrānī, *Jalā' al-naẓr*, in *Rasā'il fī waḥdat al-wujūd*, 190.

103. Al-Kūrānī, *Maṭla' al-jūd*, in *Rasā'il fī waḥdat al-wujūd*, 170. This equation of "being" with light (*nūr*), here sourced to Ibn al-'Arabī himself, is similar to 'Abd al-Wahhāb al-Sha'rānī's emphasis in his own interpretation of Ibn al-'Arabī. See El-Rouayheb, *Islamic Intellectual History*, 238–240; Winter, *Early Ottoman Egypt*, 127–133. Al-Kūrānī, in fact, follows the above explanation with a citation from al-Sha'rānī's *al-Yawāqīt wa l-jawāhir*.

104. Nazār Ḥamādī, "al-Muqaddima," in al-Sindī, *Sharḥ al-Ḥikam al-'Aṭā'iyya*, 9. Ḥamādī cites al-Murādī's *Silk al-durar* for al-Sindī's affiliation to the Naqshbandiyya.

105. Al-Sindī dated the completion of this work to 1145 (1733) and claims that he finished it in seven days while still honoring his teaching commitments. See al-Sindī, *Sharḥ al-Ḥikam al-'Aṭā'iyya*, 138.

106. Al-Sindī, *Sharḥ al-Ḥikam al-'Aṭā'iyya*, 25.

107. Al-Sindī, *Sharḥ al-Ḥikam al-'Aṭā'iyya*, 24.

108. Nafi, "Teacher of Ibn 'Abd al-Wahhāb," 218.

109. Currie, "Kadizadeli Ottoman Scholarship," 282–283.

110. Al-Jabartī, *History of Egypt*, 1: 118.

111. A common misperception would be that it was only al-Bakrī who brought "the Khalwatiyya into full identification with the sharia . . . so that the order became the Muslim orthodoxy of Egypt" (Weigert, "Shaykh Mustapha Kamal al din al Bakri," 4). For al-Bakrī's uncontroversial situation within the Khalwatiyya, see De Jong,

"Mustafa Kamal al-Din al-Bakri," 117–132. For al-Bakrī's Sufi reputation in relation to his literary production, see Ralf Elger, *Muṣṭafa al-Bakrī: Zur Selbtadarstellung eines Syrischen Gelehrten, Sufis und Dichters des 18. Jahrhunderts* (Schenefeld: EB-Verlag, 2004), and Elger, "Al-Bakrī, Muṣṭafa Kamāl al-Dīn."

112. El-Rouayheb, *Islamic Intellectual History*, 267. A source contemporary to al-Bakrī puts the number of his disciples at 100,000, a figure that De Jong calls into question. See De Jong, "Mustafa al-Bakri," 120.

113. De Jong, "Mustafa al Bakri," 125; El-Rouayheb, *Islamic Intellectual History*, 267.

114. El-Rouayheb, *Islamic Intellectual History*, 257; Voll, "Abdallah ibn Salim al-Basri and 18th Century Hadith Scholarship," 359, 369. Voll relies on al-Jabartī for al-Baṣrī's description as the "seal of ḥadīth scholars."

115. Voll, "Abdallah ibn Salim al-Basri and 18th Century Hadith Scholarship," 364–365.

116. El-Rouayheb, *Islamic Intellectual History*, 269.

117. Waugh, *Visionaries of Silence*, 34.

118. Al-Jabartī, *History of Egypt*, 2: 100.

119. Kamāl al-Dīn al-Ḥarīrī, *Tibyān waṣā'il al-ḥaqā'iq*, cited in De Jong, "Mustafa al Bakri," 118.

120. Al-Jabartī, *History of Egypt*, 1: 269–270.

121. De Jong, "Mustafa al-Bakri," 117.

122. Al-Bakrī, *Risāla fī l-ṣuḥba*.

123. Al-Jabartī, *History of Egypt*, 1: 499.

124. Al-Bakrī authored a treatise on the subject, *al-Mawrid al-'adhb li-dhawī l'wurūd fī kashf ma'nā waḥdat al-wujūd*. See El-Rouayheb, *Islamic Intellectual History*, 269.

125. Al-Bakri, [*Naẓm al-Bakrī*], fol. 38.

126. Al-Bakri, cited in Earle Waugh, *Visionaries of Silence*, 35.

127. Al-Jabartī, *History of Egypt*, 1: 488.

128. Al-Jabartī, *History of Egypt*, 1: 505.

129. In this case, Maḥammad al-Amīr al-Miṣrī, to Muḥammad b. Manṣūr al-Shāwnī, to al-Kūhan. See al-Kūhan, *Fahrasat 'imdād*, 52, 153. Al-Kūhan did not receive initiation in the Khalwatiyya, however, but remained affiliated with the Nāṣiriyya-Shādhiliyya.

130. Ibn al-Mashrī, *Rawḍ al-muḥibb*, 45, 51.

131. Al-Kattāni, *Salwat al-anfās*, I: 180.

132. Ḥarāzim, *Jawāhir al-ma'ānī*, I: 59.

133. Muthalib, "The Mystical Teachings of Muḥammad 'Abd al-Karīm al-Sammān," 15; Drewes, "Muhammad al-Samman," 75; Salih, *Sammāniyya*, 119–121. Salih's work contains a useful summary of the Sammāniyya, but it unfortunately plagiarizes other sources with false or misleading attribution (such as my own prior work *On the Path of the Prophet* when speaking of al-Tijānī's meeting with al-Sammān; see Salih, *Sammāniyya*, 132–133).

134. Mathalib, "Mystical Teachings of al-Sammān," 162.

135. Mathalib, "Mystical Teachings of al-Sammān," 178.

136. Al-Sammān, *Nafaḥāt ilāḥiyya*, 100.

137. Muthalib, "Mystical Teachings of al-Sammān," 17–19.

138. Al-Samman, *Ighathat al-lahfan wa mu'ānasat al-walhān*, cited in Muthalib, "Mystical Teachings of al-Sammān," 164.

139. Al-Samman, *al-Futuḥāt al-ilāhiyya*, cited in Muthalib, "Mystical Teachings of al-Sammān," 144.

140. Al-Sammān, *al-Futuḥāt al-ilāhiyya*, cited in Bernd Radtke, "Sufism in the 18th Century," 355.

141. Muthalib, "Mystical Teachings of al-Sammān," 130–131.

142. Al-Sammān, *al-Futuḥāt al-ilāhiyya*, cited in Muthalib, "Mystical Teachings of al-Sammān," 143.

143. Al-Samman, *Nafaḥāt*, cited in Muthalib, "Mystical Teachings of al-Sammān," 247–248.

144. Muthalib, "Mystical Teachings of al-Sammān," 265–266.

145. Al-Sammān, *Nafaḥāt*, cited in Muthalib, "Mystical Teachings of al-Sammān," 151.

146. Al-Sammān, *Nafaḥāt ilāḥiyya*, 94; Tijānī b. ʿAlī Cissé, "al-Adab bayn al-sharīʿa wa l-ḥaqīqa" (lecture, Luton, UK: Dar al-kitab wa l-hikma, September, 2018).

147. Al-Sammān, *Nafaḥāt ilāḥiyya*, 92.

148. Al-Sammān, *Nafaḥāt ilāḥiyya*, 100.

149. Al-Tāzī was the shaykh of Aḥmad b. Idrīs. Ibn Idrīs was also initiated into the Khalwatiyya by another of al-Kurdī's students, Ḥusayn al-Qanāʿī of upper Egypt. See O'Fahey, *Enigmatic Saint*, 42, 53.

150. Al-Jabartī, *History of Egypt*, 1: 496.

151. Al-Jabartī, *History of Egypt*, 2: 99–101.

152. Al-Sharqāwī, *Ḥikam al-Kurdī*, 43.

153. Al-Sharqāwī, *Ḥikam al-Kurdī*, 264.

154. Al-Sharqāwī, *Ḥikam al-Kurdī*, 96.

155. Al-Sharqāwī, *Ḥikam al-Kurdī*, 65.

156. Al-Sharqāwī, *Ḥikam al-Kurdī*, 70.

157. Al-Sharqāwī, *Ḥikam al-Kurdī*, 93.

158. Al-Sharqāwī, *Ḥikam al-Kurdī*, 97.

159. Al-Sharqāwī, *Ḥikam al-Kurdī*, 144.

160. Al-Sharqāwī, *Ḥikam al-Kurdī*, 290.

161. Al-Sharqāwī, *Ḥikam al-Kurdī*, 270.

162. Al-Sharqāwī, *Ḥikam al-Kurdī*, 286.

163. Al-Sharqāwī, *Ḥikam al-Kurdī*, 281.

164. Al-Jabartī, *History of Egypt*, 2: 100–101.

165. Muḥammad Naṣār, *al-Muqaddima*, in al-Sharqāwī, *Ḥikam al-Kurdī*, 5.

166. Al-Sharqāwī, *Ḥikam al-Kurdī*, 281.

167. Ḥarāzim, *Jawāhir al-maʿānī*, 1: 57.

168. Murphy makes a good case for translating these sciences as "the uncommon

sciences" from al-Jabarti's reference to *ʿulūm al-gharība*, but the meaning here should be more that they were not official (*rasmī*), otherwise they were widely known. See Murphy, "Ahmad al-Damanhūrī," 85–103.

169. Schimmel, *Mystery of Numbers*, 18. For the connection to the Prophet Muḥammad, the Tijānī Shaykh Ibrāhīm Niasse's exegesis of the Qurʾān narrates a story of the Prophet writing something (*khaṭṭa khaṭṭan*) to protect his companion ʿAbdallāh b. Masʿūd when Ibn Masʿūd accompanied him on a preaching mission to the jinn. See Niasse, *Fī riyād al-tafsīr*, 6: 230–232. In an interview with the author, the contemporary Shaykh Tijānī b. ʿAlī Cisse made similar claims about the esoteric sciences' connection to Prophet Idrīs and Prophet Muḥammad, emphasizing that Niasse's Wolof Qurʾān exegesis claimed the definitive support for writing talismans to be what the Prophet wrote for ʿAbdallāh b. Masʿūd. Tijānī Cisse, interview with author, Paris, France, May 2019.

170. I have been unable to locate the book mentioned by al-Jabarti, *al-Zahr al-bāsim fī ʿilm al-ṭalāsim* (al-Jabartī, *History of Egypt*, 2: 39–40), but two other related books include the fifty-page *Iḥyāʾ al-fuʾād*, and the seventy-page *Kitāb al-fayḍ al-mutawālī*. Concerning al-Damanhūrī's connection to al-Yūsī, see El-Rouayheb, "al-Damanhūrī, Aḥmad."

171. Dallal, *Islam without Europe*, 117.

172. Reichmuth, *World of Murtaḍā al-Zabīdī*, 32, 202–203. For al-Zabīdī's relationship with al-Kashnāwī, see Reichmuth, "Murtaḍā al-Zabīdī and the Africans," 137–138.

173. Michon, *Autobiography of a Moroccan Sufi*, 146–154.

174. Al-Ghazālī, *Deliverance from Error*, 75.

175. Aḥmad Zarrūq, *Taʾsīs al-qawāʿid*, cited in Niasse, *Removal of Confusion*, 30.

176. Winter, *Society and Religion in Early Ottoman Egypt*, 134–135.

177. Ibn ʿAbd al-Wahhāb, *Book of Monotheism*, chapters 7 and 8. The hadith upon which he based his first statement, however, was widely considered to refer to non-Islamic talismans used by the Arabs of "pagan ignorance" (*jāhiliyya*).

178. Al-Yūsī, *al-Qānū fī aḥkām al-ʿilm*, cited in El-Rouayheb, *Islamic Intellectual History*, 224–225.

179. Al-Nafrāwī, cited in Owusu-Ansah, *Islamic Talismanic Tradition*, 33–34. Al-Nafrāwī's chief text was the *Kitāb al-fawākih al-dawānī ʿalā Risālat ibn Abī Zayd al-Qayrawānī*, a commentary of the *Risāla* of al-Qayrawānī, a seminal text of Mālikī jurisprudence.

180. In Arabic: Muḥammad Bīr ʿAlī al-Rūmī al-Birkawī, *al-Ṭarīqa al-Muḥammadiyya wa l-sayra al-Aḥmadiyya*.

181. Birgivi, *Path of Muhammad*, 98.

182. Al-Nabulusī, *al-Ḥadīqa al-nadiyya*, 2: 147–149.

183. Al-Nabulusī, *al-Ḥadīqa al-nadiyya*, 2: 151.

184. Al-Nabulusī, *al-Ḥadīqa al-nadiyya*, 2: 144.

185. Wright, "Islamic Intellectual Traditions of Sudanic Africa."

186. For more on the work's contents and resonance, see Ernst, "Jawāher-e Kamsa," 608–609; El-Rouayheb, *Islamic Intellectual History*, 249–251. For more on the life of the

book's author, see Ernst, "Persecution and Circumspection in Shattari Sufism," 416–435; Moin, *Millennial Sovereign*, 103–104.

187. Le Gall, *Culture of Sufism*, 100.

188. Ernst, "Jawāher-e Kamsa," 608–609.

189. Reichmuth, *World of Murtaḍā al-Zabīdī*, 234.

190. The actual editing was done by 'Abd Allāh al-Yisār al-Tijānī. For more information on previous printings on the book by Tijānīs and spread around the Islamic world, see Ernst, "Jawāher-e Kamsa," 608–609.

191. Ould Abdellah, "Le Passage au Sud," 93.

192. The Shattariyya was transmitted in the Hijaz by Sighat-Allah al-Barwaji, who lived in Medina and translated *al-Jawāhir al-khams* from Persian into Arabic. Sibghat-Allah's successor was Ahmad al-Shinnawai (d. 1619), who taught Aḥmad al-Qushāshī (d. 1660), who taught Ibrahim Kūrānī. See El-Rouayheb, "Opening the Gate of Verification," 271.

193. Moin, *Millennial Sovereign*, n. 26, 276.

194. Al-'Ayyāshī, *al-Riḥla*, 1: 451.

195. Al-'Ayyāshī, *al-Riḥla*, 1: 454; al-Tijānī, *Kunnash al-riḥla*, 38.

196. This was the case for 'Umar Tāl, *Rimāḥ*, 446.

197. Biblioteca Alexandrina, Microfilm 647, MS 14. Shaykh Tijānī Cissé possesses a more legible manuscript of this text in his library in Medina-Baye Kaolack, Senegal. I am grateful to have seen this copy.

198. Tijānī b. 'Alī Cissé, interview with author, Medina-Baye Kaolack, Senegal, July 2016.

199. Al-Tijānī, *Kunnāsh al-riḥla*, 34. The first name "Aḥmad" before Sālim appears in the text, but it seems to have been crossed out. Later al-Tijānī reproduces a letter by the same scholar who refers to himself as "*al-faqīr* (the humble Sufi) Sālim."

200. Bāzhīr, *al-Jawāhir al-ḥissān*, 2. Bāzhīr here quotes from al-Muḥibbī, *Khulāṣat al-athar*. I thank a former Hamad Bin Khalifa University College of Islamic Studies graduate student, Ayaz Asadov, for procuring Bāzhīr's informative document on the history of the Āl-Shaykhān.

201. Al-Tijānī, *Kunnāsh al-riḥla*, 34–36.

202. See footnote Muḥammad al-Rāḍī Kanūn in Ibn al-Mishrī, *Rawḍ al-muḥibb*, fn. 1, 54.

203. Al-Tijānī, *Kunnāsh al-rihla*, 30.

204. Ernst, "Jawāher-e Kamsa," 608–609. See Ernst's article for a more detailed list of chapter headings.

205. Al-Ghawth, *al-Jawāhir al-khams*, 128–129.

206. In the manuscript: *lam ya'lam* (does not know); in the published version, *lam yadrī* (is not aware).

207. Qur'ān, 2:255; 108:1–3.

208. The point being that seventy years of prayer more than covers an individual, since a person is only responsible for prayer from age ten.

209. Al-Tijānī, *Kunnāsh al-riḥla*, 31.

210. Al-Tijānī, *Kunnāsh al-riḥla*, 31. This prayer is similar (but not identical) to the opening of the third (Wednesday) section of Muḥammad al-Jazūlī's (d. 1465) *Dalāʾil khayrāt.*

211. Al-Bakrī seems to have first emerged among Ḥanafī circles in the Levant, and another student Ḥasan al-Husaynī became the Ḥanafī mufti of Jerusalem. See Weigert, "Sufi Reformer," 5.

212. Among al-Bakrī's students, al-Jabarti thus mentions Muhammad b. Ahmad al-Nabulusi al-Hanbali. Al-Jabarti, *History of Egypt*, 1: 687–688.

213. Jabarti, *History of Egypt*, 1: 684.

214. This being Muhammad al-ʿAwfī (d. 1777). See al-Jabarti, *History of Egypt*, 2: 21.

215. El-Rouayheb, "al-Damanhūrī."

216. Dallal, *Islam without Europe*, 66–67. On al-Zabīdī's more conservative opinion, see Reichmuth, *World of Murtaḍā al-Zabīdī*, 288.

217. Mansour, *Morocco in the Reign of Mawlay Sulayman*, 133.

218. Mansour, *Morocco in the Reign of Mawlay Sulayman*, 140.

219. El-Rouayheb, *Islamic Intellectual History*, 358.

220. In addition to those mentioned, there is the intriguing case of Ali b. Muhammad al-Shanwīhī (d. 1776), who used to see "many visions of the Prophet," until he became too famous and then stopped seeing him. So, he withdrew from public teaching. See al-Jabarti, *History of Egypt*, 2: 4–5.

221. Al-Sindī, *Fatḥ al-ghafūr*, 15.

222. Wright, *Living Knowledge in West African Islam*, 224–228.

223. While al-Nābulusī certainly went beyond al-Birkawī's statements in many respects, such as concerning the importance of shaykh-disciple relations or the enduring validity of divine inspiration (see Allen, "Reading Mehmed Birgivi with ʿAbd al-Ghanī al-Nabulusi"), he refrained from giving an alternative definition to the "Muhammadan Way" beyond that of al-Birkawī.

224. Al-Kattānī, *Salwat al-anfas*, 3: 69.

225. Reichmuth, *World of Murtaḍā al-Zabīdī*, 307. Al-Zabīdī's initiators included Aḥmad al-Mallawī, who transmitted to him "a Maghribi line of the tariqa muhammadiyya," ʿAbdallāh al-Mirghānī, who appears to have transmitted a Naqshbandi line. See Reichmuth, *World of Murtaḍā al-Zabīdī*, 33, 44.

226. Radtke, "Ibrīziana," 126–127.

227. Andalib's words cited in Schimmel, *Pain and Grace*, 42.

228. Mir Dard, *ʿIlm al-kitāb*, cited in Schimmel, *Pain and Grace*, 42. Schimmel estimates that the vision, first recorded in 1740, must have occurred "sometime in the mid-thirties of the 18th century."

229. Radtke, "Ibriziana," 127.

230. This was already demonstrated by Radtke, "Sufism in the 18th Century," 352

231. For O'Fahey's disavowal of Trimingham's notion that eighteenth-century Sufism (Ibn Idrīs and al-Tijānī) "did not believe in personal guidance and progress along the Path," see O'Fahey, *Enigmatic Saint*, 19.

232. Nafi, "Taṣawwuf and Reform," 342, 345.

233. This is demonstrated at greater length in Wright, "Secrets on the Muḥammadan Way," 77–105.

Chapter Two: Portrait of a Scholar

1. Sukayrij, *Kashf al-ḥijāb*, 540–541.

2. As cited previously, Al-Kattānī, *Ṣalwat*, 3: 469–470.

3. Ould Abdellah, "Passage au Sud," 69–100.

4. Ibn al-Mashrī, *al-Jāmiʿ*, 86.

5. Sukayrij, *Kashf al-ḥijāb*, 741, 759.

6. Sukayrij, *Kashf al-ḥijāb*, 213. According to al-Ṭayyib al-Sufyānī (al-Tijānī's disciple in Fes), the shaykh used to recite "Glory to my Lord the Majestic and to Him praise" eleven times in the bowing position (*rukūʿ*) of the ritual prayer. See al-ʿIrāqī, *al-Jawāhir al-ghāliyya*, 13.

7. Al-Nāṣirī, *al-Istiqṣā*, 3: 213, 232.

8. El-Adnani, "Réflexions sur la naissance de la Tijaniyya," 22.

9. Al-Tijānī's legal studies were primarily under an elder scholar of ʿAyn Māḍī, al-Mabrūk b. Būʿāfiya al-Māḍāwī al-Tijānī (d. 1753). Ḥarāzim, *Jawāhir al-maʿānī*, I: 40.

10. Ibn al-Mashrī, *Rawḍ al-muḥibb*, 44.

11. Al-ʿIrāqī, *al-Risāla al-shāfiyya*, 1: 168–169. In this regard, al-ʿIrāqī related that al-Tijānī had something of a photographic memory: "memorizing whatever he heard after only hearing it once," allegedly memorizing the entire ḥadīth collections of al-Bukhārī and Muslim.

12. Ibn al-Mashrī, *al-Jāmiʿ*, 894.

13. Ḥarāzim, *Jawāhir al-maʿānī*, 1: 40. Al-Tijānī's teacher was Muhammad b. Ḥammū al-Tijānī (d. 1749), who was taught the Qurʾān by ʿIsā Būʿukkāz al-Maḍāwī al-Tijānī. According to al-ʿIrāqī, al-Tijānī had nonetheless mastered the seven different readings (*qirāʾa*) of the Qurʾān, having studied the variant readings with Imām al-Daqqāq during his first visit to Fez when he was only twenty-one. See al-ʿIrāqī, *al-Risāla al-shāfiyya*, 1: 167.

14. Al-Sufyānī, *al-Ifāda*, 45.

15. Al-Sufyānī, *al-Ifāda*, 142.

16. Ḥarāzim, *Jawāhir al-maʿānī*, 1: 92.

17. Ḥarāzim, *Jawāhir al-maʿānī*, 1: 44.

18. Al-Sufyānī, *al-Ifāda*, 108.

19. Ibn al-Mashrī, *al-Jāmiʿ*, 890.

20. Sukayrij, *Kashf al-ḥijāb*, 238.

21. The book, Ibn al-Mashrī regretted, was never written down. Ibn al-Mashrī, *al-Jāmiʿ*, 86.

22. Ḥarāzim, *Jawāhir al-maʿānī*, 1: 168.

23. Al-Sufyānī, *al-Ifāda*, 78.

24. The verb utilized by al-Tijānī here (*injabara*) indicates "compulsion" but not legal obligation. Al-Sufyānī, *al-Ifāda*, 118. Al-Tijānī says the prayer can be made up in the early morning after the sun rises and supplemented with three prayers on what the Prophet called *jawharat al-kamāl*.

25. Ḥarāzim, *Jawāhir al-ma'ānī*, 1: 147; al-Ṭaṣfāwī, *al-Fatḥ al-rabbānī*, 36.

26. Al-Sufyānī, *al-Ifāda*, 108.

27. Al-'Alawī, *Ifādat al-Tijānī*, 34.

28. Qur'ān, 5:6; ḥadīth in the collection of al-Bukhārī. The juristic opinion allowed for the faster *tayammum* (purification with sand or rock), which al-Tijānī considered only permissible in case of sickness or the absence of water, "even if the prayer-time should end." Ibn al-Mashrī, *al-Jāmi'*, 878–879.

29. Ibn al-Mashrī, *al-Jāmi'*, 909.

30. Ibn al-Mashrī, *al-Jāmi'*, 908–909.

31. Al-Sufyānī, *al-Ifāda*, 66. Al-Tijānī defended the endowments (*aḥbās*) of Fez's Qarawīn mosque-university in particular.

32. Al-Sufyānī, *al-Ifāda*, 82.

33. Ibn al-Mashrī, *al-Jāmi'*, 909.

34. Ḥarāzim, *Jawāhir al-ma'ānī*, as cited in Berque, *L'intérieur du Maghreb*, 261.

35. Ibn al-Mashrī, *al-Jāmi'*, 909.

36. Ibn al-Mashrī, *al-Jāmi'*, 910.

37. Ibn al-Mashrī, *al-Jāmi'*, 934–935.

38. Ibn al-Mashrī, *Rawḍ al-muḥibb*, 388.

39. Ibn al-Mashrī, *al-Jāmi'*, cited in al-'Alawī, *Ifādat al-Tijānī*, 27.

40. Ibn al-Mashrī, *Rawḍ al-muḥibb*, 384.

41. For example, the reason why sea creatures do not require ritual slaughter to be eaten while animals do. Ibn al-Mashrī, *al-Jāmi'*, 890.

42. Al-Sufyānī, *al-Ifāda*, 84.

43. Al-Sufyānī, *al-Ifāda*, 84. Earlier condemnations of smoking in North and West Africa, immediately preceding al-Tijānī, were pronounced by the Nāṣiriyya Sufi order and central African scholars such as Muḥammad al-Wālī al-Barnāwī (fl. 1688). See Batran, *Tobacco Smoking under Islamic Law*; van Dalen, *Doubt, Scholarship and Society*, 166–180.

44. Al-Sufyānī, *al-Ifāda*, 142.

45. For more on this issue, see Hunwick and Harrak (trans.), *Mi'rāj al-Ṣu'ūd, Aḥmad Bābā's Replies on Slavery*.

46. Al-Sufyānī, *al-Ifāda*, 80. These words of the Prophet may have been dictated to al-Tijānī by the Prophet directly, as my own preliminary search for this ḥadīth could not locate it in an earlier textual reference.

47. Al-Sufyānī, *al-Ifāda*, 87.

48. Al-Sufyānī, *al-Ifāda*, 70.

49. Al-Sufyānī, *al-Ifāda*, 81.

50. Ḥarāzim, *Jawāhir al-maʿānī*, 1: 113–114.

51. Sukayrij, *Kashf al-hijāb*, 334–335.

52. Terem, *Old Texts, New Practices*; Terem, "Redefining Islamic Orthodoxy."

53. Al-Sufyānī, *al-Ifāda*, 139. This opinion, al-Sufyani explains, was later softened by al-Tijānī and was not considered binding on al-Tijānī's students, although al-Tijānī refused to eat sugar for the rest of his life.

54. This was evidently the opinion of Ḥasan al-Yūsī. See El-Rouayheb, *Islamic Intellectual History*, 217–230.

55. Al-ʿIrāqī, *al-Risāla al-shāfiyya*, 1: 167. I have been unable to identify ʿIrāqī's reference to a "Shaykh Sijilmāsī," but it is clear that Sijilmasa was an important center of scholarship during the period, being the birthplace of the Moroccan sultan Mawlay Sulaymān, and the origin of several important scholars in Fez during the period. See Nasser, "Moroccan Purism," 398–400.

56. Ibn al-Mashrī, *Rawḍ al-muḥibb*, 44.

57. Ibn al-Mashrī, *Rawḍ al-muḥibb*, 64.

58. El-Rouayheb, *Islamic Intellectual History*, 212.

59. Ibn al-Mashrī, *Rawḍ al-muḥibb*, 44.

60. Ibn al-Mashrī, *Rawḍ al-muḥibb*, 65–66.

61. Ibn al-Mashrī, *Rawḍ al-muḥibb*, 66.

62. Ibn al-Mashrī, *Rawḍ al-muḥibb*, 65.

63. Ibn al-Mashrī, *Rawḍ al-muḥibb*, 115–118.

64. Ḥarāzim, *Jawāhir al-maʿānī*, II: 188.

65. Ibn al-Mashrī, *al-Jāmiʿ*, cited in al-ʿAlawī, Ifādat al-Tijānī, 40.

66. Ibn al-Mashrī, *Rawḍ al-muḥibb*, 65.

67. Al-Sanūsī, *al-ʿAqīda al-ṣughrā*, cited in Louis Brenner, *West African Sufi*, 58.

68. Ibn al-Mashrī, *al-Jāmiʿ*, 945.

69. Ibn al-Mashrī, *Rawḍ al-muḥibb*, 64.

70. Hadith related by Ibn ʿAbbās and narrated in al-Bukhārī. See Ibn al-Mashrī, *Rawḍ al-muḥibb*, fn. 2, 63.

71. Ibn al-Mashrī, *Rawḍ al-muḥibb*, 65.

72. Qureshi, "ʿAbd al-Ghanī al-Nābulusī's Kalām Writings," 59–72.

73. Ḥarāzim, *Jawāhir al-maʿānī*, 2: 162.

74. Ḥarāzim, *Jawāhir al-maʿānī*, 2: 162.

75. Ḥarāzim, *Jawāhir al-maʿānī*, 2: 163.

76. Al-Tijānī mentioned this in reference to the cosmological presences, or celestial worlds. Ibn al-Mashrī, *Rawḍ al-muḥibb*, 132.

77. Ibn al-Mashrī, *al-Jāmiʿ*, 245.

78. Ibn al-Mashrī, *Rawḍ al-muḥibb*, 132.

79. Niasse, *Jawāhir al-rasāʾil*, 1: 115–117. The Qurʾān verse cited here is 17:81. These ideas on divine manifestation were clearly anchored in al-Tijānī's own articulations, also suggestive of three levels of perceiving divine manifestation. See Ḥarāzim, *Jawāhir al-maʿānī*, 2: 233.

80. Ḥarāzim, *Jawāhir al-maʿānī*, 2: 233. I thank Talut Dawud for drawing my attention to this passage.

81. Ḥarāzim, *Jawāhir al-maʿānī*, 1: 74.

82. Al-Tijānī, cited in Cheikh Tidiane Cisse, *Knowing Allah, Living Islam*, 24.

83. Qurʾān, 57:4.

84. Qurʾān, 50:16.

85. Ḥarāzim, *Jawāhir al-maʿānī*, 1: 293.

86. Ḥarāzim, *Jawāhir al-maʿānī*, 1: 294.

87. Ibn Ḥanbal's statement here was in reference to the Qurʾān verse praising "whoever rejects the idols" (2:257). Ḥarāzim, *Jawāhir al-maʿānī*, 2: 27.

88. Al-Sufyānī, *al-Ifāda*, 74.

89. El-Adnani, *La Tijaniyya*, 148–149.

90. Ibn al-Mashrī, *al-Jāmiʿ*, 50.

91. Sukayrij, *Kashf al-ḥijāb*, 212.

92. Ibn ʿAjība, *al-Fahrasa*, in Michon, *Autobiography*, as mentioned in chapter 1.

93. ʿUthmān b. Fūdī thus castigated those "who claim that they possess knowledge of the unseen through written magic or by sand-writing, from the positions of the stars . . . who practice black magic to separate those who love each other, or husband from wife: all of that is unbelief." See Martin, *Muslim Brotherhoods*, 28.

94. See, for example, Ibn Fūdī's treatise on "God's Greatest Name," where he endorses the use of a three-by-three "magic square." See Ibn Fūdī, *The Book of the Great Name of Allah*.

95. Wright, *Living Knowledge*, 234–235.

96. Aḥmad Sukayrij, *Kashf al-ḥijāb*, 243.

97. Al-Burūjī, *Miftāḥ al-saʿāda*, 179–180.

98. Sukayrij, *Kashf al-ḥijāb*, 195. See the lengthy fn. 1, 195, for al-Rāḍī Kanūn's discussion of Ibn ʿAzūz's background.

99. Sukayrij, *Kashf al-ḥijāb*, 195–196.

100. Al-Būnī's text did appear in the study of esoteric sciences elsewhere in the eighteenth century, for example in al-Kashnāwī's transmission received by al-Zabīdī. See Reichmuth, "Murtaḍā al-Zabīdī and the Africans," 138.

101. Ḥarāzim, *Jawāhir al-maʿānī*, 1: 41; Ibn al-Mashrī, *al-Jāmiʿ*, 45.

102. Aḥmad Zarrūq, cited in Sukayrij, *Nayl al-amānī*, 42.

103. Earlier speculation was that this notebook transcribed secrets from a variety of sources during al-Tijānī's visit to the Middle East. See Wright, "Secrets on the Muhammadan Way," 77–105. But al-Rāḍī Kanūn suggests that the whole text was from al-Hindī, which seems logical as al-Hindī's name is the only contemporary scholar al-Tijānī mentioned in the book.

104. Ḥarāzim, *Jawāhir al-maʿānī*, I: 58–59.

105. Ḥarāzim, *Jawāhir al-maʿānī*, I: 58–59. See also Ibn al-Mishrī, *al-Jāmiʿ*, 66–67.

106. Al-Tijānī, *Kunnāsh al-riḥla*, 30.

107. Al-Mundhirī, *Ighāthat al-Lahfān*, 7, cited in al-Tijani, *al-Kunnāsh al-riḥla*, 1.

108. Al-Mundhirī, *Ighāthat al-lahfān*, 7.

109. Al-Mundhirī, *Ighāthat al-lahfān*, 7.

110. Al-Mundhirī, *Ighāthat al-lahfān*, 15. I have been unable to identify the text primarily criticized here, but it is named as *al-Nafaḥat al-rabbāniyya fī ʿilm al-rūḥāniyya*.

111. Al-Tijānī, *Kunnāsh al-riḥla*, 34.

112. Ḥarāzim, *Jawāhir al-maʿānī* (2001 edition), 197; previously cited in Wright, *Living Knowledge*, 234.

113. Ḥarāzim, *Jawāhir al-maʿānī*, cited in Ḥamdī, *Qāmūs al-muṣṭalāḥāt al-Ṣūfī*, 61.

114. Al-Mundhirī, *Ighāthat al-lahfān*, cited in al-Tijānī, *Kunnāsh al-riḥla*, 10.

115. Ibn al-Mashrī, *al-Jāmiʿ*, 815–816.

116. Ibn al-Mashrī, *al-Jāmiʿ*, cited in al-ʿAlawī, *Ifādat al-Tijānī*, 28. In this regard, later Tijānī scholars mentioned a certain prayer based on God's name "the Gracious" (*al-Laṭīf*), allegedly transmitted from the renowned ḥadīth scholar Ibn Ḥajar al-ʿAsqalānī (d. 1449, Cairo), who claimed that the prayer was capable of "turning back" even a "fixed decree" (*al-qiḍāʾ al-munbiram*). See Niasse, *Jawāhir al-rasāʾil*, 3: 36.

117. This typed manuscript, many Tijānīs report, is obtainable in Fez, Morocco, from private manuscript sellers. The copy I quote from here is contained in the archive of al-Tijānī b. ʿAlī Cissé in Medina-Baye Kaolack, Senegal. This work, in the handwriting of Sayyid ʿAlī Cissé, appears to differ from the typed version, in both content and title: *al-Kunnāsh al-maktūm al-makhzūn al-adhī lā yuṭāliʿuhu illā man lahu al-idhn* ("The treasured hidden notebook that will not be opened except by one who has permission").

118. Al-Tijānī, *al-Kunnāsh al-maktūm al-makhzūn*, 115.

119. Al-Barrāda, *Jawāhir al-maʿānī*, 1: 58–59. This is when al-Hindī instructs al-Tijānī to go to Medina after his own death to "meet the saintly pole after me . . . Muhammad al-Sammān."

120. Al-Tijānī, *Al-Kunnāsh al-maktūm al-makhzūn*, 115.

121. Al-Tijānī, *Al-Kunnāsh al-maktūm al-makhzūn*, 115–116.

122. Al-Tijānī, *Al-Kunnāsh al-maktūm al-makhzūn*, 118.

123. Ḥarāzim, *Jawāhir al-maʿānī*, 1: 139.

124. Ibn al-Mashrī, *al-Jāmiʿ*, 61.

125. This being "the famous pole" Aḥmad al-Ḥabīb al-Qamārī from Sijilmasa, Algeria. Ḥarāzim, *Jawāhir al-maʿānī*, 1: 55–56. Aḥmad al-Ḥabīb (d. 1752), also known as al-Lamatī, had already passed by the time of al-Tijānī's dream. Al-Ḥabīb, according to the Saharan biographical dictionary *Fatḥ al-shukur*, was the saintly pole of his time (*quṭb zamānih*). See Ismail Warscheid, "Sufism, Scholarly Networks," 7.

126. This being the "Malāmatī" Aḥmad al-Ṭawāsh al-Tāzī (d. 1790). Ḥarāzim, *Jawāhir al-maʿānī*, 1: 56.

127. Those who informed him of this included Muḥammad b. al-Ḥasan al-Wānjilī, from the town of Tīssa about 90 kilometers north of Fez, and the aforementioned Aḥmad al-Hindī. Ḥarāzim, *Jawāhir al-maʿānī*, I: 55.

128. This being ʿAbd al-Ṣamad al-Raḥawī of Tunis. Ḥarāzim, *Jawāhir al-maʿānī*, 1: 57.

129. Ḥarāzim, *Jawāhir al-maʿānī*, 1: 54.

130. Ibn al-Mashrī, *al-Jāmiʿ*, 61. Elsewhere, Ibn al-Mashrī reports that al-Tijānī also found al-Ṣaqillī in a worldly state: "It was in my mind that the saint could not be in a worldly state, so I left him." Ibn al-Mashrī, *Rawḍ al-muḥibb*, 45–46.

131. Mansour, 'Sharifian Sufism," 75.

132. Al-Sufyānī, *al-Ifāda*, 77.

133. Al-Sufyānī, *al-Ifāda*, 114.

134. Aḥmad al-Ṭawāsh, letter to al-Tijānī, undated manuscript scanned on the website of Muḥammad al-Kabīr al-Tijānī, representative of the Tijānī family in Morocco. http://www.tidjania.fr/documents/215-ahmadtawach. Accessed August 2018.

135. Ḥarāzim, *Jawāhir al-maʿānī*, cited in Abun-Nasr, *The Tijaniyya*, 43. I have amended Abun-Nasr's translation slightly here.

136. Ḥarāzim, *Jawāhir al-maʿānī*, 2: 91.

137. Ḥarāzim, *Jawāhir al-maʿānī*, 1: 56.

138. Ḥarāzim, *Jawāhir al-maʿānī*, 1: 57.

139. Ḥarāzim, *Jawāhir al-maʿānī*, 1: 60.

140. Muḥammad Naṣṣār, "al-Muqaddima," in al-Sharqāwī, *al-ḥikam al-Kurdiyya*, 9–10.

141. Ḥarāzim, *Jawāhir al-maʿānī*, 1: 58–59.

142. Ibn al-Mashrī, *Rawḍ al-muḥibb*, 54; *al-Jāmiʿ*, 68.

143. Among al-Sammān's reported utterances while in a state of self-annihilation, for example, was "I am Muḥammad whom you seek." See Muthalib, "Mystical Teachings," 149–150.

144. Mayeur-Jaouen, "Small World of Aḥmad al-Ṣāwī," 118.

145. Ḥarāzim, *Jawāhir al-maʿānī*, 1: 59.

146. Ḥarāzim, *Jawāhir al-maʿānī*, 1: 102.

147. Ḥarāzim, *Jawāhir al-maʿānī*, 1: 103.

148. Niasse, *Removal of Confusion*, 51.

149. Al-Sufyānī, *al-Ifāda*, 110.

150. Ibn al-Mashrī, *Rawḍ al-muḥibb*, 486.

151. Ibn al-Mashrī, *al-Jāmiʿ*, 86–87.

152. Ḥarāzim, *Jawāhir al-maʿānī*, 2: 165–166.

153. Ḥarāzim, *Jawāhir al-maʿānī*, 2: 209.

154. Ḥarāzim, *Jawāhir al-maʿānī*, 2: 199.

155. Ḥarāzim, *Jawāhir al-maʿānī*, 2: 99. The Qur'an verse cited is 48:23.

156. Ḥarāzim, *Jawāhir al-maʿānī*, 2: 19.

157. Ḥarāzim, *Jawāhir al-maʿānī*, 2: 206.

158. Al-Tijānī quoted in Cissé, *Knowing Allah, Living Islam*, 73–74. Cissé states these words "are not found in any book," suggesting that their source is an unpublished manuscript or oral tradition. According to Cissé, Ibrāhīm Niasse was very fond of them, saying, "These words are the reason for my being pleased to have him as our Shaykh."

159. Ḥarāzim, *Jawāhir al-maʿānī,* 1: 189. At the end of this passage, al-Tijānī quotes an unidentified verse of Sufi poetry.

160. Mukhtār al-Kuntī, *al-Kawākib al-waqqād fī faḍl dhikr al-mashāʾikh wa l-ḥaqāʾiq,* cited in Niasse, *Removal of Confusion,* 135.

161. Ḥarāzim, *Jawāhir al-maʿānī,* 1: 189

162. Ḥarāzim, *Jawāhir al-maʿānī,* 1: 87.

163. Chittick, *Sufi Path of Knowledge,* 19.

164. Ḥarāzim, *Jawāhir al-maʿānī,* 1: 87.

165. al-Tijānī b. ʿAlī Cisse, interview with author, Rabat, Morocco, February 2019.

166. Ḥarāzim, *Jawāhir al-maʿānī,* 2: 165.

167. Ḥarāzim, *Risālat al-faḍl wa l-imtinān,* cited in Sukayrij, *Rafaʿ al-niqāb,* 4: 1212–1213. "Ingratitude" in covering (*kafara*) over God's favors here seems a more appropriate translation for the Arabic *kufr* than "disbelief."

168. Ḥarāzim, *Jawāhir al-maʿānī,* 1: 193.

169. Ḥarāzim, *Jawāhir al-maʿānī,* 1: 181.

170. Ḥarāzim, *Jawāhir al-maʿānī,* 1: 190.

171. Ḥarāzim, *Jawāhir al-maʿānī,* 1: 186.

172. Ḥarāzim, *Risālat al-faḍl wa l-imtinān,* in Sukayrij, *Rafaʿ al-niqāb,* 4: 1218.

173. Petrone, "*Ādāb* with an Absent Master," 609–610.

174. Al-Tijānī, *Mukhtārāt min rasāʾil al-Shaykh,* 25.

175. Al-Sufyānī, *al-Ifāda,* 258.

176. Ḥarāzim, *Jawāhir al-maʿānī,* 2: 85.

177. Al-Sufyānī, *al-Ifāda,* 144.

178. Al-Sufyānī, *al-Ifāda,* 65.

179. Tāl, *Rimāḥ,* 530–531. See also al-Lamaṭī, *Pure Gold,* 533. O'Kane and Radtke's translation of these passages is slightly different than my own.

180. Mansour, *Mawlay Sulayman,* 135.

181. Sukayrij, *Kashf al-ḥijāb,* 92–93.

182. Al-Sufyānī, *al-Ifāda,* 145–146.

183. Ḥarāzim, *Risālat al-faḍl,* in Sukayrij, *Rafaʿ al-niqāb,* 4: 1217.

184. Taji-Farouki, *Ibn ʿArabi,* 4.

185. For an example of how prayer collections can be read as attempts at anti-colonial liberation in West Africa, see Wright, *Living Knowledge in West African Islam,* 256–257.

186. Al-Anṭākī, *Tadhkirat ʾūlā l-albāb*; Shaykh al-Tijānī Cissé, interview with author, Paris, France, April 2019. According to Cissé, this book was one of the last books al-Tijānī read before his passing in 1815. The book was known as one of the most comprehensive collections of pharmacology in the world to the sixteenth century. See Gran, "Medical Pluralism," 343.

187. Al-Burūjī, *Miftāḥ al-saʿāda*; al-Ḥāfiẓ al-Miṣrī, *Aḥzāb wa awrād.*

188. Tāl, *Rimāḥ,* 448–449.

189. Al-Burūjī, *Miftāh al-saʿāda,* 90. The parenthetical addition is based the oral

commentary of Ḥasan Cissé, interview with author, Medina-Baye Kaolack Senegal, August 2002.

190. Al-Ḥāfiẓ al-Miṣrī, *Aḥzāb wa awrād*, 75.

191. Niasse, *Jawahir al-rasa'il*, 1: 151; al-Ḥāfiẓ al-Miṣrī, *Aḥzāb wa awrād*, 78.

192. Al-Lamaṭī, *Pure Gold*, 423–425.

193. Kugle, *Rebel between Spirit and Law*, 148.

194. Khushaim, "Aḥmad Zarrūq," 212.

195. Kugle, *Rebel between Spirit and Law*, 148. For an alternative version of this vision, along with a full text of the prayer, see Ahmad Ali Al-Adnani (translated and edited), *Shaykh Ahmad Zarruq: The Ship of Rescue for Those Who Take Shelter in Allah, also Called al-Wazifa az-Zarruqiyyah* (South Africa: Aliya Publications, 2017). Available online at salawaat.wordpress.com. The importance of the *waẓīfa* for the nascent "Zarrūqiyya" is also discussed, along with a full English translation, in Khushaim, "Aḥmad Zarrūq," 211–221.

196. Some of these benefits were elaborated by Zarrūq himself, but most were explanations by Zarrūq's student Muḥammad al-Kharrūbī (d. 1555, Tripoli). See Adani, *The Ship of Rescue*, 5–7.

197. Al-Burūjī, *Miftāḥ al-sa'āda*, 149–156; al-Naẓīfī, *al-Durra al-kharīda*, 3: 241–243.

198. Taji-Farouki, *Ibn 'Arabi*, 30–38.

199. Ḥarāzim, *al-Jawāhir al-ma'ānī*, 2: 91. Other prayers from al-Sammān included the *Aḥzāb* of Abu Ḥasan al-Shādhilī, the *Waẓīfa* of Aḥmad Zarrūq, and the *Dalā'il al-khayrāt* of Muḥammad al-Jazūlī. The text of the *Dawr* is found in al-Ḥāfiẓ al-Miṣrī, *Aḥzāb wa awrād*.

200. Taji-Farouki, *Ibn 'Arabi*, 21, 40–41, 70–71.

201. See, for example, Al-Ḥāfiz al-Miṣrī, *Aḥzāb wa awrād*, 80–92. See also al-Tijānī b. 'Alī Cissé, interview with author, Medina-Baye Kaolack, Senegal, July 2016.

202. Al-Ghawth, *al-Jawāhir al-khams*, 287–288.

203. Ḥarāzim, *Jawāhir al-ma'ānī*, 1: 162.

204. Al-Burūjī, *Miftāḥ al-sa'āda*, 179–180.

205. *Tārīkh al-fattāsh*, concerning the travels of Askia Muhammad in Egypt, cited in Pettigrew, "Muslim Healing," 104. It remains to be seen whether the authenticated seventeenth-century *Tārīkh Ibn Mukhtār*, which the nineteenth-century version of the *Tārīkh al-fattāsh* draws upon, contains this narration. For a discussion of the problems with the *Tārīkh al-fattāsh*, see Nobili and Mathee, "New Study of the Tārīkh al-Fattāsh," 37–73. The larger work of authentication is currently underway with Mauro Nobili, Ali Diakité, and Zachary Wright, *Phantom Books of the Sudan: The Authenticated Timbuktu Chronicle of Ibn al-Mukhtār and the Tārīkh al-fattāsh of the Caliphate of Ḥamdallāhi* (British Academy Fontes Historiae Africanae, forthcoming).

206. This to 'Umar al-Sharqāwī (d. 1260); in al-Kattānī, *Salwat*, 285; also cited in Ellen Amster, *Medicine and the Saints*, 226.

207. Sukayrij, *Rafa' Niqāb*, 1209–1210.

208. O'Fahey, *Enigmatic Saint*, 38–39.

209. Batran, *Qadriyya Brotherhood*, 229. Batran mistakenly believed the *ḥizb al-sayf* to have been composed by Mukhtār al-Kuntī, unless Batran is referring to another prayer authored by al-Kuntī with the same name.

210. Ḥarāzim, *Jawāhir al-maʿānī*, 2: 91.

211. Cornell, *Realm of the Saint*, 183.

212. Tāl, *Rimāḥ*, 451.

213. Niasse, *Jawāhir al-rasāʾil*, 3: 37; see also Sukayrij, *Lubān al-lubb*, 2: 45, for reference to this connection to Sammān.

214. Ibn al-Mashrī, *al-Jāmiʿ*, 83.

215. Ibn al-Mashrī, *al-Jāmiʿ*, 83.

216. Ḥarāzim, *Jawāhir al-maʿānī*, I: 175.

217. Tāl, *Rimāḥ*, 387–388. Muḥammad al-Ḥāfīẓ includes the prayer in his *Aḥzāb wa awrād*, 93–99.

218. Al-Ghawth, *al-Jawāhir al-khams*, 68–69.

219. Al-Ghawth, *al-Jawāhir al-khams*, 68–70, 130–284.

220. Muḥammad al-Rāḍī Kanūn, in Sukayrij, *Tījān al-ghawānī*, fn. 1, 47.

221. Al-Ghawth, *al-Jawāhir al-khams*, 183–184.

222. Kumshakhānawī, *Majmūʿ aḥzāb*, 66–69.

223. Sukayrij, *Tījān al-ghawānī*, 49.

224. Muḥammad al-Rāḍī Kanūn, in Sukayrij, *Tījān al-ghawānī*, fn. 1, 47.

225. Al-Ghawth, *al-Jawāhir al-khams*, 211.

226. Al-Ghawth, *al-Jawāhir al-khams*, 190.

227. Al-Ghawth, *al-Jawāhir al-khams*, 244–245.

228. Al-Ghawth, *al-Jawāhir al-khams*, 195.

229. Al-Ghawth, *al-Jawāhir al-khams*, 202.

230. al-Tijānī Cissé, author's observation in Rabat, Morocco, March 2016.

Chapter Three: The Actualization of Humanity on the Muhammadan Path

1. In addition to the *Jawāhir al-maʿānī* cited here, see Ibn al-Mashrī, *Rawḍ al-muḥibb*, 55; Ḥarāzim, *al-Mashāhid*, 67; Ibn al-Mashrī, *al-Jāmiʿ*, 89.

2. Ḥarāzim, *Jawāhir al-maʿānī*, 1: 62. Generally, *Ṭarīqa Aḥmadiyya* here must be considered interchangeable with *Muḥammadiyya*, as "Aḥmad" is an alternative name for the Prophet Muḥammad. ʿUmar Tāl enumerated a number of divergent characteristics between *Aḥmadiyya* and *Muḥammadiyya*, but the attribution is to the Prophet Muḥammad, not Aḥmad al-Tijānī, in either case. See Tāl, *Rimāḥ*, 477–484.

3. Reichmuth, Rüsen, and Sarhan, "Humanism and Muslim Culture," 13.

4. An example of such portraits avoided here can be found in a study of the Tijāniyya in Senegal, where the twentieth-century Tijānī shaykh Mālik Sy's teachings are presented as a "rational understanding of Islam," which "brought open-mindedness to his interpretation of the rules of Islam." See Diallo, "Exploring a Sufi Tradition," 31, 38.

5. Mamdani, *Good Muslim, Bad Muslim*, 24.

6. Würsch, "Humanism and Mysticism," 92. For more on the concept of Islamic humanism, in addition to the works cited in this discussion, see Goodman, *Islamic Humanism.*

7. Reichmuth, "Humanism in Islam," in *Humanism*, 120.

8. Würsch, "Humanism and Mysticism," 91.

9. Yaḥyā b. ʿAdī, *Tahḍīb al-akhlāq* ("The Reformation of Morals"), cited in Griffith, "Commending Virtue," 91. According to Sidney (92–93), this same idea was seized upon by the Muslim court philosopher Miskawayh (d. 1030) as especially appropriate to multicultural societies under Islamic rule.

10. Cornell, "Practical Sufism," printed online at http://www.secondspring.co.uk/articles/cornell.htm. Accessed May 30, 2016.

11. Reichmuth, Rüsen, and Sarhan, "Humanism and Muslim Culture," 12.

12. Akkach, *ʿAbd al-Ghani al-Nabulusi*, 114.

13. Ibn al-Mashrī, *Rawḍ al-muḥibb*, 132.

14. Qur'an, 41:53.

15. Al-Ghazālī, *Niche of Lights*, as cited in Elkaisy-Friemuth, *God and Humans*, 136.

16. Niasse, *Fī riyād al-tafsīr*, V: 251.

17. Ḥarāzim, *Jawāhir al-maʿānī*, 2: 150.

18. Representative of this identification was Ṣadr al-Dīn al-Qūnawī, the inheritor of Ibn al-ʿArabī. See Todd, *Sufi Doctrine of Man*, 119. For al-Tijānī's discussion of the concept, see Ḥarāzim, *Jawāhir al-maʿānī*, 1: 284.

19. Ibn al-Mashrī, *Rawḍ al-muḥibb*, 70–71. According to the accompanying footnote by al-Rāḍī Kannūn, the ḥadīth mentioned is related by Abū Hurayra and found in *Ṣaḥīḥ Muslim*.

20. Niasse, *The Removal of Confusion*, 22–23.

21. See, for example, Chittick, *Sufi Path of Knowledge*, 351–352; Knysh, *Sufism*, 93–96.

22. Ḥarāzim, *Jawāhir al-maʿānī*, 2: 121–124. See also the discussion of Niasse's *al-Sirr al-akbar*, in Wright, *Living*, 152.

23. Here the shaykh begins reference to the later stages of the self's purification: (1) the self inciting to evil; (2) the self-blaming self; (3) the serene self; (4) the contented self; and (5) the self pleasing to God.

24. Ḥarāzim, *Jawāhir al-maʿānī*, 2: 210.

25. Ṣadr al-Dīn al-Qunāwī, *Murshidīya*, cited in Todd, *Sufi Doctrine of Man*, 153.

26. Ḥarāzim, *Kitāb al-irshidāt*, 23.

27. Ḥadīth cited by Ḥasan Cisse, commentary on Niasse, *Spirit of Good Morals*, 51.

28. Ḥarāzim, *Jawāhir al-maʿānī*, 2: 188.

29. Ḥarāzim, *Jawāhir al-maʿānī*, 1: 217.

30. Reference to the *ḥadīth qudsī* that begins with the words, "I was a hidden treasure, and loved to be known, so I created . . ." According to ʿAjlūnī's *Kashf al-khafāʾ* analysis of this ḥadīth: "Its meaning is correct." See Niasse, *Removal of Confusion*, fn. 15, 87.

31. Ḥarāzim, *Jawāhir al-maʿānī*, 1: 215–216.

32. Ḥarāzim, *Jawāhir al-maʿānī*, 1: 284.

33. Ḥarāzim, *Jawāhir al-maʿānī*, 1: 216. The verse cited here is Qurʾān, 17:44.

34. Qurʾān, 11:56.

35. Ḥarāzim, *Jawāhir al-maʿānī*, 1: 241. The verses cited here are Qurʾān, 22:18 and 17:44.

36. Ḥarāzim, *Jawāhir al-maʿānī*, 1: 274–275; see page 275 for alternative description of this process.

37. Ḥarāzim, *Jawāhir al-maʿānī*, 2: 127.

38. Ḥarāzim, *Jawāhir al-maʿānī*, 2: 275.

39. Ḥarāzim, *Jawāhir al-maʿānī*, 2: 128.

40. The text here admits that this refers to the "internal" (*bāṭin*) reality, while the external purpose of the human creation is to worship God, as in the Qurʾān verse, "*I have only created the Jinn and men to worship me.*"

41. Ḥarāzim, *Jawāhir al-maʿānī*, 2: 12.

42. Hadith related in al-Bukhārī and in the Musnad of Aḥmad b. Ḥanbal; see Ḥarāzim, *Jawāhir al-maʿānī*, 2: 18.

43. Qur'an, 5:54.

44. This line is not part of the original hadith quoted earlier in the text, but it is included in some alternate narrations. See Sells, *Mystical Languages of Unsaying*, 69.

45. Qurʾān, chapter 112, consists of only three lines and is one of the shortest of the Qurʾān.

46. Ḥarāzim, *Jawāhir al-maʿānī*, 2: 21–22.

47. Ḥarāzim, *Jawāhir al-maʿānī*, 2: 274.

48. Ibn al-Sāʾiḥ, *Bughyat al-mustafīd*, 201. The text attributes this opinion to the earlier Egyptian Sufi ʿAbd al-Wahhāb al-Shaʿrānī, perhaps in explanation of the ideas of Ibn al-ʿArabī.

49. Ḥarāzim, *Jawāhir al-maʿānī*, 2: 24–25.

50. al-Tijānī b. ʿAlī Cissé, telephone interview with author, January 25, 2016.

51. Ḥarāzim, *Jawāhir al-maʿānī*, 2: 149.

52. Ḥarāzim, *Jawāhir al-maʿānī*, 2: 149.

53. Al-Sufyānī, *al-Ifāda*, 85.

54. Ḥarāzim, *Jawāhir al-maʿānī*, 1: 173. The companions mentioned in conversation with Uways were ʿUmar and ʿAlī.

55. Schimmel, *And Muhammad Is His Messenger*, 130–132.

56. See Brown, *Misquoting Muhammad*, 227–229, 325. Brown's characterization of these narrations as "forged" and "concocted" seems to reflect a more contemporary/reformist textual rigor than the opinion of most classical ḥadīth scholars themselves. Earlier scholars usually did not conclude that a ḥadīth had been "made up" just because it could not be substantiated in an earlier text. The category of forged ḥadīth (*mawḍūʿāt*) normally pertains to a narration in whose line of transmission there is a known forger. See al-Sakhāwī, *al-Qawl al-bādiʿ*, cited in G. F. Haddad and Muhammad Sarkisian,

"Validity of Weak Hadith," *Living Islam* (livingislam.org, 2006). In any case, al-Tijānī apparently had similar doubts concerning some of these unsubstantiated ḥadīth, once asking the Prophet to confirm the narration in al-Jazūlī's *Dalāʾil al-khayrāt* concerning a bird created from every invocation of blessing on the Prophet (in fact, Brown's primary example of Sufis "concocting" ḥadīth). The Prophet told al-Tijānī this narration was authentic. See Ḥarāzim, *Jawāhir al-maʿānī*, 1: 163.

57. Ḥarāzim, *Jawāhir al-maʿānī*, 2: 341.

58. Ḥarāzim, *Jawāhir al-maʿānī*, 1: 171.

59. Ḥarāzim, *Jawāhir al-maʿānī*, 1: 172.

60. Ḥarāzim, *Jawāhir al-maʿānī*, 1: 171.

61. Ḥarāzim, *al-Irshidāt al-rabbāniyya*, 4.

62. Ḥarāzim, *Jawāhir al-maʿānī*, 2: 343.

63. Ḥarāzim, *Jawāhir al-maʿānī*, 1: 173.

64. Niasse, *al-Sirr al-akbar*, in Muḥammad Maigari, *al-Shaykh Ibrāhīm Aniyās*, 434. For further discussion of this topic, see Wright, *Living Knowledge*, 152. I have slightly adjusted the translation here.

65. Qurʾān, 33:6.

66. Qurʾān, 6:33.

67. Ḥarāzim, *Jawāhir al-maʿānī* 1: 266.

68. Tāl, *Rimāḥ*, 477–484.

69. Al-Sufyānī, *al-Ifāda*, 195.

70. Akansūs, *al-Jawāb al-muskit*, cited in Seesemann, "New Dawn for Sufism," 296.

71. Seesemann, "New Dawn for Sufism," 295–296. Seesemann is here summarizing Ibn Anbūja's arguments in *Mīzāb al-raḥma*.

72. Sukayrij, *Kashf al-ḥijāb*, 191. The letter here was discovered by Aḥmad ʿAbdallāwī and related to his disciple, Aḥmad Sukayrij. The idea that the one who offered many prayers on the Prophet could experience the waking vision of the Prophet was also articulated by Ibn al-Sāʾiḥ in *Bughyat al-mustafīd*. See Seesemann, "New Dawn for Sufism," 296–297.

73. Ḥarāzim, *Jawāhir al-maʿānī*, 2: 284, 325–326.

74. Valerie Hoffman similarly concludes that eighteenth- and nineteenth-century "Neo-Sufi" orders, through their emphasis on "annihilation in the Messenger," did not depart from earlier Sufism's (i.e., Ibn al-ʿArabī) understanding of the prerequisite "annihilation in God." See Hoffman, "Annihilation in the Messenger of God," 351–369.

75. Ḥarāzim, *Jawāhir al-maʿānī*, 2: 286.

76. This earlier erroneous understanding of the *Ṭarīqa Muḥammadiyya*, put forth by H. R. Gibb and Fazlur Rahman, has already been debunked. See O'Fahey and Radtke, "Neo-Sufism Reconsidered," 56, 70.

77. Meier, "A Resurrection of Muhammad in Suyuti," in *Essays on Islamic Piety and Mysticism*, 505–547.

78. Meier, "Resurrection of Muḥammad in Suyūṭī," in *Essays on Islamic Piety and Mysticism*, 529.

79. Ḥarāzim, *Jawāhir al-maʿānī*, 2: 60. Meier's assertion ("Resurrection," 515) that al-Tijānī understood Muḥammad's spirit to "rush [. . .] back from the court of the heavenly Jerusalem and (to) enter [. . .] his body only in order to return the pious person's greeting," is thus clearly mistaken.

80. Ḥarāzim, *Jawāhir al-maʿānī*, 2: 333. For earlier academic analysis of the *Jawharat al-kamāl*, see Ryan, "Mystical Theology," 211–213.

81. Qurʾān, 55:29.

82. Aḥmad al-Rifāʿī (d. 1182, Iraq) was the founder of the Rifāʿiyya Sufi order popular today in Egypt.

83. Ḥarāzim, *Jawāhir al-maʿānī*, 2: 292. Khiḍr was the mystical guide of Moses referenced in the eighteenth chapter of the Qurʾān, who like Jesus and Enoch, many Muslim believe to be still alive.

84. Ḥarāzim, *Jawāhir al-maʿānī*, 1: 166–167.

85. Tāl, *Rimāḥ*, 332. See also Ware, Wright, and Syed, *Jihad of the Pen*, 105–106, where the translation of this passage is slightly different.

86. Ḥarāzim, *Jawāhir al-maʿānī*, 1: 62.

87. For more on this subject, and on the importance of visions in Islamic history more generally, see Goldiher, "Appearance of the Prophet in Dreams," 503–509; Fahd, *La Divination Arabe*; Gouda, *Dreams and Their Meanings in the Old Arab Tradition*; Ashtiany (ed.), *Dreaming across Boundaries*; Iain Edgar, *The Dream in Islam*; Felek and Knysh (eds.), *Dreams and Visions in Islamic Societies*; Sirriyeh, *Dreams and Visions in the World of Islam.*

88. Goldziher, "Appearance of the Prophet in Dreams," 503.

89. In this dream of ʿUmar b. ʿAbd al-ʿAzīz, the Prophet decided in favor of ʿAlī, but forgave Muʿawiya. See Fahd, *Divination*, 297–298.

90. Likewise, the dream of ʿUmar b. ʿAbd al-ʿAzīz. Fahd, *Divination*, 297–298.

91. Fahd, *Divination*, 288–289.

92. McCarthy, *Theology of al-Ash'ari*, 152–155.

93. Goldziher, "Appearance of the Prophet," 503–504.

94. Ghazālī, *Remembrance of Death and the Afterlife*, 163.

95. This in the Prophet's appearance to Aḥmad al-Kharrāz (d. 899). See Schimmel, *And Muhammad Is His Messenger*, 130.

96. Chourief, *Spiritual Teachings of the Prophet*, xxiii.

97. Green, "Religious and Cultural Roles of Dreams," 298, 300, 306.

98. For more on this subject, see Kinberg, *Ibn Abi al-Dunya*; Katz, *Dreams, Sufism and Sainthood*; or Gouda's work primary based on al-Nābulusī's *Taʿtīr al-anām fī taʿbīr al-manām*: Gouda, *Dreams and Their Meanings in the Old Arab Tradition.*

99. Al-Shinjīṭī, *al-Jaysh al-kafīl*, 52.

100. Al-Shinjīṭī, *al-Jaysh al-kafīl*, 54.

101. Ibn al-ʿArabī, *Futuḥāt al-makkiyya*, cited in Chittick, *Imaginal Worlds*, 84. Al-Ghazālī's similar statement, "The mystics in their waking state now beyond the angels

and the spirits of prophets," is found in his *Deliverance from Error*. See Watt, *Faith and Practice of al-Ghazālī*, 61.

102. Ḥarāzim, *Jawāhir al-maʿānī*, 1: 67.

103. Ḥarāzim, *Jawāhir al-maʿānī*, 2: 27. The Qur'an verse cited here is 2:256.

104. Ḥarāzim, *Jawāhir al-maʿānī*, 1: 67.

105. Ḥarāzim, *Jawāhir al-maʿānī*, 1: 111.

106. Sukayrij, *Kashf al-ḥijāb*, 752.

107. Ḥarāzim, *Jawāhir al-maʿānī*, 1: 67.

108. Sukayrij, *Kāshf al-ḥijāb*, 149–150.

109. Abun-Nasr, *The Tijaniyya*, 21.

110. Ḥarāzim, *al-Mashāhid*, 24.

111. In this case, saying that water that fell back into the bucket from one's ablution did not render the rest of the water in the bucket impure. Ḥarāzim, *Jawāhir al-maʿānī*, 1: 66–67.

112. Ḥarāzim, *Jawāhir al-maʿānī*, 1: 66.

113. Al-Sufyānī, *al-Ifāda*, 84; al-Ṭaṣfāwī, *al-Fatḥ al-rabbānī*, 15.

114. Ḥarāzim, *Jawāhir al-maʿānī*, 1: 94.

115. Ḥarāzim, *Jawāhir al-maʿānī*, 1: 162, 175–178.

116. Ḥarāzim, *Jawāhir al-maʿānī*, 1: 164.

117. Ḥarāzim, *Jawāhir al-maʿānī*, 1: 161.

118. Ḥarāzim, *Jawāhir al-maʿānī*, 1: 161; Tāl, *Rimāḥ*, 434.

119. Al-Naẓīfī, *Durrat al-kharīda*, 4: 216–217. Al-Naẓīfī adds the condition of persistent recitation, "and persistence means reading it once per day."

120. Al-Naẓīfī, *Durrat al-kharīda*, 4: 219–220.

121. Ḥarāzim, *Jawāhir al-maʿānī*, 1: 167–168.

122. According to al-Tijānī, "This benefit mentioned is not obtained except by the one granted permission (directly) by my hand (*mushāfahatan*) or through an intermediary." See al-Naẓīfī, *al-Durra al-kharīda*, 4: 218

123. Al-ʿIrāqī, *Iqtiṭāf azhār*, 1: 284–284.

124. Al-Kattānī, *Salwat al-anfās*, 3: 46.

125. al-Naẓīfī, *al-Durra al-kharīda*, 4: 218.

126. Ḥarāzim, *Jawāhir al-maʿānī*, 2: 333.

127. Ḥarāzim, *Jawāhir al-maʿānī*, 2: 283.

128. Ḥarāzim, *Jawāhir al-maʿānī*, 2: 347.

129. Tāl, *Rimāḥ*, 480.

130. Ibn al-Mashrī, *Rawḍ al-muḥibb*, 306.

131. Aḥmad al-Shinqīṭī, "al-Futūḥāt al-rabbāniyya," cited in Padwick, *Muslim Devotions*, 150. I have amended the translation here based on the text available in the appendix of Muḥammad al-Ṭaṣfāwī, *al-Fatḥ al-rabbānī*, 78–99.

132. Ḥarāzim, *Jawāhir al-maʿānī*, 2: 129.

133. Ḥarāzim, *Jawāhir al-maʿānī*, 2: 273.

134. Ḥarāzim, *Jawāhir al-maʿānī*, 1: 67.

135. Sukayrij, *Kashf al-ḥijāb*, 415.

136. El-Adnani, *La Tijaniyya*, 90.

137. El-Adnani, *La Tijaniyya*, 87–89.

138. Sukayrij, *Kashf al-ḥijāb*, 212.

139. Sukayrij, *Kashf al-ḥijāb*, 744–745.

140. Sukayrij, *Kashf al-ḥijāb*, 308.

141. Sukayrij, *Kashf al-ḥijāb*, 352–353.

142. Sukayrij, *Kashf al-ḥijāb*, 358.

143. Sukayrij, *Kashf al-ḥijāb*, 402.

144. These included ʿAlī Tamāsīnī, ʿAbd al-Wahhāb b. Aḥmar, Muḥammad b. Nāṣir al-ʿAlawī, Maḥmūd al-Tunisī, Abū Yaʿzā b. ʿAlī Ḥarāzim, ʿAbd al-Raḥmān b. ʿAlī Ḥarāzim, Maḥammad b. ʿAbd al-Wāḥid Bannānī al-Miṣrī, and Muḥammad b. Aḥmad al-Jbārī. See Sukayrij, *Kashf al-ḥijāb*, 202, 244, 247, 338, 346, 357, 417, 418.

145. Sukayrij, *Kashf al-ḥijāb*, 237.

146. Sukayrij, *Kashf al-ḥijāb*, 203.

147. Sukayrij, *Kashf al-ḥijāb*, 203–204.

148. Sukayrij, *Kashf al-ḥijāb*, 403.

149. Sukayrij, *Kashf al-ḥijāb*, 348.

150. Ibn al-Sāʾiḥ, *Bughyat al-mustafīd*, cited in Sukayrij, *Kashf al-ḥijāb*, 348.

151. Ḥarāzim, *Jawāhir al-maʿānī*, 2: 234–238.

152. Al-Rāḍī Kanūn, in Ibn al-Mashrī, *Rawḍ al-muḥibb*, fn. 1, 55.

153. Al-Sufyānī, *al-Ifāda al-Aḥmadiyya*, 62; Ibn al-Sāʾiḥ, *Bughyat al-mustafīd*, 187.

154. Ḥarāzim, *Jawāhir al-maʿānī*, 2: 234.

155. Sukayrij, *Kashf al-ḥijāb*, 196–197.

156. The ensuing details are found in Sukayrij, *Kashf al-ḥijāb*, 149–200.

157. El-Adnani, *La Tijaniyya*, 53.

158. Sukayrij, *Kashf al-ḥijāb*, 155.

159. For the full text of this lengthy prayer, see Sukayrij, *Kashf al-ḥijāb*, 157–190. The prayer was later published separately by al-Tijānī Cissé: al-Damrāwī, *Yāqūtat al-maḥtāj*.

160. Sukayrij, *Kashf al-ḥijāb*, 176.

161. Sukayrij, *Kashf al-ḥijāb*, 155.

162. Sukayrij, *Kashf al-ḥijāb*, 156.

163. Sukayrij, *Kashf al-ḥijāb*, 156.

164. Sukayrij, *Kashf al-ḥijāb*, 152–153.

165. Sukayrij, *Kashf al-ḥijāb*, 153.

166. Niasse, *Jawāhir al-rasāʾil*, 1: 30–31. Niasse wrote that it was Sukayrij who transmitted the prayer to him.

167. Sukayrij, *Kashf al-ḥijāb*, 199.

168. Ḥarāzim, *al-Mashāhid*, 50–51.

169. Al-Tijānī Cisse, interview with author, Cairo, October 2016.

170. The Prophet tells Ḥarāzim to tell al-Tijānī to tell Muḥammad b. al-Mashrī that his enthusiastic announcements of al-Tijānī's *maqām* were stirring up controversy, and that he should "hold his tongue." See Ḥarāzim, *al-Mashāhid*, 42.

171. The Prophet assures al-Tijānī not to be concerned about financing the construction of the *zāwiya*, that its affair is in God's hands and that those who assisted in its construction would be with the Prophet in Paradise. See Ḥarāzim, *al-Mashāhid*, 42.

172. Ḥarāzim, *al-Mashāhid*, 42.

173. Ḥarāzim, *al-Mashāhid*, 41.

174. Sukayrij, *Kashf al-ḥijāb*, 212.

175. Ḥarāzim, *al-Mashāhid*, 27.

176. Ḥarāzim, *al-Mashāhid*, 8. According to al-Rāḍī Kanūn's footnote on a reference to the *miftāḥ al-quṭbāniyya* in Ibn al-Mishrī's *Rawḍ al-muḥibb al-fānī*, this was a prayer that guarantees the attainment of axial sainthood to anyone who recites it. It was given to al-Tijānī by a "great angel" (according to Ibn al-Mishrī), and no one prior to him or, according to Kānūn. Shaykh al-Tijānī Cisse, in an interview with the author (Medina-Baye Kaolack, Senegal, July 2010), disagreed with this latter assessment, and suggested that Shaykh Ibrahim Niasse had the prayer and transmitted it to close disciples such as Sayyid ʿAlī Cisse.

177. Ḥarāzim, *al-Mashāhid*, 50.

178. Niasse, *Removal of Confusion*, 33.

179. Ḥarāzim, *al-Mashāhid*, 50. The notion of intermediary (*wāsiṭa*) refers to the shaykh's relationship to his other followers, not between the shaykh and the Prophet, as in al-Tijānī's reported statement, "No one of our companions obtains anything except by the intermediary of Sayyid al-Ḥājj ʿAlī Ḥarāzim, and he was given that without asking for it." Al-Sufyānī, *al-Ifāda*, 113.

180. Ḥarāzim, *al-Mashāhid*, 41.

181. Ḥarāzim, *al-Mashāhid*, 67.

182. Al-Baʿqīlī, *al-Shurb al-ṣāfī*, 1: 202.

183. This was Mufaḍḍil al-Saqqāt. See Al-Sufyānī, *al-Ifāda*, 62.

184. Al-Nābulusī, *Taʿṭīr al-anām*, 3.

185. Sirriyeh, *Sufi Visionary*, 57.

186. Al-Tijānī cited in Benabdellah, *La Tijania*, 75.

187. Ḥarāzim, *Jawāhir al-maʿānī*, 2: 274.

188. Niasse, *Jawāhir al-rasāʾil*, 1: 50.

189. Niasse, *Jawāhir al-rasāʾil*, 1: 160.

190. Niasse, *Jawāhir al-rasāʾil*, 1: 20. By the eighteenth century, the Malāmityya was an idea within Sufism that the saint should be indistinguishable from the ordinary Muslim. But when it first appeared in the tenth century the term originally meant those who called blame (*malām*) on themselves so as to not be publicly identified as pious (and thus become prideful). See Karamusta, *Sufism in the Formative Period*, 48–51.

191. See, for example, Abū ʿAbd al-Raḥmān al-Sulamī (d. 1021), *Zalal al-fuqarāʾ*, in Heer and Honerkamp, *Three Early Sufi Texts*, 129–154.

192. Ḥarāzim, al-Mashāhid, 44.

193. ʿUmar Tāl, *al-Rimāḥ*, in Ware, Wright, and Syed, *Jihad of the Pen*, 103–107. Tāl's discussion here mostly draws from Ibn al-Mubārak's *al-Ibrīz*.

194. Niasse, "Eternal Islam," cited in Wright, *Living Knowledge in West African Islam*, 266.

195. Cissé, "Islam and Peace," in *Islam the Religion of Peace*, 7, 15, 28.

196. Reichmuth, "Humanism in Islam," 125.

Chapter Four: The Seal of Muhammadan Sainthood and Hidden Pole

1. Al-Sufyānī, *al-Ifāda*, 123.

2. Al-Sufyānī, *al-Ifāda*, 125.

3. Ḥarāzim, *Jawāhir al-maʿānī*, 2: 91.

4. Al-Tijānī b. ʿAlī Cisse, interview with author, Medina-Baye Kaolack, Senegal, July 2017. Al-Tijānī Cisse offers this as evidence of al-Tijānī actually being the seal, implying that later scholars to whom this claim was ascribed cannot be verified to have themselves made that claim. Other Tijānī scholars did admit of later claimants to this title, but treated them much as they treated earlier claimants.

5. Niasse, *Tanbīh al-adhkiyāʾ*, 13.

6. In one narration, however, al-Tirmidhī's wife, who was earlier told in a spiritual audition that she had obtained the same spiritual rank as her husband, is told in a dream to relay the message to al-Tirmidhī, "I have given you a seal ring." See al-Tirmidhī, *Kitāb khatm al-awliyāʾ*, as cited in Palmer, "Social and Theoretical Dimensions of Sainthood," 205.

7. Palmer, "Social and Theoretical Dimensions of Sainthood," 142–180.

8. Ḥasan b. ʿAlī Cisse, interview with author, Medina-Baye Kaolack, Senegal, February 2003. Curiously, I have yet to locate an external reference for this narration. Chodkiewicz mentions only that the work was only known through the citations of Ibn al-ʿArabī until a full text was discovered in the 1960s. See Chodkiewicz, *Seal of the Saints*, 28.

9. Al-Tijānī Cissé, "Sainthood in Islam and the Seal of the Saints," in *Knowing Allah, Living Islam*, 108–109; Radtke and O'Kane, *Concept of Sainthood in Early Islamic Mysticism*, 130–131.

10. Radtke and O'Kane, *Concept of Sainthood*, 186.

11. Al-Tijānī Cisse, "Sainthood in Islam and the Seal of the Saints," in *Knowing Allah, Living Islam*, 111. For similar narration, see Radtke and O'Kane, *Concept of Sainthood*, 187.

12. Radtke and O'Kane, *Concept of Sainthood*, 109

13. Chodkiewicz, *Seal of the Saints*, 130.

14. Ibn al-ʿArabī as quoted by al-Shaʿrānī, cited in Winters, *Society and Religion*, 129.
15. Ibn al-ʿArabī, *ʿAnqāʾ mughrib*, cited in Chodkiewicz, *Seal of the Saints*, 139.
16. Ibn al-ʿArabī, *Futūḥāt al-makkiyya*, cited in Chodkiewicz, *Seal of the Saints*, 120–121.
17. Ibn al-ʿArabī, *Fuṣūṣ al-ḥikam*, cited in Chodkiewicz, *Seal of the Saints*, 124.
18. Ibn al-ʿArabī, *ʿAnqāʾ mughrib*, 91, also cited in Chodkiewicz, *Seal of the Saints*, 122.
19. Ibn al-ʿArabī, *Futūḥāt al-makkiyya*, cited in Chodkiewicz, *Seal of the Saints*, 119.
20. Ibn al-ʿArabī, *Fuṣūṣ al-ḥikam*, cited in Chodkiewicz, *Seal of the Saints*, 125–126.
21. Ibn al-ʿArabī, *Futūḥāt al-makkiyya*, cited in Chodkiewicz, *Seal of the Saints*, 129.
22. Ibn al-ʿArabī, *Futūḥāt al-makkiyya*, cited in Chodkiewicz, *Seal of the Saints*, 117–118.
23. Chodkiewicz, *Seal of the Saints*, 140.
24. Among those who held to Ibn al-ʿArabī's exclusive claim to the title was Emir ʿAbd al-Qādir al-Jazāʾirī. See Chodkiewicz, *Seal of the Saints*, 137. Chodkiewicz saw ʿAbd al-Qādir as "representing the Akbarian tradition in its purest form."
25. Al-Qāshānī, *Glossary of Sufi Technical Terms*, 110.
26. McGregor, *Sanctity and Mysticism*, 116–117.
27. McGregor, *Sanctity and Mysticism*, 111.
28. McGregor, *Sanctity and Mysticism*, 143–147.
29. Knysh, *Ibn ʿArabi in the Later Islamic Tradition*, 81.
30. Al-Shaʿrānī, *al-Ṭabaqāt al-kubra*, cited in Chodkiewicz, *Seal of the Saints*, 135.
31. Winters, *Society and Religion*, 130.
32. Chodkiewicz, *Seal of the Saints*, 135. Sirhindī posited a saintly station beyond that of the axial saint (*quṭb*): that of the "supreme helper" (*ghawth*). See Buehler, *Revealed Grace*, 260.
33. Buehler, *Revealed Grace*, 213–214.
34. Cornell, *Realm of the Saint*, 211–222.
35. Chodkiewicz, *Seal of the Saints*, 135–136.
36. Al-ʿIrāqī, *al-Fayḍ al-rabbānī*.
37. Chodkiewicz, *Seal of the Saints*, 136.
38. Sirriyeh, *Sufi Visionary*, 133.
39. Schimmel, *Pain and Grace*, 42.
40. Muthalib, "Mystical Teachings," 11, 62. Muthalib's source-work here is based on al-Sammān's *Nafaḥāt al-ilāhiya*, as well as Purwadaksi's examination of Ṣiddīq b. ʿUmar Khan al-Madanī's *Rātib al-Sammān*.
41. Muthalib, "Mystical Teachings," 149–150.
42. Al-Zabīdī, *Tāj al-ʿarūs*, cited in Niasse, *Tanbīh al-adhkiyāʾ*, 13.
43. ʿUthmān b. Fūdī, *al-Dāliyya*, cited in Shareef, *Increase of the Spiritual Aspirant*, 269–270.
44. Shareef, *Increase of the Spiritual Aspirant*, 252–253.
45. ʿAbd al-Qādir b. Muṣṭafa, *Shukr al-wāhib al-mufīḍ li l-Muwāhib*, cited in Shareef, *Increase of the Spiritual Aspirant*, 243.
46. Batran, *Qadiriyya Brotherhood*, 124.

47. Muḥammad al-Khalīfa b. al-Mukhtār al-Kuntī, *al-Ṭarā'if wa l-talā'id*, cited in Niasse, *Tanbīh al-adhkiyā'*, 13. Here al-Kuntī cites the ḥadīth where the Prophet defined the "greater jihad" as the "jihad against the carnal self and lust."

48. Niasse, *Tanbīh al-adhkiyā'*, 17.

49. The following information is contained in al-Tijānī, *Kunnāsh al-riḥla*, 34–36.

50. For a more elaborate discussion of Ibn al-'Arabī's understanding of this saintly hierarchy, see Chodkiewicz, *Seal of the Saints*, 89–115.

51. Sukaryij includes this citation in his *Nahj al-hidāya fī khatm al-wilāya*, sourcing it to Bā 'Alawī's *Shaqq al-jayb fī ma'rifa ahl al-shahāda wa l-ghayb*. Sukayrij, *Nahj al-hidāya*, 46.

52. Al-Tijānī, *Kunnāsh al-riḥla*, 35, 36.

53. Al-Tijānī, *Kunnāsh al-riḥla*, 36.

54. Sukayrij, *Nahj al-hidāya*, 46.

55. Niasse, *Tanbīh al-adhkiyā'*, 34. Niasse mentions that parts of this passage were taken from Muḥammad Wafā, as cited in al-Sha'rānī's *Tabaqāt*, but it is unclear where the passage from Sha'rānī begins and ends.

56. Ibn al-Mashrī, *Rawḍ al-muḥibb*, 309–310.

57. Al-Sufyānī, *al-Ifāda*, 101, 133. This work's editor, Muḥammad al-Ḥāfiẓ al-Miṣrī, explains in commentary, citing Ibn Qayyim al-Jawziyya and others, that the dominant scholarly opinion holds that the spirits of beings were present before the creation of their bodies. See al-Sufyānī, *al-Ifāda*, 102–103.

58. Ḥarāzim, *al-Mashāhid*, 13

59. Ḥarāzim, *al-Mashāhid*, 42.

60. For a discussion of such ambiguity in the *Fuṣūṣ al-ḥikām*, see Chodkiewicz, *Seal of the Saints*, 123.

61. Ibn al-Mashrī, *Rawḍ al-muḥibb*, 311.

62. Ibn al-Mashrī, *al-Jāmi'*, 74.

63. Ḥarāzim, *Jawāhir al-ma'ānī*, 1: 168–169; Ibn al-Mashrī, *al-Jāmi'*, 76. The precedent merit of the companions over the saints was an opinion also held by the later Yemeni scholar Muḥammad al-Shawkānī. See Dallal, *Islam without Europe*, 119.

64. When I asked Ḥasan b. 'Alī Cisse (interview with author, Medina-Baye Kaolack, Senegal, February 2003) to explain al-Tijānī's statements concerning the companions with his own claimed rank, he told me, "He was just being humble."

65. Ibn al-Mashrī, *al-Jāmi'*, 75.

66. Ḥarāzim, *al-Mashāhid*, 52–53.

67. Ḥarāzim, *al-Mashāhid*, 42.

68. Ḥarāzim, *al-Mashāhid*, 55.

69. Tāl, *Rimāḥ*, 403.

70. Ḥarāzim, *Jawāhir al-ma'ānī*, 1: 199–200.

71. Ḥarāzim, *al-Mashāhid*, 50.

72. Ibn al-'Arabī, as cited in Niasse, *Removal of Confusion*, 114–115.

73. Niasse, *Removal of Confusion*, 115.

74. Ḥarāzim, *Jawāhir al-maʿānī*, 2: 150.

75. Ibn al-Mashrī, *Rawḍ al-muḥibb*, 305. For discussion of the spiritual station (*maqām*) of al-Tuhāmī as *quṭb*, see al-Sufyānī, *al-Ifāda*, 77.

76. Tāl, *Rimāḥ*, 403.

77. This date is also confirmed in Ibn al-Mashrī, *al-Jāmiʿ*, 77, although the year given is 1213 (1798), not 1214. In any case, both accounts have the investiture happening soon after al-Tijānī's establishment in Fez. I believe, however, that 1214 was the correct year, as the eighteenth of Safar fell on a Monday that year (according to online Gregorian-Hijri date conversions, adjusted one day for moonsighting delay) as Ḥarāzim's account indicates.

78. Ḥarāzim, *Mashāhid*, 45–48.

79. Sukayrij, *Kashf al-ḥijāb*, 198–199.

80. Ibn al-Mashrī, *al-Jāmiʿ*, 91–92.

81. Al-Tijānī's words cited in al-Tijānī b. ʿAlī Cisse, *Knowing Allah*, 109.

82. Al-Sufyānī, *al-Ifāda*, 136.

83. Ibn al-Mashrī, *Rawḍ al-muḥibb*, 306.

84. Tāl, *Rimāḥ*, 478.

85. Niasse, *Jawāhir al-rasāʾil*, 1: 47.

86. Ibn al-Mashrī, *al-Jāmiʿ*, 74–75.

87. Ḥarāzim, *Jawāhir al-maʿānī*, 2: 165.

88. Ibn al-Mashrī, *al-Jāmiʿ*, 86.

89. Ibn al-Mashrī, *Rawḍ al-muḥibb*, 304.

90. Al-Sufyānī, *al-Ifāda*, 131.

91. Tāl, *Rimāḥ*, 412–413. Tāl cites the narrations of several of al-Tijānī's direct disciples for this narration.

92. Al-Sufyānī, *al-Ifāda*, 111.

93. Ibn al-Mashrī, *al-Jāmiʿ*, 73.

94. Ibn al-Mashrī, *Rawḍ al-muḥibb*, 309–310.

95. Ḥarāzim, *al-Mashāhid*, 54–55; Ibn Mishrī, *al-Jāmiʿ*, 72.

96. Al-Sufyānī, *al-Ifāda*, 152.

97. Ibn al-Mashrī, *al-Jāmiʿ*, 75.

98. Tāl, *Rimāḥ*, 403.

99. Al-Shinqīṭī, *Al-Wāridāt*, 31–34.

100. Al-Shinqīṭī, *al-Wāridāt*, 32.

101. Al-Shinqīṭī, *al-Wāridāt*, 33.

102. Al-Shinqīṭī, *al-Wāridāt*, 34.

103. Niasse, *Tanbīh al-adhkiyāʾ*, 53.

104. Niasse, *Tanbīh al-adhkiyāʾ*, 35.

105. Niasse, *Jawahir al-rasāʾil*, 3: 26.

106. Niasse, *Jawāhir al-rasāʾil*, 1: 69.

107. For Niasse's testimony to Bamba as a saint, for example, see Wright, *Living Knowledge*, 86–87.

108. Al-Talīdī, *al-Muṭrib*, 242–244.

109. Niasse, *Tanbīh al-adhkiyā'*, 34. Niasse dates his own manuscript 1934. The appendix by Abu Bakr 'Atīq is dated 1947.

110. Al-Tijānī b. 'Alī Cisse, interview with author, Dakar, Senegal, June 2018.

111. Mansour, "Sharifian Sufism," 81.

112. Ibn al-Mashrī, *Rawḍ al-muḥibb*, 302. A similar discussion is found in Ḥarāzim, *Jawāhir al-ma'ānī*, 1: 159, where there is also reference to the claims to salvation of 'Abd al-Raḥmān al-Tha'ālabī (d. 1479, Algiers).

113. Ibn al-Mashrī, *al-Jāmi'*, 75.

114. Ibn al-Mashrī, *Rawḍ al-muḥibb*, 302.

115. Tāl, *Rimāḥ*, 420.

116. Ibn al-Mashrī, *Rawḍ al-muḥibb*, 302.

117. Qur'ān, 56:40; Al-Sufyānī, *al-Ifāda*, 85.

118. Al-Sufyānī, *al-Ifāda*, 114.

119. Ḥarāzim, *Jawāhir al-ma'ānī*, 1: 158.

120. Al-Sufyānī, *al-Ifāda*, 105.

121. Al-Sufyānī, *al-Ifāda*, 105.

122. Ḥarāzim, *Jawāhir al-ma'ānī*, 1: 153.

123. Ḥarāzim, *Jawāhir al-ma'ānī*, 1: 155–156.

124. Al-Sufyānī, *al-Ifāda*, 53

125. Al-Sufyānī, *al-Ifāda*, 110.

126. Tāl, *Rimāḥ*, 420. Tāl's narration here is on the authority of Muḥammad al-Ghālī.

127. Ibn al-Sā'iḥ, *Bughyat al-mustafīd*, cited in Sukayrij, *Kashf al-ḥijāb*, 205.

128. Al-Tijānī, *Rasā'il al-Shaykh*, 194, 201.

129. Sukayrij, *Kashf al-ḥijāb*, 145.

130. Al-Sufyānī, *al-Ifāda*, 122.

131. Sukayrij, *Kashf al-ḥijāb*, 117.

132. Al-Sufyānī, *al-Ifāda*, 101.

133. Al-Sha'rānī, *al-Ṭabaqāt al-wusṭā*, 1: 602.

134. Sukayrij, *Kashf al-ḥijāb*, 566.

135. Ibn al-Mashrī, *al-Jāmi'*, 185–186. While it appears most logical this occurrence was after al-Tijānī's investiture of the Seal of Saints in 1799, different manuscripts give alternative dates for this statement. Al-Rāḍī Kanūn's published version has 1205 A.H. (1791), as does a recent publication of Ibn al-Sā'iḥ's *Bughyat al-mustafīd* where the citation from *al-Jāmi'* is included (page 248). A handwritten manuscript of *al-Jāmi'* copied for Ibrāhīm Niasse by a Mauritanian disciple in 1939, provided to me by Ḥasan Cisse in 2003, gives the date as 1207 (1793). The published version of Niasse's *Kāshif al-ilbās*, the introduction of which cites this passage, renders the date as 1224 (1809). See Niasse, *Kāshif al-ilbās*, 28. Either all of the above dates are transcribed in error, or one of the earlier dates is correct and this command was not effected immediately (or disciples like Ḥarāzim and Ibn al-Mashrī left Fez but frequently returned to visit al-Tijānī). Ibn al-Sā'iḥ writes that this statement was the reason for Ḥarāzim's and Ibn

al-Mashrī's departure from Fez, but Ḥarāzim did not leave Fez until 1800 and Ibn al-Mashrī was with al-Tijānī in Fez at least at the time of his establishment there in 1798. See Ibn al-Sā'iḥ, *Bughyat al-mustafīd*, 211, 248; Sukayrij, *Kashf al-ḥijāb*, 238.

136. Ibrāhīm Khalīl b. Muḥammad al-Kabīr al-Tijānī and 'Abd al-Ḥalīm Luṭfī, interviews with author, Fez, Morocco, February 2003 and January 2019.

137. Al-Tijānī Cisse, interview with author, Casablanca, Morocco, July 2017.

138. Ḥarāzim, *Jawāhir al-ma'ānī*, I: 186.

139. Ḥarāzim, *Risālat al-faḍl wa l-imtinān*, in Sukayrij, *Raf' al-niqāb*, 1218, 1231.

140. Al-Sufyānī, *al-Ifāda*, 99.

141. Al-Sufyānī, *al-Ifāda*, 99.

142. Ibn al-Mashrī, *al-Jāmi'*, 91.

143. Muḥammad al-Ḥāfiẓ al-Miṣrī, commentary in Al-Sufyānī, *al-Ifāda*, 100.

144. Niasse, *Removal of Confusion*, 61.

145. Tāl, *Rimāḥ*, 422. This was presumably the testimony of al-Ghālī to Tāl. For similar statements in other primary sources, see Ḥarāzim, *Jawāhir al-ma'ānī*, 1: 153–160.

146. Tāl, *Rimāḥ*, 422.

147. Al-Sufyānī, *al-Ifāda*, 130.

148. Ḥarāzim, *al-Mashāhid*, 48.

149. Qur'ān, 33:6. Al-Tijānī's explanation of this verse was earlier included in chapter 3.

150. One such narration from Abu Dardā', in the canonical collection of al-Nisā'ī reads, "Whoever says there is no god but God enters Paradise even if he commits adultery and even if he steals." See G. F. Haddad, "Forty Hadiths on the Merit of Saying La Ilaha Ill-Allah," available online at Sunnah.org. Accessed February 2019.

151. Ḥadīth on the authority of Ibn Mas'ūd, *Ṣaḥīḥ Muslim*, volume 1, chapter 40, no. 165. http://www.theonlyquran.com/hadith/Sahih-Muslim/?volume=1&chapter=40.

152. Al-Sufyānī, *al-Ifāda*, 101. Al-Tijānī is here referencing the Qur'ān verse, 7:99.

153. Al-Sufyānī, *al-Ifāda*, 138.

154. Ḥarāzim, *Jawāhir al-ma'ānī*, 1: 159.

155. Ibn al-Mashrī, *al-Jāmi'*, 93.

156. Ḥarāzim, *Jawāhir al-ma'ānī*, 2: 215.

157. Al-Shinqīṭī, *al-Wāridāt*, 42.

158. Al-Sufyānī, *al-Ifāda*, 122. For this statement's origin in the Prophet's warning, see Ḥarāzim, *al-Mashāhid*, 55.

159. Ibn al-Mashrī, *al-Jāmi'*, 189.

160. Ḥarāzim, *al-Mashāhid*, 57.

161. Niasse, *Jawāhir al-rasā'il*, 3: 33.

162. Ḥarāzim, *al-Mashāhid*, 44.

163. Al-Tijānī's words related to Muḥammad al-Ghālī, who related them to 'Umar Tāl. See Tāl, *Rimāḥ*, 422.

164. Alexandre Knysh suggests this of al-Tijānī, together with Ibn Idrīs and the Sudanese Mahdī. Knysh, *Ibn 'Arabi in the Later Islamic Tradition*, 110.

Chapter Five: Abundant Blessing in an Age of Corruption

1. Ḥarāzim, *Jawāhir al-ma'ānī*, 1: 168.
2. Al-Sufyānī, *al-Ifāda*, 80.
3. Shuval, "Households in Ottoman Algeria," 41–42.
4. Shuval, *La ville d'Alger*, 121.
5. Clancy-Smith, *Rebel and Saint*, 65.
6. Benabdellah, *La Tijania*, 21.
7. Clancy-Smith, *Rebel and Saint*, 67–68.
8. Clancy-Smith, "Between Cairo and the Algerian Kabylia," 206, 208–209.
9. Clancy-Smith, *Rebel and Saint*, 65.
10. Al-Sufyānī, *al-Ifāda*, 87–88.
11. Al-Zayānī, *al-Turjumana al-kubra*, cited in Abun-Nasr, *The Tijāniyya*, 19.
12. Al-Azmī, *al-Ṭarīqa al-Tijāniyya*, 1: 102–106.
13. Al-Kattānī, *Salwat al-anfās*, 1: 374.
14. Al-Azmī, *al-Ṭarīqa al-Tijāniyya*, 107–108.
15. Muḥammad b. 'Abd al-Qādir al-Jazā'irī, *Tuḥfat al-zā'ir fī ta'rīkh al-Jazā'ir*, cited in al-Azmī, *al-Ṭarīqa al-Tijāniyya*, 115–116. For the date of the *Tuḥfa*'s composition, see Woerner-Powell, "'Abd al-Qādir al-Jazā'irī," 215.
16. Al-Nāṣirī, *al-Istiqṣā*, 3: 213–214. This text has the date for al-Tijānī's entrance in Fez incorrectly written as 1211 (1796).
17. This was in particular reference to his follower Muḥammad b. Mūsā al-Turkī and his tribe the Banū Aṣmīl of Algeria. Sukayrij, *Kashf al-ḥijāb*, 682.
18. Ḥarāzim, *Jawāhir al-ma'ānī*, 1: 66.
19. Al-Tijānī, *Mukhtārāt min rasā'il*, 142–143. This work's editor al-Kabīr al-Tijānī sources the letter to Sukayrij, *Kashf al-ḥijāb*.
20. Sukayrij, *Rafa' al-niqāb*, 1: 67; Al-Sufyānī, *al-Ifāda*, 118.
21. Dallal, *Islam without Europe*, 24.
22. Most famously, the Tijānī shaykh Muḥammad b. Mukhtār "Wad al-'Aliyya" (the same al-Shinqīṭī above, author of *al-Wāridāt*) who was on close terms with the Sultan 'Abd al-Ḥamīd II. See Abun-Nasr, *The Tijaniyya*, 58–59, 61.
23. Al-Tijānī, *Mukhtārāt min rasā'il*, 142. The Qur'ān verse cited is 99:8.
24. El-Adnani, "Réflexions," 22–23.
25. Al-Tijānī, *al-Kunnāsh al-asfar al-maktūm*, 84–98.
26. Al-Tijānī, *Mukhtārāt min rasā'il*, 69–70.
27. Ḥarāzim, *Jawāhir al-ma'ānī*, 1: 263.
28. Al-Tijānī, *Mukhtārāt min rasā'il*, 70.
29. Al-Tijānī, *Mukhtārāt min rasā'il*, 70.
30. Al-Sufyānī, *al-Ifāda*, 128.
31. Ḥarāzim, *Jawāhir al-ma'ānī*, as cited in Niasse, *Removal of Confusion*, 123.
32. Ḥarāzim, *Jawāhir al-ma'ānī*, 2: 85.
33. Ḥarāzim, *Jawāhir al-ma'ānī*, 2: 85–87. Al-Tijānī b. 'Alī Cisse's footnotes source

the ḥadith mentioned here to be found in Abū Na'īm's *Ḥilyat al-awliyā'* and in al-Bukārī's *Ṣaḥīḥ*, respectively.

34. Sukayrij, *Kashf al-ḥijāb*, 201–202.
35. Sukayrij, *Kashf al-ḥijāb*, 587–588.
36. Sukayrij, *Raf' al-niqāb*, 3: 729.
37. Sukayrij, *Kashf al-ḥijāb*, 585–586; *Raf' al-niqāb*, 3: 716.
38. Sukayrij, *Raf' al-niqāb*, 3: 720–721.
39. Sukayrij, *Kashf al-ḥijāb*, 668–671.
40. Sukayrij, *Kashf al-ḥijāb*, 234–235.
41. Sukayrij, *Kashf al-hijāb*, 565–566.
42. Sukayrij, *Kashf al-ḥijāb*, 609.
43. Sukayrij, *Raf' al-niqāb*, 4: 1053–1054.
44. Sukayrij refers to this figure by an alternate name in *Kashf al-ḥijāb* (696–696), Aḥmad b. 'Asākir al-Jazā'irī.
45. Sukayrij, *Kashf al-ḥijāb*, 707.
46. Sukayrij, *Raf' al-niqāb*, 4: 1323.
47. Sukayrij, *Kashf al-ḥijāb*, 244; Abun-Nasr, *The Tijaniyya*, 22.
48. Sukayrij, *Kashf al-ḥijāb*, 552–557; also Ould Abdellah, "Le passage au sud," 69–100.
49. Warscheild, "Sufism, Scholarly Networks, and Territorial Integration."
50. Batran, *Qadiriyya Brotherhood*, 117, 125; Ould Cheikh, "Man of Letters in Timbuktu," 231–232. For reference to the Kunta's economic influence in Tuwāt, see Batran, *Qadiriyya Brotherhood*, 116; Charles Stewart, "Southern Saharan Scholarship," 81.
51. Al-Bartilī, *Fatḥ al-shakūr*, 201. I thank Ismail Warscheid for pointing out the reference to Tuwāt here.
52. Al-Bartilī, *Fatḥ al-shakūr*, 203.
53. Ibn al-Sā'iḥ, *Bughyat al-mustafīd*, 187–188; Sukayrij, *Kashf al-ḥijāb*, 670.
54. Sukayrij, *Kashf al-ḥijāb*, 668.
55. Ḥarāzim, *Jawāhir al-ma'ānī*, 1: 63. The Hijri date given is the sixth of Rabī' al-Thānī, 1213.
56. Al-Azmī, *al-Ṭarīqa al-Tijāniyya*, 1: 127–136.
57. Al-'Irāqī, *al-Yawāqīt*, cited in al-Azmī, *al-Ṭarīqa al-Tijāniyya*, 1: 119. This was in the area of Fez known as Darb al-Ṭawīl.
58. Al-'Irāqī, *al-Jawāhir al-ghāliyya*, 17.
59. Sukayrij, *Kashf al-ḥijāb*, 624; al-Kattānī, *Salwat al-anfās*, 1: 467. Among al-Fihrī's teachers were the leading elder scholars of Fez: Muhammad b. al-Ḥasan al-Bannānī and 'Abd al-Qādir b. Shaqrūn. Al-Fihrī was appointed as an imam in the main mosque in Raṣīf (Fez).
60. Sukayrij, *Kashf l-ḥijāb*, 766.
61. Sukayrij, *Kashf al-ḥijāb*, 555–558; al-Kattānī, *Salwat al-anfās*, 3: 469–470.
62. Al-'Irāqī, *al-Yawāqīt*, cited in al-Azmī, *al-Ṭarīqa al-Tijāniyya*, 1: 119. The mosque was called Masjid al-Dīwān.
63. Al-Azmī, *al-Ṭarīqa al-Tijāniyya*, 1: 120.

64. Al-Azmī, *al-Ṭarīqa al-Tijāniyya*, 1: 121

65. For ʿAbbas b. Kīrān, see Sukayrij, *Rafʿ al-niqāb*, 4: 1048–1049; ʿAbd al-Salām b. Sūda, *Itḥāf al-muṭāliʿ*, in al-Muḥibbī, *Mawsūʿat aʿlām*, 7: 2602–2603.

66. Sukayrij, *Kashf al-ḥijāb*, 737–738. "The truth was clear and the falsehood dissipated" is no doubt an invocation of the Qurʾān verse 17:82.

67. Ibn al-Sāʾiḥ, *Bughyat al-mustafīd*, 173.

68. Aḥmad al-Sharīf, *al-Anwār al-qudsiyya*, cited in Vikor, *Sufi and Scholar*, 59–60.

69. Sukayrij, *Rafʿ al-niqāb*, 4: 1090.

70. Aḥmad al-ʿIrāqī, *Ibn Shaqrūn*, 52.

71. Sukayrij, *Kashf al-ḥijāb*, 759.

72. Abun-Nasr, *The Tijaniyya*, 20. Abun-Nasr associates this opinion with ʿAbd al-Salām al-Nāsirī's *Riḥla*, but the evidence is unconvincing.

73. Al-Sufyānī, *al-Ifāda*, 84.

74. Sukayrij, *Kashf al-ḥijāb*, 738. The Qurʾān verse cited is 33:69.

75. Sukayrij, *Kashf al-ḥijāb*, 763.

76. Sukayrij, *Kashf al-ḥijāb*, 308–309.

77. Sukayrij, *Kashf al-ḥijāb*, 351–356. The most famous of whom was ʿAbd al-Raḥmān Bannīs (d. 1799), described in Ibn Sūda's *Itḥāf al-muṭāliʿ* as "a scholar in many fields, who brought good to the religion." See *Itḥāf al-muṭāliʿ* in al-Muḥibbī, *Mawsūʿat aʿlām*, VII: 2466.

78. Sukayrij, *Kashf al-ḥijāb*, 298–301.

79. Sukayrij, *Kashf al-ḥijāb*, 263–271.

80. Sukayrij, *Kashf al-ḥijāb*, 265–266.

81. Sukayrij, *Kashf al-ḥijāb*, 298, 301.

82. Nasser, "Morocco Religious Purism," 432.

83. Aḥmad al-ʿIrāqī, *al-Shiʿr bi l-Maghrib*, 123.

84. Nasser, "Morocco Religious Purism," 400.

85. Mustafa ʿAklī, "Ḥamdūn b. al-Ḥājj al-Sulamī."

86. Al-Kattānī, *Salwat al-anfās*, 3: 8.

87. Al-Kūhan, *Fahrasat*, 48–50. Al-Kūhan records studying the following with Ḥamdūn b. al-Ḥājj: Bayḍāwī's *Tafsīr*, along with other works of exegesis; the ḥadith collections of Bukhārī and Abū Dāwūd, the *Shifāʾ* of Qāḍī Iyāḍ, the prophetic biographies of al-Qasṭalānī and al-Kalāʿī, the poetry of Ibn Rashīd al-Baghdādī and al-Buṣayrī, the work on rhetoric of al-Taftāzānī, and al-Sanūsī's works on logic and theology.

88. See the testimony of Ibn al-Ḥājj's Muḥammad al-Ṭālib in the introduction of Ibn al-Ḥājj, *al-Dīwān*, 9.

89. Ibn al-Ḥājj, *al-Dīwān*, 2: 438.

90. Mustafa ʿAklī, "Ḥamdūn b. al-Ḥājj al-Sulamī." See also Ibn Sūda, *Itḥāf al-muṭāliʿ*, in al-Muḥibbī, *Mawsūʿat aʿlām*, 7: 2499. His son Ṭālib's work in full, concerning Islamic law, theology, and Sufism, was called *Ḥāshiyat al-ʿallāmah Abū ʿAbd Allah Muḥammad al-Ṭālib ibn al-ʿallāmah Ḥamdūn ibn al-Ḥājj ʿalā Sharḥ al-ʿallāmah Muhammad ibn Ahmad al-Fāsī al-shahīr bi-Mayāra ʿalā Manẓūmat al-faqīh al-ḥujjah*

Abd al-Wāḥid ibn ʿĀshīr al-musammāt bi-al-Murshid al-Muʿīn ʿalā al-ḍarūra min ʿulūm al-dīn ʿalā madhhab al-Imām Mālik ibn Anas.

91. Aḥmad al-ʿIrāqī, "al-Muqadimma," in Ibn al-Ḥājj, *al-Dīwān*, 8.

92. Sukayrij, *Kashf al-ḥijāb*, 740–741.

93. Aḥmad al-ʿIrāqī, "al-Muqadimma," in Ibn al-Ḥajj, *Rasāʾil*, 7.

94. Ibn al-Ḥājj, *Rasāʾil*, 97.

95. Ibn al-Ḥājj, *Rasāʾil*, 99.

96. Al-Ḥajūjī, *Kitāb al-ittiḥāf*; cited by al-Rāḍī al-Kanūn in Sukayrij, *Kashf al-ḥijāb*, fn. 1, 741.

97. Sukayrij, *Kashf al-ḥijāb*, 741.

98. Al-Tijānī's letter cited in al-Kattānī, *Salwat al-anfās*, 3: 9.

99. Abun-Nasr, *The Tijaniyya*, 21–22.

100. Abun-Nasr, *The Tijaniyya*, 94.

101. Ḥarāzim, *al-Mashāhid*, 24; Abun-Nasr, *The Tijaniyya*, 21.

102. Al-ʿIrāqī, *al-Jawāhir al-ghāliyya*, 17.

103. Al-Tijānī's words to Muḥammad b. Ḥirz-Allāh, in Sukayrij, *Kashf al-ḥijāb*, 585–586. Al-Tijānī qualified this statement elsewhere, as Sukayrij proceeds to explain, by saying the Mahdi would attack the evil scholars, not those who were sincere.

104. Mansour, *Morocco in the Reign of Mawlay Sulayman*, 172.

105. Al-Zayānī, *al-Rawḍa*, cited in Mansour, *Morocco in the Reign of Mawlay Sulayman*, 172, 182; al-Nāṣirī, *al-Istiqsāʾ*, cited in Abun-Nasr, *The Tijaniyya*, 22.

106. Sukayrij, *Kashf al-ḥijāb*, 753. It seems the Prophet Muḥammad had assured al-Tijānī, "The affair of the *zāwiya* is in the hand of God." Ḥarāzim, *Mashāhid*, 44.

107. Oral tradition related by various Moroccan Tijānīs in Fez. Here by Ibrāhīm Khalīl Tijānī, interview with author, Fez, Morocco, May 2003.

108. Sukayrij, *Kashf al-ḥijāb*, 752.

109. Sukayrij, *Kashf al-ḥijāb*, 744.

110. This servant, Sharīf ʿAlī Bannāṣir al-Maṭīrī, developed a great love for al-Tijānī and eventually took the Tijāniyya. See al-Rāḍī Kanūn, in Sukayrij, *Kashf al-ḥijāb*, fn. 1, 745.

111. Sukayrij, *Kashf al-ḥijāb*, 745.

112. Sukayrij, *Kashf al-ḥijāb*, 746–747.

113. Sukayrij, *Kashf al-ḥijāb*, 749.

114. Sukayrij, *Kashf al-ḥijāb*, 752.

115. Al-Azmī, for example, seems to consider them authentic. Al-Azmī, *al-Ṭarīqa al-Tijānīyya*, 118–136.

116. This to Aḥmad b. al-Nadi in 1821. See Mansour, *Morocco in the Reign of Mawlay Sulayman*, n. 151, 183. In the context of al-Tijānī's earlier statement to a student, "The Nāṣirī litany will suffice you," the sultan's approval (*ijāza* itself can mean different things in different contexts) of the continued practice the Nāṣiriyya, if authentic, may not have been incompatible with his apparent affiliation to the Tijāniyya.

117. Mansour, *Morocco in the Reign of Mawlay Sulayman*, 173.

118. Nasser, "Morocco Religious Purism," 535.

119. Mansour, *Morocco in the Reign of Mawlay Sulayman*, 172.

120. The notion that the sultan used the Tijāniyya in his campaign against other Sufi orders appears rooted in French colonial sources. Henri Terrasse, for example, suggested that the sultan welcomed al-Tijānī because "he had thought to fight against the older Sufi orders by arousing a rival against them." See Terrasse, *Histoire du Maroc* (Casablanca: Éditions Atlantides, 1950), 312.

121. Al-Nāṣirī, *al-Istiqṣā'*, cited in Nasser, "Morocco Religious Purism," 504.

122. Nasser, "Morocco Religious Purism," 412.

123. Nasser, "Morocco Religious Purism," 535.

124. Mansour, "Sharifian Sufism," 82.

125. Al-Sufyānī, *al-Ifāda*, 66.

126. These included the Sharqāwī branch of the Nāṣiriyya-Shādhiliyya, the Wazzāniyya, and the Darqawiyya. See Mansour, *Morocco in the Reign of Mawlay Sulayman*, 162–171.

127. Ould Cheikh, "A Man of Letters in Timbuktu," 241

128. Vincent Cornell dates this notion in Morocco at least to the eleventh and twelfth centuries. See Cornell, *Realm of the Saint*, xxxvii.

129. Nasser, "Morocco Religious Purism," 403, 407.

130. Nasser, "Morocco Religious Purism," 400, 409, 420–421.

131. Mansour, *Morocco in the Reign of Mawlay Sulayman*, 135; Nasser, "Morocco Religious Purism," 410.

132. Mansour, *Morocco in the Reign of Mawlay Sulayman*, 134–135; Nasser, "Morocco Religious Purism," 421–422.

133. Nasser, "Morocco Religious Purism," 409, 425.

134. Al-Sufyānī, *al-Ifāda*, 75.

135. Sukayrij, *Raf' al-niqāb*, IV: 1054–1055.

136. Muḥammad Akansūs, *al-Jaysh al-'Aramram al-Khumāsī*, cited in Nasser, "Morocco Religious Purism," 502.

137. Nasser, "Morocco Religious Purism," 520.

138. Nasser, "Morocco Religious Purism," 521–522. The full text of this poem is included in Sukayrij, *Raf' al-niqāb*, IV: 1339–1341.

139. Mansour, *Morocco in the Reign of Mawlay Sulayman*, 140.

140. Nasser, "Morocco Religious Purism," 525–527; Mansour, *Morocco in the Reign of Mawlay Sulayman*, 142–143. The reference to God's attributes here concerns how to understand references to the divine throne, speech, hand, finger, or eye as mentioned in the Qur'an and ḥadīth.

141. Nasser, "Morocco Religious Purism," 527.

142. Sulaymān al-Ḥawwāt, cited in Nasser, "Morocco Religious Purism," 500–501; Mansour, *Morocco in the Reign of Mawlay Sulayman*, 143.

143. This apparently changed with the later influence of Ibrahim al-Riyāḥī. See Green, "Tunisian Reply," 155–177.

144. One of the earliest Tijānī works in Mauritania thus summarized, concerning the mystical audition (*samā'*) often leading to expressions of spiritual intoxication: "Among those of the mystical audition, there are those possessed of sensory movement, and those who are not. As for those of the movement of meaning (*ma'nawiya*), you must be among them, for this unlimited audition cannot be left aside. What the distinguished scholars (*akābir*) have left alone is the limited, trivial audition which is just singing." See Ibn Anbūja, *Mīzāb al-raḥma*, 298.

145. Abun-Nasr, *The Tijaniyya*, 164–185. Prominent early deniers (*munkirūn*) of the Tijāniyya included: Ali al-Mili, a Tunisian scholar living in Egypt; Aḥmad al-Bakkā'ī of Timbuktu; Muhammad al-Kanimī, the sultan of Bornu; and Idyayj al-Kamlayli and Muhammad b. al-Mayaba of Mauritania.

146. Al-Ghazālī, *Iḥyā' 'ulūm al-dīn*, cited in Ibn Anbūja, *Mīzab al-raḥmā*, 69.

147. Al-Junayd, cited by al-Ghazālī; Ibn Anbūja, *Mīzāb al-raḥma*, 71.

148. Ibn Anbūja, *Mīzāb al-raḥma*, 72. For more on the nine steps of *sulūk*, see Seesemann, *Divine Flood*, 87–93.

149. Qur'ān, 14:7.

150. Ibn al-'Arabī, *Futuhat al-Makkiyya*, cited in Chittick, "Futuhat al-Makkiyya," 90–123.

151. Ibn Anbūja, *Mīzāb al-raḥma*, 68.

152. Ḥarāzim, *Jawāhir al-ma'ānī*, 1: 136.

153. Ḥarāzim, *Jawāhir al-ma'ānī*, 1: 137.

154. Ḥarāzim, *Jawāhir al-ma'ānī*, 1: 138, citing the Qur'ān, 4:147.

155. Ibn al-'Arabī, *Futūḥāt al-Makkiyya*, cited in Chittick, "Futuhat al-Makkiyya," 90–96.

156. Ḥarāzim, *Jawāhir al-ma'ānī*, 1: 139.

157. Qur'ān, 34:13.

158. Ḥarāzim, *Jawāhir al-ma'ānī*, 1: 137–138.

159. Ḥarāzim, *Jawāhir al-ma'ānī*, 1: 130.

160. Ḥarāzim, *al-Mashāhid*, 15, 48, 52.

161. Knysh, *Islamic Mysticism*, 95–99.

162. Muḥammad b. Nāṣir to Ibn al-Sā'iḥ; in Sukayrij, *Kashf al-ḥijāb*, 247–248.

163. Ḥarāzim, *al-Mashāhid*, 44.

164. Ḥarāzim, *Jawāhir al-ma'ānī*, 1: 138. The Qur'ān verse cited is 14:7.

165. Sukayrij, *Raf' al-niqāb*, 4: 1081.

166. Sukayrij, *Kashf al-ḥijāb*, 504–505.

167. Al-Sufyānī, *al-Ifāda*, 80.

168. Al-Sufyānī, *al-Ifāda*, 123.

169. Al-Sufyānī, *al-Ifāda*, 123.

170. Al-Sufyānī, *al-Ifāda*, 138.

171. Sukayrij, *Shamā'il al-Tijāniyya*, 308–309; al-Sufyānī, *al-Ifāda*, 80, 92; Ḥarāzim, *Jawāhir al-ma'ānī*, 1: 97.

172. This servant was al-'Araī al-Ashhab. See Sukayrij, *Kashf al-ḥijāb*, 708.

173. Al-Sufyānī, *al-Ifāda*, 80.

174. Sukayrij, *Kashf al-ḥijāb*, 247.

175. Ibrāhīm Khalīl b. Muḥammad al-Kabīr al-Tijānī, interview with author, Fez, Morocco, November 2002.

176. Sukayrij, *Rafʿ al-niqāb*, 4: 1091.

177. Ḥarāzim, *Jawāhir al-maʿānī*, 1: 127.

178. Ḥarāzim, *Jawāhir al-maʿānī*, 1: 128.

179. This to ʿAbd al-Raḥmān b. ʿAlī Ḥarāzim al-Barrāda; Sukayrij, *Kashf al-ḥijāb*, 346.

180. Sukayrij, *Kashf al-ḥijāb*, 335–336.

181. Sukayrij, *Kashf al-ḥijāb*, 767–768.

182. Sukayrij, *Kashf al-ḥijāb*, 299–301.

183. Ḥarāzim, *Jawāhir al-maʿānī*, 2: 274.

184. Al-Ifrānī, *Tiryāq al-qulūb*, 1: 350.

185. Al-Sufyānī, *al-Ifāda*, 105.

186. Sukayrij, *Kashf al-ḥijāb*, 765.

187. Al-Sufyānī, *al-Ifāda*, 95.

188. Al-Barrāda, *Jawāhir al-maʿānī*, 1: 111–114.

189. Tāl, *Rimāḥ*, 276.

190. Al-Sufyānī, *al-Ifāda*, 96.

191. Al-Sufyānī, *al-Ifāda*, 93.

192. Ḥarāzim, *Jawāhir al-maʿānī*, 1: 163–167, 213.

193. Ḥarāzim, *Jawāhir al-maʿānī*, 1: 176.

194. Ḥarāzim, *Jawāhir al-maʿānī*, 1: 164.

195. Ḥarāzim, *Jawāhir al-maʿānī*, 1: 168.

196. Katz, "Shaykh Aḥmad's Dream," 158. The circulation of such accounts was not limited to the early nineteenth-century, however. Curiously, a Salafi-influenced website features the Saudi Shaykh ʿAbd al-ʿAzīz b. Bāz's rejection of a purported "Shaykh Ahmad's dream" spread over email, the text of which bears remarkable similarity to the nineteenth-century circulations analyzed by Katz. See https://islamqa.info/en/answers/31833/lies-about-a-dream-falsely-attributed-to-the-watchman-of-the-prophets-tomb. Accessed 16 July 2019.

197. Al-Tijānī b. ʿAlī Cisse, author's observation, Rabat, Morocco, March 2016.

Conclusion

1. Green, *Sufism*, 189.

2. As suggested by the earlier presentation of al-Sindī's teachings in chapter 1, I believe Voll's earlier reliance on al-Sindī to explain the emergence of Ibn ʿAbd al-Wahhāb's distinctive thought is misplaced. See Voll, "Muḥammad Ḥayyā al-Sindī and Muḥammad ibn ʿAbd al-Wahhab," 32–39.

3. Gaborieu, "Le mahdi oublié," 257–274.

4. Voll, "Sudanese Mahdi," 145–166.

5. Dallal, *Islam without Europe*, 20, 26.

6. Dallal, *Islam without Europe*, 55.

7. As cited in chapter 3, Ḥarāzim, *Jawāhir al-maʿānī*, 2: 129.

8. Zarcone, "Iconographie d'Ahmad al-Tijani," 93.

9. Abun-Nasr, *Tijaniyya*, 157–160; Seesemann, "Tarbiya in Darfur," 393–438; Ishara, "Spirit Possession," 505–515; Wright, "Afropolitan Sufism," 63–66.

10. For evidence of this, see Nelson Haqqani, "Muhammad al-Hafiz al-Tijani." Facebook post, https://www.facebook.com/NelsonNaqshbandiHaqqani/posts/shaykh-muhammad-al-hafiz-al-misri-al-tijani-q-al-sayyid-muhammad-al-hafiz-bin-ab/917512638371810/. Accessed 22 June 2016.

11. This according to the testimony of the Egyptian Mufti Nūḥ al-Qaḍāt. See recorded video of al-Qaḍāt at https://vmire.life/video/20Ig4ckDGfo. Accessed 17 November 2019.

12. Dollar, "Notes on the Tijāniyya in Early Republican Turkey," 30–34.

13. Clayer, "The Tijaniyya in Interwar Albania," 483–493.

14. Dollar, "Notes on the Tijāniyya in Early Republican Turkey," 30; Schleifer, "ʿIzz-īd-Din al-Qassam," 62–63, 69; Back, "Tijāniyya on Hajj Routes," 12–15; Wright, "Afropolitan Sufism," 67.

15. Ahmed, *West African ʿUlamāʾ*, 24–25; Wright, "Afropolitan Sufism," 67–69.

16. Van Bruinessen, "Controversies in Twentieth-Century Indonesia," 720–722; Wright, "Afropolitian Sufism," 64–65.

17. Danin, *Black Pilgrimage to Islam*, 82; Lliteras, "The Tijaniyya in Cape Town, 71–91; Wright, "Afropolitan Sufism," 64, 69–70.

18. Al-Sufyānī, *al-Ifāda*, 83.

19. For more on this, see Wright, "Afropolitan Sufism."

20. Schleifer, *Muslim 500*.

21. For more on this, see Petrone, "*Ādāb* with an Absent Master," 608–629. Petrone's emphasis on Niasse's allegedly divergent understandings of spiritual training (*tarbiya*) in comparison with earlier Tijānī sources could be reinterpreted based on alternative readings of the *Jawāhir al-maʿānī* and *Rimāḥ*, which both contain lengthy (and very similar to Niasse's understandings) discussions of the necessity of spiritual training with a living master.

22. For example, see Seesemann, "Takfīr Debate," 39–70; and Seesemann, "The Takfīr Debate, Part II," 65–110.

23. Tāl, *Rimāḥ*, 483.

24. Niasse, *Removal of Confusion*, 149.

25. Filali, "Différend Qadiriyya-Tijaniyya," 301–313.

26. El-Adnani, *La Tijaniyya*, 185–187.

27. Al-ʿIrāqī, *al-Jawāhir al-ghāliyya*, 125–135. A rendition of this story is found online at https://www.tidjaniya.com/en/sidi-ahmed-tidjani/companions-ahmed-tidjani

/sidi-muhammad-el-habib-tidjani-son-of-seyyidina-ahmedi-tidjani-may-allah-be-pleased-with-them. Accessed February 2019.

28. Berriane, *Ahmad al-Tijânî de Fès*, 204–205.

29. Berriane, *Ahmad al-Tijânî de Fès*, 51–91.

30. Al-Ḥāfiẓ, "Ayām fī zāwiya." I thank Fakhruddin Owaisi for providing me with a copy of this unpublished letter.

31. Author's observations during various visits to Fez (mostly on an annual basis), 2002–2019.

32. Ḥasan Cisse, interview with author, Fez, Morocco, June 2007.

33. Al-Sufyānī, *al-Ifāda*, 72.

34. Al-Sufyānī, *al-Ifāda*, 61.

35. Al-ʿIrāqī, *al-Jawāhir al-ghāliyya*, 45–49.

36. Sukayrij, *Kashf al-ḥijāb*, 338.

37. This claim is advanced on the shaykh's Facebook page, @sidialibelarabi.

38. Al-Tijānī b. ʿAlī Cisse, discussion with disciple, author's observation, Dakar, Senegal, January 2019.

39. This is discussed in greater length in Wright, "Afropolitan Sufism."

40. As cited in chapter 4, Tāl, *Rimāḥ*, 422.

BIBLIOGRAPHY

Primary Arabic Sources

ʿAbdallāh al-Tshādī, al-Ḥājj Makkī. 1977. *al-Yawāqīt wa l-jawāhir al-maḍīʾa fī taʿrīf bi l-quṭb al-maktūm*. Cairo: Maṭbaʿat al-Marawa.

Adnani, Ahmad Ali Al-. 2017. *Shaykh Ahmad Zarruq: The Ship of Rescue for Those Who Take Shelter in Allah, also Called al-Wazifa az-Zarruqiyyah*. South Africa: Aliya Publications.

Akansūs, Muḥammad. n.d. *Tarjama maʿlamat maʿālim Sūs*. 2 vols. Rabat: Imprimerie Yadip.

ʿAklī, Mustafa. n.d. "Ḥamdūn b. al-Ḥājj al-Sulamī," on al-Rābiṭa al-Muḥammadiyya li l-ʿulamāʾ fī l-mamlaka al-Maghribiyya, *Markaz al-dirāsāt wa l-abḥāth wa iḥyāʾ al-turāth*. Accessed July 1, 2019. http://www.almarkaz.ma/Article.aspx?C=3959.

ʿAlawī, ʿAbdallāh b. Muḥammad al-Mishrī al-. 1980. *Indhār wa ifāda ilā bāʾiʿ dīnihi bi-shahāda*. Kaolack, Senegal: publisher unknown.

ʿAlawī, Muṣṭafā b. Muḥammad al-. n.d. *Ifādat al-Tijānī bi-mā laysa fī kitāb Jawāhir al-maʿānī min ʿaqīda wa aqwāl al-shaykh Aḥmad al-Tijānī*. Bondoyuo, Indonesia: Fausan Press.

ʿAlawī al-Shinjīṭī, Aḥmad b. Muḥam. n.d. *Rawḍ al-shamāʾil ahl al-ḥaqīqa fī l-taʿrīf bi-akābir ahl al-ṭarīqa*. Rabat: Dar al-Aman.

Anṭākī, Dāwud al-. 2014. *Tadhkirat ʾūlā l-albāb wa l-jāmiʿ li l-ʿajāʾib al-ʿajāb*. Cairo: Maktabat al-Zahrān.

ʿAyyāshī, Abū Sālim ʿAbdallāh b. Muḥammad al-. 1971. *al-Riḥla al-ʿAyyāshiyya li l-baqāʿ al-Ḥijāziyya*. Beruit: Dār al-Kutub al-ʿIlmiyya.

Azmī, Aḥmad al-. 2000. *al-Ṭarīqa al-Tijāniyya fī l-maghrib wa l-sūdān al-gharbī*. 3 vols. Rabat: Ministry of Islamic Affairs.

Bakrī, Muṣṭafā Kamāl al-Dīn al-. n.d. *Naẓm al-Bakrī*, edited by Dār al-Kutub al-Qaymiyya. Cairo.

———. n.d. *Risāla fī l-ṣuḥba*, edited by Dār al-Kutub al-Qaymiyya. Cairo.

Bannīs, ʿAbd al-Karīm b. al-ʿArabī. *al-Wāḍiḥ al-minhāj fī nuẓm mā li l-Tāj*. Beiruit: Dār al-Kutub al-ʿIlmiyya.

Baqāsh, ʿAbd al-Karīm. 2018. *Risālat al-talīd wa l-ṭarīf fī kayfiyyat al-tawajjuh bi l-ism al-laṭīf*. Casablanca: Dar al-Rashad.

Ba'qīlī, al-Aḥsan b. Muḥammad. 1934. *al-Shurb al-ṣāfī min al-karam al-kāfī 'alā Jawāhir al-ma'ānī.* 2 vols. Casablanca: Darb Ghalaf.

———. 1981. *Tarayyāq li-man fasad qalbahu wa mazājah.* Casablanca: al-Maṭba'a al-'Arabiyya.

———. 2009. *Sūq al-asrār ila ḥaḍrat al-shāhid al-sattār.* Tunis: al-Sharika al-Tūnisiyya.

———. 2016. *Irā'at 'arā'is shumūs falak al-ḥaqā'iq al-'irfāniya bi-aṣābi' ḥaqq māhiyat al-tarbiya bi l-ṭarīqa al-Tijāniyya.* 2 vols. Rabat: Imprimerie Yadip.

Bartilī al-Walātī, Muḥammad al-. 1981. *Fatḥ al-shakūr fī marifat a'yān 'ulamā' al-Takrūr.* Beirut: Dar al-Gharb al-Islami.

Bartilī al-Walātī al-Shinqīṭī, Muḥammad Yaḥyā b. Muḥammad al-Mukhtār al-. 2018. *Fatḥ al-wadūd bi-sullim al-ṣu'ūd 'alā marāqī al-su'ūd.* Beirut: Dar Aldeyaa.

Bāzhīr, Munīr b. Sālim. 2015. "al-Jawāhir al-ḥissān min tarājim al-sādat Āl Shaykhān." Unpublished paper. Hadramawt, Yemen.

Birgivi, Muhammad. 2005. *The Path of Muhammad, a Book on Islamic Morals and Ethics [translation of al-Ṭarīqa al-Muḥammadiyya wa l-sayra al-Aḥmadiyya].* Translated by Tosun Bayrak. Bloomington, IN: World Wisdom.

Būnī, Aḥmad b. 'Alī. 1985. *Shams al-ma'ārif al-kubra wa laṭā'if al-'awārif.* Beirut: al-Maktaba al-Sha'biyya.

Burūjī, Abu Bakr Zayd al-Fūtī al-Jalluwī al-. 1988. *Miftāḥ al-sa'āda al-abadiyya fī maṭālib al-Aḥmadiyya.* Tunis: M. al-Manār.

Cissé, 'Alī b. al-Ḥasan. c. 1939. *Kunnāsh al-maktūm al-makhzūn.* Medina-Baye, Senegal: Shaykh Tijānī Cissé Archive.

Cissé, al-Tijānī b. 'Alī (Cheikh Tidiane). 2013. *Islam the Religion of Peace.* Translated by Zachary Wright. Singapore: Light of Eminence.

———. 2014. *Knowing Allah, Living Islam.* Translated by Zachary Wright. Singapore: Light of Eminence.

Cissé, Ḥasan b. 'Alī. 2001. *The Spirit of Good Morals by Shaykh al-Islam Ibrahim Niasse, Translation and Commentary.* Detroit, MI: African American Islamic Institute.

———. 2007. "al-Ṭarīqa al-Tijāniyya: al-khaṣā'iṣ wa al-mamayyizāt." Forum for the Followers of the Tijaniyya, Fez, Morocco, June 29, 2007.

Damanhūrī, Aḥmad. 1786. *Iḥyā' al-fu'ād bi-ma'rifat khawāṣṣ al-a'dād.* McGregor Collection MIUH92-A20, University of Michigan.

Damrāwī, Muḥammad b. al-'Arabī al-. 1996. *Yāqūtat al-maḥtāj fī l-ṣalāt 'alā ṣāḥib al-mi'rāj.* Casablanca: al-Najah al-Jadida.

Ghawth, Muḥammad b. Khaṭīr al-Dīn Khawāja al-'Aṭṭār al-. 1900. *Jawāhir al-khams.* Morocco: 'Abd-Allāh al-Yasār al-Tijānī.

Ghazālī, Abū Ḥāmid al-. 2000. *al-Munqidh min al-ḍalāl, al-Ghazālī's Path to Sufism: His Deliverance from Error.* Translated by R. J. McCarthy. Louisville, KY: Fons Vitae.

———. 2004. "The Elaboration of the Marvels of the Heart." In *Knowledge of God in Classical Sufism: Foundations of Islamic Mystical Theology*, edited by John Renard, 298–326. New York: Paulist Press.

———. 2016. *The Remembrance of Death and the Afterlife: Kitāb dhikr al-mawt wa-mā baʿdahu*. UK: Islamic Texts Society.

Ḥāfiẓ al-Miṣrī, Muḥammad al-. 1937. *Ayām fī zāwiya Saydī Aḥmad al-Tijānī*. Cairo.

———. 2007. *Aḥzāb wa awrād al-quṭb al-rabbānī wa l-ʿārif al-ṣamadānī sayyidunā wa mawlānā al-shaykh Aḥmad al-Tijānī al-sharīf al-ḥasanī*. Cairo: al-Zawiya al-Tijaniyya al-Kubra.

Ḥamdī, Ayman. 2000. *Qāmūs al-muṣṭalāḥāt al-Ṣūfī: dirāsa turātha maʿ sharḥ iṣṭalaḥāt ahl al-safāʾ min kalām khātim al-awliyāʾ*. Cairo: Dar Quba.

Ḥarāzim al-Barrāda, ʿAlī. n.d. *Kitāb al-irshādāt al-rabbāniyya bi l-futuḥāt al-ilahiyya min fayḍ al-ḥaḍra al-Aḥmadiyya al-Tijāniyya ʿalā matn al-Hamziyya fī madḥ khayr al-bariyya*. Beirut: al-Maktaba al-Shabiyya.

———. 1938. *al-Mashāhid*. Medina-Baye Kaolack, Senegal: Archive al-Tijānī Cisse.

———. 2001. *Jawāhir al-maʿānī wa bulūgh al-amānī fī fayḍ Sayyidī Abī l-ʿAbbās al-Tijānī*. Beirut: Dār al-Fikr.

———. 2011. *Jawāhir al-maʿānī wa bulūgh al-amānī fī fuyūḍ saydī Abī l-ʿAbbās Ahmad al-Tijānī*. 2 vols. Cairo: al-Sharika al-Dawliyya.

———. 2012. *Jawāhir al-maʿānī wa bulūgh al-amānī fī fayḍ al-shaykh Abī l-ʿAbbās al-Tijānī*. Rabat: Dār al-Amān.

Ḥudaykī, Muḥammad b. Aḥmad al-. 2011. *al-Riḥla al-Ḥijāziyya*. Rabat: al-Rābiṭa al-Mūhammadiyya li l-ʿUlamāʾ.

Ibn ʿAbd al-Wahhāb, Muḥammad. n.d. *Kitab Tawhid: The Book of Monotheism*. Translated by Abdul Malik Mujahid. Riyadh: Dar-us-Salam.

———. 2013. *al-Rasāʾil al-shakhṣiyya*. Riyad: Markaz al-Turāth li l-barmajiyyāt.

Ibn al-ʿArabī, Muḥyī al-Dīn. 1971. *ʿAnqāʾ mughrib fī khatm al-awliyāʾ wa shams al-Maghrib*. Beirut: Dar al-Kutub al-Ilmiyya.

———. 1980. *The Bezels of Wisdom, Fuṣūṣ al-ḥikam*. Translated by R. W. J. Austin. New York: Paulist Press.

———. 2018. *The Openings Revealed in Makkah: al-Futūḥāt al-Makkīyah, Books 1 and 2*. Translated by Shu'ayb Eric Winkel. New York: Pir Press.

Ibn al-Farid, ʿUmar. n.d. *Diwān Ibn al-Farid*. Fez: al-Bilabil al-Batha.

Ibn al-Ḥājj al-Sulamī, Ḥamdūn. 1995. *al-Dīwān al-ʿām li-Ḥamdūn bin al-Ḥājj al-Sulāmī*. Rabat: Maṭbaʿ al-maʿārif al-jadīda.

———. 2010. *Rasāʾil Abī l-Fayḍ Ḥamdūn b. al-Ḥājj al-Sulamī*. Fez: Info Print.

Ibn al-Mashrī, Muḥammad. 2013. *al-Jāmiʿ li-durar al-ʿulūm al-fāʾiḍa min biḥār al-quṭb al-maktūm*. Rabat: Dār al-Amān.

———. 2013. *Rawḍ al-muḥibb al-fānī fīmā talaqqaynāh min shaykhinā Abī l-ʿAbbās al-Tijānī*. Rabat: Dār al-Amān.

Ibn al-Sāʾiḥ, Muḥammad al-ʿArabī. n.d. *al-Jawāb al-kāfī wa l-bayān al-shāfī*. Rabat: Imprimerie Yadip.

———. 2009. *Bughyat al-mustafīd li sharḥ muniyat al-murīd*. Casablanca: Dār al-Rashād.

Ibn Anbūja, ʿUbayda. 2000. *Maydān al-faḍl wa l-afḍāl fī shamm rāʾiḥat jawharat al-kamāl*. Cairo: Madbula al-Saghir.

———. 2018. *Mīzāb al-raḥma al-rabbāniyya fī l-tarbiya bi l-ṭarīqa al-Tijāniyya*. Beirut: Dar Sadr.

Ibn Fūdī, Uthmān. 2009. *The Book of the Great Name of Allah*. Translated by Muhammad Shareef. Sudan: Sankore Institute of Islamic-African Studies.

Ifrānī, al-Ḥusayn b. Aḥmad al-. 2016. *Tiryāq al-qulūb min adwāʾ al-ghafla wa l-dhunūb*. 2 vols. Rabat: Imprimerie Yadib.

ʿIrāqī, Aḥmad. 2008. *al-Shiʿr bi l-Maghrib zamān al-ʿAlawiyīn, min 1171 ilā 1238 hijriyya*. Fez: Info Print.

———. 2017. *Aʿlām maghribiyya fī l-fikr wa l-adab: al-ʿallāma al-adīb ʿAbd al-Qādir b. Aḥmad b. Shaqrūn al-Fāsī*. Fez: Info-Print.

ʿIrāqī, Idrīs b. Muḥammad b. ʿĀbid al-. n.d. *Iqtiṭāf azhār al-ḥadīqa fīmā li-muʾallifah min al-shuyūkh fī ʿilmay al-sharīʿa wa l-ḥaqīqa*. 2 vols. Casablanca: Anas al-ʿIrāqī.

———. n.d. *al-Kanz al-ghaẓīfī fī bayān baʿḍ khawāṣṣ wa kayfiya dhikr wa kitābat al-ḥizb al-sayfī*. Casablanca: Anas al-ʿIrāqī.

———. n.d. *Maṭālaʿ anwār al-jamāl fī bayān mā kaman fī jawharat al-kamāl*. Casablanca: Anas al-ʿIrāqī.

———. 1992. *al-Fayḍ al-rabbānī fīmā tadūr ʿalayh al-tarbiya ʿind al-Shaykh al-Tijānī*. Casablanca.

———. 2009. *al-Risāla al-shāfiyya fī fiqh al-ṭarīqa al-Aḥmadiyya al-Tijāniyya*. 2 vols. Casablanca: Anas al-ʿIrāqī.

———. 2011. *Ikhtiṣār irshād al-khāṣṣ wa l-ʿām li-bayyān faḍl baʿḍ al-ayām wa l-layālī wa l-shuhūr wa l-aʿwām*. Casablanca: Anas al-ʿIrāqī.

———. 2016. *al-Jawāhir al-ghāliyya fī l-jawāb ʿan al-asʾila al-karzāziyya*. Casablanca: Anas al-ʿIraqi.

———. 2017. *Nayl al-irātha fī l-jawāb ʿan al-asʾila al-thalātha*. Casablanca: Anas al-ʿIrāqī.

———. 2018. *Tuḥfat al-nāẓir fīmā yaḥtāj ilayh al-ḥājj wa l-zīʾir*. Casablanca: Anas al-ʿIrāqī.

Jabartī, ʿAbd al-Raḥmān al-. 1994. *al-Jabartī's History of Egypt: ʿAjāʾib al-ātār fī l-tarājim wa l-akhbār*. Translated by Thomas Philipp and Moshe Perlmann. Stuttgart: Franz Verlag.

Kanūn, Muhammad al-Rāḍī. n.d. *al-Madad al-rabbānī bi-tarjamat al-ʿallāma al-quṭb saydī al-ḥājj al-Ḥusayn al-Ifrānī*. Rabat: Imprimerie Yadip.

Kattānī, Muḥammad Jaʿfar al-. 2014. *Salwat al-anfās wa muḥādathat al-akyās mi-man uqbira min al-ʿulamāʾ wa l-ṣulaḥāʾ bi-madīnat Fās*. 4 vols. Rabat: Dār al-Amān.

Kanūn, Muḥammad Fatḥā b. Muḥammad. 2007. *Ḥall al-ʿaqfāl li qurrāʾ jawharat al-kamāl*. Beirut: Dar al-Kutub al-ʻIlmiyya.

Kanūn, Muhammad al-Rāḍī. n.d. *Nisā' Tijāniyyāt*. Rabat: al-Rāḍī Kanūn.

Kattānī, 'Abd al-Kabīr b. Hāshim al-. 2014. *Rawḍ al-anfās al-'āliya fī ba'ḍ al-zawāyā al-Fāsiyya*. Rabat: Dār al-Amān.

Kūhan, 'Abd al-Qādir al-. 2012. *Fahrasat 'imdād dhawī l-ista'dād ilā ma'ālim al-rawāya wa l-isnād*. Beirut: Dār al-Kutub al-'Ilmiyya.

Kumshakhānawī, Aḥmad Ḍiyā' al-Dīn Efendi. n.d. *Majmū' aḥzāb wa awrād al-Shaykh al-Akbar Ibn 'Arabī*. Beruit: Kitāb Nāshirūn.

Kūrānī, Ibrāhīm b. Ḥasan al-. 2007. *Rasā'il fī waḥdat al-wujūd*. Cairo: Maktabat al-Thaqāfa al-Dīniya.

———. 2013. *I'māl al-fikr wa l-riwāyāt fī sharḥ ḥadīth innamā l-'amāl bi l-niyyāt*. Beirut: Dar al-Kutub al-'Ilmiyya.

Lamaṭī, Aḥmad b. al-Mubārak al-. 2007. *Pure Gold from the Words of Sayyidī 'Abd al-'Azīz al-Dabbāgh (Al-Dhahab al-Ibrīz min Kalām Sayyidī 'Abd al-'Azīz al-Dabbāgh)*. Translated by John O'Kane and Bernd Radtke, *Basic Texts of Islamic Mysticism*. Leiden: Brill.

Maigari, Muhammad. 1981. *al-Shaykh Ibrāhīm Aniyās al-Sinighālī ḥayātuhu wa arā'uhu wa ta'ālīmuhu*. Beirut: Dār al-'Arabiyya.

Miftāḥ, 'Abd al-Bāqī. 2009. *Shaykh Aḥmad al-Tijānī wa atbā'uh*. Beirut: Dar al-Kutub al-'Ilmiyya.

Muḥibbī, Muḥammad. 2008. *Mawsū'at a'lām al-Maghrib tata'lluf min tis'at nuṣūṣ turāthiyya yunshir ba'ḍihā li-awal marra wa tatarjum li-abraz al-shakhṣiyyāt al-maghribiyya ḥasab tasalsal sanawāt wafiyyātihim min bidāyat al-Islām ila nihāyat al-qarn al-rābi' 'ashar al-Hijrī*. 10 vols. Tunis: Dar al-Gharb al-Islami.

Muḥibbī, Muḥammad Amīn b. Faḍlallāh al-. 1966. *Khulāṣat al-athar fī a'yān al-qarn al-ḥādī 'ashar*. 4 vols. Beirut: Maktabat Khayyāṭ.

Mundhirī Sulayfī, 'Umar al-. 2016. *Ighāthat al-lahfān fī taskhīr al-amlāk wa l-jān*. Beirut: Dār al-Mīzān.

Muzīn, Muḥammad. 2012. *Tārīkh madīnat Fās min al-ta'sīs ilā awākhir al-qarn al-'ashirīn, al-thawābit wa l-mutaghayyirāt*. 2 vols. Fez: Sipama.

Nābulusī, 'Abd al-Ghanī al-. 1940. *Ta'ṭīr al-anām fī ta'bīr al-manām*. Cairo: Muṣṭafā al-Ḥalabī.

———. 2011. *Al-Ḥadīqa al-nadiyya sharḥ al-Ṭarīqa al-Muḥammadiyya wa l-sayra al-Aḥmadiyya* Beirut: Dār al-Kutub al-'Ilmiyya.

Nāṣirī al-Salāwī, Aḥmad b. Khālid al-. 2015. *al-Istiqṣā li-akhbār duwal al-Maghrib al-aqṣā*. 3 vols. Beirut: Dār al-Kutub al-'Ilmiya.

Naẓīfī, Muḥammad al-. n.d. *al-Ṭīb al-fā'iḥ wa l-wird al-sāniḥ fī ṣalāt al-fātiḥ*. Medina-Baye, Senegal: Cheikh Tidiane Cisse.

———. 1984. *al-Durra al-kharīda sharḥ al-yāqūta al-farīda*. 4 vols. Beirut: Dar al-Fikr.

Niasse, Ibrāhīm b. 'Abd-Allāh. n.d. *Jawāhir al-rasā'il wa yaliya ziyāda al-jawāhir al-ḥāwī ba'ḍ 'ulūm wasīla al-wasā'il*. 3 vols. Nigeria: Aḥmad Abī al-Fatḥ.

———. 1933. al-Sirr al-akbar wa-l-kabrīt al-aḥmar. In *Falke MS 0595*. Evanston, IL: Northwestern.

———. 1974. *Tanbīh al-adhkiyā' fī kawn al-shaykh al-tijānī khātim al-awliyā'*. Kano, Nigeria: al-Ḥājj Thānī Ya'qūb.

———. 1988. *Diwāwīn al-sitt*. Dakar: Muḥammad Ma'mun Niasse.

———. 1988. *Jāmi' al-jawāmi' al-dawāwīn*. Dakar: Muḥammad Ma'mun Niasse.

———. 1988. *Majmū' riḥlāt al-shaykh Ibrāhīm*. Dakar: Muhammad Ma'mūn Niasse.

———. 2001. *Kāshif al-ilbās 'an fayḍa al-khatm Abī al-'Abbās*. Cairo: al-Sharika al-dawliyya.

———. 2006. *Pearls from the Divine Flood: Selected Discourses from Shaykh Al-Islam Ibrāhīm Niasse*. Translated by Zachary Wright. Atlanta, GA: African American Islamic Institute.

———. 2006. *Sa'āda al-anām bi aqwāl shaykh al-islām*. Cairo: al-sharika al-dawliyya li-l-ṭibā'a.

———. 2010. *Fī riyāḍ al-tafsīr li-l-Qur'ān al-karīm*. 6 vols. Tunis: al-Yamāna.

———. 2010. *The Removal of Confusion Concerning the Flood of the Saintly Seal Aḥmad al-Tijānī: A Translation of the Kāshif al-ilbās*. Translated by Zachary Wright, Muhtar Holland, and Abdullahi Okene. Louisville, KY: Fons Vitae.

———. 2016. *Spirit of Good Morals: Rūḥ al-adab*. Translated by Talut Dawud. Atlanta, GA: Fayda Books.

Niasse, Muḥammad b. 'Abdallāh. 2014. *al-Juyūsh al-ṭulla' bi l-murhafāt al-quṭṭi' ilā Ibn Mayyāba akhī al-tanaṭṭu'*. Cairo: Dar al-Salam.

Qādirī, 'Abd al-Salām b. al-Ṭayyib al-. 1932. *Kitāb al-maqṣad al-Aḥmad fī al-ta'rīf bi-Sayyidinā Ibn 'Abd Allāh Aḥmad*. Fez: s.n.

Qāshānī, 'Abd al-Razzāq al-. 1991. *A Glossary of Sufi Technical Terms*. Translated by Nabil Safwat. London: Octagon Press.

Riyāḥī, Ibrāhīm al-. n.d. *Mibrad al-ṣawārim wa l-asinna fī l-radd 'alā man akhraj al-shaykh al-Tijānī 'an dā'irat ahl al-sunna*. Rabat: cheikh-skiredj.com.

Sammān, Muḥammad 'Abd al-Karīm al-. n.d. Nafaḥāt ilāḥiyya fī kayfiyat al-ṭarīqa al-Muḥammadiyya. Riyadh: King Saud University.

Sha'rānī, 'Abd al-Wahhāb al-. 2017. *al-Ṭabaqāt al-wusṭā*. Cairo: Dar al-Ihsan.

Sharqāwī, Abdallāh al-. 2007. *Sharḥ al-ḥikam al-ṣūfiyya wa hiya ḥikam al-'ārif bi-Llāh al-shaykh Maḥmūd al-Kurdī al-Khalwatī*. Cairo: Dārat al-Karaz.

Shinjīṭī, Muḥammad b. Muḥammad al-Saghīr al-. 1961. *al-Jaysh al-kafīl bi-akhdh al-thār mimman sall 'alā l-shaykh al-Tijānī sayf al-inkār*. Cairo: Mustafa Halabi.

Shinnāwī, Aḥmad. n.d. Sharḥ al-Jawāhir al-khams. Alexandria, Egypt: Biblioteca Alexandrina.

Shinqīṭī, Muḥammad b. al-Mukhtār Aflaj al-. 2013. *al-Wāridāt: al-durr al-manẓūm min fuyūḍ wārith al-quṭb al-maktūm Sīdī Aḥmad al-Tijānī*. Beirut: Books-Publisher.

Sufyānī, Muḥammad al-Ṭayyib al-. 2007. *al-Ifāda al-Aḥmadiyya li-murīd al-sa'āda al-abadiyya*. Taghzūt, Algeria: Dar al-Tijani.

Sukayrij, Aḥmad b. al-'Ayyāshī. n.d. *Bustān al-ma'ārif fīmā awradah al-wārid min al-laṭā'if 'ind baḍ al-mawāqif*. Rabat: Imprimerie Yadip.

———. n.d. *al-Ijāda ʿalā l-Ifāda*. Rabat: Muḥammad al-Rāḍī Kanūn.

———. n.d. *Lubān al-lubb wa huwa kitāb yaḍum majmūʿa min al-fawāʾid al-nafīsa jamaʿahā al-ʿārif bi-Llāh al-ʿallāma al-qāḍī al-ḥājj Aḥmad Sukayrij ayām dirāsatih bi l-Qarawiyīn*. Archive Tijānī b. ʿAlī Cissé.

———. n.d. *Nahj al-hidāya fī khatm al-wilāya*. Rabat: Imprimerie Yadip.

———. n.d. *Nūr al-sirāj fī sharḥ Iḍāʾat al-dāj*. Rabat: Imprimerie Yadip.

———. n.d. *Shamāʾil al-Tijāniyya*, edited by Muḥammad al-Rāḍī Kanūn. Rabat.

———. n.d. *Tījān al-ghawānī fī sharḥ Jawāhir al-maʿānī*. Rabat: Dar al-Aman.

———. n.d. *al-Yawāqīt al-Aḥmadiyya al-ʿirfāniyya wa l-laṭāʾif al-rabbāniyya fī l-ajwiba ʿan baʿḍ al-asʾila fī l-ṭarīqa al-Tijāniyya*. Rabat: Imprimerie Yadib.

———. 2012. *Kashf al-ḥijāb ʿamman talāqī maʿ al-Shaykh al-Tijānī min al-aṣḥāb*. Rabat: Dar al-Iman.

———. 2014. *Rafʿ al-niqāb baʿda kashf al-ḥijāb ʿamman talāqā maʿa l-shaykh al-Tijānī min al-aṣḥāb*. 4 vols. Rabat: Maṭbaʿat al-Maʿārif al-Jadīda.

———. 2016. *Jināyat al-muntasib al-ʿānī fīmā nasabah bi l-kadhib li l-Shaykh al-Tijānī*. Rabat: Imprimerie Yadib.

———. 2016. *Nayl al-amānī fī l-ṭibb al-rūḥānī wa l-juthmānī*. Rabat: Imprimerie Yadip.

———. 2019. *al-Īmān al-ṣaḥīḥ fī l-radd ʿalā muʾallif al-jawāb al-ṣarīḥ*. Rabat: Maṭbaʿ al-maʿārif al-jadīda.

Sūrā Bābā Jāw al-Sharqīyya Indūnīsiyā, Muḥammad b. Yūsuf. 2002. *al-Fayḍ al-rabbānī fī baʿḍ khaṣāʾiṣ sayyidinā Abī l-ʿAbbās Aḥmad b. Maḥammad al-Tijānī*. Indonesia: Keluarga Besar Attijaniyah.

Tāl, ʿUmar b. Saʿīd al-Fūtī. 1983. *Voilà ce qui est arrivé—Bayân mâ waqaʿa d'al-Ḥâǧǧ ʿUmar Al-FÛtî: Plaidoyer pour une guerre sainte en Afrique de l'ouest au XIXe siècle*. Translated by Mohamed Mahibou and Jean-Louis Triaud, *Fontes historiae Africanae*. Paris: Editions du Centre national de la recherche scientifique.

———. 2001. *Rimāḥ ḥizb al-raḥīm ʿala nuḥūr ḥizb al-rajīm*. Beruit: Dār al-Fikr.

Talīdī, ʿAbdallāh al-. 2012. *al-Muṭrib bi-mashāhīr awliyāʾ al-Maghrib*. Beirut: Dār al-Bashāʾir al-Islāmiyya.

Ṭaʿmī, Muḥyī al-Dīn al-. 2008. *Ṭabaqāt al-Tijāniyya*. Cairo: Maktabat al-Jundi.

Ṭaṣfāwī, Muḥammad b. ʿAbdallāh al-Shāfiʿī al-. n.d. *al-Fatḥ al-rabbānī fīmā yaḥtāj ilayh al-murīd al-Tijānī*. Casablanca: Dar al-Kitab.

Tijānī, Aḥmad b. Maḥammad al-. n.d. *Kunnāsh al-aṣfār al-maktūm*. Medina-Baye Kaolack, Senegal: Archive Cheikh Tidiane Ali Cissé.

———. n.d. *al-Kunnāsh al-maktūm al-makhzūn al-adhī lā yuṭāliʿuhu illā man lahu al-idhn*. Medina-Baye Kaolack, Senegal: Archive Cheikh Tidiane Ali Cissé.

———. n.d. *Kunnāsh al-riḥlāh al-ḥijāziyya*. Medina-Baye Kaolack, Senegal: Archive Cheikh Tidiane Ali Cissé.

———. 2009. *Mukhtārāt min rasāʾil al-shaykh saydī Aḥmad b. Maḥammad al-Tijānī*. Rabat: Maṭbaʿat al-Karāma.

Tijānī, Ṣalāḥ al-Dīn al-. 1999. *Kashf al-Ghuyūm ʿan baʿd asrār al-Quṭb al-Muktūm.* Cairo: Dar al-Taysir.

Tirmidhī, Muḥammad b. ʿAlī al-Ḥakīm. 2009. *Nawādir al-uṣūl fī maʿrifat aḥādīth al-rasūl.* 2 vols. Cairo: Maktaba al-Imām al-Bukhārī.

Yūsī, al-Ḥasan al-. n.d. *Kitāb al-fayḍ al-mutawālī fī Muthallath al-Imām al-Ghazzālī al-musammá bi-ʿIqd al-farāʾid fī mā lil-Muthallath min al-fawāʾid.* Cairo: Maktabat Aḥmad ʿAlī al-Malījī.

———. 2020. *The Discourses: Reflections on History, Sufism, Theology, and Literature (al-Muḥāḍarāt fī l-adab wa l-lugha).* Translated by Justin Stearns, *Library of Arabic Literature.* New York: New York University Press.

Zayānī, Abū l-Qāsim b. Aḥmad al-. 1967. *al-Tarjumāna al-kubrā fī akhbār al-maʿmūr barran wa baḥran.* Rabat: Wizārat al-Anbāʾ.

Secondary Sources in European Languages

Abun-Nasr, Jamil M. 1965. *The Tijaniyya, a Sufi Order in the Modern World.* Oxford: Oxford University Press.

Adnani, Jilali El. 2000. "Les origines de la Tijâniyya: Quand les premiers disciples se mettent à parler." In *La Tijâniyya: Une confrérie musulmane à la conquête de l'Afrique*, edited by Jean-Louis Triaud and David Robinson. Paris: Karthala.

———. 2000. "Reflexions sur la naissance de la Tijaniyya." In *La Tijâniyya: Une confrérie musulmane à la conquête de l'Afrique*, edited by Jean-Louis Triaud and David Robinson, 19–33. Paris: Karthala.

———. 2007. *La Tijâniyya, 1781–1881: Les origines d'une confrérie religieuse au Maghreb.* Rabat: Marsam.

———. 2018. "La confrérie Tijaniyya: Entre instrumentalisations et usages politiques." *Journal of the History of Sufism* 7.

Ahmed, Chanfi. 2015. *West African ʿulamāʾ and Salafism in Mecca and Medina, Islam in Africa.* Leiden: Brill.

Ahmed, Sumayya. 2016. "Desert Scholarship: The Zawiya Library of the Nasiriyya Sufi Order." In *Libraries at the Heart of Dialogue of Cultures and Religions: History, Present, Future*, edited by T. Courau and F. Vandermarcq, 103–109. Cambridge, UK: Cambridge Scholars Publishing.

Akkach, Samer. 2007. *ʿAbd al-Ghanī al-Nābulusī: Islam and the Enlightenment.* Oxford, UK: Oneworld.

———. 2012. *Intimate Invocations: al-Ghazzī's Biography of ʿAbd al-Ghanī al-Nābulusī (1641–1731).* Leiden: Brill.

Allen, Jonathan. 2019. "Reading Mehmed Birgivî with ʿAbd al-Ghanī al-Nābulusī: Contested Interpretations of Birgivî's al-Ṭarīqa al-Muḥammadīya in the 17th–18th Century Ottoman Empire." In *Early Modern Trends in Islamic Theology: ʿAbd *al-Ghanī al-Nābulusī and His Network of Scholarship*, edited by Lejla Demiri and Samuela Pagani, 153–170. Tübingen: Mohr Siebeck.

Amster, Ellen. 2014. *Medicine and the Saints: Science, Islam, and the Colonial Encounter in Morocco*. Austin: University of Texas Press.

Andre, Capitaine P. J. 1924. *L'islam noir*. Paris: Geuthner.

Ashtiany, Mohsen. 2008. *Dreaming across Boundaries*. Cambridge, MA: Harvard University Press.

Back, Irit. 2015. "From West Africa to Mecca and Jerusalem: The Tijāniyya on Hajj Routes." *The Journal of the Middle East and Africa* 6 (1): 1–15.

Baldick, Julian. 1993. *Imaginary Muslims: The Uwaysi Sufis of Centrall Asia*. London: I.B. Tauris.

Batran, Aziz. 2001. *The Qadiriyya Brotherhood in West Africa and the Western Sahara: The Life and Times of Shaykh al-Mukhar al-Kunti (1729–1811)*. Rabat: Institut des Etudes Africaines.

———. 2003. *Tobacco Smoking under Islamic Law, Controversy over Its Introduction*. Baltimore, MD: Amana Publications.

Benabdellah, Abdelaziz. 1995. *Le Soufisme Afro-Maghrebin aux XIXe et XXe siecles*. Rabat: Media Strategie.

———. 1999. *La Tijania: Une voie spirituelle et sociale*. Marrakesh: Al Quobba Zarqua.

Berque, Jacques. 1958. *Al-Yousi: Problems de la culture marocaine au XVII siecle*. Paris: Mouton.

———. 1978. *L'intérieur du Maghreb: XVe-XIXe siècle, bibliothèque des histoires*. Paris: Gallimard.

Berriane, Johara. 2015. *Ahmad al-Tijânî de Fès: Un sanctuaire soufi aux connexions transnationales*. Paris: L'Harmattan.

Bey, Ali. 1816. *The Travels of Ali Bey*. London: Longman.

Blum, Charlotte, and Humphrey Fisher. 1993. "Love for Three Oranges, or, the Askiya's Dilemma: The Askiya, al-Maghili and Timbuktu, c. 1500 A.D." *Journal of African History* 34 (1): 65–91.

Bobboyi, Hamid. 1995. "Shaykh Abd Allah al-Barnawi and the World of Fez Sufism: Some Preliminary Observations." In *Fès et l'Afriques, Relations Economiques, Culturelles et Spirituelles*, edited by Institut des Études Africaines Université Mohammed V, 115–124. Casablanca: Imprimerie an-Najah al-Jadida.

Bousbina, Said. 1988. "Analyse et commentaire du livre, Rimāḥ ḥizb al-raḥīm 'alā nuḥ̄ ur ḥizb al-rajīm" d'al-Hājj 'Umar al-Fūtī de Tāɪɪ." D.E.A., Université de Paris I Panthéon-Sorbonne.

———. 1989. "Les merites de la Tijaniyya d'apres 'Rimah' d'al-Hajj 'Umar." *Islam et Societes au Sud du Sahara* 3: 253–260.

Brenner, Louis. 1984. *West African Sufi: The Religious Heritage and Spiritual Search of Cerno Bokar Saalif Taal*. London: C. Hurst.

———. 1988. "Sufism in Africa in the Seventeenth and Eighteenth Centuries." *Islam et Societes au Sud du Sahara* 2: 80–93.

———. 2000. "Sufism in Africa." In *African Spirituality: Forms, Meanings, and Expressions*, edited by Jacob K. Olupona, 324–349. New York: Crossroads.

Brigaglia, Andrea. 2001. "The Fayda Tijaniyya of Ibrāhīm Nyass: Genesis and Implications of a Sufi Doctrine." *Islam et sociétés au sud du Sahara* 14/15: 41–56.

———. 2009. "Learning, Gnosis and Exegesis: Public Tafsir and Sufi Revival in the City of Kano (Northern Nigeria), 1950–1970." *Welt Des Islams* 49 (3–4): 334–366.

———. 2014. "Sufi Revival and Islamic Literacy: Tijani Writings in Twentieth-Century Nigeria." *Annual Review of Islam in Africa* 12 (1): 102–111.

Brown, Jonathan. 2015. *Misquoting Muhammad: The Challenge and Choices of Interpreting the Prophet's Legacy*. London: One World.

Brown, Kenneth. 1972. "Profile of a Nineteenth-Century Moroccan Scholar." In *Scholars, Saints and Sufis: Muslim Religious Institutions in the Middle East since 1500*, edited by N. Keddie, 127–148. Berkeley: University of California Press.

Buehler, Arthur. 1998. *Sufi Heirs of the Prophet: The Indian Naqshbandiyya and the Rise of the Mediating Sufi Shaykh*. Columbia: University of South Carolina Press.

———. 2011. *Revealed Grace: The Juristic Sufism of Ahmad Sirhindi* Louisville, KY: Fons Vitae.

Burke, Edmund, III. 1972. "The Moroccan 'Ulama,' 1869–1912." In *Scholars, Saints and Sufis: Muslim Religious Institutions in the Middle East since 1500*, edited by N. Keddie, 93–125. Berkeley: University of California Press.

Chih, Rachida. 2000. "Les debuts d'une tariqa, la Halwatiyya." In *Le Saint and Son Milieu, ou Comment lire les sources hagiographiques*, edited by Rachida Chih and Denis Gril, 137–149. Cairo: IFAO.

Chittick, William. 1989. *The Sufi Path of Knowledge: Ibn al-'Arabi's Metaphysics of Imagination*. Albany: State University of New York Press.

———. 1991. "Ibn 'Arabi and His School." In *Islamic Spirituality, Manifestations*, edited by Seyyed Hossein Nasr, 49–79. New York: Crossroads.

———. 1992. *Faith and Practice of Islam: Three Thirteenth-Century Sufi Texts*. Albany: State University of New York Press.

———. 1993. "Two Chapters from the Futuhat al-Makkiyya." In *Muhyiddin Ibn 'Arabi—A Commemorative Volume*, edited by S. Hirtensteen and M. Tiernan, 90–123. Shaftsbury, UK: Element.

———. 1994. *Imaginal Worlds: Ibn al-'Arabi and the Problem of Religious Diversity*. Albany: State University of New York Press.

———. 1998. *The Self-Disclosure of God: Principles of Ibn Al-'Arabī's Cosmology, SUNY Series in Islam*. Albany: State University of New York Press.

———. 2007. *Science of the Cosmos, Science of the Soul: The Pertinence of Islamic Cosmology in the Modern World*. Oxford, UK: Oneworld.

———. 2015. "The Quran and Sufism." In *The Study Quran: A New Translation and Commentary*, edited by Seyyed Hossein Nasr, 1737–1750. New York: HarperCollins.

Chodkiewicz, Michel. 1992. *Emir Abd el-Kader, Ecrits spirituels*. Paris: Editions du Seuil.
———. 1993. *An Ocean without Shore, Ibn 'Arabi, the Book, and the Law*. Albany: State University of New York Press.
———. 1993. *Seal of the Saints: Prophethood and Sainthood in the Doctrine of Ibn 'Arabī*. Translated by Liadain Sherrard. Cambridge, UK: Islamic Texts Society.
Chourief, Tayeb. 2011. *Spiritual Teachings of the Prophet*. Translated by Edin Lohja. Louisville, KY: Fons Vitae.
Clancy-Smith, Julia. 1990. "Between Cairo and the Algerian Kabylia: The Rahmaniyya Tariqa, 1715–1800." In *Muslim Travellers: Pilgrimage, Migration, and the Religious Imagination*, edited by Dale Eickelman and James Piscatori, 200–216. Berkeley: University of California Press.
———. 1997. *Rebel and Saint: Muslim Notables, Populist Protest, Colonial Encounters: Algeria and Tunisia, 1800–1904*. Berkeley: University of California Press.
Clayer, Nathalie. 2009. "The Tijaniyya: Reformism and Islamic Revival in Interwar Albania." *Journal of Muslim Minority Affairs* 29 (4): 483–493.
Corbin, Henry. 1958. *Imagination creatrice dans le Soufisme d'Ibn Arabi*. Paris: Flammarion.
Cornell, Vincent. 1996. *The Way of Abu Madyan: The Works of Abu Madyan Shu'ayb*. Cambridge, UK: Islamic Texts Society.
———. 1998. *Realm of the Saint: Power and Authority in Moroccan Sufism*. Austin: University of Texas Press.
———. 2004. "Practical Sufism: An Akbarian Basis for a Liberal Theology of Difference." *Journal of the Ibn Arabi Society* 36.
Currie, James. 2015. "Kadizadeli Ottoman Scholarship, Muḥammad Ibn 'Abd al-Wahhāb, and the Rise of the Saudi State." *Journal of Islamic Studies* 26 (3): 265–288.
Curry, John. 2010. *The Transformation of Muslim Mystical Thought in the Ottoman Empire: The Rise of the Halveti Order, 1350–1650*. Edinburgh: Edinburgh University Press.
Dallal, Ahmad. 1993. "The Origins and Objectives of Islamic Revivalist Thought." *Journal of the American Oriental Society* 113 (3): 341–359.
———. 2018. *Islam without Europe: Traditions of Reform in Eighteenth-Century Islamic Thought*. Chapel Hill: University of North Carolina Press.
Danin, Robert. 2002. *Black Pilgrimage to Islam*. New York: Oxford University Press.
Danner, Victor. 1991. "The Shadhiliyyah and North African Sufism." In *Islamic Spirituality, Manifestations*, edited by Seyyed Hossein Nasr, 26–48. New York: Crossroads.
De Jong, Frederick. 1987. "Mustafa Kamal al-Din al-Bakri (1688–1749): Revival and Reform of the Khalwatiyya tradition?" In *Eighteenth-Century Renewal and Reform in Islam*, edited by Nehemia Levtzion and John Voll, 116–132. Syracuse: Syracuse University Press.

Depont, Octave, and X. Coppolani. 1897. *Les conferies religieuses Musulmanes*. Algiers.
Diagne, Souleymane Bachir. 2004. "Islam in Africa: Examining the Notion of an African Identity within the Islamic World." In *A Companion to African Philosophy*, edited by Kwasi Wiredu, 374–384. Malden, MA: Blackwell.
Diallo, Samba Amadou. 2008. "Retour sur les conditions historiques et sociologiques de la fondation de la Tijaniyya." *Afrika Zamani* 15–16: 125–154.
———. 2011. "Exploring a Sufi Tradition of Islamic Teaching: Education and Cultural Values Among the Sy Tijāniyya of Tivaouane (Senegal)." *Social Compass* 58 (1): 27–41.
Dollar, Cathlene. 2012. "An "African" Tarika in Antatolia: Notes on the Tijāniyya in Early Republican Turkey." *Annual Review of Islam in Africa* 11: 30–34.
Douglas, Elmer, and Ibrahim Abu-Rabiʿ. 1993. *The Mystical Teachings of al-Shadhili, Including His Life, Prayers, Letters, and Followers: A Translation of Ibn al-Sabbagh's Durrat al-Asrar wa Tuhfat al-Abrar.* Albany: State University of New York Press.
Drague, George. 2015. *Esquisse d'histoire religieuse du Maroc*. Paris: L'Harmattan.
Drewes, G. 1992. "A Note on Muhammad al-Samman, His Writings, and 19th-century Sammaniyya Practices, Chiefly in Batavia." *Archipel* 43: 73–88.
Edgar, Iain. 2011. *The Dream in Islam, from Qur'anic Tradition to Jihadist Inspiration*. New York: Berghahn Books.
Elger, Ralf. 2004. *Muṣṭafa al-Bakrī: Zur Selbtadarstellung eines Syrischen Gelehrten, Sufis und Dichters des 18. Jahrhunderts*. Schenefeld: EB-Verlag.
———. 2014. "Al-Bakrī, Muṣṭafā Kamāl al-Dīn." In *Encyclopedia of Islam, Three*, edited by Kate Fleet, Gudrun Kramer, Denis Matringe, John Nawas, and Everett Rowson. Leiden: Brill.
Elkaisy-Friemuth, Maha. 2006. *God and Humans in Islamic Thought: Abd al-Jabbar, Ibn Sina and al-Ghazali*. London: Routledge.
Ernst, Carl W. 1997. *The Shambhala Guide to Sufism*. 1st ed. Boston, MA: Shambhala.
———. 1999. "Persecution and Circumspection in Shattari Sufism." In *Islamic Mysticism Contested: Thirteen Centuries of Controversies and Polemics*, edited by Frederick De Jong and Bernd Radtke, 416–435. Leiden: Brill.
———. 2008. "Jawāher-e Kamsa." *Encyclopedia Iranica* 14 (6).
Fahd, Toufic 1966. *La Divination Arabe* Leiden: Brill.
———. 1966. "The Dream in Medieval Islamic Society." In *The Dream and Human Societies*, edited by Gustave Von Grunebaum and Robert Caillois, 351–363. Berkeley: University of California Press.
Fāl, al-Tijānī b. al-Hādī b. Mawlūd. 2008. *Ṭawāliʿ al-suʿūd fī hayā wa manāqib ghulām al-Tijānī abī l-suʿūd*. Rabat: Dar Abi Raqraq.
Felek, Ozgen, and Alexander Knysh, eds. 2012. *Dreams and Visions in Islamic Societies* Albany: State University of New York Press.

Filali, Kamel. 1997. "Le différend Qadiriya-Tidjaniya en Algérie." *Revue d'Histoire Maghrébine* 24 (87–88): 304–314.

———. 1999. "Quelques modalités d'opposition entre marabouts mystiques et élites du pouvoir, en Algérie à l'époque ottomane." In *Islamic Mysticism Contested: Thirteen Centuries of Controversies and Polemics*, edited by Frederick De Jong and Bernd Radtke, 248–266. Leiden: Brill.

Gaboriue, Marc. 2009. "Le mahdi oublié de l'Inde britannique: Sayyid Ahmad Barelwi (1786–1831), ses disciples, ses adversaires." *Revue des Mondes Musulmans et de la Méditerrané* 91–94: 257–274.

Geertz, Clifford. 1968. *Islam Observed: Religious Development in Morocco and Indonesia*. New Haven: Yale University Press.

Gellner, Ernest. 1969. *Saints of the Atlas, The Nature of Human Society Series*. Chicago: University of Chicago Press.

Goldiher, Ignaz. 1912. "The Appearance of the Prophet in Dreams." *Journal of the Royal Asiatic Society* 44 (2): 503–506.

Goodman, Lenn. 2003. *Islamic Humanism*. Oxford: Oxford University Press.

Gouda, Yehia. 1991. *Dreams and Their Meanings in the Old Arab Tradition*. New York: Vantage Press.

Gran, Peter. 1979. "Medical Pluralism in Arab and Egyptian History." *Social Science & Medicine* 13 (4): 339–348.

———. *Islamic Roots of Capitalism: Egypt, 1760–1840*. Cairo: American University in Cairo Press.

Green, Arnold H. 1984. "A Tunisian Reply to a Wahhabi Proclamation: Texts and Contexts." In *In Quest of an Islamic Humanism*, edited by Arnold H. Green, 155–177. Cairo: American University in Cairo Press.

Green, Nile. 2003. "The Religious and Cultural Roles of Dreams and Visions in Islam." *Journal of the Royal Asiatic Society* 13 (3): 287–313.

———. 2012. *Sufism: A Global History*. Malden, MA: Blackwell.

Griffith, Sidney. 2012. "Commending Virtue and a Humane Polity in 10th Century Baghdad: The Vision of Yaḥya ibn ʿAdī." *Islamochristiana* 38: 77–100.

Guabli, Brahim El. 2018. "Refiguring Pan-Africanism through Algerian-Moroccan Competitive Festivals." *Interventions, International Journal of Postcolonial Studies* 20 (7): 1053–1071.

Gubara, Dahlia. 2014. "Al-Azhar and the Orders of Knowledge." PhD dissertation, History, Columbia University.

Gutelius, David. 2004. "Sufi Networks and the Social Contexts for Scholarship in Morocco and the Northern Sahara, 1660–1830." In *The Transmission of Learning in Islamic Africa*, edited by Scott Steven Reese, 15–38. Leiden: Brill.

Hamel, Chouki El. 2002. *La vie intellectuelle Islamique dans le sahel ouest Africain*. Paris: L'Harmattan.

Hamet, Ismael. 1923. *Histoire du Maghreb*. Paris: Editions Leroux.

Hammoudi, Abdallah. 1980. "Sainteté, pouvoir et société: Tamgrout aux XVIIe et XVIIIe siècles." *Histoire, Sciences Sociale* 35: 615–639.

Hanretta, Sean. 2009. *Islam and Social Change in French West Africa: History of an Emancipatory Community.* Cambridge: Cambridge University Press.

Hanson, John, and David Robinson. 1991. *After the Jihad: The Reign of Ahmad al-Kabir in the Western Sudan.* East Lansing: Michigan State University Press.

Haq Ansari, Abdul. 1998. "Shaykh Ahmad Sirhindi's Doctrine of 'Wahdat al-Shuhud'." *Islamic Studies* 37 (3): 281–313.

Haykal, Bernard. 2003. *Revival and Reform in Islam: The Legacy of Muhammad al-Shawkani.* Cambridge: Cambridge University Press.

Heer, Nicholas, and Kenneth Honerkamp, eds. 2003. *Three Early Sufi Texts: al-Tirmidhī's Treastise on the Heart and al-Sulamī's Stations of the Righteous and the Stumblings of Those Aspiring.* Louisville, KY: Fons Vitae.

Hiskett, Mervyn. 1980. "'The Community of Grace' and Its Opponents, the 'Rejecters': A Debate about Theology and Mysticism in Muslim West Africa with Special Reference to Its Hausa Expression." *African Language Studies* 17: 99–140.

———. 1994. *The Sword of Truth: The Life and Times of the Shehu Usman Dan Fodio.* Evanston, IL: Northwestern University Press.

Hoffman, Valerie J. 1995. *Sufism, Mystics, and Saints in Modern Egypt.* Columbia: University of South Carolina Press.

———. 1999. "Annihilation in the Messenger of God: The Development of a Sufi Practice." *International Journal of Middle East Studies* 31: 351–369.

Hofheinz, Albrecht. 1996. "Internalising Islam: Shaykh Muḥammad Majdhūb, Scriptural Islam, and Local Context in Early Nineteenth-Century Sudan." PhD dissertation, University of Bergen.

Hunwick, John. 1973. "An Introduction to the Tijani Path: Being an Annotated Translation of the Chapter Headings of the Kitab al-Rimah of al-Hajj 'Umar." *Islam et sociétés au sud du Sahara* 6: 17–32.

———. 1984. "Ṣāliḥ al-Fullānī: The Career and Teachings of a West African ʿĀlim in Medina." In *In Quest of an Islamic Humanism*, edited by A. H. Green, 139–154. Cairo: American University in Cairo Press.

———. 1996. "Sub-Saharan Africa and the Wider World of Islam: Historical and Contemporary Perspectives." *Journal of Religion in Africa* 26 (3): 230–257.

———. 2003. *Timbuktu and the Songhay Empire: al-Saʿdi's Taʾrikh al-Sudan Down to 1613, and Other Contemporary Documents.* Leiden: Brill.

Hunwick, John, and Fatima Harrak. 2000. *Miʿrāj al-Ṣuʿūd, Aḥmad Bābā's Replies on Slavery.* Rabat: Imprimerie El-Maarif Al-Jadida.

Ishihara, Minako. 2010. "Spirit Possession and Pilgrimage: The Formation and Configuration of the Tijjānī Cult in Western Oromoland." In *Proceedings of the 16th International Conference of Ethiopian Studies*, edited by Svein Ege, Harald

Aspen, Birhanu Teferra, and Shireraw Bekele, 248–259. Wiesbaden, Germany: Harrassowitz.

———. 2015. "The Role of Women in the Tijāniyya, from Three Oromo Religious Centers in Western Ethiopia." *Annales d'Éthiopie* 30: 21–43.

Kane, Ousmane. 1989. "La Confrerie 'Tijaniyya Ibrāhīmiyya' de Kano et ses liens avec la zawiya mere de Kaolack." *Islam et Societes au Sud du Sahara* 3: 27–40.

———. 1996. "La Tidjaniyya." In *Les Voies D'Allah*, edited by Alexandre Popovic and Gilles Veinstein, 475–478. Paris: Éditions Fayard.

———. 1999. "La polémique contre le soufisme et les ordres soufis en Afrique de l'Ouest post-coloniale." In *Islamic Mysticism Contested: Thirteen Centuries of Controversies and Polemics*, edited by Frederick De Jong and Bernd Radtke, 324–340. Leiden: Brill.

———. 2000. "Muḥammad Niasse (1881–1956) et sa replique contre le pamphlet anti-tijani de Ibn Mayaba." In *La Tijaniyya: Une confrerie musulmane a la conquete de l'Afrique*, edited by Jean-Louis Triaud and David Robinson, 219–235. Paris: Karthala.

———. 2016. *Beyond Timbuktu: An Intellectual History of Muslim West Africa*. Cambridge, MA: Harvard University Press.

Karamustafa, Ahmet. 2007. *Sufism: The Formative Period*. Berkeley: University of California Press.

Karrar, Ali Salih. 1992. *The Sufi Brotherhoods in the Sudan*. London: C. Hurst.

Katz, Jonathan. 1994. "Shaykh Ahmad's Dream: A 19th-Century Eschatological Vision." *Studia Islamica* 79: 157–180.

———. 1996. *Dreams, Sufism and Sainthood: The Visionary Career of Muhammad al-Zawawi*. Leiden: Brill.

Khushaim, Ali Fahmi. 1971. "Aḥmad Zarrūq: His Life and Works." PhD dissertation, School of Oriental Studies, University of Durham.

———. 1976. *Zarrūq the Ṣūfī, a Guide in the Way and a Leader to the Truth: A Biographical and Critical Study of a Mystic from North Africa*. Tripoli: Libyan General Company for Publication.

Kinberg, Leah. 1993. "Literal Dreams and Prophetic Hadits in Classical Islam: A Comparison of Two Ways of Legitimization." *Der Islam* 70 (2): 279–300.

———. 1994. *Ibn Abi al-Dunya: Morality in the Guise of Dreams, a Critical Edition of Kitab al-Manam*. Leiden: Brill.

Knysh, Alexander. 1999. *Ibn 'Arabi in the Later Islamic Tradition: The Making of a Polemical Image in Medieval Islam*. Albany: State University of New York Press.

———. 2000. *Islamic Mysticism: A Short History*. Leiden: Brill.

———. 2017. *Sufism: A New History of Islamic Mysticism*. Princeton, NJ: Princeton University Press.

Kugle, Scott. 2006. *Rebel between Spirit and Law: Ahmad Zarruq, Sainthood, and Authority in Islam*. Bloomington: Indiana University Press.

Last, Murray. 1967. *The Sokoto Caliphate*. New York: Humanities Press.

Le Gall, Dina. 2005. *Culture of Sufism: Naqshbandis in the Ottoman World, 1450–1700*. Albany: State University of New York Press.

———. 2010. "Recent Thinking on Sufis and Saints in the Lives of Muslim Societies, Past and Present." *International Journal of Middle East Studies* 42: 683.

Le-Chatalier, A. 1887. *Les Confreries Religieux Musulmans*. Paris: E. Leroux.

Leconte, Franck. 1995. *Une Exégese Mystique Du Coran Au Xviiiem Siecle Dans Le Sud-Ouest De La Mauritanie (al-Gibla): Aḍ-Ḏahab Al-Ibrīz Fī Tafsīr Kitāb Allāh Al-'azīz De Muḥammad Ibn Al-Muḫtār Al-Yadālī (1685–1753)*. n.p.

Levtzion, Nehemia. 1994. "Patterns of Islamization in Africa." In *Islam in West Africa: Religion, Society and Politics to 1800*, I: 207–216. Aldershot, Hampshire, UK: Variorum.

———. 1997. "Eighteenth-Century Sufi Brotherhoods: Structural, Organizational and Ritual Changes." In *Islam: Essays on Scripture, Thought and Society: A Gestschrift in Honour of Anthony Johns*, edited by Peter Riddel and Tony Street, 147–160. Leiden: Brill.

———. 2000. "Islam in the Bilad al-Sudan to 1800." In *The History of Islam in Africa*, edited by Nehemia Levtzion and Randall Pouwels, 63–92. Athens: Ohio University Press.

Levtzion, Nehemia, and John Voll. 1987. *Eighteenth-Century Renewal and Reform in Islam*. Syracuse, NY: Syracuse University Press.

Lings, Martin. 1973. *A Sufi Saint of the Twentieth Century, Shaikh Ahmad al-Alawi, His Spiritual Heritage and Legacy*. Britain: Unwin Brothers.

Lliteras, Susana. 2006. "The Tijāniyya Tariqa in Cape Town." *Journal of Islamic Studies* 26.

Loimeier, Roman. 2005. "Is There Something Like 'Protestant Islam'?" *Die Welt des Islams* 45 (2): 216–254.

———. 2013. *Muslim Societies in Africa: A Historical Anthropology*. Bloomington: University of Indiana Press.

Low, Michael. 2008. "Empire and the Hajj: Pilgrims, Plagues, and Pan-Islam under British Surveillance, 1865–1908." *International Journal of Middle East Studies* 40 (2): 269–290.

Ly-Tall, Madina. 1991. *Un Islam militant en Afrique de l'ouest au XIXe siècle: La Tijaniyya de Saïku Umar Futiyu contre les pourvoirs traditionnels et la puissance coloniale, racines du présent*. Paris: ACCT IFAN/Cheikh Anta Diop, Editions l'Harmattan.

Lydon, Ghislaine. 2009. *On Trans-Saharan Trails: Islamic Law, Trade Networks, and Cross-Cultural Exchange in Nineteenth-Century Western Africa*. Cambridge: Cambridge University Press.

Maïga, Aboubakr Ismaïl. 2003. *La culture et l'enseignement islamiques au Soudan occidental de 400 à 1100 h sous les empires du Ghana, du Mali et du Songhay*. Niamey: Nouvelle Impr. du Niger.

Mamdani, Mahmood. 2004. *Good Muslim, Bad Muslim: America, the Cold War, and the Roots of Terror.* New York: Pantheon Books.

Mansour, Mansour Hasan. 1994. *The Maliki School of Law: Spread and Domination in North and West Africa, 8th–14th Centuries.* San Francisco, CA: Austin & Winfield.

Mansour, Mohamed El. 1990. *Morocco in the Reign of Mawlay Sulayman.* Cambridgeshire: MENA Press.

———. 1991. "Sharifian Sufism: the Religious and Social Practice of the Wazzani Zawiya." In *Tribe and State: Essays in Honour of David Montgomery Hart*, edited by E. G. H. Joffe and C. R. Pennel, 69–83. Cambridgeshire: MENA Press.

———. 2012. "Wazzān, and Wazzāniyya." In *Encyclopedia of Islam*, 2nd ed. Leiden: Brill.

Marcus-Sells, Ariela. 2019. "Science, Sorcery, and Secrets in the Fawāʾid nūrāniyya of Sīdi Muḥammad al-Kuntī." *History of Religions* 58 (4): 432–464.

Marsot, Afaf Lutfi al-Sayyid. 1973. "The Political and Economic Functions of the ʿUlamāʾ in the 18th Century." *Journal of the Economic and Social History of the Orient* 16 (2-3): 130–154.

———. 1977. "The Wealth of the Ulama in late Eighteenth Century Cairo." In *Studies in Eighteenth-Century Islamic History*, edited by Thomas Naff and Roger Owen, 205–216. Carbondale: Southern Illinois University Press.

Martin, B. G. 1976. *Muslim Brotherhood in Nineteenth-Century Africa.* Cambridge: Cambridge University Press.

Mayeur-Jaouen, Catherine. 2017. "The Small World of Aḥmad al-Ṣāwī (1761–1825), an Egyptian Khalwatī Shaykh." In *The Piety of Learning: Islamic Studies in Honor of Stefan Reichmuth*, edited by Michael Kemper and Ralf Elger, 103–144. Leiden: Brill.

Mbaye, Ravane. 2004. *Pensée et action d'El Hadji Malick Sy: Vie et oeuvre.* 3 vols. Beruit: Al Bouraq.

McCarthy, Richard. 1953. *The Theology of al-Ashʿari.* Beirut: Imprimerie Catholique.

———. 2000. *Al-Ghazali's Path to Sufism.* Louisville, KY: Fons Vitae.

McGregor, Richard. 2004. *Sanctity and Mysticism in Medieval Egypt: The Wafāʾ Sufi Order and the Legacy of Ibn ʿArabī.* Albany: State University of New York Press.

Meier, Fritz. 1999. *Essays on Islamic Piety and Mysticism.* Translated by John O'Kane. Leiden: Brill.

Melliti, Imed. 1994. "La ruse maraboutique: Le statut du Hayal et du Itlaq dans L'hagiographie des Tijaniyya." *Annuaire d l'Afrique du Nord* 33: 241–252.

Michon, Jean-Louis. 1999. *The Autobiography of a Moroccan Sufi: Ahmad ibn ʿAjiba (1749–1809).* Translated by David Streight. Louisville, KY: Fons Vitae.

Mohammed, Ahmed Rufai. 1993. "The Influence of the Niass Tijaniyya in the Niger-Benue Confluence Area of Niger." In *Muslim Identity and Social Change in Sub-Saharan Africa*, edited by Louis Brenner, 116–134. Bloomington: Indiana University Press.

Moin, Azfar. 2012. *The Millennial Sovereign: Sacred Kingship and Sainthood in Islam*. New York: Columbia University Press.

Moos, Ebrahiem. 2011. "The Literary Works of Shaykh Sīdī Al-Mukhtār Al-Kuntī: A Study of the Concept and Role of 'Miracles' in al-Minna fī i'tiqād ahl al-sunna." Master's thesis, Historical Studies, University of Cape Town.

Murata, Sachiko, and William Chittick. 1994. *The Vision of Islam*. St. Paul, MN: Paragon House.

Muritānī, Muḥammad b. 'Abd-Allāh. 1989. *Radd bi al-ḥadīth wa al-Qu'rān 'ala mā fī kitāb Maygharī al-Nayjīrī min al-zūr wa al-buhtān*. Kano, Nigeria: Zawiya Ahl al-Fayda al-Tijaniyya.

Murphy, Jane H. 2010. "Ahmad al-Damanhūrī and the Utility of Expertise in Early Modern Ottoman Egypt." *Osiris* 25: 85–103.

Muthalib, Abdul. 2007. "The Mystical Teachings of Muḥammad 'Abd al-Karīm al-Sammān: An 18th Century Ṣūfī." PhD dissertation, Institute of Islamic Studies, McGill University.

Nafi, Basheer M. 2002. "Taṣawwuf and Reform in Pre-Modern Islamic Culture: In Search of Ibrāhīm al-Kūrānī." *Die Welt des Islams* 42 (3): 307–355.

———. 2006. "A Teacher of Ibn 'Abd al-Wahhāb: Muḥammad Ḥayāt al-Sindī and the Revival of Aṣḥāb al-Ḥadīth's Methodology." *Islamic Law and Society* 13 (2): 208–241.

Nasser, Rachied El-. 1983. "Morocco, From Kharijism to Wahhabism: The Quest for Religious Purism." PhD dissertation, History, University of Michigan.

Neveu, Francois Edouard de. 1846. *Ordres Religieux chez les Musulmans de l'Algerie*. Paris: A. Guyot.

Nobili, Mauro, and Mohamed Mathee. 2015. "Towards a New Study of the So-Called Tārīkh al-fattāsh." *History in Africa: A Journal of Method* 42: 37–73.

Norris, H. T. 1964. "The Wind of Change in the Western Sahara." *Geographical Journal* 130 (1): 1–14.

———. 1967. "Ṣanhājah Scholars of Timbuctoo." *Bulletin of the School of Oriental and African Studies, University of London* 30 (3): 634–640.

———. 1969. "Znāga Islam during the Seventeenth and Eighteenth Centuries." *Bulletin of the School of Oriental and African Studies, University of London* 32 (3): 496–526.

———. 1990. *Sufi Mystics of the Niger Desert: Sidi Mahmud and the Hermits of Air*. Oxford: Clarendon Press.

O'Fahey, R. S. 1990. *Enigmatic Saint*. Evanston, IL: Northwestern University Press.

O'Fahey, R. S., and Bernd Radtke. 1993. "Neo-Sufism Reconsidered." *Islam* 70: 52–87.

Ould Abdellah, A. Dedoud. 2000. "Le passage au sud: Muḥammad al-Hafiz et son heritage." In *La Tijâniyya: Une confrérie musulmane à la conquête de l'Afrique*, edited by Jean-Louis Triaud and David Robinson, 69–100. Paris: Karthala.

Ould Bah, Mohamed El Mokhtar. 1981. *La littérature juridique et l'évolution du malikisme en Mauritanie*. Vol. 19, *Publications de l'Université de Tunis, Faculté des lettres et sciences humaines de Tunis*. Tunis: Université de Tunis.

Ould Cheikh, Abdel Wedoud. 2008. "A Man of Letters in Timbuktu: al-Shaykh Sidi Muhammad al-Kunti." In *The Meanings of Timbuktu*, edited by Shamil Jeppie and Souleymane Diagne, 231–248. Cape Town: HSRC Press.

Owusu-Ansah, David. 1991. *Islamic Talismanic Tradition in Nineteenth-Century Asante*. Lewiston, NY: Edwin Mellen Press.

———. 2000. "Prayers, Amulets, and Healing." In *The History of Islam in Africa*, edited by Nehemia Levtzion and Randall Lee Pouwels, 477–488. Athens: Ohio University Press.

Paden, John. 1973. *Religion and Political Culture in Kano*. Berkeley: University of California Press.

Padwick, Constance. 1961. *Muslim Devotions: A Study of Prayer Manuals in Common Use*. London: SPCK.

Palmer, Aiyub. 2015. "The Social and Theoretical Dimensions of Sainthood in Early Islam: al-Tirmidhī's Gnoseology and Foundations of Ṣūfī Social Praxis." PhD dissertation, Near Eastern Studies, University of Michigan.

Peskes, Esther. 1999. "The Wahhābiyya and Sufism in the Eighteenth Century." In *Islamic Mysticism Contested: Thirteen Centuries of Controversies and Polemics*, edited by Frederick De Jong and Bernd Radtke, 145–161. Leiden: Brill.

Petrone, Michele. 2016. "Ādāb with an Absent Master: Sufis and Good Manners in the Tijaniyya." In *Ethics and Spirituality in Islam: Sufi adab*, edited by Francesco Chiabotti, Eve Feuillebois-Pierunek, Catherine Mayeur-Jaouen, and Luca Patrizi, 608–629. Leiden: Brill.

Pettigrew, Erin. 2014. "Muslim Healing, Magic, and Amulets in the 20th-Century History of the Southern Sahara." PhD dissertation, History, Stanford University.

Piga, Adriana. 2004. "Un apercu sur les confreries Soufies au Senegal contemporain: Le role socio-culturel de la Tidjaniyya Niassene." In *Confreries Soufies oufies d'Afrique: Nouveaux roles, nouveaux enjeux*, edited by Institute des Etudes Africaines, 152–176. Rabat: Institut des Etudes Africaines.

Qureshi, Jawad. 2019. "Some of ʿAbd al-Ghanī al-Nābulusī's Kalām Writings." In *Early Modern Trends in Islamic Theology*, edited by Lejla Demiri and Samuela Pagani, 59–72. Tübingen: Mohr Siebeck.

Radtke, Bernd. 1994. "Ijtihad and Neo-Sufism." *Asiatische Studien* 19 (3): 909–921.

———. 1996. "Sufism in the 18th Century: An Attempt at a Provisional Appraisal." *Die Welt des Islams* 36 (3): 326–364.

———. 1997. "Ibriziana: Themes and Sources of a Seminal Sufi Work." *Sudanic Africa* 7: 113–158.

———. 2000. "Fritz Meier's Unpublished Papers and the Tijāniyya." *Sudanic Africa* 11: 125–130.

Radtke, Bernd, and John O'Kane. 1996. *The Concept of Sainthood in Early Islamic Mysticism*. London: RoutledgeCurzon.

Radtke, Bernd, John O'Kane, Knut Vikor, and Rex O'Fahey. 2000. *The Exoteric Ahmad Ibn Idris; A Sufi's Critique of the Madhahib and the Wahhabis: Four Arabic Texts with Translation and Commentary*. Leiden: Brill.

Razi, Najm al-din. 1982. *The Path of God's Bondsmen from Origin to Return*. Translated by Hamid Algar. New York: Caravan Books.

Reichmuth, Stefen. 2000. "Islamic Education in Sub-Saharan Africa." In *The History of Islam in Africa*, edited by Nehemia Levtzion and Randall Pouwels, 419–440. Athens: Ohio University Press.

———. 2002. "Arabic Literature and Islamic Scholarship in the 17th/18th Century: Topics and Biographies: Introduction." *Die Welt des Islams* 42 (3): 281–288.

———. 2004. "Murtaḍā al-Zabīdī and the Africans: Islamic Discourse and Scholarly Networks in the Late Eighteenth Century." In *The Transmission of Learning in Islamic Africa*, edited by Scott Reese, 121–153. Leiden: Brill.

———. 2009. *The World of Murtaḍā al-Zabīdī*. Cambridge, UK: Gibb Memorial Trust.

———. 2012. "Humanism in Islam between Mysticism and Literature." In *Humanism in Muslim Culture*, edited by Stefan Reichmuth, Jörn Rüsen, and Aladdin Sarhan, 115–126. Taipai: National Taiwan University Press.

Reichmuth, Stefan, Jörn Rüsen, and Aladdin Sarhan. 2012. "Humanism and Muslim Culture: Historical Heritage and Contemporary Challenges." In *Humanism in Muslim Culture*, edited by Stefan Reichmuth, Jörn Rüsen, and Aladdin Sarhan, 11–24. Taipai: National Taiwan University Press.

Rémi, Dewière. 2018. "La Légitimité des Sultans Face à l'Essor de l'Islam confrérique au Sahel Central (XVIe–XIXe siècles)." *Journal of the History of Sufism* 7: 15–30.

Renard, John. 2004. *Knowledge of God in Classical Sufism: Foundations of Islamic Mystical Theology*. Mahwah, NJ: Paulist Press.

Robinson, David. 1985. *The Holy War of Umar Tal: The Western Sudan in the Mid-Nineteenth Century*. Oxford: Clarendon Press.

———. 2000. *Paths of Accommodation: Muslim Societies and French Colonial Authorities in Senegal and Mauritania, 1880–1920, Western African Studies*. Athens: Ohio University Press.

Robinson, David, and Jean-Louis Triaud. 1997. *Le temps des marabouts: Itinéraires et stratégies Islamiques en Afrique Occidentale Française V.1880–1960, Hommes et sociétés*. Paris: Karthala.

Rouayheb, Khaled El-. 2006. "Opening the Gate of Verification: The Forgotten Arab-Islamic Florescence of the 17th Century." *International Journal of Middle East Studies* 38 (2): 263–281.

———. 2013. "al-Damanhūrī, Aḥmad." In *Encyclopedia of Islam*, 3rd ed. Leiden: Brill.

———. 2015. *Islamic Intellectual History in the Seventeenth Century: Scholarly Currents in the Ottoman Empire and the Maghreb*. New York: Cambridge University Press.
Ryan, Patrick. 2000. "The Mystical Theology of Tijani Sufism and Its Social Significance in West Africa." *Journal of Religion in Africa* 30 (2): 208–224.
Salih, Abdulgalil Abd Allah. 2015. *The Sammāniyya: Doctrine, History and Future*. Khartoum: Abdulgalil Salih.
Sall, Ibrahim. 1999. *Le guide du parfait Tijani aspirant a la perfection*. Beirut: al-Bouraq.
Samb, Amadou Makhtar. 1994. *Introduction a la Tariqah Tidjaniyya ou Voie Spirituelle deCheikh Ahmad Tidjani*. Dakar: Imprimerie Saint-Paul.
Samb, Amar. 1972. *Essai sur la contribution du Sénégal a la littérature d'expression Arabe*. Vol. 87, *Mémoires de l'Institut fondamental d'Afrique noire*. Dakar: IFAN.
Schimmel, Annemarie. 1975. *Mystical Dimensions of Islam*. Chapel Hill: University of North Carolina Press.
———. *Pain and Grace: A Study of Two Mystical Writers of Eighteenth-Century Muslim India*. Leiden: Brill.
———. 1985. *And Muḥammad Is His Messenger: The Veneration of the Prophet in Islamic Piety*. Chapel Hill: University of North Carolina Press.
———. 1993. *The Mystery of Numbers*. New York: Oxford University Press.
Schleifer, Abdallah. 1979. "The Life and Thought of 'Izz-Id-Din al-Qassam." *Islamic Quarterly* 23 (2): 61–81.
———, ed. 2013. *The Muslim 500: The 500 Most Influential Muslims*. Amman, Jordan: The Royal Islamic Strategic Studies Center.
Schmidt, Elizabeth. 2005. *Mobilizing the Masses: Gender, Ethnicity, and Class in the Nationalist Movement in Guinea, 1939–1958, Social History of Africa*. Portsmouth, NH: Heinemann.
Sedgwick, Mark J. 2005. *Saints and Sons: The Making and Remaking of the Rashīdi Aḥmadi Sufi Order, 1799–2000*. Vol. 97, *Social, Economic, and Political Studies of the Middle East and Asia*. Leiden: Brill.
———. 2005. *Sufism, the Essentials*. Cairo: American University in Cairo Press.
Seesemann, Rüdiger. 2000. "The History of the Tijaniyya and the Issue of Tarbiya in Darfur (Sudan)." In *La Tijâniyya: Une confrérie musulmane à la conquête de l'Afrique*, edited by Jean-Louis Triaud and David Robinson, 393–437. Paris: Karthala.
———. 2004. "Nach Der 'flut': Ibrāhīm Niasse (1900–1975), Sufik Und Gesellschaft in Westafrika." Universität Bayreuth.
———. 2004. "The Shurafa' and the 'Blacksmith': The Role of the Idaw 'Alī of Mauritania in the Career of the Senegalese Shaykh Ibrāhīm Niasse (1900–1975)." In *The Transmission of Learning in Islamic Africa*, edited by Scott Steven Reese, 72–98. Leiden: Brill.

———. 2006. "African Islam or Islam in Africa? Evidence from Kenya." In *The Global Worlds of the Swahili: Interfaces of Islam, Identity and Space in 19th-and 20th-Century East Africa*, edited by Roman Loimeier and Rüdiger Seesemann, 229–250. Berlin: Lit.

———. 2009. "Three Ibrāhīms: Literary Production and the Remaking of the Tijaniyya Sufi Order in Twentieth-Century Sudanic Africa." *Die Welt des Islams* 49: 299–333.

———. 2011. *The Divine Flood: Ibrāhīm Niasse and the Roots of a Twentieth-Century Sufi Revival*. Oxford: Oxford University Press.

———. 2015. "A New Dawn for Sufism? Spiritual Training in the Mirror of Nineteenth-Century Tijānī Literature." In *Sufism, Literary Production, and Printing in the Nineteenth Century*, edited by Rachida Chih, Catherine Mayeur-Jaouen, and Rüdiger Seesemann. Würzburg: Ergon Verlag.

Seesemann, Rüdiger, and Benjamin Soares. 2009. "'Being as Good Muslims as Frenchmen': On Islam and Colonial Modernity in West Africa." *Journal of Religion in Africa* 39: 91–120.

Sells, Michael. 1994. *Mystical Languages of Unsaying*. Chicago: University of Chicago Press.

Shahin, Emad. 1997. *Political Ascent: Contemporary Islamic Movements in North Africa*. Boulder, CO: Westview Press.

Shareef, Muhammad. 2013. *The Increase of the Spiritual Aspirant in Gratitude of the Benefactor for the Divine Overflowing Given to Those He Favors*. Sennar, Sudan: Sankore Institute.

Shuval, Taj. 1998. *La ville d'Alger ver la fin du XVIIIe siècle: Population et cadre urbain*. Paris: CNRS Éditions.

———. 2000. "Households in Ottoman Algeria." *Turkish Studies Association Bulletin* 24 (1): 41–64.

Sindī, Muḥammad Ḥayāt al-. n.d. *Fatḥ al-ghafūr fī waḍ' al-aydī 'alā l-ṣudūr*. www.al-mostafa.com.

———. 2010. *Sharḥ al-Ḥikam al-'Aṭā'iyya*. Beirut: Dār Maktabat al-Ma'ārif.

Sirriyeh, Elizabeth. 1999. *Sufis and Anti-Sufis: The Defense, Rethinking and Rejection of Sufism in the Modern World, Curzon Sufi Series*. Richmond, Surrey: Curzon.

———. 2005. *Sufi Visionary of Ottoman Damascus*. London: Routledge.

———. 2015. *Dreams and Visions in the World of Islam: A History of Muslim Dreaming and Foreknowing*. London: I.B. Tauris.

Skali, Faouzi. 2014. *Saints et Sanctuaires de Fès*. Rabat: Marsam.

Soares, Benjamin F. 2005. *Islam and the Prayer Economy: History and Authority in a Malian Town*. Ann Arbor: University of Michigan Press.

Stewart, Charles. 1976. "Southern Saharan Scholarship and the Bilad al-Sudan." *Journal of African History* 17 (1): 73–93.

Taji-Farouki, Suha. 2006. *Ibn 'Arabi: Prayer for Spiritual Elevantion and Protection.* Oxford, UK: Anqa Publishing.

Terem, Etty. 2014. *Old Texts, New Practices: Islamic Reform in Modern Morocco.* Stanford, CA: Stanford University Press.

———. 2017. "Redefining Islamic Orthodoxy: Fatwās and Anxieties of Moroccan Modernity." Conference on Texts, Knowledge, and Practice: The Meaning of Scholarship in Muslim Africa, Harvard University.

Terrasse, Henri. 1950. *Histoire du Maroc: Des origines à l'établissement du Protectorat français.* Casablanca: Éditions Atlantides.

Thurston, Alexander. 2018. "Polyvalent, Transnational Religious Authority: The Tijaniyya Sufi Order and Al-Azhar University." *Journal of the American Academy of Religion* 86 (3): 789–820.

Todd, Richard. 2014. *The Sufi Doctrine of Man: Ṣadr al-Dīn al-Qūnawī's Metaphysical Anthropology* Leiden: Brill.

Triaud, Jean-Louis. 1989. "Khalwa and the Career of Sainthood. An Interpretive Essay." In *Charisma and Brotherhood in African Islam*, edited by Donal B. Cruise O'Brien and Christian Coulon, 53–66. Oxford: Clarendon Press.

———. 2000. "La Tijâniyya, une confrérie musulmane pas comes les autres?" In *La Tijâniyya: Une confrérie musulmane à la conquête de l'Afrique*, edited by Jean-Louis Triaud and David Robinson, 9–17. Paris: Karthala.

Trimingham, J. Spencer. 1998. *The Sufi Orders in Islam.* New York: Oxford University Press.

van Bruinessen, Martin. 1999. "Controversies and Polemics Involving the Sufi Orders in Twentieth-Century Indonesia." In *Islamic Mysticism Contested: Thirteen Centuries of Controversies and Polemics*, edited by Frederick De Jong and Bernd Radtke, 705–728. Leiden: Brill.

van Dalen, Dorrit. 2016. *Doubt, Scholarship and Society in 17th-Century Central Sudanic Africa.* Leiden: Brill.

Vaughan, Rupert. 1992. "Al-asrar fi nahj al-Islam: Muslims and Secret Sciences in West Africa circa 1100 to 1880." PhD dissertation, Princeton University.

Vikor, Knut. 1995. "The Development of Ijtihad and Islamic Reform, 1750–1850." Third Nordic conference on Middle Eastern Studies, Joensuu, Finland.

———. 1995. *Sufi and Scholar on the Desert Edge: Muḥammad b. 'Alī al-Sanūsī and His Brotherhood.* Evanston, IL: Northwestern University Press.

Voll, John. 1975. "Muḥammad Ḥayyā al-Sindī and Muḥammad ibn 'Abd al-Wahhab: An Analysis of an Intellectual Group in Eighteenth-Century Madīna." *Bulletin of the School of Oriental and African Studies, University of London* 38 (1): 32–39.

———. 1979. "The Sudanese Mahdi: Frontier Fundamentalist." *International Journal of Middle East Studies* 10 (2): 145–166.

———. 1980. "Hadith Scholars and Tariqahs." *Journal of Asian and African Studies* 15 (3–4): 264–273.

———. 1994. *Islam: Continuity and Change in the Modern World*. Syracuse, NY: Syracuse University Press.

———. 2002. "Abdallah ibn Salim al-Basri and 18th Century Hadith Scholarship." *Die Welt des Islams* 42 (3): 356–372.

———. 2016. "Scholars in Networks: 'Abd al-Ghanī al-Nābulusī and His Travels." In *The Heritage of Arabo-Islamic Learning*, edited by Maurice Pomerantz and Aram Shahin, 333–351. Leiden: Brill.

Ware, Rudolph, III. 2011. "Slavery in Islamic Africa." In *The Cambridge World History of Slavery, vol. 3, AD 1420—AD 1804*, edited by David Eltis and Stanley Engerman, 47–80. Cambridge: Cambridge University Press.

———. 2014. *The Walking Qur'an: Islamic Education, Embodied Knowledge, and History in West Africa*. Chapel Hill: University of North Carolina Press.

Ware, Rudolph, III, Zachary Wright, and Amir Syed. 2018. *Jihad of the Pen: The Sufi Literature of West Africa*. Cairo: American University in Cairo Press.

Warscheild, Ismail. 2018. "Sufism, Scholarly Networks, and Territorial Integration in the Early Modern Sahara (Algeria, Mauritania, Mali), 1600–1800." West Africa and the Maghreb: Reassessing Intellectual Connections in the 21st century, Cambridge, MA.

Watt, Montgomery. 1953. *Faith and Practice of al-Ghazali*. London: Unwin Brothers.

Waugh, Earle. 2008. *Visionaries of Silence*. Oxford: Oxford University Press.

Wehr, Hans. 1980. *A Dictionary of Modern Written Arabic*. Beirut: Librarie du Liban.

Weigert, Gideon. 1999. "Shaykh Mustapha Kamal al din al Bakri—A Sufi Reformer in Eighteenth-Century Egypt." *Bulletin of the Israeli Academic Center in Cairo* 24: 1–7.

Willis, John Ralph. 1979. "The Writings of al-Hajj 'Umar al-Futi and Shaykh Mukhtar b. Wadiat Allah: Literary Themes, Sources and Influences." In *Studies in West African Islamic History.* Vol. 1, *The Cultivators of Islam*, edited by John Ralph Willis, 177–210. London: Frank Cass.

———. 1989. *In the Path of Allah, the Passion of Al-Hajj 'Umar: An Essay into the Nature of Charisma in Islam*. London: Frank Cass.

Winter, Michael. 1982. *Society and Religion in Early Ottoman Egypt: Studies in the Writings of 'Abd Al-Wahhab Al-Sharani*. Vol. 4, *Studies in Islamic Culture and History.* New Brunswick, NJ: Transaction Books.

Wise, Christopher. 2011. *Ta'rīkh al-fattāsh: The Timbuktu Chronicles*. Trenton, NJ: Africa World Press.

Woerner-Powell, Tom. 2011. "'Abd al-Qādir al-Jazā'irī, Migration, and the Rule of Law: A Reply to Certain Persons of Distinction." *Studia Islamica* 106 (2): 214–240.

Wright, Zachary. 2005. *On the Path of the Prophet: Shaykh Ahmad Tijani (1737–1815) and the Tariqa Muḥammadiyya*. Atlanta, GA: African-American Islamic Institute.

———. 2010. "The Kāshif al-ilbās of Shaykh Ibrāhīm Niasse: Analysis of the Text." *Islamic Africa* 1 (1): 109–123.

———. 2012. "The History of Islamic Identity in West Africa." *Orient: German Journal for Politics, Economics and Culture of the Middle East* 53 (1): 18–23.

———. 2013. "Sufism in West Africa." *Sufi Journal of Mystical Philosophy and Practice* 84: 30–35.

———. 2015. *Living Knowledge in West African Islam*. Leiden: Brill.

———. 2015. *On the Path of the Prophet: Shaykh Ahmad Tijani (1737–1815) and the Tariqa Muḥammadiyya*, 2nd ed. Atlanta, GA: Fayda Books.

———. 2018. "Secrets on the Muhammadan Way: Transmission of the Esoteric Sciences in 18th Century Scholarly Networks." *Islamic Africa* 9: 77–105.

———. 2018. *Sur la voie du Prophète: Le Cheikh Ahmad Tijani et la Tariqa Muhammadiyya*. Translated by Benoit Schirmer. Wattrelos, France: Éditions Tasnim.

———. 2019. "Afropolitan Sufism: The Contemporary Tijāniyya in Global Contexts." In *Global Sufism: Boundaries, Structures, and Politics*, edited by Francesco Piraino and Mark Sedgwick, 55–74. London: Hurst.

———. 2020. "The Islamic Intellectual Traditions of Sudanic Africa, with Analysis of a 15th Century Timbuktu Manuscript." In *Handbook of Islam in Africa*, edited by Fallou Ngom, Mustapha Kurfi, and Toyin Falola. London: Palgrave.

Würsch, Renate. 2012. "Humanism and Mysticism—Inspirations from Islam." In *Humanism in Muslim Culture*, edited by Stefan Reichmuth, Jörn Rüsen, and Aladdin Sarhan, 89–100. Taipai: National Taiwan University Press.

Yapp, Malcolm. 1987. *The Making of the Modern Near East, 1792–1923*. London: Longman.

Zarcone, Thierry. 2018. "Au sujet d'une iconographie d'Ahmad al-Tijani: Image de dévotion et hagiographie visuelle." *Journal of the History of Sufism* 7: 93–112.

Zargar, Cyrus. 2011. *Sufi Aesthetics: Beauty, Love, and the Human Form in the Writings of Ibn 'Arabi and 'Iraqi*. Columbia: University of South Carolina Press.

INDEX

ʿAbbās b. Kīrān, 54, 187, 196
ʿAbbās b. Muḥammad b. Kīrān al- (d. 1855), 186
ʿAbd al-Fattāḥ, Saʿīd, 227n96
ʿAbd al-Mālik (Mawlay) (d. 1793), 183
ʿAbd al-Qādir b. Muṣṭafa ("Dan Tafa"), 149
ʿAbd al-Qādir b. Shaqrūn (d. 1804), 185, 187
ʿAbd al-Wahhāb b. Aḥmar, 130
abdāl ("substitutes"), 150. *See also* Saints, Seal of (*khātim al-awliyāʾ*)
ʿAbdallāh (Mawlay), 183
ʿAbdallāh al-Sharīf (d. 1678), 165
Abū (Abī) Samghūn, Algeria, 177, 178
Abū Ḥanīfa, 57
Abun-Nasr, Jamil, 9, 10–11, 187
actualization (*taḥqīq*) of humanity. *See taḥqīq al-insāniyya* (actualization of humanity)
actualization (*taḥqīq*) of Islamic identity. *See taḥqīq* (actualization/realization) of Islamic identity
Adnani, Jilali El, 9–10, 129
Aghwāṭī, Saḥnūn b. al-Ḥājj al-, 183
aḥadiyya (unique oneness of God), 119. *See also tawḥīd* (oneness of God)
Aḥlāfī, Muḥammad b. al-Dāwdī al-, 182
Aḥmad b. Ḥanbal (d. 855), 69, 195
Aḥmad ʿAbdallāwī (d. 1910), 186
Aḥmad Bābā al-Massūfī (d. 1627), 28
Aḥmad Bābā al-Timbuktī (fl. 1694), 28
Aḥmad b. Idrīs (d. 1837), 30–31, 50, 94, 163
Aḥmad b. Ismāʿīl, 182–183
Aḥmad b. Uways, 25
Aḥzāb wa awrād (al-Ḥāfiẓ al-Miṣrī), 89, 92
ʿĀʾisha bt. Abī Bakr, 47
Akansūs, Muḥammad (d. 1877), 116, 202, 206, 221n48
Akkach, Samer, 102
ʿAlawī, Muḥammad b. Nāṣir al-, 200
Albania, Tijāniyya in, 212
Algeria: French colonization and Tijāniyya, 213; French conquest of Algiers, 179; Ottoman rule in, 175–179, 184; spread of Tijāniyya in, 182–184
ʿAlī b. Abī Ṭālib, 47, 97, 113, 147, 151
ʿAlī al-Khawāṣṣ, 162–163
ʿAlī Qarabāsh (d. 1686), 34
Amlās, ʿAlī, 129, 166
amulets and talismans, 132
ʿAndalīb, Nāṣir al- (d. 1758), 51, 52, 148
Ansar al-Din (Islamist group), 226n57
Anṭākī, Dāwud al- (d. 1599), 89, 240n186
ʿAqīda al-ṣughra (al-Sanūsī), 28
Aqīt family, 27, 226n60
aqṭāb (axial or perfected saints). *See* saints, perfected (*aqṭāb*; sing. *quṭb*)
ʿArabī b. al-Sāʾiḥ, al-, 112
asceticism (*zuhd*), 81–82. *See also* self-purification

Ash'arī, Abū Ḥasan al- (d. 936), 63
Ash'arī theology, 32, 61, 63. *See also* orthodoxy
asmā' al-Idrīsiyya, al- ("Idrīsī names"), 96–98
'Asqalānī, Ibn Ḥajar al- (d. 1449), 238n116
awtād ("stakes"), 150. *See also* Saints, Seal of (*khātim al-awliyā'*)
axial saints (*aqṭāb*; sing. *quṭb*). *See* saints, axial (*aqṭāb*; sing. *quṭb*)
'Ayn Māḍī, Algeria, 176, 178, 179, 213
'Ayyāshī, Abū Sālim 'Abdallāh al- (d. 1679), 44
Azharī, Muḥammad b. 'Abd al-Raḥmān al- (d. 1793), 36, 79, 176
'Aẓīmābādī, Muḥammad (d. 1905), 29
Azmī, Aḥmad al-, 177

Bā-'Alawī, 'Abd al-Raḥmān al-Saqqāf (d. 1713), 33–34
Bā-'Alawī, (Aḥmad) Sālim b. Shaykhān (d. 1636), 44–45, 150
Baghdādī, Sidi Maḥmūd al-, 25, 26
Bakrāwī, Idrīs al-, 184
Bakrī, Muḥammad b. 'Alī al- (d. 1585), 27, 125–126, 226n61
Bakrī, Muṣṭafā al- (d. 1749): disciples of, 229n112; as Seal of Saints, 37, 148; shaykh-disciple relations of, 86; transmission of ideas through, 28, 31, 34–36, 228n111; visionary experiences by, 40, 139
Bamba, Aḥmad, 164
Bannānī, Aḥmad al- (d. 1889), 127, 131, 204
Bannānī, Aḥmad b. Maḥammad al-, 188, 189
Bannānī al-Maṣrī, Maḥammad b. 'Abd al-Wāḥid al-, 189
Bannīs, Aḥmad, 130
Ba'qīlī, al-Ḥasan al- (d. 1948), 213
Barnāwī, Muḥammad al-Wālī al- (fl. 1688), 235n43
Barrāda family, 184
Barwajī al-Shaṭṭārī, Sibghat-Allāh al- (d. 1606), 43, 45
Baṣrī, 'Abdallāh b. Sālim al- (d. 1722), 34
Birkawī, Mehmed al- (Mehmed Birgivi, d. 1573), 42, 50
Book of Five Jewels, The (al-Ghawth). See *Jawāhir al-khams, al-* (al-Ghawth)
"Bosom Rose" (*Wardat al-juyūb*), 125–126
Brown, Jonathan, 244n56
Bughyat al-Mustafīd (Ibn al-Sā'iḥ), 13
Būnī, Aḥmad al-, 71, 237n100
Burnāwī, 'Abdallāh b. 'Abd al-'Azīz al- (d. 1677), 24–25
Burnāwī, 'Abdallāh b. 'Abd al-Jalīl, 24, 30
Burūjī, Abū Bakr al-, 89, 92
Buṣayrī (Buṣīrī), Muḥammad al- (d. 1294), 106, 114–115, 208

Chittick, William, 2, 84, 198–199
Chodkiewicz, Michel, 145, 146
"Circle of Lights" (*Dawr al-anwār*), 133–134
Cissé, 'Alī, 215
Cissé, Ḥasan, 212, 214, 215
Cissé, Muḥammad al-Māḥī, 215
Cissé, Tijānī b. 'Alī: avoidance of night in Fez, 168; on benefit of Tijāniyya, 98, 207; on divine essence, 85; on Ḥarāzim as intermediary with Prophet, 135; influence of today, 212–213; on leadership of Tijāniyya, 215; on living with non-Muslims, 141; publication of *Jawāhir al-ma'ānī*, 12; on al-Tijānī as Seal of Saints, 164
colonialism: accusations of collaboration of Sufi orders, 9, 213; conquest of Algiers, 179; effects of on Tijāniyya,

213–214, 216; effects of on *'ulamā'* (scholars), 19, 213–214; jihads against, 102; use of "humanism" in, 101. *See also* corruption of the age
Cornell, Vincent, 102, 147
corruption of the age: in leaders of the East, 124–125; and modern appeal of Tijāniyya, 215–216; in Muslim societies, 179–182, 206–207, 262n196; open rebellion cautioned against, 178–179; reflected in Labbāda's dream, 204; and spread of Tijāniyya, 182–184; Turks in Algeria, 175–179, 184. *See also* colonialism

Dabbāgh, 'Abd al-'Azīz al- (d. 1719): on *Ḥizb al-baḥr*, 91; influence of in Fez, 30; Qur'ān interpretation by, 59; on ranks of visionaries, 152; on sacredness of human being, 103; on seeking mediation of saints, 88; students of, 39–40, 50; on *tawḥīd* of gnostics, 66; visionary experiences of, 24. See also *Ibrīz, al-* (al-Lamaṭī)
Dabbāgh, Sharīf Muḥammad b. al-Hadi al- (d. 1867), 26
Dalā'il al-khayrāt (al-Jazūlī): circulation of in North Africa, 80; in curriculum at Qarawiyīn University, 195–196; al-Tijānī's commendation of, 23, 224n31; transmission of from al-Sammān, 241n199; and visionary experiences, 204, 244n56
Dallal, Ahmad, 4, 5, 210
Damanhūrī, Aḥmad al- (d. 1778), 41, 49
Damrāwī, Muḥammad al-'Arabī al- (d. 1798): esoteric sciences studied by, 71; murder of, 179; on prayer on the Prophet, 116–117; visionary experiences by, 131–134, 158, 166
Dāmūnī, Muḥammad al- (d. 1785), 92–93
Dardīr, Aḥmad al- (d. 1786), 36
Darqawiyya, 21, 176, 223n11
Dasūqī, Ibrāhīm al- (d. 1277), 91
dawr al-a'lā ("the highest station"), 92–93
Dawr al-anwār ("Circle of Lights"), 133–134
Dhahab al-ibrīz (al-Lamaṭī). See *Ibrīz, al-* (al-Lamaṭī)
divine decree and contentment, 202
divine decree and free-will, 75, 238n116
divine manifestation, people of (*ahl al-tajalla*), 132. *See tajalla* (divine manifestation); visionary experiences
divine manifestation (*tajalla*). See *tajalla* (divine manifestation)
divine reward and punishment, 170–171, 173–174
divine transcendence (*tanzīh*). See *tanzīh* (divine transcendence)
Durr al-manẓūm wa khulāsat al-sirr al-maktūm, al- (al-Kashnāwī), 28–29

egocentrism, 180–181
eighteenth century. *See* colonialism; corruption of the age; Islamic scholarly networks in eighteenth century
epistemological strategies of *taḥqīq*, 4–5, 219 (n. 15)
esoteric sciences (*'ulūm al-asrār*): controversy over, 41–42; definition of, 41, 230n168; divine decree and free-will, 75, 238n116; in eighteenth century, 41–48; greatest name of God, 76–77; al-Kashnāwī on, 28–29; misuse of, 88; sacred words and spiritual beings, 74–75; secret names of God, 91; al-Tijānī's studies of, 70–74. *See also* knowledge of God (*ma'rifa*)

faḍl Allāh (grace or bounty of God). *See* grace of God (*faḍl Allāh*)
false Sufism, 87–89

Fāsī, Ibn al-Ḥājj al-ʿAbdarī al- (d. 1336), 122
Fāsī, Muḥammad b. al-Ṭayyib al- (d. 1757), 224n18
Fātiḥa, al- (opening chapter of Qurʾān), 206
fear and hope, balance of, 171–173. *See also* orthodoxy
Fihrī, ʿAbd al-Wāḥid al-Fāsī al- (d. 1799), 184, 257n59
fiṭra (innate human disposition), 106–107. *See also rūḥ* (spirit or soul)
free-will and divine decree, 75, 238n116
Fullānī, Ṣāliḥ al-, 29, 37, 184, 226n79
Futūḥāt al-Makkiya (Ibn al-ʿArabī), 146

Ghālī, Muḥammad al- (d. 1829), 130, 131
Ghawth, Muḥammad al- (fl. 16th c.), 43, 44, 45, 93, 97. See also *Jawāhir al-khams, al-* (al-Ghawth)
Ghazālī, Abū Ḥāmid al- (d. 1111): epistemological divisions of, 219n15; on esoteric sciences, 41; on human being, 103; in Moroccan curriculum, 195; on types of gratitude, 198; on visionary experiences, 122, 123
Ghazzī, Kamāl al-Dīn al-, 148
gnosis (*maʿrifa*). *See* knowledge of God (*maʿrifa*)
Goldziher, Ignaz, 121
grace of God (*faḍl Allāh*): emphasis on in Tijāniyya, 198, 206; individuals as instruments of, 175
gratitude (*shukr*): in earlier Sufism, 198–199; as path to God, 201, 207; in practice, 202–206; al-Tijānī on, 199–201
grave visitation (*ziyāra*): in orthodox Islam, 88; al-Tijānī's restrictions on, 87, 88, 194–195
greatest name of God, 76–77, 135–137
Green, Nile, 209
hadīth (prophetic narrations): forged or weak, 114, 244n56; study of, 46, 49; transmission chains, study of, 4–5, 219n16
Hafian, Faissal al-, 222n52
Ḥāfiẓ al-ʿAlawī, Muḥammad al-Shinqīṭī al- (d. 1830), 29, 53, 183, 185
Ḥāfiẓ al-Miṣrī, Muḥammad al- (d. 1978), 89, 92, 169, 211–212, 214
Ḥajūjī, Muḥammad al- (d. 1952), 213
Hallāj, Manṣūr al- (d. 922), 114
Ḥamdūn b. al-Ḥājj (d. 1817): approval for Wahhābīs by, 49; knowledge network of, 29; poem to King Saʿūd, 196; scholarship of, 189–190; in sultan's council, 185; al-Tijānī consulted by, 54; in Tijāniyya, 8, 188, 190–191
Ḥarāzim al-Barrāda, ʿAlī (d. 1804): as intermediary (*wāsiṭa*), 134–135, 138, 249n179; as *khalīfa* of al-Tijānī, 132–133, 214; spiritual rank of, 167; tensions with Ibn al-Mashrī, 167; writing of *Jawāhir al-maʿānī*, 11–12, 220n39. *See also* Ḥarāzim al-Barrāda, ʿAlī (d. 1804), as source; Ḥarāzim al-Barrāda, ʿAlī (d. 1804), visionary experiences; *Jawāhir al-maʿānī* (Ḥarāzim); *Jawāhir al-maʿānī* (Ḥarāzim), as source
———, as source: contentment with divine decree, 81; God's grace and gratitude, 199; Hidden Pole, 152–153; Muḥammadan reality, 114–115; shaykh-disciple relations, 86–87, 168–169; supplication, 153–154; *taḥqīq* (verification) and *tadqīq* (scrutiny), 2–3; visionary experiences, 123, 124, 128–129, 134–138; *waḥdat al-wujūd* (oneness of being), 68–69. *See also* Ḥarāzim al-Barrāda, ʿAlī (d. 1804); Ḥarāzim al-Barrāda, ʿAlī (d. 1804),

visionary experiences; *Jawāhir al-maʿānī* (Ḥarāzim), as source; Tijānī, Aḥmad b. Maḥammad al- (d. 1815), writings and teachings
———, visionary experiences: Idrīsī names, 97; instructions from Prophet to al-Tijānī, 124–125, 200–201; investiture of al-Tijānī as Hidden Pole, 156–157; investiture of al-Tijānī as Pole of Poles, 154; meeting with Shamharūsh, 93–94; rebuke of a disciple by Prophet, 172; station of al-Tijānī, 152, 153; various, 134–138. *See also* Ḥarāzim al-Barrāda, ʿAlī (d. 1804); Ḥarāzim al-Barrāda, ʿAlī (d. 1804), as source; Tijānī, Aḥmad b. Maḥammad al- (d. 1815), visionary experiences; visionary experiences
Ḥasan b. ʿAlī b. Abī Ṭālib, 51, 148
Hāshim, Alfa (d. 1931), 212
Ḥātimī, al-. *See* Ibn al-ʿArabī, Muḥyī al-Dīn (d. 1240)
Hidden Pole (*al-quṭb al-maktūm*). *See* saints, Hidden Pole (*al-quṭb al-maktūm*)
hierarchy of saints, 44–45, 149–151, 198, 251n32. *See also* sainthood, axial (*quṭbāniyya*); saints; saints, axial (*aqṭāb*; sing. *quṭb*); Saints, Seal of (*khātim al-awliyāʾ*)
Ḥifnī (Ḥifnāwī), Muḥammad al- (d. 1767), 34, 35–36, 39
Hindī, Aḥmad ʿAbdallāh al- (d. 1774): "great secret" from, 76; initiation of al-Tijānī by, 7, 72–73; instructions to al-Tijānī regarding al-Sammān, 238n119; transmission lines from, 45; transmission of Idrīsī names by, 96
historiography, 14–15
hizb al-baḥr ("Orison of the Sea"), 90–91
hizb al-mughnī, 183–184
hizb al-sayf ("Orison of the Sword"), 93–94, 184
hope and fear, balance of, 171–173. *See also* orthodoxy
human condition, reality of, 103–106
human potentiality, 109–113. *See also* *taḥqīq al-insāniyya* (actualization of humanity)
human spirit and divine love, 106–109
humanism, Islamic, 101–103, 243n9

Ibn ʿAjība, Aḥmad (d. 1809), 41, 70
Ibn Anbūja (d. 1867), 116, 198
Ibn al-ʿArabī, Muḥyī al-Dīn (d. 1240): actualization (*taḥqīq*), 2; on blessings, 199; dating of "Muḥammadan reality" to, 114; *dawr al-aʿlā* ("the highest station"), 92–93; on divine manifestation, 84; on esoteric sciences, 41–42; on gratitude, 198–199; humanity's reflection of divine attributes, 104; Idrīsī names, 96–97; influence of on al-Kurdī, 40; saintly rank of, 161–162, 163–164, 167; on Seal of Saints, 143–144, 145–146; as Seal of Saints, 148; *tajalla* (divine manifestation), 32–33, 228n103; verification of visions, 122, 123; *waḥdat al-wujūd* debate, 31–32
Ibn ʿAṭā-Allāh (d. 1309), 33, 208
Ibn ʿAzūz, ʿAbdallāh (d. 1790), 71, 132
Ibn al-Fuḍayl, Muḥammad, 182, 183
Ibn Ḥajar Haythamī (d. 1566), 121–122
Ibn Kathīr, 195
Ibn al-Mashrī (Mishrī) al-Sāʾiḥī, Muḥammad (d. 1809): miracles of, 130; visionary experiences by, 158; writing of *Rawḍ al-muḥibb* and *al-Jamiʿ*, 12–13
———, as source: al-Damrāwī, 133; esoteric sciences, 70; following Sharīʿa, 56; promises of salvation, 165;

rank of Hidden Pole, 162; tensions with Ḥarāzim, 167; al-Tijānī as Hidden Pole, 152; al-Tijānī's legal methodology, 58, 59; al-Tijānī's miracles, 54; al-Tijānī's visions, 128
Ibn Masʿūd, ʿAbdallāh, 231n169
Ibn al-Sāʾiḥ, Muḥammad al-ʿArabī (d. 1898), 13, 97, 112, 221n48
Ibn Taymiyya, 195
Ibrāhīm b. Sulaymān (Mawlay), prince, 196
Ibrīz, al- (al-Lamaṭī), 24, 59, 88, 91, 120–121
Idrīs, Prophet (Enoch), 41, 246n83
Idrīsī, ʿAbdallāh b. Ibrāhīm al- (d. 1678), 22–23
Idrīsī names (*al-Asmāʾ al-Idrīsiyya*), 96–98
Ifāda al-Aḥmadiyya, al- (al-Sufyānī), 13, 56, 188
Ifrānī, al-Ḥusayn al-, 204–205
Ighāthat al-lahfān (al-Mundhirī), 73–74
Iḥyā ʿulūm al-dīn (al-Ghazālī), 195
ijtihād (legal judgments). *See* Islamic law, legal opinions
insān al-kāmil, al- (perfect man), 104, 147–148
"Invocation of the Unseen concerning the Aḥmadan Reality" (*ṣalāt al-ghaybiyya fī l-ḥaqīqa al-Aḥmadiyya*), 127
ʿIrāqī, Aḥmad al-, 187
ʿIrāqī, Idrīs al- (d. 2009), 148, 184, 215
Islamic humanism, 101–103, 140–141, 243n9. *See also taḥqīq al-insāniyya* (actualization of humanity)
Islamic law, legal opinions: on ablution (*wuḍūʾ*), 57, 235n28; influenced by visions, 58, 125, 178; methodology of, 29–30; permissibility of, 49; on slavery, 60–61; on sugar, 60–61, 236n53; on tobacco, 28, 59, 226n71, 235n43. *See also* Sharīʿa; Tijānī, Aḥmad b. Maḥammad al- (d. 1815), intellectual development
Islamic scholarly networks in eighteenth century: introduction, 18–20; overview, 208–209; discourses of, 210–211; Egypt and Hijaz, 30–31; "esoteric sciences" (*ʿulūm al-asrār*), 41–48; al-Kūrānī al-Kurdī legacy, 31–34; al-Kurdī, 38–40; Muṣṭfā al-Bakrī and Egyptian Khalwatiyya, 34–36; al-Sammān, 36–38; scholarly developments in, 4–6; Shādhiliyya in North Africa, 21–23; *Ṭarīqa Muḥammadiyya*, forms of, 48–52; *Ṭarīqa Muḥammadiyya* in Sub-Saharan Africa, 24–30. *See also* Sammān, Muḥammad al- (d. 1775)
isolation (*khalwa*), 81–82
Istiqṣā li-akhbār duwal al-Maghrib al-aqṣā, al- (al-Nāṣirī), 14

Jabartī, ʿAbd al-Raḥmān al-, 34, 36, 38–39
Jabartī, Ḥasan al-, 28
Jabbārī, ʿAbd al-Ḥaqq al-, 196
Jaʿfar al-Ṣādiq (d. 765), 93
Jalāʾ al-naẓr (al-Kūrānī), 32, 227n96
Jāmiʿ, al- (Ibn al-Mashrī): al-Tijānī's legal opinions in, 56
Jamiʿ, al- (Ibn al-Mashrī), 12–13. *See also* Ibn al-Mashrī al-Sāʾiḥī, Muḥammad (d. 1809); Ibn al-Mashrī al-Sāʾiḥī, Muḥammad (d. 1809), as source
Jawāhir al-khams, al- (al-Ghawth), 43–48, 73–74, 96–97. *See also* Ghawth, Muḥammad al- (fl. 16th c.)
Jawāhir al-maʿānī (Ḥarāzim), 11–12, 220n39, 221n45, 221n48, 222n52. *See also* Ḥarāzim al-Barrāda, ʿAlī (d. 1804); Ḥarāzim al-Barrāda, ʿAlī

(d. 1804), as source; *Jawāhir al-maʿānī* (Ḥarāzim), as source; Tijānī, Aḥmad b. Maḥammad al- (d. 1815), writings and teachings
———, as source: "greatest name," 76; human condition, 103, 105; Idrīsī names, 96, 97; Khalwatī chain of initiation, 79; miracles (*karāmāt*), 112–113; misguidance of God, 170–171; Muḥammadan reality, 115; prayers given to al-Tijānī, 127; supplication, 153–154; al-Tijānī's arrival in Fez, 184; al-Tijānī's encounter with al-Hindī, 72–73; al-Tijānī's legal opinions, 56; visions by disciples, 131–132. *See also* Ḥarāzim Barada, Ali; *Jawāhir al-maʿānī* (Ḥarāzim); Tijānī, Aḥmad b. Maḥammad al- (d. 1815), writings and teachings
Jawharat al-kamāl ("Jewel of Perfection"), 127
Jaysh al-kafīl, al- (al-Shinjīṭī), 122
Jazāʾirī, ʿAbd al-Qādir al-, 213
Jazāʾirī, Muḥammad b. ʿAbd al-Qādir al-, 177
Jazūlī, Muḥammad al- (d. 1465), 94, 147–148, 224n21
Jazūliyya (Dalāʾiliyya), 22–23, 147–148, 224n21
Jesus, Prophet, 146, 150, 151
Jilānī, ʿAbd al-Qādir al- (d. 1166), 113, 147, 161, 165
Jinn: in House of Mirrors, 192; Shamharūsh, 93–94; al-Tijānī's visions of, 71. *See also* spirits (*rūḥāniyyāt*)
Junayd, al-, 171, 198

Kanūn (Genoune), Muḥammad al-Rāḍī, 12, 45, 96
karāmāt (miracles). *See* miracles (*karāmāt*)
Kashf al-ḥijāb (Sukayrij), 13, 185–187
Kāshif al-ilbās (I. Niasse), 13, 71
Kashnāwī, Muḥammad al-, 28, 41
Kattānī, Muḥammad Jaʿfar al- (d. 1927), 8, 14, 127, 189
Katz, Jonathan, 206, 262n196
"Key of Axial Sainthood, The" (*miftāḥ al-quṭbāniyya*), 137, 249n176
Khalwatiyya: conformance to Sharīʿa, 228n111; in Egypt, 34–36, 127; al-Kurdī in, 40; shaykh-disciple relations in, 86; Suhrawardī in chain of authorities, 96; threatened by Ottomans, 176; al-Tijānī in, 7, 21, 31, 79–80
khātim al-walāya (Seal of Sainthood). *See* Sainthood, Seal of (*khātim al-walāya*)
Khiḍr (guide of Prophet Moses), 24, 34, 94, 119, 246n83
Khilāfa (vicegerency), 103–104
Khulāṣat al-athar (Muḥibbī), 150
Kitāb al-irshādāt al-rabbāniyya (Ḥarāzim), 13
Kitāb al-maqṣad al-Aḥmad (al-Qādirī), 11
Kitāb sīrat al-awliyāʾ (al-Tirmidhī), 144
knowledge of God (*maʿrifa*): and capacity to become agent of Divine action, 103–104; human capacity for, 109; intrinsic to spirit, 107–109, 244n40; and Seal of Sainthood, 146; and self-annihilation, 83–85. *See also* esoteric sciences (*ʿulūm al-asrār*); Ḥarāzim al-Barrāda, ʿAlī (d. 1804), visionary experiences; self-annihilation (*fanāʾ*); Sufism; *taḥqīq* (actualization/realization); *taḥqīq* (actualization/realization), promise of sainthood; *tajalla* (divine manifestation); *tanzīh* (divine transcendence); *tawḥīd* (oneness of God); Tijānī, Aḥmad b. Maḥammad

al- (d. 1815), visionary experiences; Tijānī, Aḥmad b. Maḥammad al- (d. 1815), writings and teachings; Tijāniyya; visionary experiences; *waḥdat al-wujūd* (oneness of being)
Knysh, Alexander, 10
Koçi, Ḥāfiẓ Ṣabrī (d. 2004), 212
Korah (Qārūn), 123–124
Kūhan, ʿAbd al-Qādir al- (d. 1837), 36, 189
Kunnāsh al-aṣfar (al-Tijānī), 179
Kunnāsh al-maktūm (al-Tijānī), 76. *See also* Tijānī, Aḥmad b. Maḥammad al- (d. 1815), writings and teachings
Kunnāsh al-riḥla (al-Tijānī): on Arabic letters and spiritual beings, 74–75; as primary source, 13–14; study of *al-Jawāhir al-khams*, 44–48; transmission of text from al-Hindī, 72–73, 237n103. *See also* Tijānī, Aḥmad b. Maḥammad al- (d. 1815), intellectual development; Tijānī, Aḥmad b. Maḥammad al- (d. 1815), writings and teachings
Kuntī, Muḥammad b. al-Mukhtār al-, 195
Kuntī, Mukhtār al- (d. 1811), 26, 84, 94, 149, 242n209
Kuntī-Qādiriyya scholarly lineage, 30, 227n85
Kuntiyya-Qadiriyya, 26, 183
Kūrānī al-Kurdī, Ibrāhīm b. al-Ḥasan al- (d. 1693): knowledge network of, 45, 50–51; legacy of, 30–34, 227n96, 228n101, 228n103; study of *Al-Jawāhir al-khams*, 43, 45
Kurdī, Maḥmūd al- (d. 1780): influence of on al-Tijānī, 38–40, 78–80; influences on, 28; initiation of al-Tijānī by, 7; lieutenant of al-Ḥifnī, 36; receival of prayer from Khiḍr, 94; on smoking, 59; teaching of *dawr al-aʿlā*, 92; visionary experiences by, 59

Laḥlū, Muḥammad, 184, 188, 205
Lallā Mannāna (d. 1815), 204
Lamaṭī, Aḥmad b. al-Mubārak al-, 71. See also *Ibrīz* (al-Lamaṭī)
laylat al-qadr ("night of power"), 89, 196

Maghīlī, ʿAbd al-Karīm al- (d. 1505), 26
magic squares, 41. *See also* esoteric sciences (*ʿulūm al-asrār*)
Mahdī, 147, 149, 151, 163, 191–192
Mahdist community, 209–210
Maḥmūdiyya, 25–26, 225n48
Makkī, Abū Ṭālib al- (d. 996), 94
Malāmatī, 140, 200, 249n190
Mālik (Imam), 42; on position of hands in prayer, 50
Mālikī school: on ablution (*wuḍūʾ*), 57, 235n28; curriculum of, 55–56, 195; in Morocco, 49; on position of hands in prayer, 50
Mamdani, Mahmood, 101–102
maʿrifa (gnosis). *See* knowledge of God (*maʿrifa*)
Mashāhid (Ḥarāzim), 14, 134–138, 154, 155–157. *See also* Ḥarāzim al-Barrāda, ʿAlī (d. 1804), as source; *Jawāhir al-maʿānī* (Ḥarāzim), as source; Tijānī, Aḥmad b. Maḥammad al- (d. 1815), writings and teachings
Maṭlaʿ al-jūd (al-Kūrānī), 32, 227n96, 228n101
mawlid (birthday) of Prophet, 196
Māzirī, Muḥammad al-, 182
Mazzūr, al-Ḥasan, 214
Mehmed Birgivi (or Birkawī, d. 1573), 42, 50
miftāḥ al-quṭbāniyya ("The Key of Axial Sainthood"), 137, 249n177
Miftāḥ al-saʿāda (al-Burūjī), 89, 90, 93

Mir Dard, 148
miracles (*karāmāt*): hiding of, 139–140, 249n190; by non-Muslims, 140–141; of al-Tijānī, 54, 113, 124, 204–205; of al-Tijānī's disciples, 130–131. *See also* Tijānī, Aḥmad b. Maḥammad al- (d. 1815), visionary experiences; visionary experiences
Mirandola, Pico della (d. 1494), 102
Mirghānī, Muḥammad al- (d. 1853), 163, 164
misguidance of God (*makr Allāh*), 170–172. *See also* orthodoxy
Miskawayh (d. 1030), 243n9
Mīzāb al-raḥma, 198
Moses (Mūsā), Prophet, 123–124
Muḥammad (Mawlay), sultan (r. 1757–90), 49, 189
Muḥammad, Prophet: esoteric sciences connected to, 41, 231n169; spiritual reality (*al-ḥaqīqa al-Muḥammadiyya*) of, 114–119; spiritual reality and actualization of true knowledge, 119–121. *See also* visionary experiences
Muḥammad b. ʿAbd al-Salām (d. 1823), 224n18
Muḥammad b. ʿAbd al-Wahhāb: knowledge network of, 30–31, 33–34, 209; marginality to scholarship, 210; on *ṭarīqa* of Prophet, 19; on use of amulets, 42. *See also* Wahhābī movement; Wahhabis; Wahhabism
Muḥammad b. ʿAbdallāh, 214
Muḥammad Aḥmad ("Sudanese Mahdī"), 209–210
Muhammad Baghrūʿu, 28
Muhammad Bello b. ʿUthmān Fūdī, sultan of Sokoto, 43
Muḥammad b. Faqīra, 188
Muḥammad b. al-Nāṣir, 168, 200, 203
Muḥammad b. Nāṣir al-ʿAlawī, 200
Muḥammad b. Nāṣir al-Darʿī (d. 1674), 21, 161. *See also* Nāṣiriyya
Muḥammad al-Ṭālib, 190
Muḥammad b. ʿUthmān (d. 1791), 177
Muḥammadan Sufism. *See Ṭarīqa Muḥammadiyya*
Muḥaqqiq (verifier): definition of, 2; *wird* (litany) and self-purification of, 82–83. *See also taḥqīq* (actualization/realization)
Mukhtārāt min rasāʾil al-shaykh ("Selected Letters" of al-Tijānī), 13
Mukhtaṣar (Sīdī Khalīl), 195
Mundhirī al-Sulayfī, ʿUmar b. Masʿūd al- (d. 1747), 73
Murād Shāh (d. 1487), 96
Murīdiyya, 127
Murshid al-muʿīn (Ibn ʿĀshir), 195
Mursī, Abū l-ʿAbbās al- (d. 1287), 128
Mūsā (Moses), Prophet, 123–124
Musabbaʿāt al-ʿashr, al- ("Ten-Sevens"), 94–95
Musaqqam, al-Ḥājj, 132
Music and dance, 21, 196, 223n11. *See also* Sharīʿa
Muʿtazilite school, 63
mystical audition (*samāʿ*), 261n144. *See also* visionary experiences

Nābulusī, ʿAbd al-Ghānī al- (d. 1731): on incantations (*ruqya*), 42–43; on Islamic humanism, 102; knowledge network of, 28, 31, 34; on Seal of Saints, 148; on *Ṭarīqa Muḥammadiyya*, 50, 233n223; as visionary and scholar, 122; on visions and dreams, 139
Nafrāwī, Aḥmad b. al-Ghunaym al- (d. 1713), 42
Naqshbandiyya, 34, 45, 127, 143, 212
Nāṣirī, Aḥmad al- (d. 1897), 14, 54–55, 177–178, 194

Nāṣiriyya, 21–22, 23, 183, 235n43
Nawawī, Yaḥya al- (d. 1277), 42–43
Naẓīfī, Muḥammad al- (d. 1951), 126, 213, 247n119
Niasse, ʿAbdallāh (d. 1922), 12, 216
Niasse, Ibrāhīm b. ʿAbdallāh (d. 1975): on abrogation of Sufi orders, 169; avoidance of night in Fez, 168; on concept of the seal, 143, 159; on contentment with divine decree, 81; *Dawr al-anwār* transmitted by, 134; on living with non-believers, 141; manuscript of *Jawāhir* owned by, 12; on Pole of Poles, 155; Prophet's being and the cosmological presences of creation, 115; on sacred composition of human being, 103; as source, 71; on al-Tijānī's claim to being Seal of Saints, 163–164; and Tijāniyya growth, 216; as Tijāniyya leader, 8, 15, 212–213, 215, 220n29; on visions, 139–140; warnings against slaves of desires, 172–173; witnessing of miracle, 113; words to French historian, 14
"Night of power" (*laylat al-qadr*), 89, 196
"Night of the Hidden Pole" (*laylat al-katmiyya*), 156, 253n77
Norris, H. T., 25
numerology (*ḥisāb abjada*), 45–46. *See also* esoteric sciences (*ʿulūm al-asrār*)

Orthodoxy: and civil behavior sought from Wahabbis, 196–197; and divine realization, 102–103; and esoteric sciences, 73; and experiential understanding of *tawḥīd*, 66; and grave visitation, 88; and Nāṣiriyya, 21–22; and Prophet's enduring spiritual presence, 118–119, 122; tensions with Sufism over divine reward and punishment, 170–171, 173–174; tensions with Sufism over misguidance of God (*makr Allāh*), 170–172; and *waḥdat al-wujūd* (oneness of being), 32, 190. *See also* Sharīʿa; *waḥdat al-wujūd* (oneness of being)
Ottoman government, 175–179, 184

Palestine, Tijāniyya in, 212
paradigmatic sainthood (*quṭbāniyya*). *See* sainthood, axial (*quṭbāniyya*)
perfect man (*al-insān al-kāmil*), 104, 147–148
Pole of Poles (*quṭb al-aqṭāb*). *See* saints, Pole of Poles (*quṭb al-aqṭāb*)
prayer for gratitude (*ṣalāt al-shukr*), 200
"Prayer of Opening" (*ṣalāt al-fātiḥ*). *See* *ṣalāt al-fātiḥ* ("Prayer of Opening")
prayer on the Prophet (*ṣalāt ʿalā l-nabī*). *See* *ṣalawāt* (blessings on the Prophet)
prayers (*ṣalāt*): position of hands in, 50; reciting *basmala* in, 125; al-Tijānī on proper form of, 57, 235n24, 235n28; al-Tijānī's, 54, 234n6. *See also* Sufi prayers
prayers, Sufi. *See* Sufi prayers

Qāḍī Iyāḍ b. Mūsā (d. 1149), 214
Qādiriyya, 25, 94, 143, 149, 183, 212
Qaranī, Uways al-, 114
Qarawiyīn University, curriculum at, 55–56, 195–196
Qārūn (Korah), 123–124
Qāshānī, ʿAbd al-Razzāq al- (d. 1330), 146–147
Qassām, ʿIzz al-Dīn al- (d. 1935), 212
Qudwā, al- (Ibn Uways), 25–26
Qūnawī, Ṣadr al-Dīn al-, 2, 104
Qurʾān, power of, 206
Qushāshī, Aḥmad al- (d. 1660), 43, 45, 50–51, 148

Qushayrī, ʿAbd al-Karīm al- (d. 1074), 40
quṭb (axial or perfected saint). *See* saints, axial (*aqṭāb*; sing. *quṭb*)
quṭb al-aqṭāb (Pole of Poles). *See* saints, Pole of Poles (*quṭb al-aqṭāb*)
quṭb al-maktūm, al- (Hidden Pole). *See* saints, Hidden Pole (*al-quṭb al-maktūm*)

Radtke, Bernd, 51
Rafʿ al-niqāb (Sukayrij), 13, 185
Raḥmāniyya (Khalwatiyya), 176
Rawḍ al-muḥibb (Ibn al-Mashrī), 12, 165. *See also* Ibn al-Mashrī al-Sāʾiḥī, Muḥammad (d. 1809); Ibn al-Mashrī al-Sāʾiḥī, Muḥammad (d. 1809), as source
Rāzī, Fakhr al-Dīn al- (d. 1210), 96
Realization (*taḥqīq*). *See taḥqīq* (actualization/realization)
Rekkāniyya, 183
Retreat (*khalwa*), 81–82
Rifāʿī, Aḥmad al- (d. 1182), 119, 246n82
Rimāḥ (Tāl), 13, 88, 96, 140–141. *See also* Tāl, ʿUmar Fūtī; Tāl, ʿUmar Fūtī, as source
Risāla (al-Qayrawānī), 195
Risāla fī l-ḥikam (al-Kurdī), 39, 40
Riyāḥī, Ibrāhīm al- (d. 1850), 54, 70, 90, 130, 136, 216
Rouayheb, Khaled El-, 4, 227n96
"Ruby of Necessity in the Prayer on the Master of Ascension, The" (*Yāqūtat al-maḥtāj fī ṣalāt ʿalā ṣāḥib al-miʿrāj*), 133, 134
"Ruby of Realities, The" (*Yaqūtat al-ḥaqāʾiq*), 117–118, 127
Rūḥ (spirit or soul): and divine love, 106–109, 244n40; and Muḥammadan reality, 115, 118
ruqya (incantations), 42–43. *See also* esoteric sciences (*ʿulūm al-asrār*)

Ṣaddīq, Muḥammad b. al- (d. 1935), 164
Ṣāfiyya Labbāda (d. 1785), 204
Saḥnūn al-Tanukhi (d. 784), 183
sainthood, axial (*quṭbāniyya*): context of al-Tijānī's assertions of, 142–143; hierarchy of saints, 149–151; hierarchy of saints criticized, 198; not to be sought, 81; prayer for, 137, 249n176; promised to disciples, 3–4, 166, 207, 217; al-Tijānī on "pole of poles" (*quṭb al-aqṭāb*), 128. *See also* saints, *awliyāʾ*; saints, axial (*aqṭāb*; sing. *quṭb*); saints, Hidden Pole (*al-quṭb al-maktūm*); saints, Pole of Poles (*quṭb al-aqṭāb*); Saints, Seal of (*khātim al-awliyāʾ*)
saints, *awliyāʾ*: ʿAlī b. Abī Ṭālib as, 97; cannot alter Sharīʿa, 58; female, 204; as inheritors of Prophet, 38; respect for, 78; verification of knowledge through visions by, 121–122; visiting graves of, 87, 88, 194–195. *See also* sainthood, axial (*quṭbāniyya*); saints, axial (*aqṭāb*; sing. *quṭb*); saints, Hidden Pole (*al-quṭb al-maktūm*); saints, Pole of Poles (*quṭb al-aqṭāb*); Saints, Seal of (*khātim al-awliyāʾ*); *taḥqīq* (actualization/realization); *taḥqīq al-insāniyya* (actualization of humanity)
———, axial (*aqṭāb*; sing. *quṭb*): al-Bakrī as, 34, 37; bodily presence (*dhāt*) of, 112; al-Dabbāgh as, 24; hierarchy of, 44–45, 149–151, 251n32; hierarchy of criticized, 198; al-Hindī as, 76, 238n119; intercession granted to, 155; Mawlay ʿAbd al-Mālik as, 183; not infallible, 200; al-Sammān as, 30, 36; supreme helper (*ghawth*), 251n32; al-Tamāsīnī as, 166–167; al-Tijānī as, 2–4; Wazzānī shaykhs as, 23. *See also* sainthood, axial (*quṭbāniyya*); saints,

awliyā'; saints, Hidden Pole (*al-quṭb al-maktūm*); saints, Pole of Poles (*quṭb al-aqṭāb*); Saints, Seal of (*khātim al-awliyā'*); *taḥqīq* (actualization/ realization); *taḥqīq al-insāniyya* (actualization of humanity)
———, Hidden Pole (*al-quṭb al-maktūm*): features of, 157–158; humility of, 160, 173; as intermediary between Prophets and saints, 158–160; rank above others, 154, 161–162; rank not to be spoken of, 200–201; and Seal's intimate proximity to Prophet, 143; al-Tijānī's attainment of, 155–157; al-Tijānī's claim as, 152–153, 173–174; al-Tijānī's claim as, verification of, 158. *See also* sainthood, axial (*quṭbāniyya*); saints, *awliyā'*; saints, axial (*aqṭāb*; sing. *quṭb*); saints, Pole of Poles (*quṭb al-aqṭāb*); Saints, Seal of (*khātim al-awliyā'*)
———, Pole of Poles (*quṭb al-aqṭāb*): al-Mursī as, 128; al-Tijānī as, 153–155. *See also* sainthood, axial (*quṭbāniyya*); saints, *awliyā'*; saints, axial (*aqṭāb*; sing. *quṭb*); saints, Hidden Pole (*al-quṭb al-maktūm*); Saints, Seal of (*khātim al-awliyā'*)
———, Seal of (*khātim al-awliyā'*): 'Alī b. Abī Ṭālib as, 147; al-Bakrī as, 37; in earlier Sufism, 143–149, 167, 250n6; hierarchy of saints, 149–151; hierarchy of saints criticized, 198; humility of, 160; previous claims to, 161–164; relationship of to Mahdi, 147, 149; *rijāl al-ghayb* (hidden hierarchy), 149–150; al-Tijānī's claim as, 142–143, 168; al-Tijānī's claim as, proximity to Prophet, 151–153; types of seals, 148–151. *See also* sainthood, axial (*quṭbāniyya*); saints, *awliyā'*; saints, axial (*aqṭāb*; sing. *quṭb*); saints, Hidden Pole (*al-quṭb al-maktūm*); saints, Pole of Poles (*quṭb al-aqṭāb*)
Salafi-Wahhabi circles, 207. *See also* Wahhabis
Ṣalāt 'alā l-nabī (prayer on the Prophet). See *ṣalawāt* (blessings on the Prophet)
Ṣalāt al-fātiḥ ("Prayer of Opening"): centrality of in Tijāniyya, 116–119; explanation of, 114; history of, 125–127; merit of, 126–127, 135, 206, 247n119, 247n122. *See also* Sufi prayers
Ṣalawāt (blessings on the Prophet): and Muḥammadan reality, 114–119; al-Sammān's emphasis on, 36–37; al-Shinnāwī on, 48; al-Zabīdī's emphasis on, 50
Ṣāliḥ al-Fullānī, 184
salvation promised: to Nāṣirī followers, 21; to Tijānī followers, 165–166, 207; warnings against relying on promises, 165, 170, 171–172
Salwat al-anfās (al-Kattānī), 8, 14, 24, 25, 177, 191
Sammān, Muḥammad al- (d. 1775): as axial saint, 30, 36; companionship with al-Tijānī, 30, 95; influence of al-Sindī on, 34; influence of on al-Tijānī, 36–38, 51, 80; initiation of al-Tijānī by, 7; knowledge network of, 29; prayers from, 92, 241n199; on Seal of Saints, 148; teachings of ignored, 209–210; treatise on *Ṭarīqa Muḥammadiyya*, 31; visionary experiences by, 37, 148, 239n143. *See also* Islamic scholarly networks in eighteenth century
Sammāniyya, 209–210
Sanūsī, Muḥammad b. Aḥmad al- (d. 1842), 130, 188
Sanūsī, Muḥammad b. 'Alī (d. 1859), 50, 187, 209, 224n18

Sanūsī, Muḥammad b. Yūsuf al- (d. 1490), 28, 61–64
Ṣaqillī, Aḥmad al- (d. 1764), 36, 77–78
Ṣarsī, ʿAlī (d. 1628), 23
Saʿūd, king of Arabia, 196–197
Sayyid Aḥmad Shahīd Barelwi (d. 1831), 209
schools of jurisprudence (*madhāhib*), 49–50
Seal of Sainthood (*khātim al-walāya*). *See* Saints, Seal of (*khātim al-awliyāʾ*)
Seesemann, Rüdiger, 6, 15, 116, 221n45
self-annihilation (*fanāʾ*): and knowledge of God (*maʿrifa*), 83–85; in the Prophet, 37–38, 117–118, 245n74, 245n76; and realization of *tawḥīd*, 68–69; al-Sammān in state of, 239n143. *See also* knowledge of God (*maʿrifa*); *taḥqīq* (actualization/realization); *tajalla* (divine manifestation); *tanzīh* (divine transcendence); *tawḥīd* (oneness of God); Tijāniyya; visionary experiences; *waḥdat al-wujūd* (oneness of being)
self-purification: ignored by later students, 209–210; and path of gratitude, 201; serene self (*nafs muṭmaʾinna*), 105, 243n23; al-Tijānī on, 81–83; and worship of God, 105–106
Shādhilī, Abū Ḥasan al-, 190
Shādhiliyya: Darqawiyya, 21, 176, 223n11; *Ḥizb al-baḥr* ("Orison of the Sea"), 90–91; Jazūliyya (Dalāʾiliyya), 22–23, 147–148, 224n21; Nāṣiriyya, 21–22, 23, 235n43; paradigmatic sainthood (*quṭbāniyya*) in, 143; *ṣalāt al-fātiḥ* used in, 127; Wazzāniyya, 22–23, 77–78, 165, 188, 224n19, 224n24. *See also* Sufi orders; Sufi orders, named
Shāfiʿī, al- (Imam), 42
Shāh Walī-Allāh (d. 1762), 30–31, 122, 209
Shamāʾil al-Muḥammadiyya, al- (M. al-Tirmidhī), 214
Shamharūsh (jinn), 93–94
Shanwīhī, ʿAlī b. Muhammad al-, 233n220
Shaʿrānī, ʿAbd al-Wahhāb al- (d. 1565), 27, 42, 43, 143–144, 147
Shaʿrāwī, Muḥammad al- (d. 1998), 212
Sharāybī, ʿAbbās al-, 186–187, 188
Sharḥ al-Ḥikam al-ʿAṭāʾiyya (M. Ḥ. al-Sindī), 33, 228n105
Sharīʿa: Ottoman ignoring of, 176; saints cannot alter, 58, 140; Sufism conforming to, 1, 22, 56–58, 195, 197. *See also* Islamic law, legal opinions; orthodoxy
Sharqāwī, Abdallāh al- (d. 1812), 39
Shaṭṭāriyya, 43, 45
Shawkānī, Muḥammad al- (d. 1839), 30–31
shaykh-disciple relations: in Khalwatiyya, 86; between Prophet and al-Tijānī, 135–136; in Tijāniyya, 85–87, 168–169, 172–173, 203–204
Shifāʾ, al- (Qāḍī Iyāḍ), 214
Shinjīṭī, Muḥammad b. Muḥammad al-Saghīr al-, 122
Shinnāwī, Aḥmad al- (d. 1619), 43, 44, 45, 46, 47–48
Shinqīṭī, ʿAbd al-Raḥmān b. Aḥmad al- (d. 1809), 29, 53, 183, 184–185, 188
Shinqīṭī, Muḥammad b. al-Mukhtār al- (d. 1882), 162–163, 164, 172
Shinqīṭī, Muḥammad al-Ṭālib Jadd al-, 183
Shirāzī, ʿAlī, 96
Sindī, Muḥammad (d. 1727), 30
Sindī, Muḥammad Ḥayāt al- (d. 1750), 30, 33, 34, 50, 209, 228n105
Sirāj al-wahhāj, al- (Ibn al-Mashrī), 133

Sirhindī, Aḥmad (d. 1624), 34, 51, 147–148, 251n32
Sirriyeh, Elizabeth, 148
slavery, legal opinions on, 60–61, 204
soul. See *rūḥ* (spirit or soul)
speculative theology, limits of, 61–66
spirits (*rūḥāniyyāt*), 71, 73, 74–75. *See also* jinn; *rūḥ* (spirit or soul)
spiritual guide, 85–87. *See also* shaykh-disciple relations
spiritualism (*ʿilm uṣūl al-rūḥāniyya*), 73
Sūdānī, Būjamʿa al-, 60, 204, 224n31
Sufi orders: accusations of collaboration with colonial powers, 9, 213; relations of earlier orders with Tijāniyya, 167–169; threatened by Ottomans, 176. *See also* Sufi orders, named; Sufism; Tijāniyya
Sufi orders, named: Kuntiyya-Qādiriyya, 26, 183; Naqshbandiyya, 34, 45, 127, 143, 212; Qādiriyya, 25, 94, 143, 149, 212; Raḥmāniyya (Khalwatiyya), 176; Rekkāniyya, 183; Sammāniyya, 209–210; Shaṭṭāriyya, 43, 45; Suhrawardiyya, 25, 96; Wafāʾiyya, 147. *See also* Khalwatiyya; Shādhiliyya; Tijāniyya
Sufi prayers: *al-Asmāʾ al-Idrīsiyya* ("Idrīsī names"), 96–98; "Circle of Lights" (*Dawr al-anwār*), 133–134; circulation of in North Africa, 80; *dawr al-aʿlā* ("the highest station"), 92–93; *Ḥizb al-baḥr* ("Orison of the Sea"), 90–91; *Ḥizb al-mughnī*, 183–184; *Ḥizb al-sayf* ("Orison of the Sword"), 93–94, 184; "Invocation of the Unseen concerning the Aḥmadan Reality" (*ṣalāt al-ghaybiyya fī l-ḥaqīqa al-Aḥmadiyya*), 127; "Jewel of Perfection" (*Jawharat al-kamāl*), 127; "The Key of Axial Sainthood" (*miftāḥ al-quṭbāniyya*), 137, 249n176; *Kunnāsh al-aṣfar*, 179; *al-Musabbaʿāt al-ʿashr* ("Ten-Sevens"), 94–95; "The Ruby of Necessity in the Prayer on the Master of Ascension" (*Yāqūtat al-maḥtāj fī ṣalāt ʿalā ṣāḥib al-miʿrāj*), 133, 134; "The Ruby of Realities" (*Yaqūtat al-ḥaqāʾiq*), 117–118, 127; *Wardat al-juyūb* ("Bosom Rose"), 125–126; *waẓīfa* (daily office) of Zarrūq, 91–92. *See also ṣalāt al-fātiḥ* ("Prayer of Opening"); *wird* (litany)
Sufism: conformance to Sharīʿa, 1, 22, 56–58, 195, 197; and human attributes, 104–105; as remedy for limits of rational theology, 64–66; steps of (*sulūk*), 202–203; tensions with orthodoxy over divine reward and punishment, 170–171, 173–174; tensions with orthodoxy over misguidance of God (*makr Allāh*), 170–172. *See also* esoteric sciences (*ʿulūm al-asrār*); Islamic scholarly networks in eighteenth century; knowledge of God (*maʿrifa*); self-annihilation (*fanāʾ*); Sharīʿa; *taḥqīq* (actualization/realization); *taḥqīq* (actualization/realization), promise of sainthood; *tajalla* (divine manifestation); *tanzīh* (divine transcendence); *Ṭarīqa Muḥammadiyya*; *tawḥīd* (oneness of God); Tijāniyya; visionary experiences; *waḥdat al-wujūd* (oneness of being)
Sufism, false, 87–89
Sufism, Muḥammadan. *See Ṭarīqa Muḥammadiyya*
Sufyānī, al-Ṭayyib al- (d. 1843), 13, 188–189
Sugar, prohibition of, 60–61, 203, 236n53
Suhrawardī, ʿUmar (d. 1234), 96
Suhrawardiyya, 25, 96

Sukayrij, Aḥmad (d. 1944), 13, 15, 213. *See also* Sukayrij, Aḥmad (d. 1944), as source
———, as source: "Circle of Lights," 133–134; council audience, 185–187; esotericism, 71, 72; Ḥarāzim as intermediary, 124; Ḥarāzim as *khilāfa*, 167; *Ḥizb al-sayf*, 94; "Idrīsī names," 97; Mawlay Sulaymān, 192–194; Special Seal, 150. *See also* Sukayrij, Aḥmad (d. 1944)
Sulaymān (Mawlay), sultan (r. 1792–1822): asylum requested from, 184; consul sought from Mannāna by, 204; council of scholars in, 185–187; delegation to Saudi king, 196–197; gift of house to al-Tijānī, 8, 178, 192; Islamic studies under, 49; in Nāṣiriyya, 22, 194; purification of rural practices, 88–89, 194–196; regard for Ibn al-Ḥājj, 189; seeking of vision of Prophet, 130, 192–193
Sulaymān (Soloman), Prophet, 74–75
Susilo Yudhoyono, 212
Suyūṭī, Jalāl al-Dīn al- (d. 1505), 118, 122
Sy, Mālik, 212, 216

Tadhkirat ʾūlā l-albāb (al-Anṭākī), 89, 240n186
Tadillisī, Yaḥyā al-, 27, 225n57
Taḥqīq (actualization/realization): centrality of in Tijāniyya, 1; definition of, 2; epistemological strategies of, 4–5, 219n15; gratitude (*shukr*) as means to, 207; relationship to *waḥdat al-wujūd*, 69; and spread of Tijāniyya, 216, 217. *See also* knowledge of God (*maʿrifa*); saints, *awliyāʾ*; saints, axial (*aqṭāb*; sing. *quṭb*); self-annihilation (*fanāʾ*); Sufism; *taḥqīq* (actualization/realization), promise of sainthood; *tajalla* (divine manifestation); *tanzīh* (divine transcendence); *tawḥīd* (oneness of God); Tijāniyya; visionary experiences; *waḥdat al-wujūd* (oneness of being)
———, promise of sainthood: and being special loved ones of Prophet, 169–170; and salvation, 165–166; strivings to actualize promise, 166–168; warnings against relying on promise, 171–172. *See also* knowledge of God (*maʿrifa*); sainthood, axial (*quṭbāniyya*); saints, axial (*aqṭāb*; sing. *quṭb*); self-annihilation (*fanāʾ*); *taḥqīq* (actualization/realization); *tajalla* (divine manifestation); *tanzīh* (divine transcendence); *tawḥīd* (oneness of God); Tijānī, Aḥmad b. Maḥammad al- (d. 1815), writings and teachings; Tijāniyya; visionary experiences; *waḥdat al-wujūd* (oneness of being)
Taḥqīq (verification): as conceptual framework, 210–211; definitions of, 16, 19–20, 101, 223n4; in *al-Jawāhir al-khams*, 46–47; by scholars and jurists, 49–50; through visions, 121–122
Taḥqīq al-insāniyya (actualization of humanity): overview, 100–101, 138–141; human potentiality, 109–113; human spirit and divine love, 106–109; Islamic humanism, 101–103; Muḥammadan reality and prayer on the Prophet, 114–119; reality of human condition, 103–106; vision of the Prophet and disciple verification, 119–123; visionary experiences, 16; visionary experiences of Aḥmad al-Tijānī, 123–129; visionary experiences of al-Damrāwī, 131–134; visionary experiences of al-Tijānī's disciples, 129–131; visionary experiences of Ḥarāzim, 134–138

Tāj al-Dīn ʿUthmānī (d. 1640), 34
Tajalla (divine manifestation): in creation, 84–85; al-Kūrānī on, 32–33, 228n103; people of (*ahl al-tajalla*), 132; al-Sammān on, 37–38; al-Tijānī on, 66–68, 236n79. *See also* knowledge of God (*maʿrifa*); self-annihilation (*fanāʾ*); Sufism; *taḥqīq* (actualization/realization); *tanzīh* (divine transcendence); *tawḥīd* (oneness of God); Tijāniyya; visionary experiences; *waḥdat al-wujūd* (oneness of being)
Tāl, ʿUmar al-Fūtī: as leader, 212, 216; transmission of *al-Jawāhir al-khams*, 43; writing of *Rimāḥ*, 13
———, as source: *Ḥizb al-baḥr* ("Orison of the Sea"), 90; Ibn al-ʿArabī's claimed rank, 162; miracles by non-Muslims, 140–141; *al-Musabbaʿāt al-ʿashr* ("Ten-Sevens"), 94–95; promises of salvation in Tijāniyya, 165; Prophet as guarantor of Tijāniyya, 128; visions of Prophet, 120–121; visiting graves, 88
Talismans and amulets, 41–42. *See also* esoteric sciences (*ʿulūm al-asrār*)
Tamāsīnī, ʿAlī al- (d. 1844), 130–131, 166–167, 182, 214–215
Tanzīh (divine transcendence): al-Bakrī on, 35; al-Kūrānī on, 32. *See also* knowledge of God (*maʿrifa*); self-annihilation (*fanāʾ*); Sufism; *taḥqīq* (actualization/realization); *tajalla* (divine manifestation); *tawḥīd* (oneness of God); Tijāniyya; visionary experiences; *waḥdat al-wujūd* (oneness of being)
Tārikay, Aḥmad al-, 25
Taʾrīkh al-sūdān (al-Saʿadī), 27
Ṭarīq al-Ḥaqq ("The Path of Truth"), 211–212
Ṭarīqa Aḥmadiyya, 100, 242n2. See also *Ṭarīqa Muḥammadiyya*
Ṭarīqa Maḥmūdiyya, 25–26
Ṭarīqa Muḥammadiyya: divergent understandings of, 19–20; in eighteenth century, 28, 50–52; as means of spiritual realization, 116–119; as path of bountiful grace, 202; al-Sammān on, 37, 38; in sixteenth century, 25, 225n52; in Sub-Saharan Africa, 24–30; Tijānī form of, 1–2, 6–7. *See also* Sufism; Tijāniyya
Tarjumāna al-kubrā, al- (al-Zayānī), 14
Taʿṭīr al-anām (al-Nābulusī), 139
Tawḥīd (oneness of God): differing understandings of verification, 19; mystical experience of, 64–65, 83–85; and relationship with spirits, 73; al-Tijānī's teachings on, 62–65. *See also* *aḥadiyya* (unique oneness of God); esoteric sciences (*ʿulūm al-asrār*); knowledge of God (*maʿrifa*); self-annihilation (*fanāʾ*); Sufism; *taḥqīq* (actualization/realization); *tajalla* (divine manifestation); *tanzīh* (divine transcendence); Tijāniyya; visionary experiences; *waḥdat al-wujūd* (oneness of being)
Tāwudī b. Sūda al-, 37, 204
Ṭayyib, al- (Mawlay) (d. 1767), 23
Ṭayyib b. Kīrān al-, 185–188, 191
Ṭayyib al-Sufyānī, 184
Tāzī, ʿAbd al-Wahhāb al- (d. 1792), 38–39, 50, 230n149
Tāzī, Aḥmad al-Ṭawāsh al- (d. 1790), 78
"Ten Sevens" (*al-Musabbaʿāt al-ʿashr*), 94–95
Tijānī, Aḥmad b. Maḥammad al- (d. 1815): overview, 208–209; ancestry of, 7, 219n24; approachability of, 203–205; arrival in Fez, 184–188, 191–195, 197–198; claim to be Seal

of Saints, 2–4, 142–143; conflicts with Turkish authorities, 177–178; in council of scholars, 187–188; education of, 7, 54–57, 234n9, 234n11, 234n13; Khalwatiyya contacts of, 36; knowledge networks of, 211; in Medina, 30–31; miracles (*karāmāt*) of, 113, 124, 204–205; private asceticism, 60–61, 203, 236n53; in Saharan Tūwāt, 30, 183, 227n85; Shādhiliyya influence on, 23, 224n31, 224n32; al-Sindī's influence on, 34; study of *al-Jawāhir al-khams*, 44–48, 46; as *tafsīr* authority, 187–188; teaching career of, 54. *See also* Islamic scholarly networks in eighteenth century; Tijānī, Aḥmad b. Maḥammad al- (d. 1815), intellectual development; Tijānī, Aḥmad b. Maḥammad al- (d. 1815), visionary experiences; Tijānī, Aḥmad b. Maḥammad al- (d. 1815), writings and teachings; Tijāniyya

———, intellectual development: overview, 53–54, 98–99; esoteric sciences, 70–74; esoteric sciences, greatest name, 76–77; esoteric sciences, sacred words and spirits, 74–75; Islamic law, 54–58; Islamic law, legal methodology, 58–59; Islamic law, smoking and slavery, 59–61; speculative theology, limits of, 61–66; Sufi path, early steps, 77–80; Sufi path, etiquette and self-purification, 80–83; Sufi path, "false" Sufism, 87–89; Sufi path, knowledge of God, 83–85; Sufi path, prayers, 89–98; Sufi path, spiritual guide, 85–87; *waḥdat al-wujūd* (oneness of being), 66–69. *See also* Tijānī, Aḥmad b. Maḥammad al- (d. 1815); Tijānī, Aḥmad b. Maḥammad al- (d. 1815), visionary experiences; Tijānī, Aḥmad b. Maḥammad al- (d. 1815), writings and teachings; Tijāniyya

———, visionary experiences, 123–129; confirmation of descent from Prophet, 219n24; and formation of legal opinions, 58, 125, 178; gifting of *ṭarīqa* in, 3–4, 7, 100–101; on his being Hidden Pole, 161–162; investiture as Hidden Pole, 156–157; *Jawāhir al-maʿānī* ordered preserved, 11–12, 221n45; ordered to remain in Fez, 191; Prophet as guarantor for disciples, 128, 213; Prophet's advice to sultan, 193; spiritual station defined, 152; and Sufi prayers, 125–128. *See also* miracles (*karāmāt*); Sufi prayers; Tijānī, Aḥmad b. Maḥammad al- (d. 1815); Tijānī, Aḥmad b. Maḥammad al- (d. 1815), intellectual development; Tijānī, Aḥmad b. Maḥammad al- (d. 1815), writings and teachings; Tijāniyya; visionary experiences

———, writings and teachings: advice to sultan, 193; asking forgiveness, 180; authorization (*ijāza*) to Ḥarāzim, 167; calamities and tribulations, 179–180, 181–182; dependence on God, 76–77; facility of Sufi path, 202–203; faith and gratitude, 199; fear and hope, 171–172; following Sharīʿa, 56–58; glorifying sanctity of saints, 194–195; God's grace, 175; God's love, 107, 110–112; God's unique oneness (*aḥadiyya*), 119; his proximity to Prophet, 151–152; human reality, 104, 105–106; humanity of infidels, 102; Ibn al-Ḥājj, 191; jihad (fighting), 181–182; jurisprudential errors, 57–58; knowledge of God, 83–85; knowledge of *tawḥīd*, 64–65;

Kunnāsh al-maktūm, 76; learning for laity, 187–188, 205; meaning of Sufism, 1; miracles, 205; monasticism, 205; Muḥammadan reality, 114–115, 116; *al-Musabbaʿāt al-ʿashr*, 95; other Sufi orders, 168–169; others' claims to high rank, 161–162; path of gratitude, 201; promises to disciples, 169–170; Prophet's life in grave, 118–119, 246n79; Prophet's rank, 119–120; reward of *al-Fātiḥa*, 206; *rūḥ* and human realization, 107–109, 244n40; saints, Hidden Pole, 8–9, 153, 155, 159, 160; saints, "pole of poles" (*quṭb al-aqṭāb*), 128; saints, Seal of Saints, 158; saints and sainthood, 23, 78, 81, 142; *ṣalāt al-fātiḥ*, 127; self-purification, 81–83; shaykh-disciple relations, 168, 172; spiritual guides, 85–87; Turks in Algeria, 176, 178–179; venal scholars, 191–192; visiting graves, 194–195; warnings against relying on promises of salvation, 165, 170, 171–172; warnings against staying near him, 168, 254n135. *See also* Ḥarāzim al-Barrāda, ʿAlī (d. 1804), as source; *Jawāhir al-maʿānī* (Ḥarāzim), as source; *ṣalāt al-fātiḥ* ("Prayer of Opening"); Tijānī, Aḥmad b. Maḥammad al- (d. 1815); Tijānī, Aḥmad b. Maḥammad al- (d. 1815), intellectual development; Tijānī, Aḥmad b. Maḥammad al- (d. 1815), visionary experiences; Tijāniyya

Tijānī, ʿAlī Bilʿarābī al-, 215

Tijānī, ʿAmmār al-, 213

Tijānī, Bashīr b. Muḥammad b. Aḥmad al-, 12

Tijānī, Maḥammad b. Mukhtār al-, 71–72

Tijānī, Muḥammad al-Ḥabīb b. Aḥmad (d. 1853), 213, 215

Tijānī, Ṣalāḥ al-Dīn al-, 227n96

Tijāniyya: appeal of, accent on God's grace, 198; appeal of, actualization of religious identity, 207, 215–217; appeal of, actualization of religious identity, 3; appeal of, promises made by, 165–166; appeal of, spiritual realization, 130–131, 170–171, 207; centrality of prayer on the Prophet, 116–119; companionship as spiritual training (*tarbiya*), 203–204; discussion of saintly rank within, 201; distinguishing characteristic of, 6, 77; early tensions within, 129, 172–173; formation and spread of, 2, 8–9, 100–101, 182–184, 211–213, 215–217, 220n28; historical context of, 175; knowledge networks in formation of, 5–6; leadership of after al-Tijānī, 214–215; literature and sources on, external, 14–15; literature and sources on, primary, 11–14; literature and sources on, secondary, 9–11; as methodology of *taḥqīq*, 138–139; and other Sufi communities, 167–169; popularity of today, 215–217; promises made by, 165–166; saintly seal, 150–151; Salafi-inspired attack against, 11; shaykh-disciple relations, 85–87, 168–169, 172–173, 203–204; spread of and Arabic literature, 15, 223n70; visionary experience in foundation of, 121–123, 134; visiting graves (*ziyāra*), 87, 88, 194–195; as way of gratitude (*shukr*), 202; *wird* (litany), 7, 204–205, 220n26; women in, 204. *See also* Islamic scholarly networks in eighteenth century; Sufi prayers; Sufism; *taḥqīq* (actualization/realization); *taḥqīq* (verification); *Ṭarīqa Muḥammadiyya*; Tijānī, Aḥmad b. Maḥammad al- (d. 1815); Tijānī, Aḥmad b.

Maḥammad al- (d. 1815), intellectual development; Tijānī, Aḥmad b. Maḥammad al- (d. 1815), visionary experiences; Tijānī, Aḥmad b. Maḥammad al- (d. 1815), writings and teachings; *wird* (litany)
Tīmī, Ibrāhīm al-, 94
Tirmidhī, Ḥakīm al- (d. 905–910), 143–145, 163–164, 250n6
Tirmidhī, Muḥammad al- (d. 892), 214
Tlemcen, Algeria, 177, 178
tobacco, legal opinions on, 28, 59, 226n71, 235n43
Tuhāmī (Mawlay), 165
Tunisī, Maḥmūd al-, 70–71, 183
Tunisī, Muḥammad al-, 93
Turkey, Tijānī activists in, 212
Turkī, Aḥmad al-Baghdādī al-, 178–179
Tustarī, Sahl al- (d. 896), 114
Tuwāt, Algeria, 183
Tuwātī, Aḥmad al-, 182, 183–184
Tuzānī, Muḥammad b. ʿAbdallāh al- (d. 1778), 23

ʿUjaymī, Ḥasan al-, 37, 50–51
ʿulamāʾ (scholars): effects of colonialism on, 19, 213–214; under Ottoman rule, 176; pre-colonial prestige of, 18. *See also* Islamic scholarly networks in eighteenth century
ʿUthmān b. al-ʿAffān, 47
ʿUthmān b. Fūdī (d. 1817), 30–31, 70, 149, 237n93

Van Dalen, Dorrit, 226n71
vicegerency (*khilāfa*), 103–104
visionary experiences: by Amlās, 129, 166; by al-ʿAndalīb, 51, 148; attributed to scholars of Timbuktu, 26–27; by Būjamʿa, 204; by al-Dabbāgh, 24; by al-Damrāwī, 131–134, 158, 166; and disciple verification, 119–123; of guidance in worldly affairs, 123–125, 135; by Ibn al-Mashrī, 158; by al-Idrīsī, 22–23; of juristic guidance, 125; by jurists, 50, 233n220; by al-Kurdī of Khiḍr, 94; by Maḥammad b. Mukhtār al-Tijānī of spirits, 71; by Mawlay Sulaymān, 192–193; by Muḥammad al-Bakrī, 125–126; by Muṣṭafā al-Bakrī, 34–35; mystical audition (*samāʿ*), 261n144; promised to disciples, 130, 248n144; related to *Dalāʾil al-khayrāt* (al-Jazūlī), 204, 244n56; by al-Sammān, 37–38, 148, 239n143; scholarly acceptance of, 121–122; by Tamāsīnī, 166–167; by al-Tijānī, 123–129; by al-Tijānī of jinn, 71; by al-Tijānī's disciples, 129–131; by al-Tīmī, 94; al-Yūsī's treatment of, 21–22; by Zarrūq, 92. *See also* esoteric sciences (*ʿulūm al-asrār*); Ḥarāzim al-Barrāda, ʿAlī (d. 1804), visionary experiences; knowledge of God (*maʿrifa*); miracles (*karāmāt*); self-annihilation (*fanāʾ*); Sufism; *taḥqīq* (actualization/realization); *taḥqīq* (actualization/realization), promise of sainthood; *tajalla* (divine manifestation); *tanzīh* (divine transcendence); *tawḥīd* (oneness of God); Tijānī, Aḥmad b. Maḥammad al- (d. 1815), visionary experiences; Tijāniyya; *waḥdat al-wujūd* (oneness of being)
Voll, John, 4, 5

Wafāʾ, ʿAlī (d. 1405), 147, 167
Wafāʾ, Muḥammad (d. 1363), 143–144, 147, 163
Wafāʾiyya, 147
waḥdat al-wujūd (oneness of being): al-Bakrī's explanation of, 35; Ibn al-Ḥājj on, 190; al-Kūrānī's

explanation of, 31–32, 228n101; relationship to *taḥqīq* (actualization/realization), 69; al-Sammān's avoidance of subject, 37–38; al-Sindī's treatment of subject, 33–34; al-Tijānī's explanation of, 66–69. *See also* knowledge of God (*maʿrifa*); self-annihilation (*fanāʾ*); Sufism; *taḥqīq* (actualization/realization); *tajalla* (divine manifestation); *tanzīh* (divine transcendence); *tawḥīd* (oneness of God); Tijāniyya; visionary experiences

Wahhābī movement: approval of in Fez, 49; *tawḥīd* (oneness of God), understanding of, 19–20. *See also* Muḥammad b. ʿAbd al-Wahhāb; Wahhabis; Wahhabism

Wahhabis: as "bad" Muslims, 101–102; Moroccan delegation to, 196–198; rejection of al-Tijānī's teachings, 207. *See also* Muḥammad b. ʿAbd al-Wahhāb; Wahhābī movement; Wahhabism

Wahhabism: early marginality of, 210; influence of on Mawlay Sulaymān alleged, 194–195; prohibitions by, 196. *See also* Muḥammad b. ʿAbd al-Wahhāb; Wahhābī movement; Wahhabis

Walī al-Burnāwī, Muḥammad al- (fl. late 17th c.), 28

Wardat al-juyūb ("Bosom Rose"), 125–126

waẓīfa (daily office) of Zarrūq, 91–92

Wazzānī, al-Ṭayyib al-, 77–78

Wazzānī, al-Tuhāmī b. Muḥammad al-, 155

Wazzāniyya, 22–23, 77–78, 165, 188, 224n19, 224n24

West African scholars: as global representatives of Tijāniyya, 212–213, 214–215; influence of in Fez, 24–26, 29–30, 211; in Timbuktu, 26–28, 225n57

wird (litany): of gnostics, 82; heedlessness in reciting, 137, 249n176; of Khalwatiyya, 40; proper recitation of, 204–205; al-Tijānī's following of, 23; Tijāniyya *wird* contents, 220n26; Tijāniyya *wird* from Prophet, 7; *wird al-saḥar* (daytime litany) of al-Bakrī, 34–35. *See also* Sufi prayers

wird al-saḥar (daytime litany) (al-Bakrī), 34–35

women in Tijāniyya, 204

Yaḥyā b. ʿAdī, 102

Yamanī, ʿAbdallāh al-, 202

Yamanī, Aḥmad al- (d. 1712), 24–25, 26, 225n41

Yaqūtat al-ḥaqāʾiq ("The Ruby of Realities"), 117–118, 127

Yāqūtat al-maḥtāj fī ṣalāt ʿalā ṣāḥib al-miʿrāj ("The Ruby of Necessity in the Prayer on the Master of Ascension"), 133, 134

Yūsī, al-Ḥasan al-, 21–22, 41, 42, 62, 140

Zabīdī, Murtaḍā al- (d. 1791): *ijāza* granted to Ibn al-Ḥājj by, 189; knowledge network of, 26, 37, 224n18, 233n225; in Nāṣiriyya, 22; restriction of *ijtihād*, 49; on *ṣalwāt*, 50; on Seal of Saints, 148–149; study of esoteric sciences by, 41

Zarrūq, Aḥmad (d. 1493): on saying blessings on Prophet, 116; warnings against esoteric sciences, 41, 71, 72; *waẓīfa* (daily office) of, 91–92

Zayānī, Abū l-Qāsim al- (d. 1833), 14, 177, 191, 196

ziyāra (grave visitation). *See* grave visitation (*ziyāra*)

ISLAMIC CIVILIZATION AND MUSLIM NETWORKS

Zachary Valentine Wright, *Realizing Islam: The Tijaniyya in North Africa and the Eighteenth-Century Muslim World* (2020).

Michael Muhammad Knight, *Muhammad's Body: Baraka Networks and the Prophetic Assemblage* (2020).

Kelly A. Hammond, *China's Muslims and Japan's Empire: Centering Islam in World War II* (2020).

Alex Dika Seggerman, *Modernism on the Nile: Art in Egypt between the Islamic and the Contemporary* (2019).

Babak Rahimi and Peyman Eshaghi, *Muslim Pilgrimage in the Modern World* (2019).

Simon Wolfgang Fuchs, *In a Pure Muslim Land: Shiʿism between Pakistan and the Middle East* (2019).

Gary R. Bunt, *Hashtag Islam: How Cyber Islamic Environments Are Transforming Religious Authority* (2018).

Ahmad Dallal, *Islam without Europe: Traditions of Reform in Eighteenth-Century Islamic Thought* (2018).

Irfan Ahmad, *Religion as Critique: Islamic Critical Thinking from Mecca to the Marketplace* (2017).

Scott Kugle, *When Sun Meets Moon: Gender, Eros, and Ecstasy in Urdu Poetry* (2016).

Kishwar Rizvi, *The Transnational Mosque: Architecture, Historical Memory, and the Contemporary Middle East* (2015).

Ebrahim Moosa, *What Is a Madrasa?* (2015).

Bruce B. Lawrence, *Who Is Allah?* (2015).

Edward E. Curtis IV, *The Call of Bilal: Islam in the African Diaspora* (2014).

Sahar Amer, *What Is Veiling?* (2014).

Rudolph T. Ware III, *The Walking Qurʾan: Islamic Education, Embodied Knowledge, and History in West Africa* (2014).

Saʿdiyya Shaikh, *Sufi Narratives of Intimacy: Ibn ʿArabī, Gender, and Sexuality* (2012).

Karen G. Ruffle, *Gender, Sainthood, and Everyday Practice in South Asian Shiʿism* (2011).

Jonah Steinberg, *Ismaʿili Modern: Globalization and Identity in a Muslim Community* (2011).

Iftikhar Dadi, *Modernism and the Art of Muslim South Asia* (2010).

Gary R. Bunt, iMuslims: Rewiring the House of Islam (2009).

Fatemeh Keshavarz, *Jasmine and Stars: Reading More Than "Lolita" in Tehran* (2007).

Scott Kugle, *Sufis and Saints' Bodies: Mysticism, Corporeality, and Sacred Power in Islam* (2007).

Roxani Eleni Margariti, *Aden and the Indian Ocean Trade: 150 Years in the Life of a Medieval Arabian Port* (2007).

Sufia M. Uddin, *Constructing Bangladesh: Religion, Ethnicity, and Language in an Islamic Nation* (2006).

Omid Safi, *The Politics of Knowledge in Premodern Islam: Negotiating Ideology and Religious Inquiry* (2006).

Ebrahim Moosa, *Ghazālī and the Poetics of Imagination* (2005).

Miriam Cooke and Bruce B. Lawrence, eds., *Muslim Networks from Hajj to Hip Hop* (2005).

Carl W. Ernst, *Following Muhammad: Rethinking Islam in the Contemporary World* (2003).

www.ingramcontent.com/pod-product-compliance
Lightning Source LLC
Chambersburg PA
CBHW030522230426
43665CB00010B/727
* 9 7 8 1 4 6 9 6 6 0 8 2 0 *